SHOCK XPRESS

1

Edited By
STEFAN JAWORZYN

Editorial Consultant:
Stephen Jones

TITAN BOOKS
LONDON

SHOCK XPRESS 1

ISBN 1 85286 392 7

Published by
Titan Books Ltd
58 St Giles High Street
London
WC2H 8LH

First edition August 1991
10 9 8 7 6 5 4 3 2 1

Printed and bound in England by Hillman Printers (Frome) Ltd.

A CIP record for this publication is available from the British Library.

Picture credits:
Amblin, American General, American International Pictures, Archaeopteryx Corp., Avco-Embassy Pictures, Barber Dann Films Ltd, Barber International, BFI, Blue Dolphin, Braveworld Ltd, Brooksfilms, Castle Premier Releasing, The Cannon Group, Cinema Associates Inc, Circle Films, Murray Close, Columbia/Tri-Star Pictures, Commonwealth United Entertainment Inc, Connoisseur, Corgi Books, Crown International Pictures, DAC/Penta, Dimension Pictures, Attila Dory, Dreamland Productions, EMI, Entertainment Film Distributors, *Famous Monsters of Filmland*, The Filmgroup, First Independent, Buddy Giovinazzo, Grand National Film Distributors, GTO Films, Hemdale Film Distributors Ltd, Hemisphere Pictures, ICA Projects, Joseph Green Pictures, Dick Jude, George Kuchar, Guy Maddin, Sean Manchester/Holy Grail, Maniac Productions Inc, Mark IV Pictures Incorporated, MGM/UA Home Video, Miracle Films Ltd, Mogul Video, *Monster Mania*, Morgan Creek Productions, New Line Cinema, New World Pictures, Orion Pictures Corporation, Palace Pictures, Palace Video, Pathé, Abe Perlstein, Planet Film Distributors, Prism Entertainment, Rank Film Distributors, Recorded Picture Company, Replay Video, Rochelle/Navaron Films, Jack Stevenson, Towers of London (Films) Ltd Productions, Troma, 20th Century-Fox, United Artists Corporation, United International Pictures, Oliver Upton, Vipco Video, The Walt Disney Company, Warner Bros, Werkstattkino/Erich Wagner, Kjell Wirum, Firooz Zahedi.
Any omissions will be corrected in future editions.

Front cover photo:
The Blob © 1988 Braveworld/Tri-Star Pictures.

Back cover photos:
Top: *The Sect* © 1991 DAC/Penta.
Middle: *The Laughing Dead* © 1989 Archaeopteryx Corp. Photo: Abe Perlstein.
Bottom: *Prom Night* © 1980 Avco Embassy Pictures Corp.

CONTENTS

For Michael and Alex

ACKNOWLEDGEMENTS:
BFI/Mark Finch, Larry Buchanan, Capital Home Video,
Carolco, Connoisseur Video/Ian Gilchrist, Corbett & Keane
Publicity, David Cox, Brian Curran, DDA/Jonathan Rutter,
Entertainment in Video, First Independent, Frontline PR,
Guild Video, Mick Hamer, Michael Helms, Hollywood Book
and Poster Shop, David Hyman, ICA Press Office, George
Kuchar, Guy Maddin, Medusa, New Line Cinema, New
World Pictures, Orion Pictures, Palace Video, Psychotronic
Video/Bal & Mike, Rank Film Distributors, Steve Roe, 20th
Century-Fox, UIP, Warner Home Video, Winsor-Beck, and
everyone who offered advice or encouragement.

Special thanks to all the staff of Titan Books for their work
on the project, and to Stephen Jones and David Sutton,
without whom this would not have been possible.

Some back issues of *Shock Xpress* magazine are still available.
All enquiries should be addressed to *Shock Xpress*,
c/o Titan Books. Please enclose a SAE or IRC.

XPRESSWAY TO YOUR SKULL

AN 'INTRODUCTION'

BY STEFAN JAWORZYN

In one of my ceaseless attempts to avoid writing an introduction to this book I found myself sorting through a heap of what can only be termed 'stuff' - incomprehensible missives from people who write their names and addresses on their envelopes but not their letters, orders for things I don't have, 'YOU CAN STOP THE ROT' Conservative Party flyers, hate mail, you know the kind of heap - when out tumbled the 103rd edition of *Gore Gazette*. 'TEN FUCKING YEARS & STILL MAKING ENEMIES!' it screamed. Well, we've got some catching up to do (the first issue of *Shock Xpress* magazine appeared in July 1985), but I can only hope Rick Sullivan's *Weltanschauung* will apply to *Shock* in years to come.

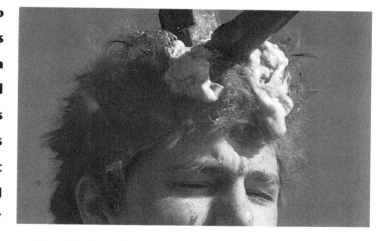

Though I always favoured Bill Landis' astonishing explorations of the lowlife milieu in *Sleazoid Express*, *Gore Gazette* has remained dedicated to scum cinema for a decade, no mean feat considering the frequent dearth of interesting exploitation material. While *Sleazoid* and Bill Landis hit self-destruct through a too-literal immersion in the whole trash ethos (an increasing disillusion with the hypocrisy of main-stream cinema, a gradual need to experience something *harder*...), Sullivan's publication has remained a consistent voice of discontent operating on the fringes of cinematic spew. But for me (and a good few of the writers appearing in this volume) *Sleazoid Express* embodied everything that an all-encompassing obsession with moral turpitude should be. One can only gloomily reflect on the fact that the circle of Britain's 'noted' genre critics (from youthful pedants and opportunists to ageing misanthropes) comprise dullards whose qualifications might induce reader catatonia but who could never even *collectively* aspire to the apocalyptic revelations contained in a single issue of Landis' magazine...

What does all this have to do with *Shock Xpress*? Nothing, immediately. I guess what I believe is that exploitation cinema is an easy area to, ahem, *exploit*, and especially to misrepresent. Frequently it's done by the wrong people for the wrong reasons. Inept directors and poorly executed movies are now a blatant - and lucrative - target, and ground which is far from fallow has been more than overworked. What a successful exploitation picture and/or publication *should* do is to so infuse the reader with glimpses into the weird and twisted that they become infected, that an overall perspective emerges which the viewer or reader is part of *and can never escape...*!

There are still publications (all of which are, significantly, fanzines) that maintain the standards set by Bill Landis - the ability to draw the reader into a kind of hermetically sealed world of sleaze: *Subhuman* and the early issues of *Grindhouse* in the USA and *Sheer Filth* in Britain come immediately to mind. Each contains a reasonably eclectic selection of material, but presents a whole somehow *more* than equal to the sum of its parts... The same effect can be obtained from consuming a particularly demented exploitation film. Ironically it wasn't until the last two issues of *Shock Xpress* magazine (particularly the final issue) that I felt it achieved the much desired thematic unity (or conceptual continuity - call it what you will) I'd been striving for.

Well, I've had two years since the last issue to pon-der and pontificate the significance of 'what it's all about'. My abhorrence for most recent major studio genre 'product' (for that it is) and disillusion with much of the current independent movie scene certainly hasn't helped me maintain a healthy perspective. (I'm hard pressed to think of a really stunning independent feature since *Henry, Portrait of a Serial Killer*.) I suspect part of the problem lies in the fact that the early '80s were a staggering time for exploitation cinema (in Britain present mainly through unrated videos) and it's taken some sobering up to the fact that the flood of warped material has, through censorship, been effectively stemmed from widespread consumption in Britain, and has also, to a certain extent, *ceased to be produced...*

This volume contains pieces encompassing various aspects of exploitation cinema, written by some of my favourite commentators on the genre - I won't say I hope there's something here for everyone, because that wouldn't be true. It's a personal choice which took me a long time to make: my major aims were to cast my nets wider than the more obvious horror material and to strike a balance between contemporary and 'vintage' or historical subject matter. Given the repressive nature of modern day Britain, censorship was an issue that obviously had to be addressed. Maybe there's something here to make a few friends - and there *must* be something to make a few enemies! And if the spirit of Bill Landis and *Sleazoid Express* lives on *anywhere* in these pages then at least *I'm* happy. ∎

Stefan Jaworzyn, April 1991

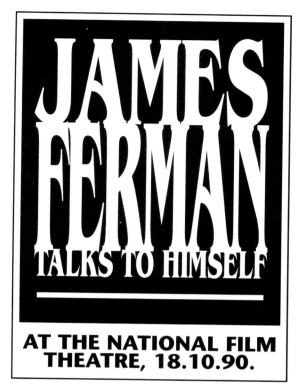

AT THE NATIONAL FILM THEATRE, 18.10.90.

James Ferman is the head of the British Board of Film Classification. Here he talks about his position and that of the BBFC. This piece is followed by an interview with Ferman conducted by journalist, academic and anti-censorship campaigner Julian Petley.

I'm a poacher turned gamekeeper. I was a television director for seventeen and a half years, before I joined what was then the British Board of Film Censors in 1975. I've now been there for fifteen years, which I never thought I would be when I joined; I thought I'd do it for five years or so and then go back to directing or producing. It's been an extraordinary time because there have been a number of major problems - the Williams Committee who investigated us and talked about reorganisation in the late '70s, the video nasties scare, sex shops, club cinemas and, of course, the Video Recordings Act, and now cable and satellite TV. The result is that we've grown, with really very little preparation at each stage, from eleven people on one floor at 3 Soho Square doing about 350 films a year to sixty-eight people in the whole of the building. There's a lot of building work going on around us all the time and a sense of martyrdom in the staff, so it's been tough going. We now do about 360-370 films a year plus about 4,000 videos and, on a purely voluntary basis, because we have no statutory role there, Sky

Movies. They asked us to see all their movies and tell them what time slots they were suitable for, as well as seeing if there were any problems with the versions they'd bought. We try not to become like a factory farm, though. The place is staffed by people who love film, several have worked for the BFI, a lot have come out of media jobs, though the one thing employees must not have done is to have worked on the commercial side of the film and video industry because there must be no conflicts of interest.

I applied for the job because it was suggested that I do so, and I discovered that they were looking for someone who not only knew their way around a cutting room but was also in some way concerned with social problems, and in 1975 I was running a series of courses at the Polytechnic of Central London on community mental health which were looking at the prevention of various social problems.

When I came into the Board it was a time of enormous ferment; my predecessor (Stephen Murphy), who'd come from the IBA as a backroom boy, had found that the whole thing had become too stormy and preferred to go back to the IBA. The storms weren't of his making - almost as soon as he arrived he got *The Devils*, *A Clockwork Orange*, *Last Tango in Paris*, *Straw Dogs* and so on, one after the other. There was constant pressure and press interest, and when I joined they said they wanted me to see if I could re-establish the Board and make it acceptable again. It took a lot of work over several years, but I hope we succeeded. Part of my motivation when I joined there was based on the fact that I thought that some of the principles of censorship in the past were not acceptable to me as a director. I also said in my interview that I never again wanted to go to the cinema and see a film which had been butchered in the name of censorship, including cuts to the soundtrack. We reduced the number of films cut, though I should point out that we do not make the cuts ourselves - we tell the company what's necessary and they resubmit their version. They can discuss the matter with us, and every cut is negotiable. We try to help the company to

James Ferman.

James Woods deals with CIC's initial print of **Videodrome**.

language, nudity and sexuality. But I remember in my first week at the Board being called in by some examiners to have a look at a scene in which a woman takes her clothes off and gets in a shower. I thought the issue at stake was her nudity and the way in which the camera was exploiting it, but then lo and behold a hand reached into the shower and slashed her repeatedly across the breasts. I was half way up the wall with horror, and the examiners said to me, "That's what we call a slasher movie. We see one every three weeks or so, and you'll get used to them." I also discovered, within the first months of joining, porno-rape, which was a staple of sex films in those days; the woman is raped at gunpoint or knifepoint and halfway through, without fail, she begins to enjoy it and at the end she throws her arms round the rapist and thanks him for this glorious, liberating experience. We had a lot of discussions about this kind of thing, and I said that such scenes were not really acceptable because the message is that when a woman says "no" she really means "yes." Now I know the idea of sensory messages is problematic but the 'deprave and corrupt' test of the Obscene Publications Act (which in fact we were not yet under in 1975) does talk about things that make people morally bad, and scenes such as these did seem to me to have that capacity. We did bring films within the Obscene Publications Act in 1977 because at the time films were being prosecuted on account of one individual scene, which would be prosecuted under the common law indecency test; the film didn't have to be taken *as a whole*, which the OPA required, so it seemed very important that we should get film treated in the same way as theatre, for example, was treated - as a significant work of art, even if it was a slasher movie. We achieved this in 1977, and one of the first things we did was to clamp down on porno-rape; we don't allow it at all now, and we have gone back and taken it out of films passed uncut before that date.

With the video nasties, people suddenly began seeing on video what they hadn't been able to see in the cinema because of cuts or bans by the Board. There was a particular fuss because any child could take these films out of the video shop. So we were approached by the video industry, or rather the respectable side of it, who said that they would like the Board to bring in a classification system. I said we'd be happy to do that, but told them I was worried about how it would be enforced in the shops. They said that they wanted the categories to be advisory, but we argued that if we were attaching our certificates to individual tapes we wanted shops to abide by our decisions and not, for instance, to rent or sell '18' tapes to children. The industry was very reluctant to accept this and went away for a few months to think about it. After the HMV shop in Oxford Street was raided and had its 'adult' shelves cleared by Scotland Yard they came back and were prepared to go along with us. So we set up a working party on video which, after a year, came up with a code of practice which the British Videogram Association said they would adopt. It was a very slow business, and the one thing they said they wouldn't adopt was any control of packaging and advertising which we had said was a good idea because of the quite outrageous packaging which was then around, for example *The Driller Killer*. Anyway, they didn't want to go along with that at the time. RCA/Columbia and Warners began submitting videos to us on a purely voluntary basis, and then lo and behold the 1983 General Election came along. During

do good cuts, to do a good job. Anyway, I said at my interview that I actually cared about bringing a modern set of principles to censorship, principles that could be defended in public, unlike a lot of past practice. I also told them about my whole history of dealing with censorship on television, where I had some pretty stormy confrontations over *The Wednesday Play* and *Play for Today*, and also a documentary which I did for ATV about religious freedom, which ran into problems over our coverage of the Northern Ireland dimension. In fact, it was the first TV film about Northern Ireland to be banned, though it was eventually broadcast with major cuts and alterations: we lost about seventeen minutes out of a fifty-two minute documentary. Oddly enough my reporter was Paul Johnson, then a left-wing radical and deputy editor of the *New Statesman*, and the programme was defended by Peter Black in the *Daily Mail*, which was in those days still capable of being a campaigning newspaper!

Anyway, when I joined the Board none of the problems were anything like those I'd encountered in television; there was far greater latitude in terms of

the campaign Channel 4 ran a documentary called *A Gentleman's Agreement* which basically said the BVA's code of practice depends on people abiding by it, and that gentleman's agreements work very well in Britain when they apply to gentlemen, of which there are very few in the video industry. Somebody in the Government saw that programme and thought that there were votes to be gained by making the arrangement statutory, although Willie Whitelaw had said that he thought video censorship, like film censorship, should be done on an internal, industry basis, and the rest is history.

Anybody who has studied semiotics or worked in film theory will know that the audience completes the film, the film is never solely what the author intended. It is always a mental and emotional transaction with each individual member of the audience, who may well respond quite differently one from the other. So each person completes the film in their own personal way; this is a fundamental tenet of semiotics and it's been borne out through research. There was a researcher in New York in the late '70s who was concerned about all the fuss that was being made about

sexual violence in films, so he decided to set up an experiment to see whether or not people really were turned on by scenes of sexual violence. He doubted that they were. Anyway, he got together a whole load of scenes of erotic sex and violent sex, including porno-rape, and he showed these to a test audience of statistically sampled men in the age range eighteen to sixty. The test was physiological - he attached a glove to the penis which measured the degree of penile tumescence - and he got a very reassuring result: the more tender, erotic content there was in a scene the more these men were turned on, the more violent the less they were turned on. But then he began to wonder if everyone would react the same and he went to a prison and repeated the test on convicted rapists, a very large number of them, and he got exactly the opposite result. So we have to bear in mind always that some people are turned on by violence, while others loathe it. If you show the same film to different kinds of audiences you will get different results.

When *Lethal Weapon 2* was made, the editor told me about how this film and others, especially sequels, are test screened in the USA. If audiences don't respond to

Sylvester Stallone helps the BBFC with the editing of **Rambo III.**

a scene they would simply cut out the chat and bring the various scenes closer together. Inevitably a lot of characterisation would go, even key elements of the plot would go, and the violence would come thicker and faster - just to get the buzz going in the cinema. Take the scene where Mel Gibson kills the two baddies after his girlfriend had been murdered - they cut that down till the audience stood up and cheered Gibson's actions, and that was in a test screening at a cinema near Watts; not an NFT-type audience I suspect!

One of our basic guidelines is to balance the rights of the robust majority against the needs of the vulnerable minority. Unfortunately, the Board, long before my time, passed the first two Bruce Lee films with the nunchaka scenes intact. Lo and behold, by the time the third one came out, teenagers were going onto the football terraces with home-made nunchakas tucked in their belts, there were fights with nunchakas on the pier at Brighton, the papers were making a terrible fuss, and my predecessor had to admit that the Board might have made a mistake and cut them out of the next two Bruce Lee films. When we discovered some years later that the first two had become part of the standard repertoire and were constantly doing the rounds we decided that we had to be consistent, so we took them out of those too. Because our status is unofficial when it comes to film, as opposed to video, where we are a statutory body, we can and do change our minds about films. We restore cuts, as in the case of *Last Tango*, or we call back films and make new ones, as in the case of sexual violence. And when films came onto video we had to rethink our policy on films that had first been seen by the Board ten, twenty or thirty years earlier, and, on the whole, most of the cuts have been restored on video. The trouble with videos is that they're out there on the shelf in vast numbers, unlike films, where there are a relatively small number of prints. So you can't withdraw the videos if we decide we want to change a decision on a particular title, but we can pass a different version for the same company, or a different company, three years later if we want to. The decisions we make are the decisions of the moment; like anybody else in authority we're totally fallible, but we make the best decisions that we can at that particular moment.

We've rethought our weapons policy quite a bit, particularly post-Hungerford, when we were under terrible pressure about weapons. We now have a policy about knives. We passed *First Blood* and *Rambo II* uncut, and the latter included what used to be called the Bowie knife but is now known as the Rambo knife. By the time the film was due out these knives were in the windows of weapon and survival shops all over England. There was also a magazine advertising weapons which contained pictures of Stallone wearing or brandishing them; this was ready to go out even before we'd classified the film, so as a result we were very much more cautious with the third Rambo film than the second one - we had to rethink our policy.

Rejected videos are very rare. At the end of September 1990 we'd passed 17,011 videos, with another 1,504 that had been passed pending packaging approval; we've only rejected twenty-eight, most of them because we feel that they fall foul of the law, the 'deprave and corrupt' test. We always consult our lawyers on these matters, but there are a lot of videos on the DPP's list that have been convicted by juries and we're not allowed to pass anything that infringes the criminal law. We have to assess the decisions of

Michael Gambon escapes the unkindest cut of all in **The Cook, the Thief** *and so on...*

juries and apply the law as best we can, and there's a video appeals committee which has nothing to do with the Board and can overrule our decisions. On *Visions of Ecstasy* the committee agreed with us that the video was blasphemous at law; now I believe the case may go to the European Court, and it will be fascinating to see what they think, since there isn't a blasphemy law in much of Europe. On *International Guerrillas*, on the other hand, the committee disagreed with us that it was libellous, Salman Rushdie himself said he was prepared to set the libel aside, and so the video was passed with an '18'. So there is a system of checks and balances. But mostly when a video is cut it's cut to category. Very few of the films that have recently been contentious in America have been cut in Britain - *The Cook, The Thief, His Wife and Her Lover, 9½ Weeks, Crimes of Passion, Tie Me Up! Tie Me Down!, Santa Sangre, Angel Heart* and so on. In general though, if you look at what happens to films in the USA and Britain which *are* cut, then they cut the sex and we cut the violence. So I don't think there's as much censorship here as some people think.

The Driller Killer has never been submitted to the Board as a video; it had so many prosecutions as a video nasty that I suppose nobody thought it worthwhile to do so. It seems to me to be a film about psychiatric breakdown, but the middle sequence would be a problem. I think we would trim the *process* of the violence in a lot of those street killings because of the gloating quality of some of them. Our general approach to violence is that we will allow the occasion of the violence, and we try always to allow the price of the violence, provided the shots of dead bodies and wounds are not too prurient. We're worried about the process of violence when it's a turn-on, when directors get their cameras in close on details of woundings, when audiences are intended to get off on the process of inflicting pain.

We see a huge range of films, and we do not give 'name' directors an easier ride compared to unknown

(Left) James Woods and Deborah Harry appear on a National Viewers and Listeners Association quiz show. (**Videodrome** actually, but you already knew that, didn't you...)

ones. Very often we discover a terrific film by an unknown director, and that creates a real buzz round the Board. What we do have to apply is the artistic defence, which is written into the Obscene Publications Act; if we think a film is of artistic merit, whoever it's by, then it might be possible to overlook details that would not be overlooked in a film without artistic merit. We've never cut a Cronenberg or a Scorsese film, for instance. There were terrible, maiming cuts in the video of *Videodrome*, but those were made by CIC who were hoping to put it out; we've now passed it uncut in a rerelease from the same company. In those days the video industry was running very scared because so many companies were being dragged through the courts in the early '80s, before the Video Recordings Act came in. We don't give anybody legal protection, though, because we, or a video company, can be prosecuted even for a certificated video. We accepted that because we wanted to preserve our independent, non-governmental status, and the *quid pro quo* for that was that we can be prosecuted for dropping a clanger over any section of the criminal law. I would rather be independent and vulnerable at law than a government lackey. But in the fifteen years I've been at the Board I can't remember a single instance of political censorship, which is interesting when you consider the kind of pressure that television has been under, especially regarding Northern Ireland. The government has never ever got in touch with any of us, including Lord Harewood, who might easily have been telephoned by the Home Secretary had he wanted to, to pressure us to make a particular decision. Of course, there's always the Sword of Damocles hanging over us, in that Parliament could de-designate us as the classifying body for video if they thought we weren't doing a good job. Once we were designated, they let us get on with it, and I gather that various Ministers told Lord Harewood that they were surprised at how well the job was being done. We're not leaned

THERE ARE THOSE WHO KILL VIOLENTLY !

DRILLER KILLER

on by government to do the kind of things that people fear. I suppose the mechanism is there if they chose to pack the Board. We fought against that possibility in 1985; we were designated a long time after the Act was passed, almost a whole year, and the papers began running stories asking why hadn't the Board been designated yet. The reason for this is that we would not allow the government to appoint our President and Vice President - they have the right to approve, but they had to be our appointees. ■

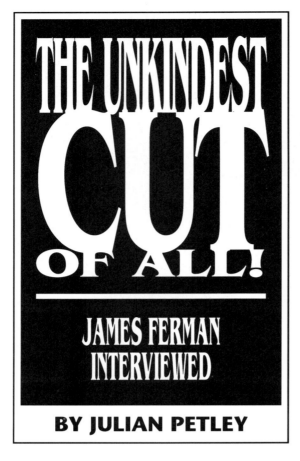

THE UNKINDEST CUT OF ALL!

JAMES FERMAN INTERVIEWED

BY JULIAN PETLEY

The perennially cheerful James Ferman.

SX: How did the Video Packaging Review Committee (VPRC) and the Video Advertising Review Committee come about, and how voluntary are the controls on advertising and packaging?

JF: When I originally wrote a video code of practice in 1982 I suggested that it include packaging and advertising because these were things that had really brought the industry into disrepute in the first place, not the contents of the tapes, which very few had actually seen. However, in the first instance the British Videogram Association (BVA, the main distributors' body) was not keen on the idea. After a while various companies, who were concerned about the industry's image, came to us and said that they'd like to bring in a voluntary system of control of packaging and advertising, and asked if we would administer the packaging side. It's only part of the Board's job to help the industry clean up its image if the industry asks it to do so. The companies suggested that we should withhold a video's certification until the packaging had been approved. I talked to our lawyers about this and they said we couldn't do that, as the certificate is statutory. I then talked to the Home Office, and they said that we could only carry out this scheme if the companies concerned are *willing* to have certification withheld - if they protest and tell us that we've got no legal right to withhold certification then we've got to give them one, providing of course the video itself is okay.

The VPRC has been in operation since December 1987. There are three industry representatives at each meeting, two from the BVA and one independent. Also in regular attendance are representatives from the BBFC, the Video Standards Council and the Advertising Standards Authority. The packaging side is administered by the BBFC. Packaging is submitted separately from the video itself and is first vetted by the Board's examiners, whose decisions must be ratified by the VPRC. The VPRC logo can appear only on those sleeves passed by the Committee, and videos not carrying the logo will not be stocked by those retailers who are members of the Video Standards Council (ie the vast bulk of major retailers).

I think that most major wholesalers are doing likewise, and we make companies aware of all this. They can, however, withdraw from the scheme at any time, and about twenty (mostly suppliers of mail order sex videos) have done so. The scheme has Home Office support and is registered with the Office of Fair Trading as a recognised restrictive trade practice. The courts have approved the logo as an indication of testing and approval under the Trade Descriptions Act.

SX: Do you see the Board as responding to public opinion, or as playing a more active role than that? And how do you judge what is public opinion anyway?

JF: We have the fairly tricky function of reading society aright, and occasionally we have played safe with what we take to be public opinion. Take the Michael Ryan affair for instance. Now, we know that there is no evidence that Ryan even had a video machine. But when we came to look at *Rambo III* we began to analyse what all the fuss was about and what the meaning of the Michael Ryan case was. (*In what the media referred to as 'The Hungerford Massacre', Ryan went berserk and shot thirty people, sixteen of whom died. Ed.*) We also examined very carefully what the film was actually doing. The number of shots in that film

apprehension, you see the firing, and then you see his suffering. It was structured in such a way that that was the pleasure you were being offered. On the basis of that we said that, yes, post-Hungerford, we do have a duty to be more cautious. *Rambo III* is not just a *Boys' Own* fantasy military adventure. The way in which the press covered Hungerford *was* disgraceful, but the press is a symptom of something. The tabloids have their finger on a pulse that we who read *Time Out* and *The Guardian* don't like to acknowledge - look at the results of public opinion polls and elections. The emotions which come out of the tabloids are redolent of something in society and of the way in which these images work on people. If people are worried in a kind of inarticulate way about weaponry and woundings both in society and on film, and they're making an unconscious connection between the two, are we, because we can't find justification for saying 'case proven', justified in disregarding them?

Having spent my first ten years at the Board teaching examiners that each film must be judged on its own merits, and the context that counts is the context of the film itself, it's quite a turnabout to say that the context may be wider than the film itself; it's the social context, the media context, the kind of media climate the film is coming into. That was the thing about the video nasties: it wasn't so much the individual film after film of bodies being cut up, zombies eating flesh and so on. That's why we said, "Wait a minute, is this all the video industry is about, and what is it doing to people to keep on seeing these images? First of all it devalues the images themselves, and what is it doing to people's sensibilities?"

SX: Some of the cuts which the Board requires in films and videos are very small indeed. Is there any point in all this fiddling about with one second here, two seconds there?

JF: Sometimes even cutting even a few seconds from a film can make a huge difference. I was a director for seventeen years, and I know that every frame counts in the cutting room. I don't know whether the cutting of individual films can solve this problem. We're in a bind, we all now recognise there's a problem; there's no doubt that films have popularised weapons more than we realised five years ago and I think that we were to some extent responsible for not taking that seriously enough at the beginning. The popular press is very fond of saying that the effect of a film is to trigger behaviour, but there's almost no evidence that any film has ever triggered any behaviour. It may have triggered some psychopath somewhere, but as the people from the Tavistock Clinic said to us, somebody who is predisposed to psychopathic behaviour can be triggered by the sight of a boiled egg in a dish. People who are mentally disturbed are triggered by very odd things, very unlikely and unpredictable attitudes; it's the drip-drip-drip effect. Capital punishment came to an end after about thirty years of world, and especially Hollywood, cinema which was very much influenced by the whole Freudian/Marxist complex that crime is not the fault of the individual but the fault of society and upbringing, so we must understand the criminal in order to help him. Then the Hollywood Production Code was thrown out in 1968 and the revenge drama came in, spaghetti westerns, urban vigilante films, all declaring that the beast must die. And now, all around the world, there's a new generation who've been having that message drummed into them for the last fifteen

(Above left) The infamous rape scene from **Death Wish.**

(Below left) Who was that masked man? Jeff Goldblum, actually, in a part he'd probably rather forget...

which glamorise weaponry was very worrying. And then there's the problem of what one of my examiners called 'the typical Rambo sequence' - he lines someone up in his sights, then you get the man looking scared, then you get Rambo firing, then you get a blood spurt. The whole thing is set up so you are actually geared through editing to enjoy the suffering of someone who is *warned* they are going to suffer: so you see his

Perhaps it wasn't such a step from **The Exorcist** *to* **Repossessed** *for Linda Blair after all...*

SX: I'd like to talk about some individual cases of videos that have not received certificates. What about *The Exorcist*?

JF: This is one that worries us a lot, and Warners have asked us about it. The trouble with video is that you can't control the age of the viewers at all, and there are so many well documented stories about teenagers having hysteria from this film. It's a very scary story for an age group with maximum superstition, and we've been very cautious about it. We discussed religious fantasy at one of the Video Consultative Council meetings, and a Bishop said that he didn't think that one could simply label this stuff fantasy, it has a tremendous power to disturb and persuade, particularly the young. We've gone very cautiously in this area, and there are three films from the early '70s to which we haven't given certificates. On video *The Exorcist* has never been officially submitted to us, although Warners have rung up from time to time and said, "What do you think?", and we've said that on the whole we don't think the time is yet right. But they don't seem to be pressing very hard. I discouraged them because I didn't think we could pass it uncut, and when you get a classic film you really don't want to cut it apart. It's got a unique power to disturb the religiously inclined young. The power comes from the fact that it's terribly persuasively done.

SX: What about the original *Death Wish*?

JF: This has been submitted on video but we've never passed it. We would probably pass the TV version. The rape was much, much stronger than any of us remembered, because it was so long since we'd seen it. *Death Wish II* is out now on video, but only in the cut cinema version, where again the problem was rape. Our problem with *Death Wish*, post-Hungerford, was firstly the rape. *Death Wish* is very much better made and edited than *II*, the rape is very expertly put together, the shots are very brief but quite horrendous, and there are some moments which are in no doubt a turn-on. There is now evidence to suggest that some people are turned on by sexual violence, so now we have to worry even about a rape which is deliberately ugly because it may be getting to those people. Ever since the late '70s we've had a very clear policy that it is wrong to present rape erotically or as a spectator sport, but it never struck me that it is wrong to worry about ugly rape, which I'd always taken as showing people what rape was really like, rape from the side of the victim. *The Accused* presents an interesting example. If the rape had come at the beginning, as it does in *Death Wish II*, it would have been a totally different film. One's sympathies are so structured by the time one gets to it, it's so difficult to identify at all with the main man in the dock, you're seeing a lot of it through the eyes of a boy who's decided to appear in the witness box, and the music plays a very significant role too. Just at the moment the film might become a turn-on, the music becomes tragic and dominates the scene. To cut something that's *meant* to be over the top so that it's no longer too *far* over the top, is very difficult. I have to say that I personally don't think that this film is depraving or corrupting, but the courts have the last word. A lot of the fuss in 1984, before the Video Recordings Act came into effect, was that kids were watching these movies, and so when it went before a magistrate or jury they were concluding that the likely audience was young teenagers. The point is, do we actually *want* younger teenagers watch-

years, and they believe that we should bring back capital punishment. Those people are now having their prejudices reinforced by public entertainment, now they see that message wherever they go. The fact that Mel Gibson takes a very brutal revenge on two criminals after he discovers that his girlfriend has been killed in *Lethal Weapon 2*, that he takes the law into his own hands and kills quite brutally like a criminal himself, and the fact that he is the *hero*, is symptomatic of the public morality of films now. This was Bronson vigilantism in spades from a very sympathetic, engaging character, and we said that that's not on for a '15' film and insisted that they take it out.

ing this bloody spectacle? I can appreciate that. If it had been absolutely certain that *The Evil Dead* was only being seen by adults, I doubt whether there would have been many convictions.

SX: What has been refused certification recently?

JF: *The Trip* remains banned on film and video. It's been rejected three times on film and twice on video. When LSD came back on the scene a few years ago at the time of Operation Julie we felt in the wrong hands the film could be a tremendous advertisement for LSD. We confirmed the most recent rejection in 1988, before contemporary worries about acid house parties. On the video front we've rejected *Hidden Rage*, in which an AIDS victim takes his revenge by raping women and so giving them AIDS. The rapes are presented in a titillating, eroticised fashion, and anyway, it's hardly helpful to the cause of trying to change the image of rape victims to show them infected with AIDS; this kind of thing appeals to the lowest common denominator of public prejudice. There's also *Curfew*, in which a family is terrorised by two escaped prisoners - even in the soft version which we saw, there's rape, forced dancing on broken glass, and repeated degradation and mutilation, all presented solely for entertainment; *Evil Protégé* (aka *Butcher, Baker, Nightmare Maker*), *A Coming of Angels* and *Slumber Party Massacre II*. ∎

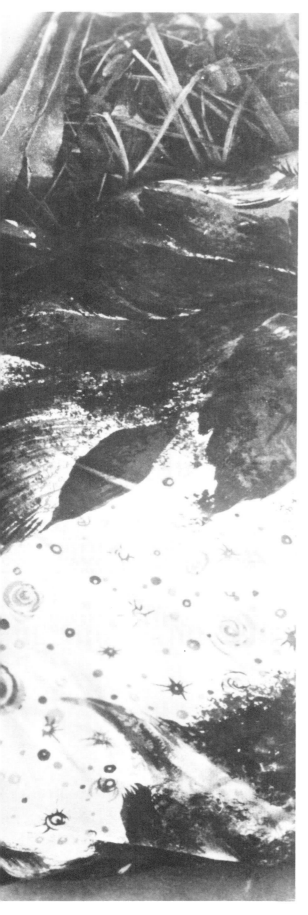

SHOCKING ASIA

EXPLOITATION CINEMA IN THE PHILIPPINES

BY DAVID TAYLOR

My introduction to the realities of the Filipino exploitation movie industry came one afternoon in 1972, in the foyer of the Hotel Intercontinental in Makati, Manila's main business district. I was sitting having coffee with my mother, when a ramshackle flatbed truck pulled into the hotel forecourt. A couple of bored-looking Filipino youths off-loaded a 16mm camera and a set of portable lighting rigs and trundled them into the foyer. A few minutes later a car pulled up behind the truck and exuded a group of Americans: two men and one woman. With little in the way of rehearsal, the oldest of the group

A victim of (gasp) **The Blood Drinkers.**

KUNG FU GIRLS ON THE RAMPAGE..!

Deadly with their hands... Deadlier with their bodies..!

TARGET INTERNATIONAL PRESENT

WONDER WOMEN

NANCY KWAN, ROSS HAGEN   MARIA DE ARAGON, ROBERTA COLLINS, SHIRLEY WASHINGTON   ROBERT O'NEIL   ROSS HAGEN

explained to his two companions that he wanted them to run through the hotel foyer and through the revolving doors into the forecourt. The two actors went through their paces with the antiquated camera rolling noisily in the background.

The director didn't seem happy with the result. In a moment of wild improvisation, he collared a young Filipino and suggested that the youth get caught in the revolving doors as the two Americans exited, to be left spinning helplessly in their wake. The two actors seemed happy with this decision, as did the young Filipino, who could obviously see stardom beckoning. The crew did a further two takes, after which the Americans bundled back into their car and took off, leaving the 'crew' to load the equipment back onto the lorry.

The entire episode took no more than twenty-five minutes and during that time absolutely no explanation was made to anyone in the hotel as to what the hell was going on. It was only on closer questioning of a bellboy that I learned permission had been granted by the hotel management some days earlier for the crew to shoot the scene as part of a film to be entitled *The Terrible Transplants of Dr Tsu*.

It was over thirteen years later, when I was living in London, that I finally got to see the movie that was being made that day. It had been eventually released under the title *Wonder Women* in 1973 - something of a schlock classic starring an over-the-hill Nancy Kwan as a mad scientist who has genetically engineered an army of Amazon martial arts experts, along with the inevitable gaggle of malformed mutants in her laboratory's cellar - although my role as an 'innocent bystander' had been relegated to the cutting room

floor. All that remains of the sequence (which begins with the two actors trashing one of the hotel rooms in a decidedly unconvincing kung fu fight) is a long shot of the couple running from the hotel, filmed from the roof of Rustans department store opposite. The scene acts as a prologue for one of the longest and most tedious car chases in modern cinema.

Only then was I able to put names to the people who had been making the movie all those years ago - the young American actor was the immortal Ross Hagen and the director was Robert Vincent O'Neil, noted auteur of *The Psycho Lover* (1970), *Blood Mania* (1970) and *Angel* (1984). I guess I missed my chance for an exclusive interview.

As they say, that's entertainment...

The Philippines is a collection of over 7,000 islands clustered together in the Pacific Ocean, just off the coast of China, and their history is one of colonisation and re-colonisation. Discovered by the Portuguese, the islands have in their time been taken over by the Spanish, the Japanese and the Americans, only being granted their independence by Douglas MacArthur after helping to repel the Japanese after the Second World War. (The Filipino role in this conflict was portrayed, rather fancifully, in Eddie Romero's *The Raiders of Leyte Gulf* [1963] and *The Ravagers* [1965] starring John Saxon.) It was in the same year as *Wonder Women* was being shot that President Ferdinand Marcos, who had served as the country's leader since 1965, decided to declare martial law in an effort to maintain power - something he succeeded in doing for the next fourteen years. The corrupt (and then some) Marcos years and the 'bloodless revolution' which saw his demise were, for most people, the events which really put the Philippines onto the world map.

This strange history has had very peculiar effects on the country and its culture. Thanks to the Spanish influence, it is the only Southeast Asian country that is predominantly Roman Catholic. Spanish folklore has also been fused with the native Filipino to provide a hybrid canon of myths and legends. The American presence has westernised the country to a high degree, with most Filipinos able to speak at least a smattering of English.

Like most of the people of Asia, the Filipinos have been in love with movies almost from the first moment they set eyes on them. But their indigenous style of film-making differs greatly from the explosive pyrotechnics of the Chinese and the methodical *longueurs* of the Japanese. The combined influence of religion, politics and Western popular culture has had an undeniable effect on all aspects of the local film industry.

As we shall see...

It all began with Gerardo de Leon.

Affectionately known in the industry as Manong, Gerry de Leon was arguably the Philippines' first major international film director. The seventy films he directed between the late '50s and his death in 1981 comprised historical epics like *Noli Me Tangere* (1961) and *El Filibusterismo* (1962) (both based on the novels of the Philippines' finest author, Jose Rizal), socially conscious films like *The Moses Padilla Story* (1961) (wherein a young man returning to his home province of Negros is radicalised by the corruption which has sprung up in his absence) and psychological dramas like *Lilet* (1971)

(concerning a doctor's psychoanalysis of a young female amnesiac, which uncovers a past history of incest and inherited insanity). Yet even while he was carving out this niche as the David Lean of Filipino cinema, he was far better known internationally as the co-director of the *Blood Island* movies.

In 1959, de Leon directed the first true Filipino exploitation movie - *Terror is a Man*. A basic variation on H.G. Wells' *The Island of Dr Moreau* (which was to provide a staple plotline for Filipino exploitation movies for years afterwards, cropping up as *The Twilight People* and *Superbeast* [both 1972] to name but two), it was aimed squarely at the lucrative international market by employing the talents of foreign actors like Francis Lederer and Greta Thyssen in the story of a scientist attempting to transform a tiger into a human being. It was one of the first films to employ a 'horror horn' to warn the faint-hearted (and the easily nauseated) of an imminent autopsy sequence (interestingly enough, *Superbeast* also threw in an actual autopsy for good measure - what the hell, it beats paying for make-up and effects!).

The success of *Terror is a Man*, both locally and internationally, led de Leon to further horror titles, including *The Blood Drinkers* (aka *Vampire People*, 1966) and *Dugo Ng Vampira* (aka *Creatures of Evil*, aka *Curse of the Vampires*, 1970). With the help of producer/director Eddie Romero, who had already entered the international film market with the aforementioned *The Raiders of Leyte Gulf* and *The Ravagers*, he also created the *Blood Island* trilogy, comprising *Brides of Blood* (aka *Island of Living Horror*, 1968), *The Mad Doctor of Blood Island* (aka *Tomb of the Living Dead*, 1969) and *Beast of Blood* (aka *Beast of the Dead*, 1970), co-directing all but the last of them.

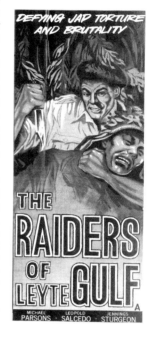

(Above right) A blood drinker in **The Blood Drinkers.**

(Below right) Complete chaos in **Dugo Ng Vampira.**

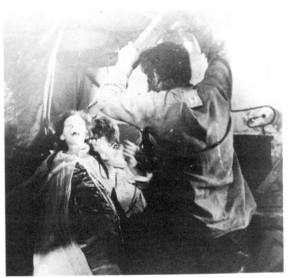

Whilst all of these films gained at least some exposure abroad, often under wilfully misleading titles and wholly inappropriate advertising campaigns (American cinema patrons were given free plastic wedding rings when they went to see *Brides of Blood*!), what was notable was how they tapped into the Filipino psyche. For most Western viewers, the labyrinthine plotting and deliberate pacing of both *The Blood Drinkers* and *Dugo Ng Vampira* was a rather quaint novelty, transposing traditional vampire motifs into a Southeast Asian setting. Yet if one looks beyond the admittedly primitive film techniques being employed (the bizarre colour tinting of the black and white *The Blood Drinkers* is particularly distracting) and the tendency to lapse into the most gratuitous conventions of melodrama, both films offer a

fascinating insight into their makers. Ronald Remy as the bald-headed, sunglassed vampire Marco in *The Blood Drinkers* can be seen as the last ghost of the Spanish aristocracy, literally bleeding the proletariat dry until the inevitable revolution complete with rampaging villagers carrying burning crosses. *Dugo Ng Vampira* is an even more perversely Catholic movie, presenting vampirism as a form of forbidden sexuality that transcends familial and gender barriers. Warped Catholic icons present themselves in the form of a ruby-lipped Madonna and the inevitable purgative crucifix. It is also worth pointing out that like most Catholic countries, with their concentration on the sanctity of the Virgin Mary, the Philippines is a tacitly matriarchal society - which adds an extra *frisson* to the scenes of Mary Walter as the vampire mother shackled up in the cellar, whilst above her head the family unit slowly disintegrates in a welter of incest and bloodlust. The idea of forbidden and aberrant sexuality also informs both *Brides of Blood*, wherein the mad scientist is shown to be impotent until his unnatural experiments transform him into a slaving monster with decidedly voracious sexual desires, and *The Mad Doctor of Blood Island*, where the Chlorophyll Monster created by Dr Lorca (Ronald Remy again) is revealed to be horny as well as thorny. The message is clear - playing at being God can ruin your sex life!

(Just as an aside... The actor Ronald Remy, who starred in many of the de Leon features, had been something of a matinée idol in the '60s. By the early '70s Remy had faded as a screen star, but assumed the mantle of television presenter for an eclectic variation of *The Dating Game*, the American precursor to *Blind Date*, called *Rhoda and Me*. The titular Rhoda was a talking computer that tabulated the suitability of the contestants for each other [and had a neat line in salacious remarks], but was actually about as convincing a depiction of modern technological hardware as Ted V.

Mikels' corpse grinding machine.)

It seems fair to assume that the thematic consistency of these films was more down to Gerry de Leon than Eddie Romero. When Romero assumed the full writer/ producer/ director mantle for *Beast of Blood*, the resulting film continued the misadventures of the chlorophyll monster with a routine horror scenario that simply upped the ante on gore. Subsequent collaborations between Romero and *Blood Island* star John Ashley were similarly disappointing. *Beast of the Yellow Night* (1971) had a promising concept - sleazeball Ashley makes a deal with the devil in exchange for his life, agreeing to turn into a cannibalistic monster every so often to devour the souls of victims and bring them to hell with him on judgement day. The notion that Ashley would gradually assume the different identities of his victims was a fascinating idea, but was all but ignored by the film-makers.

(Another aside... It's rather amusing that no one who has watched the British video release of *Beast of the Yellow Night* [billed on the box simply as *Beast*] has ever commented on the fact that two of the reels have been transposed. One can only assume that no one noticed...)

In 1972, the team made *The Twilight People*, an entertaining (primarily for the wrong reasons) but fairly dismal monster movie, with Ashley helping to lead a revolt by some unconvincing manimals against their maker (the flying Bat Man is a hoot!). Still, it did have the benefit of an appearance by the ever-wonderful Pam Grier as a cat woman. By 1973, Ashley and Romero had hit their collaborative nadir with *Beyond Atlantis*, a dreadful mess combining pearl poachers, fish men with ping-pong ball eyes and an undersexed mermaid.

It was fairly soon after this that Ashley packed his bags and returned to Hollywood (where he still produces for the cinema and television) and Eddie Romero all but abandoned exploitation movies in favour of loftier subjects like *Aguila* (1980), an impressive attempt to reconcile the modern Filipino with their history wherein the main character travels from youth under Spanish occupation to old age during the Marcos regime, and *Palaban* (1980), a study of sexual alienation. In 1982, he brought John Saxon (who had starred in his movie *The Ravagers* almost two decades earlier) back over to play the lead in *Desire*, the soapy tale of an interracial marriage.

There is, however, one interesting codicil to John Ashley's short career in the Philippines. In Mark Thomas McGee's book *Beyond Ballyhoo: Motion Picture Promotion and Gimmicks*, Ashley talks about his Filipino movies thus: "I did one other horror movie over there that was never released here called *Witchcraft*. In this picture we did an autopsy on a real body. Which was very unique. It was enlightening to me. For a couple of bottles of Johnny Walker we went to the local barrio and got the body of some prisoner who had just been killed in a fight. We were able to film the autopsy. And the whole sequence is in the film. I'm talking about the skull coming off and everything." This particular film is unfamiliar to me (and let's face it, it doesn't sound like the sort of movie one could forget) and I would venture a guess that it was probably never released in the Philippines either. It would be nice to think that it *was* released somewhere.

The Vietnam War had a crucial impact on the Philippines. At the time of the war, the islands had gained their independence from the USA but were still of tactical importance as a Southeast Asian base for the American airforce engaged in combat. The omnipresent (albeit largely imaginative) threat of an imminent communist invasion was used as a lever to maintain US presence in the country.

The war also had an impact on the local film industry. The terrain of the Philippines was considered a suitable substitute for North Vietnam or Cambodia (if you squinted real hard), which made it a natural for location shoots. Hollywood, after all, was still stinging over the critical scorn that had been heaped on the Hollywood Hills locations used for the dismal *The Green Berets* (1968). The Philippines also had a successful track record as a location for other movies about combat in the Pacific - most notably John Barwell's *Huk!* (1956), Cornel Wilde's *Beach Red* (1967) and Robert Aldrich's *Too Late the Hero* (1970). Thus in 1970 Jack Starrett, who was later to carve out a niche making blaxploitationers like *Slaughter* (1972) and *Cleopatra Jones* (1973) as well as the superior *Race with the Devil* (1975), transplanted the cast and crew of *The*

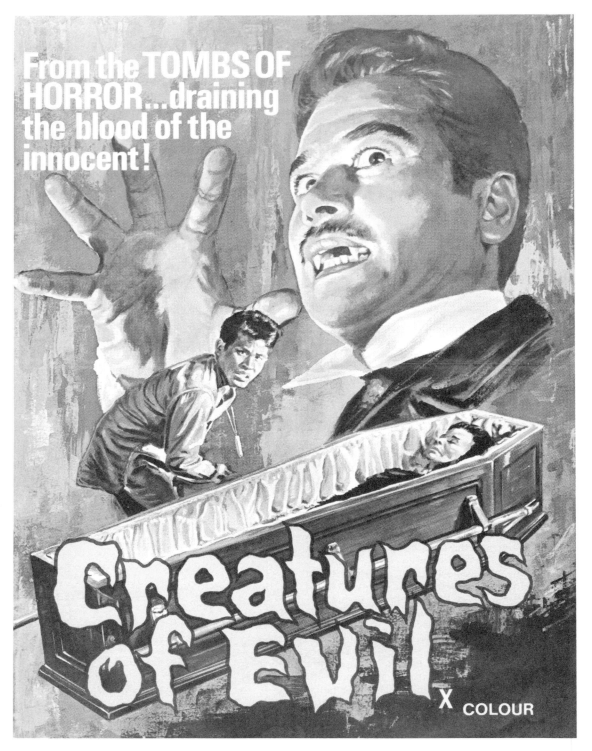

From the TOMBS OF HORROR...draining the blood of the innocent!

Creatures of Evil

X COLOUR

Dugo Ng Vampira, *aka* Creatures of Evil.

Losers over to Manila for the shoot.

The Losers is reputed to be the first movie to show soldiers in combat in Vietnam. Whether this is true or not is a moot point - but it deserves at least a footnote in the history of modern cinema for grafting the anti-Vietnam sentiments of the biker movie sub-genre with an actual war film. William Smith stars as the leader of a gang of Hell's Angels conscripted to carry out a suicide mission to rescue a presidential aide being held captive by the Communists in Cambodia. Despite this promising premise, *The Losers* remains something of a disappointment, torn as it is between presenting an all-out action extravaganza and a sober meditation on the futility of war. It did, however, set the tone for things to come...

Sidney J. Furie's *The Boys in Company C* (1978) was the first major Vietnam movie to take advantage of a Filipino location shoot. The anti-war sentiments that had been pretty much suppressed in *The Losers* were now allowed to dictate the action. Following a group of raw recruits from the draft board through to the front line and depicting not only the graphic horrors of war but the ineptitude and corruption of the American military machine, the film has sadly been all but forgotten in the veritable welter of Vietnam epics that followed in its wake.

Of course there was more than verisimilitude on Hollywood's mind when it transported cast and crew to such a far flung outpost to simply shoot a movie. For one thing, the Philippines had supplanted both Spain and Italy as the cheapest place in the world to make films, thanks to generous Government support engendered by a need to alleviate the country's flagging economy. Aside from which, any film with a Vietnam setting was able to call upon the services of the Philippines' armed forces, with their vast stock of operational American military hardware, to add even more realism to the action.

It was the grand folly of *Apocalypse Now* (1979) which put paid to a lot of this. Whereas most film units treated the generosity of the Government with a considerable amount of respect, Francis Ford Coppola's attempts to create the ultimate war experience caused more than a few questions to be asked in gubernatorial circles. Aside from his wilful misuse of high explosives in the jungle terrain, stories began running in the press about the alleged 'loss' of certain helicopters. True or not, the various rumours that floated down the Pagsanjan River (the location for most of the film and one of the country's most popular tourist attractions) were a continuing source of concern/amusement in the national newspapers. The film quickly became referred to as *Apocalypse When* and, perhaps inevitably, *Apocalypse Never*.

The trouble was that although Coppola might have been able to fix the Government and the army, he couldn't fix either the weather or the environment.

Shooting overran into the monsoon season and a particularly ferocious typhoon decimated the sets and equipment. Actors were quitting with monotonous regularity, unwilling to put up with the gruelling conditions imposed by the location. Then shooting was delayed still further when Martin Sheen suffered a heart attack and had to be rushed back to Manila for medical treatment.

(Quick aside... A friend of mine, who had a small non-speaking role as an American officer during the 'Playboy bunnies' sequence, confirmed the stories of real misery on the set. He spent four days upriver with several hundred other extras, most of the time sheltering from the torrential rain under plastic bags supported by twigs, for which he received a haircut [standard American military short-back-and-sides], his meals [bowl of rice and fish] and the equivalent of around £50 [which got stolen]. To add insult to injury, his own scene was excised from the final cut.)

To alleviate boredom between halts in the shooting and, no doubt, to attempt to increase positive PR for the film, Coppola and whichever actors were still managing to stay sane in the jungle would travel down to Manila and appear on a local television chat show, *Seeing Stars with Joe Quirino*. JQ, as the host was affectionately known, was a former newspaper gossip columnist who had gained enough popularity to warrant his own TV spot. All visiting celebrities were rushed onto the set - a mock-up of JQ's living room, complete with a whole partyload of 'pals' chatting aimlessly by the bar - to deliver a breathless plug for their latest venture while perched on the edge of his *chaise longue*. So often could Coppola be seen skulking

(Left) *'Meaningful' looks are exchanged between* **The Blood Drinkers.**

in the background that he became like some sizeable and belligerent item of furniture.

(Scurrilous aside... Another noteworthy guest on *Seeing Stars* in the late '70s was former British beauty queen Helen Morgan, who had recently been stripped of her Miss World title. Lord only knows how or why Ms Morgan ended up in Manila, but she certainly stayed long enough to shoot one tawdry feature film with the unlikely title of *Arrest the Nurse Killer!* [1977]. This early stalk and slash vehicle had our Helen as a nurse working in Manila being pursued round a variety of tourist spots by a gibbering maniac with a penchant for dicing female members of the medical profession. It is probably to Ms Morgan's unending relief that said feature, which ended up as the third highest grossing local film of the year, was never released in her home country - at least, to the best of my knowledge...)

After the events surrounding the shooting of *Apocalypse Now*, it came as no real surprise when Oliver Stone's *Platoon* (1986) eschewed massive pyrotechnics and airborne combat sequences in favour of a more subtle and low key approach. The horrendous helicopter crash on the Philippines location of *Delta Force 2* in 1989 perhaps bore out the wisdom of Stone's decision.

It wasn't only the producers of Hollywood war epics who had their beady eyes trained on the Philippines. Any number of low budget movie moguls could see the financial advantages of a Manila shoot - perfect weather (given the right time of year), colourful locations and, most importantly, cheap labour.

It was in the early '70s that Roger Corman came up with the idea of hiring Gerry de Leon and Eddie Romero to helm low budget films on his behalf, to cash in on the then popular craze for prison movies. If American gaols were hellholes, then how much worse would a Southeast Asian prison be? The answer was

(*Right*) *A fistful of offal...***The Mad Doctor of Blood Island.**

(sort of) provided by *Women in Cages* (1972), wherein a young American woman is framed for drug smuggling and hurled into prison, where she runs the usual gauntlet of vicious lesbian warders (Pam Grier again), jailhouse catfights and other sundry humiliations before the inevitable break for freedom. Sadly, despite the increased production values afforded by the injection of American cash, de Leon and Romero could add nothing to this resolutely American scenario to lift it out of the rut. It is almost impossible to differentiate between *Women in Cages* and any of the other Philippines-based prison movies of the period being made by American directors, including Jack Hill's *The Big Doll House* (1971) and *The Big Bird Cage* (1972), Richard Jackson's *The Big Bustout* (1973), and *Sweet Sugar* (aka *Chaingang Girls*, 1972) directed by Michael Levesque, fresh from *Werewolves on Wheels* (1971).

The same applies to most of the other American movies being made in the Philippines at the time, among them *Superbeast* and *Daughters of Satan* (1972), two films shot back-to-back by producer Aubrey Schenck (the latter notable only for starring Tom Selleck as a reincarnated Spanish conquistador and being directed by Hollingsworth Morse, the man behind the odious kiddie movie *Pufnstuf* [1970]). These films really could have been shot anywhere, by anyone, with little perceivable difference. (I imagine that the same holds true for *The Golden Viper* [1983] starring Eartha Kitt and *Night of the Cobra Woman* [1972] directed by ex-Warhol collaborator Andrew Mayer and starring the delightfully named Joy Bang, but I've unfortunately never seen them.)

One exception to this rule was *The Deathhead Virgin* (1972), a peculiar little horror film that appears never to have been theatrically released in either the UK or USA and doesn't even warrant a passing mention in any of the usually reliable textbooks. The plot concerns a deep sea diver and professional treasure hunter played by Jock Gaynor (who is himself presumably a

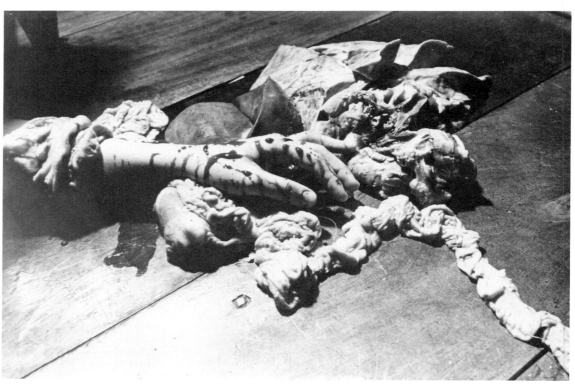

professional diver since he also claims credit for directing the underwater sequences) who, in the course of exploring a shipwreck, unleashes a malevolent sea siren who has been trapped aboard the submerged vessel. Despite the tedium of some sequences (there is a lot of wandering aimlessly along beaches), the film does have a certain oblique charm and an undeniably original monster: a voluptuous island maiden with a skull face. *The Deathhead Virgin* was written and produced by Ward Gaynor (presumably some relation to Jock) and directed by Norman Foster. (Can anyone tell me if this is the same Norman Foster who directed *Mr Moto* and *Charlie Chan* movies in the '30s and '40s?) (*Norman Foster died in 1976 at the age of seventy-six, his last film being* Brighty of the Grand Canyon *in 1967, so it seems unlikely... Ed.*)

Although much of his later work falls into the trap of being far too Americanised to be of much real interest, one other Filipino director that has to be mentioned is Cirio H. Santiago. In the '60s, Santiago ran his own production company which was responsible for, among other things, *The Blood Drinkers*. In the early '70s, he affiliated himself with Roger Corman alongside de Leon and Romero, working on everything from *Women in Cages* to *Up From the Depths* (1979) in a production capacity. Whilst his own directorial efforts - including horror movies like *Vampire Hookers* (aka *Sensuous Vampires*, aka *Cemetery Girls*, 1978) and *Demon of Paradise* (1987), *Mad Max* clones like *Wheels of Fire* (aka *Desert Warrior*, 1985) and

Equalizer 2000 (1987), sexploitation items like *Fly Me* (1973) and *Cover Girl Models* (1975), and straight action films like *TNT Jackson* (1975) and the *Silk* series (1986 and on) - are efficient enough as standard exploitation fare, they offer the viewer precious little else. Even his Filipino movies, like the tasteless rape/revenge melodrama *Ang Galing Galing Mo ... Mrs Jones* (1980) (described by the Philippines' leading film critic Isagani R. Cruz as having 'not a single good sequence') resort to American genre conventions to make their point.

Whilst the established Filipino film industry was enjoying its brief flirtation with Hollywood in the early '70s, a whole new generation of film-makers were beginning to flex their creative muscle. Without a doubt the leader of this brat pack was Celso Ad Castillo, a former writer of Filipino 'komiks' (as in many countries, young Filipino artists weaned on comic books quickly realised that the form offered the ideal forum for presenting radical and controversial concepts in a relatively blameless context). Castillo began adapting his 'komiks' stories for the screen, spearheading what was to become known locally as the 'bomba movie' genre (the term roughly translates as 'bold movies').

Early Castillo efforts included *Nympha* (1970), which insisted on directly associating sexual congress with religious fervour, and *Kill Barbara with Panic* (1973), a supernatural revenge drama wherein a ghost returns to

The Godlike genius of Gerry de Leon and Eddie Romero manifests itself as the Chlorophyll Monster in **The Mad Doctor of Blood Island***.*

graphically persecute her former husband and his mistress. What had been implicit within the films of Gerry de Leon a decade previously was now fully explicit, with no subject too extreme or repellent to receive full widescreen depiction. In 1977, Castillo received widespread critical and popular acclaim for his film *Burlesk Queen*, which starred former teen idol Vilma Santos in the title role of a sleazy Manila stripper. For a few, however, Castillo had gone too far - not only was he presenting one of the country's best loved starlets as a complete slut, he was also using this 'smut' to tacitly illustrate the moral failings of the Marcos regime. When the film picked up ten major awards, including Best Film, at the annual Metro Manila Film Festival (which also, incidentally, would have guaranteed Castillo a cash incentive of $16,000 and exemption from paying the local entertainment tax) it was the last straw. The Metro Manila Commission, sponsor of the Festival, recalled all the awards and declared the judges' decision null and void.

It was in 1981 that Castillo released what remains his definitive work to date, *Uhaw Na Dagat*. Reputed to be one of the most expensive Filipino productions ever to be mounted and certainly one of the best-looking, the film took over a year to complete on location at remote island settings. An eclectic mixture of absurdist comedy, horror imagery and twisted religious iconography, the film centres around three young sisters living alone on an idyllic island paradise and awaiting the return of their Godlike father figure. Intruders into this veritable Eden include a soldier named Crisanto, the film's obvious Christ figure who is seduced by one of the sisters before revealing himself to be her brother, a travelling freak show comprising dwarves and a giant cannibal, and last but not least a satanic pirate (played by Eddie Garcia, star of *Beast of Blood*). Castillo's penchant for the bizarre extends beyond incest into outright bestiality when the half-human giant is openly seduced by one of the sisters. He also includes disturbing scenes of the dwarves dancing naked and the ritual sacrifice of a live goat. The intense cross-cutting of the finale - as various groups dispersed around the island conspire to murder each other - becomes so rapid as to dissolve into total abstraction. As might be expected, the film was heavily censored on its initial release, only emerging in a complete version on videocassette.

The only other Filipino director to rival Castillo's notoriety is the late Lino Brocka, whose films have been screened at The London Film Festival and on Channel Four. Striving for *cinéma vérité*, but frequently resorting to outright melodrama, Brocka's movies are possibly the most socially conscious in Filipino film history. His most famous films are *Maynila, Sa Mga Kuko Ng Liwanag* (1975), the story of a young boy from the provinces who travels to Manila looking for work and gradually drifts into a life of crime, and *Macho Dancer* (1985), about a young homosexual employed as a male stripper. Brocka served time for being a dissident and both these films were banned by the Government. (Mind you, judging by current British legislation, I wouldn't expect *Macho Dancer* to turn up on UK screens in the near future...)

The generation that saw the emergence of Castillo and Brocka also spawned a few other notable talents, many of whom dabbled in fantasy (or at least pseudo-fantasy) subjects. Ismael Bernard's *Himala* (1982) starred Nora Aunor (another former teen heart-throb) as a peasant girl who has a Lourdes-like vision of the Virgin Mary and develops miraculous healing powers.

As a result Aunor's sleepy backwater town is suddenly overrun with pilgrims; crime proliferates, prostitution springs up, and eventually the young girl is violated by her followers. This neo-Sodom is ultimately cleansed by a second Flood.

Far less oblique is Mike De Leon's *Alpha Kappa Omega Batch '81* (1982), about a bunch of university fraternity brothers whose elaborate hazing rituals move from harmless pranks into elaborate and lethal torture sessions. In one gross recreation of Stanley Milgram's famous psychology experiment, neophyte frat brats are strapped into wet chairs and dealt increasingly powerful electric shocks everytime they fail to deliver the correct answer to the question "Did martial law help our country?" In another scene, an amusing pastiche of *Cabaret*, the Marcos Government is directly equated with the German National Socialist Party. Hardly surprisingly, the Government came down hard on the film and would not allow it to be released - but help came from a most unexpected quarter when Imee Marcos, daughter of Ferdinand and Imelda, defied her parents and the law by personally arranging for a private première. The film was subsequently screened as part of the Director's Fortnight at Cannes. Another controversial De Leon feature was *Kisapmata* (1981). Based on the short story 'The House On Zapote Street' by journalist and author Nick Joaquin (who also penned the story collection *Tropical Gothic* and the hard-boiled crime novel *Cave and Shadows*), the film probes into the reasons why a loving father unaccountably killed his daughter, son-in-law, wife and finally himself. Based on a real-life event, the film starts as pseudo-documentary and gradually builds into a thundering slab of *grand guignol*.

Less successful were three 'komiks' adaptations in the shape of Mike Relon Makiling's *Mag-Toning Muna Tayo* (1981), a banal comedy about demonic possession, Antonio Jose Perez' *Haplos* (1982), an ineffective spectral love story, and Joey Gosiengfiao's *Ang Kambal Sa Uma* (1979) which, as Isagani R. Cruz puts it, 'meanders through attempted rapes, mistaken identities, contrived confrontations, numberless minor characters, as well as morbid rat scenes.'

In 1981, the same year that Celso Ad Castillo was scandalising audiences with *Uhaw Na Dagat*, Eddie Romero made a return to fantasy films with *Kamakalawa*. A brave attempt to place Filipino folklore and mythology onto the big screen, but unfortunately unable to supply anything remotely approaching a special effect, the film was hamstrung from its inception. Things weren't helped by a confused and confusing plotline that contrasted a feud between the gods and the continuing war between two earthbound tribes. The film proved reasonably popular at the box office and was even placed in competition at the 1982 Manila International Film Festival, but was critically lambasted and soon forgotten.

The trouble was that *Kamakalawa* simply couldn't live up to its audiences' expectations. In the same way that Chinese fantasy expert Tsui Hark had to employ British and American effects technicians to give him the expertise to make *Zu: Warriors of the Magic Mountain* and *A Chinese Ghost Story*, Romero badly needed an injection of real screen magic.

He was also working in competition with one of the mainstays of the Filipino film industry - Fernando Poe Jr. For over three decades, Poe had remained one of the Philippines' top box office draws as both an actor

Considering he was partially responsible for The A-Team, *John Ashley ought to be* proud *to have appeared in such classics as* **Beast of the Yellow Night**...

and a director. Looking like a cross between James Garner and Elvis Presley, Poe had, and indeed still has, the ability to switch from genre pictures to straight drama with bewildering ease, whether in front or behind the camera. It must be said, however, that his attempts at making westerns tested audience patience to the maximum.

In the early '80s, Poe embarked on a series of films charting the adventures of the Panday (played by Poe himself), an archetypal mythic Filipino hero who has died and been resurrected to battle evil. In rapid succession, Filipino audiences were treated to *Pagbabalik Ng Panday* (1980), *Panday II* (1981) and *Ang Panday Ikatlong Yugto* (1982). With the help of superior special effects and lively scripts, the Panday has fought through myriad adventures with all manner of demons, including duwende (malevolent elves), taong-lawin (bird people), diwata (giant ogres) and sundry non-specific monsters. (As was noted before, many of these creatures have been adopted direct from Spanish folklore. Unfortunately, no one has yet attempted to present the Filipino demon known as a mananangal on the screen - it lurks in house rafters and sucks out the livers of sleeping victims with its tongue.) Whilst obviously aimed squarely at the juvenile audience, the Panday movies were brisk and fun in a manner not often found in the rest of Filipino cinema.

But to conclude...

No article about Filipino exploitation movies would be complete without at least a passing nod to one man without whom all this might well not have been possible. A true icon of the Filipino film industry, whether as a villain or comic actor, the shambling, rotund figure and evil leer of Vic Diaz has graced more of the movies featured in this article than I can be bothered to count. Suffice it to mention just a few of my favourite Diaz performances: as the Devil in *Beast of the Yellow Night*; as the slimy South Vietnamese Army Officer-cum-drug smuggler in *The Boys in Company C*; and as the bumbling jeepney driver in *Wonder Women*. Diaz vanished from the screen a few years ago following the murder of his son, a promising classical guitarist, outside a Manila nightclub. Recent reports, however, would suggest that he is making something of a comeback. Vic, wherever you are, this writer salutes you. ∎

THE POSITIVE VALUE OF NEGATIVE ENERGY

JOHN WATERS INTERVIEWED

BY DAMON WISE

John Waters' Dreamland years are well documented and, as his own publicist, most reliably by the director himself. Post-*Polyester* matter has become a little vague, though the truth is John Waters has achieved almost all the aims of his precocious youth with his customary anti-social grace and still managed to bust a few more taboos that presented themselves in the meantime. The softening of source material and mainstream acceptance should not disguise the fact that Waters still cares deeply for his 'underground' (such as it is) following and works hard to accommodate their preferences.

Waters and Divine on the set of Hairspray.

Those who see Waters as a spent force probably never watched those early movies closely enough. Waters has never been less than candid about his motives and now he's arrived at a pretty enviable crossroads in his career, having constructed a so-called star vehicle (the irony!) for teen idol Johnny Depp and made a 'straight' success of *Hairspray*'s Ricki Lake. With the loss of Divine, Edith Massey and David Lochary, Waters is looking firmly forward, not to recreate his trashy past in Vistavision.

This interview took place at London's St James' Club

during a brief promotional visit in 1990 to publicise *Cry-Baby* and take part in a *Guardian* Lecture at the National Film Theatre. Waters' current movie plans are under wraps, though the director has revealed that the setting is contemporary and a spokesperson suggests that a number of people still stand to be shocked by the subject matter. Whatever his choice of sacred cow, it's good to know that John Waters still knows the positive value of negative energy...

SX: I've brought you some clippings...
JW: Oh good.
SX: This one's about Tourette Syndrome.
JW: They have a conference every year, did you know that? I'd love to go but I'm too afraid. They'd all be sitting there, going, "FUCK! FUCK! FUCK!" (*Feigns embarrassment.*) "Oh, I'm *so* sorry, I don't know *what* came over me..."
SX: This is about a guy called Gary David...
JW: I know about this guy! I was in Australia when all this was going on! I kept seeing him on TV and I thought, "Who *is* this guy?" They call him the Self-Mutilator.
SX: The other's just a paltry piece. It's about a guy who collected thousands of pairs of children's corduroy shorts.
JW: Oh. That's easy. Not so hard to find them.
SX: My favourite, which I wish I'd clipped out at the time, was about a forty year-old man who buggered his eighty year-old father and killed him. But they couldn't prosecute because they couldn't prove that his father hadn't consented.
JW: Yeah, but in America it's illegal 'cause it's aiding and abetting a suicide. Which is murder. The English are more liberal.

SX: Well, to start with, in *Polyester*, Francine's daughter comes in banging herself on the furniture, shouting, "I'm having an abortion and I can't wait." Now you've got a character in *Cry-Baby* who's knocked up and hopes it's triplets. Now, what's...
JW: It's both extremes of the same thing. It's a reversal, because in all the real JD movies the unwed mother was the girl that was punished for acting bad, y'know? So I wanted to have an unwed mother that loved being one, 'cause it was just a reversal of the usual cliché. I must admit that in the middle of it I thought, suppose somebody thinks this is pro-life or something? Which *never* entered my mind. I hate pro-life people. I'm pro-*death*, y'know? It's the same thing - you're right - because in *Polyester* that was the one thing that the producers really hated.
SX: Is that what earnt it an 'X'?
JW: No, we had an 'R' for *Polyester*.
SX: It had an 'X' here.
JW: But that made 'em really nervous 'cause it was so anti-family. And 'family' is a word now used in America as a code word for *hate*. And which I'd really get upset about if I had a family 'cause it's a perfectly nice word that they've used and disguised as a way to, like, fascistly judge other people and their morals. It's always the 'something' Family Association...

Tab Hunter and Divine get to grips with semiotics in **Polyester.**

Polyester ₓ

GTO FILMS

Divine about to strut his stuff in **Pink Flamingos**.

SX: In a way, you seem to have hit this 'new global consciousness' bang on the head.

JW: Well, we'll see...

SX: What did you do for Earth Day?

JW: Nothing. I hate Earth Day. I hate the idea that it's on my goddamn birthday too, which really makes me *mad*! My birthday is Earth Day, they've *ruined* my birthday. I've nothing against all the things they're for. I *hate* the smugness of it.

SX: One thing that upset me the other day, I was watching a panel show (*Donahue*) which had Lisa Bonet talking about breast-feeding her child...

JW: Oh shit. Right there. Go ahead...

SX: ...and River Phoenix preaching vegetarianism. It's back to '69 in many ways.

JW: Well, I hate New Age really, really a lot. And that's what it is, rotten little New Age people with their filthy little crystals. And it's bad enough, old hippies when you see 'em now, but new ones are really offensive and there's plenty of 'em.

SX: Have you heard about John Denver's Symposium?

JW: No?

SX: It's a kind of New Age seminar, where amongst other things, people are encouraged to 'follow your bliss'.

JW: FOLLOW YOUR B-LISS! That's the most obscene sentiment I've ever heard! But in America, you know what they say now, these new liberal phrases? Fat peo-

ple aren't fat, they're 'people of size'. Crippled people are 'physically challenged'. It's this New Hippyism.

SX: In some ways, the upbeat nature of your last two films coincides with that. I know it's parody, but...

JW: Well, I don't know that it's parodying too much. Like Ecstasy - I feel so mature 'cause I've never taken that drug - but *I* never understood why anybody would wanna take a drug that would make everybody love everybody. That sounds like going to hell.

SX: I had to shake somebody off at a club once who was caressing my jacket.

JW: I know! "I *hate* you", I feel like saying.

SX: You're fairly vocal about this kind of thing. Will you be using your next movie to...

JW: *But*, I hate that kind of thing because it's so...

SX: Reactionary?

JW: Yes, I'm a reactionary against it. However, I'm perfectly compassionate in my real life. I mean, I generally try to understand most people's behaviour.

SX: Do you ever feel burdened by your past?

JW: No, I don't feel burdened by my past. No. The only thing I've noticed is that there are some critics who, on *Cry-Baby*, said, "Well, we just really wish it was more like *Pink Flamingos*." I remember their reviews of *Pink Flamingos* and they *hated* it! Y'know? Which...it doesn't *bother* me. I don't say to them, "But you *hated* that."

SX: You've been getting quite a lot of cosy press

lately. Do you ever long for the days of *bad* press?

JW: I got bad press on *Cry-Baby*. A really mean one, a mean review that hurt from people on *The Village Voice*. It was time in my career for people to be mean to me. I knew that. I was following *Hairspray*, a film that got, in my career, the best reviews of any movie. Real, like, 98% good reviews. It was modestly successful worldwide and I followed it very quickly, without Divine. I knew it was gonna happen. I was ready for it.

Nevertheless, mean reviews *do* hurt. I do read reviews and I'm fairly thick-skinned. I've been doing it for a long time, I've gotten some of the meanest reviews in the history of reviews!

SX: Cameos have long been a part of your movies since *Desperate Living* with Liz Renay...

JW: Well, Liz was kind of my very first star name from outside. Maybe that's hard to imagine now, what *kind* of star, but...

SX: Presumably you would have had Mr Ray in *Pink Flamingos* if you could.

JW: That's true. He would have been the first one, the first *outside* one.

SX: Now people have gone overboard on this. How will you top *Cry-Baby*?

JW: Maybe I won't use any. That's entered my mind. I won't try to top it because I've *never* tried to top something. I didn't try to top *Pink Flamingos*. As soon as you try to top something it doesn't work. It's boring, it's old hat, you did that once. I've certainly... There are people I've thought of that I'd like to put in a movie. But if they're not good... There's a lot of people that I wouldn't tell you who read for *Cry-Baby*. Star names. People of the same type - names you wouldn't *believe* - read for me. But it's too mean to tell who they are. 'Cause I didn't use 'em and it's too mean to the people who got the parts and don't know that anyone else ever was thought of.

But most of the time they *were* the first choices. The few that weren't, I'm glad the people I wanted didn't make it. 'Cause I really like how it turned out. But they were people that...you would be amazed. *I* was amazed that they would come in and read for me. People I had known about since I was a kid. They'd leave and Pat, my friend, and I would just look at each other and think, my God...

SX: I thought there'd be two ways you could improve on it. I thought, for the next one, you could have Prince Edward, Myra Hindley and Jeff Stryker or...

JW: Well, I had dinner with Jeff Stryker (*Jeff Stryker is a male model who features prominently in gay hardcore magazines and movies - DW*). Did you read that?

SX: No.

JW: I thought you'd read that. I don't know if that ever was reported. I had dinner with Jeff and I have a good Jeff Stryker story for you.

You go out with Jeff and you should see people's faces. When they see me and Jeff Stryker having dinner, they go, "Oh my God!", and I say, "Oh, hi, do you know Jeff Stryker?" They say, "No. Nice to meet you." And you see them trying to fake it, so *easily*: "Hello, so nice..." And then *running* right out. Pee Wee Herman called me two days later and said, "So! I heard you were out with Jeff Stryker for dinner!" I mean, gossip spread so quickly on that, y'know?

So, I'm with Greg Gorman and Jeff. And Jeff's really nice, he looks very handsome, just like he does in the movies, kind of a guy from the mid-west who makes a lot of money and has *no* interest in being in anything

but porno movies. He says, "Ah'm lucky. Ah point to it an' it stands uhp!" He talks like that. Very *innocently*, though. He has a Corvette, a dirty, beat-up Corvette - everything you'd think, y'know?

SX: Had you ever considered him for the Johnny Depp role in *Cry-Baby*, or is he too old?

JW: No, I didn't think of him in the Johnny Depp role, I thought of him for future reference. But then I realised, he has no *desire* to be in anything but porno, y'know?

So he said, "I got this new movie I made, I want you to see it." I thought, well...alright. So we go back to Greg's house and we put on Jeff's new movie, which he says is a solo film. I know what that means, it means him jerkin' off. But it was him jerkin' off for, like, forty minutes, looking round at the camera, saying, "EAT MY ASSHOLE! SUCK MY DICK!" And he's sitting right next to me, on the couch, while we're watching this movie. And I thought, "If I look over at Greg, I'm gonna start laughing." What does Miss Manners say you do in this situation? It was totally not sexual at all. It was like an actor showing his new work.

Then right in the middle of it Jeff said, "Thuh's that thickness ah wus talkin' about." Meaning his dick! And I couldn't look. It seemed like it was on for a hundred hours. I thought, "*Please* come. This is taking *so* long." He finally came - in the movie - and I applauded. I didn't know what else...what do you do? I mean, it's like 'Bolero' - finally this record's over. And then I

Ricki Lake, Johnny Depp and Traci Lords in Cry-Baby.

just said, "Keep up the good work."

But he would say things like, "This colour's *terrible* - I have to get you a colour-corrected print!" Like any actor watching his stuff. It was really strange.

And Myra I just wrote about in something for *Vanity Fair*. And who was the other one you were saying?

SX: Prince Edward.

JW: My mother would like that.

SX: You were talking about Mary Bell when I came in...

JW: Well, I'm still fascinated by what happened. Last time I was here she was...pregnant?

SX: I sent you a copy of *News of The World*. Did you get it?

JW: Yes. Yes. But what happened since? Anything? Nothing?

SX: They didn't follow it up. I think there was no real interest in the story, to be honest.

JW: People don't know who she is here. They don't in America either. But you know why. She was totally upstaged by Myra Hindley. It happened a little before and then when Myra came along it was just, "Who cares?"

SX: That's showbusiness.

JW: Yeah. It's like Warhol's assassination being upstaged by Bobby Kennedy's. But...what was it? She was pregnant, then left and her boyfriend said she was gonna get an abortion or something?

SX: There was talk of her joining a satanic cult.

JW: Well, did she?

SX: I don't know. Basically, satanic cults are pretty much in vogue over here.

JW: Every time I meet teenagers I ask them if they've been listening to records backwards. I finally met one, a friend of mine, who said he used to, for real! He used to, like, think that the Devil was talking to him! I *loved* that. 'Cause it's such bullshit, that stuff. Have you seen this book, *Say You Love Satan*?

SX: No.

JW: It's a good one. It's about teenage lunatic satanists in America. But the cover is really good...to *anyone*, it's the best argument against taking drugs.

SX: It's a great way of getting rid of heavy metal fans.

JW: Yeah. Oh, heavy metal... I always ask about Mary Bell as soon as I get here, to see if anything's happened. So...nothing? That was two years ago, so she's had a low media profile.

But there is a Myra Hindley book. I don't know if I talked about this last time. I don't think I did, 'cause I think I bought it when I was here last time. But it's a really good one. It's called *Inside The Mind Of A Murderess* and it's a biography of her in *jail*, since it happened. That was fascinating. 'Cause it's not so much the crime, it's everything afterwards.

SX: Do you think criminality's on the wane these days?

JW: It's very popular in America. I mean, it shocks me. The number three best-selling book is the most *horrible* true crime story. It's called *Perfect Victim*, about this poor woman that was kept in a box for seven years and fucked by the family. Literally kept in a *box*. I thought, "*This* is what everybody's *reading*?" That's really scary...

SX: Did it bother you making *Hairspray* and *Cry-Baby*, the fact that you couldn't bring the Manson family into them?

JW: No, I never would do that - put the Manson family in - y'know? Well, maybe some. But only the

ones I know... I wouldn't put Tex in. He wouldn't do it anyway, he's not into that, he's a Jesus freak. But I'm really close now with Leslie. I would never do that to her, that would be exploiting them.

SX: I meant mentioning them, not physically using them.

JW: Oh. There was a clue (*in* Cry-Baby). It got cut. There was an address on a mailbox that really showed that was a Manson address. I've had a clue in every one of 'em.

SX: Was there one in *Hairspray*?

JW: Yeah, I'm trying to remember what it was. You can barely see it. It was a name at Tilted Acres. It said 'Coming Soon' and there was a name that was a false name that two of the Family used when they were arrested. I mean, *talk* about obscure! But *I* knew...

SX: Last time you told me about a trial you went to with a nurse accused of...

JW: Stuffing turds? Yeah, well she got off but no one ever heard from her again. I read this tiny article in the paper. No one knew about this trial. I went with my friend Pepper and we were sitting there and there was this nurse accused of stuffing *turds* down her patient's throat. And we were the *only* people that walked in. The prosecutor saw and thought, "Oh Christ - he's here..."

Anyway, though the patient died, she wasn't charged with murder 'cause she was an old-ager. And someone has to get up and testify about finding turds in people's... Aw, it was *so* awful that you wanted to start laughing, it was so creepy and horrible.

And you know how when you can't laugh and start to? It was a horrible thing but I thought, "Oh God! Why did we come? We're the *only* people! How embarrassing!" And they're all thinking, "You perverts..."

So then she got on the stand and part of her defence was that she was having her period. So it got even *worse*.

SX: What happened to her?

JW: They found her guilty but all she got was three weekends in jail or something. But as she was leaving, she was flipping out, crying, and her mother was trying to calm her down. She was shouting, "What did I do? I didn't do anything!!!" It was a really weird day.

SX: But those turds - were they...?

JW: Their own! 'Cause she'd come in and be pissed off that they had, y'know... And then she said that her father did it to her when she was young and that she thought it was the proper thing to do. It was really creepy.

SX: Have you been to anything to beat that recently?

JW: Well, I went to...ah...nothing that's really topped that. I went for one day of Richard Ramirez's 'Nightstalker' trial. He's *scary*. I went to the McMartin case a lot, y'know, the child molesting case? The Ray Buckey case. Have I been to anything else? That was the last two I remember...

I think the best thing I've done lately, y'know that kind of thing of ultimate voyeurism was... I was just driving down the street and I saw this tiny little church, but I mean *really* black. Really Southern, where people were speaking in tongues and had 'the spirit'. They had nurses there to help people who were speaking in tongues. I just pulled over and as I walked up I thought, I *can't* go in. I was like a Martian. And then this nurse came out and she said, (*blandly*) "Come in, son. Would you like to witness?" So I went right in and sat down. There was a lady right next to me, completely speaking in tongues, like her head was

gonna start spinning round.

SX: Was this before *Cry-Baby*?

JW: This was, like, two weeks ago. And she was going, like, "AIIIYEEAAYAIIEE." It was *so* great. Then one turned round and said, (*softly*) "You're the movie man, aren't you?", and I thought, "I can't *believe* I'm recognised in this place!" But it was really great and only in Baltimore, I think, is it that open. I mean, somewhere that you really...it's almost *rude* to go in. I would *never* have gone in unless I'd been invited. But once I was in there...it was like *Wise Blood*, y'know? There was, like, one old, dirty, crooked sacred heart on the wall. That was the only decoration. It was *really* poor. But there were people really dressed up. Older black ladies with big hats on. It was really nice.

SX: Did you stay long?

JW: I stayed a half hour. It *seemed* long. I thought, I just want to get out of here before one person, maybe, doesn't like that I'm here. But I felt *throbbing* voyeurism! I was so interested that I couldn't leave. And I was with somebody who was out in the car, saying, I don't *believe* he went in there!

And I also went to a bar that was good. You walked in and there was a mentally retarded doorman, a hillbilly, that was, like, chug-a-lugging bags of potato crisps, just...(*makes gurgling noise*). And then you walked in and it was all black people, but they were not young, they were, like, burglars and their girlfriends. I mean *scary* ones, right? With all rap music playing. But the disc jockey was a 300lb white hillbilly girl and her 500lb mother who had no teeth and

looked like the big, bad wolf. And they were playing all black rap records. And then they would go over and dance with the scary black older men, these hugely fat white women. I thought, what *is* this? It doesn't mix. And then the door swung open to the bathroom and out came the manager, a *raving* queen! And I thought, I don't *believe* this. It was like *Last Exit to Baltimore*! It was really good.

SX: How did you find it?

JW: I just go to neighbourhoods that I've never been to in my life in Baltimore. And there *are* a lot of them. It's hit or miss. I go with two people I know that are very low-key. We don't ever attract attention to ourselves. We really dress down and we never react to each other while we're in the place. We run out to the car and go *crazy*, but the whole time we're in there we just act very cool and never show any surprise. You just try to blend in as much as you can. *Then* go crazy later. That's what I've been into a lot lately and I *always* do that right before I start to write a new movie. It's exploring. It'll leak in somewhere. I don't know if any of that stuff I just told you will be in this movie but any of that certainly could be. Because it really impressed me and I had fun, y'know?

We went last night, when I was in Amsterdam, to the red light district, which I'd never been to before. It was *huge*. I love hookers in windows, I think that's *such* a nice idea. Especially antique windows that are old and pretty, y'know?

SX: Did you see anything that shocked you?

JW: Yes. Oh, well, the Hash Museum and places like

The 'bad seeds' from **Cry-Baby**. *Which one is Traci Lords?*

JOHN WATERS' *Female Trouble* STARRING DIVINE · DAVID LOCHARY · MARY VIVIAN PEARCE · MINK STOLE · AND AS EDA EDITH MASSEY · A DREAMLAND PRODUCTION FROM SALIVA FILMS, INC. A DIVISION OF NEW LINE CINEMA CORP · 1975 FROM NEW LINE CINEMA

If there's one person who truly embodies the spirit of 'golden age' Waters, it must be the late Edith Massey.

that. Yeah, it shocked me. I mean, I'm sure to everyone in Europe who's seen it a million times, it's no big deal, but what was shocking to me was that, in America, the red light districts are scary and there's drugs and everything but these *weren't*. These were in pretty neighbourhoods. It's *very* un-American. To have sex and not be in a dirty place...

SX: Have you ever had any strange reactions to Pepper's pregnancy in *Cry-Baby*? I didn't know quite what was coming in there. The thing is, I was in America shortly before Christmas and I was taken into a triple-X bookstore - which was closed - because someone told me about a magazine called *Preggo*, which I refused to believe existed.

JW: Called what?

SX: *Preggo*.

JW: Like, dirty magazines with pregnant women? Oh, there always has been them.

SX: But seeing Pepper, I thought, "Oh my God..."

JW: I know, it makes Ricki Lake crazy. I always threaten her. There's a magazine called *Jumbo* - have you ever seen that? It's, like, nude fat women. I always show it to her and make her *crazy* and embarrassed.

SX: How does she react?

JW: She just laughs. She just goes (*averts eyes*), "Oh my God!" Jean Hill had her picture in once and she got thousands of letters. 'Cause if you're a chubby-chaser, she's Marilyn Monroe. I read some of those

letters and they were *un*-believable. Dirty letters from fat-worshippers. They just wanna *knead* it, I mean, like *bread*. Not N-E-E-D...

SX: Did you have a part for Jean in *Cry-Baby*?

JW: She was in it in a little part that got cut, that was really almost like a glorified extra. Jean's been ill. She's fine now. She was very sick, physically, for a long time. She just directed a play in Baltimore.

SX: Directed?

JW: Yeah.

SX: I suppose you don't argue with her, really.

JW: Well, she'll sit on you! I'll tell you, though, the one great memory I have of Jean is that she was at the première (*of Cry-Baby*) and Patty Hearst said, "God, do I wanna meet her!" And I loved seeing those two meet. Patty Hearst and Jean Hill. There's a great picture of 'em together, actually.

SX: Mink's part in *Cry-Baby*'s pretty small too, even by your standards...

JW: Yeah, it was and she'll certainly be in a bigger one next time. Y'know, it just *happens* that way. I mean, I didn't purposely do it. She was in it a little more but I cut it, nothing to do with Mink. In the beginning we showed 'em selling cigarettes outside the school but it was too early to introduce a secondary character. It was the second shot of the movie - you didn't even know who the main ones were.

And you find this out. It had nothing to do with Mink. I think that, certainly, Mink's part was very important, socially, with me because it could predict that I was gonna quit smoking, now that I look back on it. I was the most obsessive smoker in the world. And that was the first negative thing I've had about cigarettes in a movie.

SX: Do you miss it?

JW: Oh, every day. I hate non-smokers. I could never love a non-smoker. Yeah, I miss it every day. I'm not *crazy* about it every day but there are times...I eat toothpicks all the time now.

SX: Why did you give up? Was it your health?

JW: I don't know. I smoked five packs a day. I coughed so much it scared me, y'know? I didn't wanna die. 'Cause you die in your fifties or you live to be old. That's what happens. And, I don't know, I was just sick of it. I didn't enjoy it any more. I was *such* an addict. I mean, I *would* have shot one up in a year. Y'know, literally mainlined a carton of Kools, it was coming to that.

Way before I quit I ate the last one. Before I went to this place to get these shots - I got these shots to quit - I walked around the block, smoked my last five Kools then ate the last one. I was with my producer, she wasn't really prepared. I didn't tell her I was going to. And she was so terrified that I would *kill* someone if I didn't have a cigarette. She had to take me home because after you got these shots you couldn't walk.

SX: Serious.

JW: Yeah.

SX: In that respect, you're pretty well-preserved. You've come through a pretty rocky era that... Well, some people never made it, people like Curt McDowell.

JW: Cookie died this year.

SX: I heard she'd been ill.

JW: Yeah, it's hideous though. Stiv Bators just died, did you know that? I talked to his girlfriend. Y'know he was hit by a car and just went home and things were normal. And he went to sleep and never woke up. Stiv had jumped off so many stages, it was *nothing* getting hit by a car, he figured.

SX: It's so un-rock 'n' roll. I felt sorry for him.

JW: It really bothered me for some reason, because all the other deaths are so horrible, then just some freak thing like that...

SX: Is that why your last two films have been so upbeat?

JW: I don't know. I don't know that I can calculate this. I'm sure a psychiatrist can figure it out. I can tell, by looking back, when I was happy and when I wasn't happy. I think I was probably the least happy in my life the years I made *Desperate Living*. But I don't sit down...I just write the next movie. I'm sure it's in there, somewhere. Just all the people dying affects me in a way... The worst thing about it is if you ever feel like you're getting used to it.

That's why I'm very much *for* radical gay people. Otherwise you're just being like the Jews, going along with walking to the ovens. Y'know? I understand why that happened, but is it the same? I don't know - I'm not Jewish, so I probably shouldn't make the comparison...

SX: Do you think we've seen the death of excess?

JW: No, because there always will be excess. It'll be weirder in other ways, y'know, but basically...no, I think if they cured AIDS even, I don't think it would go back to like what it was. I think it's a shame, I think youth *needs* excess. I think it's horrible that kids can't fuck. No wonder they take crack and go wilding, they can't fuck! No wonder they're nuts!

SX: You seem to approve, tacitly, of rap.

JW: I *do* like rap. I don't like the anti-gay or the anti-women rap, I hate all that, but I do like it. I'm for it. I think it's something new. I mean, it's based in everything that's old but it's the only new thing since punk. I like it. I listen to it. I buy it. It's the only new music I've bought for at least ten years.

SX: Anything in particular?

JW: I like Queen Latifah. I like Heavy D. Those are my favourites right now. I like girl rappers. I didn't used to like rap, I mean, I'm really old. I'm likin' rap *way* too late, I realise that.

SX: Do you think delinquency's quite sordid these days?

JW: They don't have delinquents any more. You'd be *happy* if your kid called up saying he got busted for stealing hubcaps. How touching! I don't know any... All the people I know who have kids have turned out pretty good. If I had a kid I'd be really uptight. I'd be *terrified*. I went to this junkie park that they have in Zurich, y'know, this new kind of experimental let's-make-all-drugs-legal thing. Which I was always *for*, and then I saw it. And I don't know if I'm for it any more.

It's the only thing...either I'm getting old or it's the only thing that *really* bothered me that I've seen in a long time. Because, of course, in America we're used to junkies being scary people, black people - people we *aren't*, people we can't identify with. Here it was all white, young kids. Hundreds of 'em, like...like roaches. Shootin' up. Takin' the water out of mud puddles to clean the needles and they're givin' out free needles everywhere.

I mean, like, 2,000 of 'em in this little area. And, to me, it was like the Woodstock of heroin, y'know? If you were a lonely kid who hadn't tried drugs and didn't have friends and came across this you'd think, "Ahh, something to belong to, a family, a tribe." So that's why I'm against it. Although...it goes on, we just don't see it, but this you can see. It may be great

to like, take kids to walk by it and they will *never* take drugs in their life.

It shocked me. It was way beyond *Christiane F.*

SX: Was there ever a time when you thought, "This is it, no more drugs?"

JW: No, not consciously. I stopped smoking pot 'cause it made me nervous. I never got into coke that much. I mean, I *did* it in the height of the coke years when somebody offered me some every once in a while, though I don't think I ever *bought* cocaine in my whole life. I liked the high of it for five minutes but then it just made me have too much to drink and it didn't last long enough. It just made me...I don't know, I have enough energy as it is, y'know? I didn't need this fake energy.

And LSD, God knows, that's the last thing I want. And speed I love, but you have to be *young* for that kind of excess, y'know? What other drugs are popular? I never took Ecstasy, 'cause I don't want to be too lovey dovey. What else is there? Heroin I did. I tried it.

SX: You tried it?

JW: Oh yeah, of course. I had to shoot up *once*. But I never liked that high. I never liked downers. And the very first time I ever did it somebody took the needle out and this huge black bubble rose in my arm - like an abscess - and I thought (*wails*), "Ohhh, this is not me!" I'm not mechanical. You have to be mechanical to know how to shoot up. To get into needle fetishes you have to also like changing a tyre, fiddling around with a motor. I don't like to do this.

SX: Did you use a needle? How did you cope with that?

JW: Someone did it for me. Oh, I *never* did it myself. I think I did it maybe twice or something. And I did it because I knew it was the *worst* thing you could do. That's why I did it. Luckily I didn't like the high. My idea of a good time's not sittin' around itching and puking.

SX: Is that what happened?

JW: Yeah, everybody pukes. You're supposed to *like* puking. *I* didn't. And sitting around itching with people nodding out... No, I'd rather take a big Black Beauty and go out. A diet pill, y'know?

That was more my speed. *Then.* A long time ago. If I took a diet pill now they'd have to take me to a mental institution. I can't *imagine* being on speed now.

SX: Do you think there are too many wonderful things to experience without taking LSD?

JW: Yes. In a way, no. LSD I don't regret taking. If I had a kid I'd be uptight if he took it. When I left this park I thought, "Thank God I'll never have children." To worry that they could end up here. But people have asked me to do anti-drug ads and I say, "Are you kidding?" I can't be a hypocrite. I never *ever* had a bad drug experience. Drugs never hurt my life but people I did 'em with are dead. From it. So maybe I was lucky.

At a certain period I didn't think they were bad for me, I think it certainly opens up a whole new world of mental stimulation. Not heroin. Pot made me laugh more, though I think it makes you stupid in the end so it makes you satisfied with less. LSD I certainly don't regret. I remember wonderful trips with Divine doing Dionne Warwick imitations with a three-day beard and shower curtains as earrings, doing the entire *Once in a Lifetime* album. Lip-synching. We were laughing *so* hard. You know what I mean? A very early memory that was...important, y'know? A *good* memory.

I never had a bad trip, though. But, then, I stopped at a point, I think, when I knew I *would've* had a bad one. ■

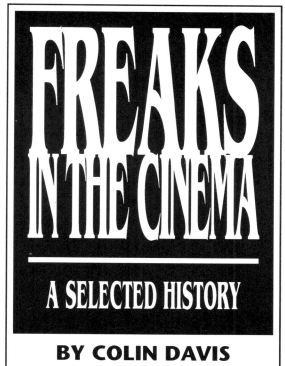

FREAKS IN THE CINEMA

A SELECTED HISTORY

BY COLIN DAVIS

First, let's define our terms. A freak is a person who is the wrong shape or size, usually from birth, sometimes because of disease. A three-eyed Martian is not a freak, only a normal Martian in the 'wrong' place. A freak must be *possible*. The Amazing Colossal Man does not qualify because no known radiation causes instant growth, and anyway he is too big - a 30' man could not exist. Most of the freaks mentioned here are not only possible, but really freaks, offscreen.

Naturally the first picture that comes to mind is Tod Browning's *Freaks* (1932), notorious for casting actual circus oddities. Thanks to Britain's paternalistic censors, it was

The freaks in Freaks.

House of the Damned

RONALD FOSTER / MERRY ANDERS / RICHARD CRANE / ERIKA PETERS / WRITTEN BY HARRY SPALDING PRODUCED AND DIRECTED BY MAURY DEXTER   AN ASSOCIATED PRODUCERS INC. PRODUCTION   RELEASED BY 20th CENTURY-FOX

not shown here until 1963. Browning is always credited with sympathetic treatment, showing the freaks as innocent and exploited, but the film's climax undermines our empathy. The freaks pursue the normal villains through a thunderstorm, and the armless-legless man, knife in his teeth, wriggling through the mud like a monstrous caterpillar lit by flickering lightning, is just one of many horrors. Only afterwards do we wonder what he could actually do.

Perhaps the weirdest sight is Johnny Eck the Half Man, whose body terminates below the ribs; he scuttles about on his hands. Born Eckhardt in Baltimore in 1910, he retired in 1940 after a career plagued by crooked agents and managers. At one time he did a stage act with a magician called Raboid Rasha, who apparently sawed a man in half. The man's legs (a midget concealed in a pair of trousers) then ran off, pursued by his upper half (Johnny, walking on his hands). Eck seems to have enjoyed black humour; he once posed for a joke 'car wreck' picture, in which he was a maimed corpse. All freaks want to be treated like ordinary people, but there are limits: as recently as 1988 Johnny Eck was assaulted by burglars (*Eck died on 5 January 1991 at the age of eighty-nine. Ed*).

Also appearing in *Freaks* are pinheads, dwarfs, a human skeleton, a bearded lady and the Hilton sisters, British born Siamese twins who later starred in their own film. It's a pity more actors didn't go into politics in those days - perhaps a *real* pinhead could have got to be President.

Another cast of real freaks was seen in *House of the Damned* (1963), directed by Maury Dexter, who made the decent little SF movie *The Day Mars Invaded Earth*. An apparently haunted house turns out to be the refuge of shy freaks whose manager has died. They include another half-man, a limbless woman and giant Richard Kiel in an early role.

She Freak (1966) was a much sleazier effort, but then it was directed by David Friedman, producer of Herschell Gordon Lewis gore epics. It is a sketchy rip-off of *Freaks*, with freaks again turning on and mutilating a scheming woman who has betrayed them. Apart from a dwarf, no freaks are glimpsed until the last moments, and the best thing about *She Freak* is the padding - real carnival footage which provides an authentic backdrop for the tedious drama.

The Mutations (1972) was also pretty sleazy, but certainly delivered its freaks, real and fictional. Donald Pleasence and deformed assistant Tom Baker make human-plant hybrids, culminating in a terrific Venus Flytrap man. Botched experiments end up in a freak show, run by Michael Dunn, himself a well-known screen dwarf. Among the other performers are Esther Blackman the Alligator Lady and the amazing Popeye, who can pop his eyes right out of their sockets.

The Sentinel (1976) managed to be even sleazier despite its relatively high budget. When the hosts of hell are unleashed at the climax, some are the work of make-up man Dick Smith but most are genuine freaks, displayed for no other purpose than to horrify. In the context their physical ugliness is clearly meant to be the expression of spiritual evil. This must be the most tasteless treatment of freaks in cinema; take a bow, director Michael Winner.

The Elephant Man (1980) employs real freaks in the squalid show where the eponymous hero - and he is a hero - is discovered. The Elephant Man was of course a real person, Joseph Merrick (1862-1890), perhaps the most famous freak of all; in the film he is John Hurt underneath Chris Tucker's superb make-up. This is that rare thing, a film about the real situation of a freak. The vast majority of cinema freaks are not people with their own lives and problems, merely henchmen or monsters. Their position has been similar to that from which black actors have to some extent escaped.

Freaks, although the human oddities were central to the story, was really a kind of morality play, but two obscure movies made in 1950, whatever their artistic failings, did treat freaks as people. William Castle, yet to become the king of horror gimmickry, made *It's a Small World* starring midget Paul Dale. 'Something's got to give', proclaimed the ads, 'When the emotions and longings of a man are pent-up in the body of a child!' The poster shows Dale trying to chat up a normal sized Lorraine Miller.

Chained for Life, starring the Hilton sisters of *Freaks*, looks archaic, the format recalling those wonderful '30s cautionary tales like *Cocaine Fiends*. The Hamilton twins (Hilton sisters) work in a cheap vaudeville show, their singing act (close harmony - what else?) interspersed with jugglers, accordionists and trick cyclists. The publicity men cook up a scheme: a handsome young trick shooter will marry one of the twins - on stage of course. He agrees, keen to share increased box-office receipts, encouraging the girl to believe he really loves her. When he deserts her after the wedding, her sister shoots him with his own gun and goes on trial for murder. The judge lets her off since he can't sentence her innocent sister with her. A similar publicity marriage and desertion involving the Hiltons actually took place in the '30s. Quite pretty in their youth, they looked all of their forty-two years in 1950, which doesn't help the romance. They died broke in 1964.

Violet and Daisy Hilton can't act, reciting their lines without expression, and the rest of the cast are little better. Dialogue is laughable, as is the creaking plot, with its artistic dream sequence where the engaged twin dreams she is no longer joined to her sister. Yet our laughter is constrained by the reality of the Hilton's plight, and the solemn discussions of their restricted life are hard to mock.

There are rumours of a recent hardcore pornographic movie starring Siamese twins. The mind, as they say, boggles.

The Ape Woman (1963) was actress Annie Girardot in make-up, but the film was based on a true story. A showman discovers a girl covered in hair and eventually marries her to stop her leaving. When she dies giving birth to a hairy baby, he exhibits the embalmed corpses. The real life ape woman was a Mexican, Julia Pastrana (1832-1860).

Mask (1985) was another true-life tale: Cher is the mother of a teenage son afflicted with a rare ailment causing his facial bones to enlarge. Since the human face is symmetrical, unlike the Elephant Man's, the effect is strange rather than repulsive.

Rondo Hatton also had an enlarged face, but in his case it was real, the result of another disease, acromegaly, a pituitary gland disorder. A former newspaperman born in 1894, Hatton had important parts in four pictures, beginning with *Pearl of Death* (1944) in which, as the back-breaking Oxton Creeper, he clashes with Basil Rathbone's Sherlock Holmes. In *Jungle Captive* (1945) he is Moloch, helping Otto Kruger revive Paula the Ape Woman from *Captive Wild Woman* (1943) and *Jungle Woman* (1944). He's another assistant in *The Spider Woman Strikes Back* (1946), where he's

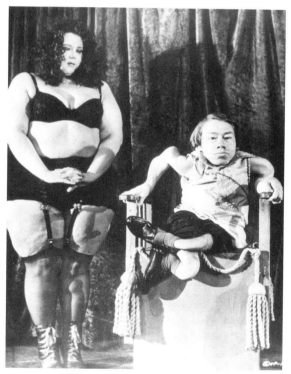

(Left and below) Some of **The Mutations.**

Mario the Monster Man, helping Gale Sondergaard in a complicated plot involving carnivorous plants needing blood to which Brenda Joyce seems set to donate. *House of Horrors* (1946) gave Rondo, if not top billing, the main role, as the Creeper, rescued from drowning by sculptor Martin Kosleck. The grateful Creeper is willing to kill for Kosleck, and does. The high spot of the film has Kosleck ranting about a bad review by a hostile critic, to which Rondo remarks in his expressionless gravel voice, "You don't like the guy?" We just know there's one critic who won't be around for the annual

Rondo Hatton.

Earth Stood Still* (1951) featured one of SF cinema's icons, Gort the robot. In the claustrophobic silver suit was 7'7" Lock Martin, former doorman at Grauman's Chinese Theatre - that's the one with the stars' footprints outside. Like many giants he was not strong: you never see him pick up Patricia Neal. She was placed in his arms before cameras rolled.

In 1953 Johnny Weissmuller, post-Tarzan paunch decently covered in the role of Jungle Jim, met *Killer Ape*, played by 7'7" Max Palmer in false nose and teeth. The same year brought *Invaders from Mars*, a low budget picture which has acquired a modest but secure reputation. Even for '50s American SF this is exceptionally paranoiac, with little Jimmy Hunt watching the invaders take over the minds of the adults. The Martian soldiers, in their furry green suits, are played by Lock Martin *and* Max Palmer, while their leader, a tentacled head in a globe, is a midget, Luce Potter, or rather her head with rubber attachments. When the giants manhandle Earthmen, they are actually lifting midget stand-ins, exaggerating the size difference and compensating for their own relative weakness. Midgets are often used as stand-ins for children in stunts kids would not be allowed to undertake.

The Brain That Wouldn't Die (1959) is one of those films loved by bad movie buffs. The mad scientist, busy combing sleaze clubs for a body to fit his fiancée's severed head, forgets the discarded experiment in the closet. Encouraged by the head, it breaks out, to be revealed as circus giant Eddie Carmel, in some really tacky make-up.

Herschell Gordon Lewis, apart from making his own pioneering genre pictures, tried to cobble together a film from *Terror at Halfday*, an abandoned project by Bill Rebane (responsible for *The Giant Spider Invasion*). He failed. The resulting disaster, *Monster a Go-Go* (1965), features Henry Hite (real name Mullens) as a returned astronaut enlarged by radiation. Having taken the trouble to hire a giant, the makers waste Hite, showing him for barely a moment in the same shot as a normal man.

1977 saw the first of the *Star Wars* blockbusters, in which 7'2" former hospital porter Peter Mayhew donned the hairy suit of Chewbacca, a sort of giant Skye terrier on two legs. Nice to see a British giant up there for a change.

The most celebrated giant in the cinema is Richard Kiel, a former teacher and nightclub bouncer. His lanky 7'2" frame, filling out over the years, has appeared in a long list of films and TV series, sometimes in starring parts. In *Eegah!* (1962) he was a caveman found in suspended animation in the desert, where he chases the hero's dune buggy. Since the hero is Arch Hall Jr, son of the director and star of masterpieces like *Wild Guitar* (1962), we might wish Kiel got to club him, but Arch's girlfriend shaves him and tames him.

Kiel was back in *House of the Damned*, mentioned previously, and in *The Human Duplicators* (1965) he graduated to a speaking part. As the alien Kolos he oversees the creation of android duplicates of key humans in the usual world takeover plan. He fails, but not before duplicating hero George Nader, for which, one surmises, he uses wood.

In 1977 Kiel achieved fame as Jaws in *The Spy Who Loved Me*, tangling with Roger Moore's lightweight James Bond and delicious Russian agent Barbara Bach. Jaws, the indestructible colossus last seen disposing of a shark with his steel dentures, is pretty much a parody even for a Bond film, and in *Moonraker* (1979) he is

awards. Rondo's last movie was *The Brute Man* (1946, the year he died), in which he played a handsome scientist rendered ugly by a lab accident. Also present is the clichéd figure of the blind girl (Jane Adams) who doesn't fear the monster. Hatton received little publicity during his career, often being unmentioned on the posters, but posthumously has acquired something of a cult following.

Next time *Mighty Joe Young* (1949) shows up on TV, watch for the wrestlers who have a tug-of-war with the giant ape in the nightclub. The one introduced as the Swedish Angel is obviously acromegalic. In *The Monster Maker* (1944) J. Carroll Naish injects Ralph Morgan with acromegaly, causing him to hide in dark rooms, perhaps so we won't see the lousy make-up. *Doomwatch* (1972), from the popular TV series, had a whole population, on an offshore island polluted by chemicals, turn all lumpy faced. A Green horror film! At least the make-up was fairly accurate. Most giants have some degree of acromegaly - Richard Kiel is an example - which brings us neatly to our next category.

Giants go back to the beginning of cinema. One of Harold Lloyd's silent comedies has him locked in gaol with 7' John Aasen, who looks gigantic and holds his own in the comedy. In more modern times *The Day the*

(Previous page) Tod Browning with the Earles family, who appear in **Freaks**.

(Above right) Richard Kiel blasts off in **The Humanoid**.

(Below right) John Merrick (John Hurt) steps out in **The Elephant Man**.

played for comedy, falling in love with a diminutive French girl and changing sides to save Bond. Kiel has almost no dialogue as Jaws but, while he isn't going to win an Oscar, he handles the comic villainy quite well.

He never had another part as important as Jaws, though in *The Humanoid* (1979) he played the name part as Golob, a giant goodie turned into a giant baddie by Barbara Bach. *War of the Wizards* (1980), also known as *The Phoenix*, was a typical Oriental fairy tale - albeit less fun than some - with the giant bird of the title, rock-men and Kiel as a large villain.

Kiel logged many TV appearances, including an episode of *The Monkees*, and he was a guest on the late Russell Harty's chat show. Much of his film work was non-genre, such as *The Mean Machine* (1974) and *So Fine* (1981), where he gets to dance in a disco and sing (dubbed) opera. In recent years Kiel has dropped from sight, which can't be easy when you're that big.

Literally hundreds of dwarfs and midgets have appeared on screen; after all, theirs is the commonest of physical anomalies. A dwarf is usually taken to be large-headed or short-limbed, a midget to be normally proportioned but tiny. The terms get used interchangeably and we won't differentiate here.

The Terror of Tiny Town (1938) is another favourite bad film, having achieved the distinction of appearing in the egregious Medveds' 'Golden Turkey' selections and in *Shock Xpress* no.2's list of fifty most boring movies. It is an ordinary B-western except for the entire cast being midgets, among them ex-vaudevillian Billy Curtis, who appeared in a number of films including *The Wizard of Oz* (1939) and the 1950 Jungle Jim entry *Pygmy Island*. In *The Thing* (1951), when vegetable monster James Arness is cooked in the electric arc and shrinks to nothing, his intermediate self is Billy Curtis. Billy's most important part was in *High Plains Drifter* (1973) where, as Mordecai, he helps returned murder victim Clint Eastwood clean up the town.

The Wizard of Oz employed crowds of midgets to play the Munchkins and in *A Midsummer Night's Dream* (1935) assorted goblins littered the camply beautiful forest sets. *Tarzan the Ape Man* (1932) featured a whole tribe of midgets in blackface to menace the explorers. Johnny Weissmuller, in his debut as Tarzan, arrives with a posse of elephants just in time to rescue Maureen O'Sullivan from the gorilla pit. Some strange pictures exist of members of the cast encountering a bird creature which, it seems, is Johnny Eck in a suit. These might be scenes cut from the finished picture, but were more likely publicity shots.

In *Superman and the Mole Men* (1951) George Reeves faces invaders from beneath the earth, midgets in furry rompers, while *Invasion of the Saucer Men* (1957) brings more invaders, this time from outer space, the midgets here being clad in lovely suits by Paul Blaisdell, creator of many flamboyant '50s monsters.

To prove that dwarf casts are not the prerogative of popular film came Werner Herzog's *Even Dwarfs Started Small* (1970). In an institute for dwarfs controlled by ordinary people, the inmates revolt over conditions. However, their own society breaks up as they realise their essential powerlessness, and their activities degenerate into random nastiness, ending in the symbolic crucifixion of a monkey.

Perhaps the longest career of any film dwarf has been that of Angelo Rossitto, born in 1905. Having begun in silents, he played a notable part in *Freaks* and went on to films starring many of the big names of fantasy and horror, including three of the inimitable Monogram B-

Angelo Rossitto lives it up in **Mad Max Beyond Thunderdome.**

movies which helped pay for Bela Lugosi's morphine habit. In *Spooks Run Wild* (1941) poor Bela is a mere foil for the East Side Kids, but the following year, in *The Corpse Vanishes*, he and Angelo get down to some serious villainy, kidnapping young brides to make a serum to keep Bela's own old wife looking young. British distributors, thinking the title a bit strong for us in wartime, changed it to *The Case of the Missing Brides*. No horror films were made here during the war; this seems to have been official policy. In case you think things have changed, consider the daft behaviour of the BBC during the Gulf War.

In 1947 Rossitto joined Lugosi again for *Scared to Death*, in colour no less. So confused do the actors appear, the *Psychotronic Encyclopedia* wondered if more than Bela had indulged in certain substances. The narration is by a dead person, anticipating *Sunset Boulevard* in this respect if, perhaps, no other. Rossitto had appeared with another horror great, Boris Karloff, in *Mr Wong in Chinatown* (1939), and in 1944 he joined Basil Rathbone in *Sherlock Holmes and the Spider Woman*. Very loosely based on *The Sign of Four*, this features Angelo as a black dwarf operating out of Gale Sondergaard's suitcase. As already mentioned, she had the help of Rondo Hatton in the unrelated *The Spider Woman Strikes Back*.

The ineffable Al Adamson, in *Dracula vs Frankenstein* (1971), provided work for several, er, veterans. J. Carroll Naish, shrivelled and chair-bound, is assisted in his wicked deeds by an equally sick looking Lon Chaney Jr and by Angelo, who at least had the satisfac-

(Above right) Michael Dunn in **The Mutations**.

tion of outliving the others. The same year he acted in another Adamson atrocity, *Brain of Blood*, this time assisting Kent Taylor in brain transplants. Taylor had plenty of experience of cheap movies, but hero Grant Williams at least had his moment of glory in *The Incredible Shrinking Man* (1957). That picture contained an interesting cop-out when the hero, by now about 3' tall, has a heart-to-heart with a lady midget about the problems of smallness. Instead of using a real midget, they employed an ordinary actress. Was this because it would have cost more to make her the same size as Williams, or because they thought a midget didn't look conventionally pretty enough?

In 1980 Rossitto donned a suit to play an alien in *Galaxina*, a so-so SF comedy chiefly notable for the title android being played by Dorothy Stratten, who was messily murdered by her estranged husband on the day of the film's première. Angelo was still going strong in 1985. In *Mad Max Beyond Thunderdome* he forms part of a warrior team, astride the shoulders of an armoured thug in this savage post-holocaust world.

Harry Earles, a little older than Rossitto, made few films, but his performances are possibly the most memorable of any dwarf actor. In the silent *The Unholy Three* (1925) he poses as a baby, helping villain Lon Chaney Sr (disguised as an old woman) in jewel robbery and murder. The sound remake (1930) allowed him to be even more sinister as the evil infant, but also posed a similar problem to that which limited Bela Lugosi's career. Earles has a strong German accent and is often hard to understand.

His other major role was in *Freaks* and when, telling his friends of the beautiful trapeze artist's attempts to poison him, he mockingly repeats her enquiries about his health, he makes a truly chilling effect. The pathetic lady midget who pines for him was played by his sister Daisy Earles.

Apart from these triumphs Earles was just another screen midget, uncredited in such fleeting appearances as his part in the Laurel and Hardy film *Blockheads* (1938).

Michael Dunn (1934-1973) managed to get some respectable parts, but all too often languished in the usual evil dwarf role. His best known performance was on TV, as villainous Dr Loveless in the '60s series *The Wild, Wild West* (1965-1970), with Dr Loveless' son played by spooky Paul Williams, not exactly a dwarf but pretty damn titchy. Williams was effective as the ageless Swan, bargaining for William Finley's soul in *Phantom of the Paradise* (1974), Brian De Palma's rock version of *Phantom of the Opera*, for which he also wrote the songs. Much less worthwhile is his psycho killer in the obscure *Stone Cold Dead* (1980).

To return to Michael Dunn, he appeared in AIP's confusing *Murders in the Rue Morgue* (1971), which is said to have suffered from tampering by the studio. In 1973 he was in *Werewolf of Washington*, a good satire, too slapdash to be first rate. The President's press secretary (Dean Stockwell) gets bitten by a werewolf while on a European trip, and on his return things get hairy at the White House. All too plausibly, the official response is to cover up and deny it all. As Dr Kiss, Dunn operates a basement mad science lab with a secret entrance in the gents.

The Mutations, already mentioned, was hardly an advance, but the following year the busy Dunn hit rock bottom playing your usual lecherous dwarf henchman in *Frankenstein's Castle of Freaks* (1973), the Count being played by Rossano Brazzi a long way from *South Pacific*. Like most cheap Italian horrors, it is *really* cheap, but at least there's plenty of nudity (not Michael Dunn - don't get excited).

My candidate for weirdest film dwarf is Hervé Villechaise, who had his own TV success in *Fantasy Island* (1977). His slanting eyes and high voice had already added to the fun in several films, beginning with an obscure gore comedy, *Malatesta's Carnival* (1973). In the Bond movie *The Man with the Golden Gun*

(1974) he was a sidekick to villain Christopher Lee, and the same year he went to Canada to make the little seen *Seizure*. Jonathan Frid (*House of Dark Shadows*) is an author whose creations come to life. Hardly original, but the characters are startling: Martine Beswick as the Queen of Evil (worth the price of admission alone), Henry Baker the huge black executioner, and Villechaise as - wait for it - an evil dwarf. Among those who die are Troy Donahue and Mary Woronov. The scene everyone remembers is when Baker crushes someone's head in his hands like a rotten pumpkin. The director was Oliver Stone, destined for bigger things.

Billy Barty had been in *Pygmy Island* along with Billy Curtis and others; a step up was Roger Corman's *The Undead* (1956), which gave him the enviable role of familiar to witch Allison Hayes (*Attack of the Fifty Foot Woman*). Unable to afford a proper studio, Corman filmed in a converted supermarket. This tale of a prostitute returning to a previous, medieval life features such Corman stalwarts as Richard Devon (as the Devil) and Dick Miller, with great pseudo-Shakespearean dialogue by Charles Griffith.

Willow (1988), an old fashioned fairy tale adventure, gave Barty a leading part; the little people share the heroic adventures on equal terms. A good fairy tale should have a giant, and here he is played by André the Giant, a paunchy middle-aged wrestler whose cautious efforts can be seen by late night TV grappling fans.

Buck Rogers in the 25th Century (1979), pilot for the ensuing TV series, featured the cute robot obligatory in modern space opera. Inside the suit as Twiki (ugh!) was midget Felix Silla, but the talking was done by Mel Blanc, the voice of Bugs Bunny and most of the others in Warner cartoons.

Talking of cute robots leads inevitably to R2D2 of *Star Wars*, with his (its?) vacuum cleaner body and telephone dialling voice. Just as Chewbacca is played by a British giant, the robot's shell is inhabited by British midget Kenny Baker, who can also be seen - properly - in *The Elephant Man*, where he helps John Hurt escape from Freddie Jones' freak show.

In the actor stakes we can walk tall - well, be proud, anyway - for Baker is by no means the only tiny Briton in films. In *The Masque of the Red Death* (1964), perhaps the best of Corman's Poe films, the dwarf jester Hop Toad (Skip Martin) takes a spectacular revenge on a nobleman in Vincent Price's castle. Persuading the man to wear an ape costume to a ball, Hop Toad sets him alight as he swings on a chandelier. The scene, and the character of the jester, come from another Poe story, 'Hop Frog'.

Skip Martin played a circus dwarf, Mr Big, in *Psycho-Circus* (1967), an unremarkable mystery with an interesting cast, including Christopher Lee as a lion tamer, Klaus Kinski, Suzy Kendall and Victor Maddern. *Horror Hospital* (1973) furnishes stiff competition for its supporting cast in the shape of Michael Gough, giving one of his most outrageous performances as a mad scientist zombifying guests at his health spa. Skip Martin, as henchman Frederick, rises to the task with the help of some good lines. Leading new arrivals past a room drenched with blood, he mildly observes, "I hope you'll be tidier than the people who had that room." In the end he changes sides and dies nobly helping the youngsters to escape.

A few years ago David Rappaport was probably the best known dwarf in this country, thanks to his success on children's TV as Shades, wearing specs Elton John

The Mini-Tones

Star Wars midgets in their day job...

would have been proud of. He was among several dwarfs, including Kenny Baker, to appear in Terry Gilliam's *Time Bandits* (1981). The disreputable gang, with names like Fidget and Vermin, wander through space-time with schoolboy hero Craig Warnock, encountering among others Ralph Richardson's Supreme Being, Sean Connery as Agamemnon and Ian Holm's Napoleon, obsessed with his own shortness.

Rappaport, in a solo TV appearance, explained his philosophy of life and how he coped with his situation, even finding some advantages in being small. Ironically, he committed suicide within a year, unable to carry on when faltering career and personal relationships were added to the problem he was born with.

Countless dwarfs have made single or occasional appearances, often unbilled, without achieving celebrity. Mad ventriloquists almost form their own sub-genre; if a dummy is required to move, the easiest method is to put a midget inside. In *Dead of Night* (1945) Michael Redgrave's classic demented ventriloquist is helped on his way by a perambulating dummy, and in the hilarious *Devil Doll* (1963) Bryant Halliday is similarly afflicted, though he has asked for it, imprisoning a human soul in Hugo the dummy.

La Rose Ecorchée (1969), released here as *Ravaged*, employed the hackneyed theme of kidnapped girls 'donating' their faces to restore the beauty of the villain's disfigured wife or daughter. In this picture, not one but two dwarf henchmen assist in the evil doings and, being randy little chaps, are open to bribery by their beautiful captives.

I Don't Want to be Born (1976) was one of those movies Joan Collins put behind her for the more cultural opportunities provided by *Dynasty*. She is a stripper, which gives us the chance to assess her forty-three year old form (pretty good) while she rejects the advances of dwarf George Claydon, who then puts a curse on her new baby. The infant limbers up by slashing faces with a nappy pin, and goes on to murder Dad

(Ralph Bates), the doctor (Donald Pleasence) and finally Joan. At the moment of the child's exorcism, the dwarf drops dead on stage. Well, it makes a change from the Krankies.

A large category, already touched on, covers the products of the make-up artist's craft - a craft some think has taken over horror movies to an excessive degree. Since Hiroshima the word 'mutant' has been much bandied about. The atom bomb came on the scene (the only time it's ever been used in war, and it had to be the good guys), and monster movies had a ready made rationale. Most of the '50s big bug pictures blamed radiation. A real mutant is *born* different, because of something happening to its parents, whereas a film mutant like the Paul Blaisdell creation in *The Day the World Ended* (1956) gets a lungful of radiation and promptly starts sprouting a third eye and an extra pair of arms. *World Without End* (1955) used the idea correctly: astronauts hit a time-warp and, on twenty-first century Earth, find that the usual nuclear war has created some extremely ugly cavemen. The giant spider, on the other hand, is impossible; a 200lb spider, not having an external skeleton, would collapse under its own weight.

Strictly speaking, all congenital freaks are mutants, like the Hunchback of Notre Dame in his various screen incarnations (Lon Chaney Sr 1923, Charles Laughton 1939, Anthony Quinn 1956). Similar-looking but less sympathetic is Victor Maddern in *Blood of the Vampire* (1958), cheerfully assisting Donald Wolfit's blood draining activities. He does eventually turn on his master, being unwilling to torture Barbara Shelley. Is he stupid or what?

This sort of ugliness is a visible token of the character's wickedness, as in *The Redeemer* (1978), whose psycho, butchering classmates at a reunion, has double thumbs, a peculiarity shared by Lon Chaney Sr in his circus melodrama *The Unknown* (1927).

Some people (we all know some) are not exactly freaks, merely grotesque, like the denizens of John Waters' film world. The one and only Divine was more startling than most circus freaks, but in a suit, without wig and make-up, he was just a fat man. The huge-breasted women in Russ Meyer's pictures are startling too, but again it is a lot to do with presentation. Chesty Morgan, on the other hand, has to be called a freak. In the early '70s her 73" bust crowded the screen in two of Doris Wishman's primitive films. In *Deadly Weapons* (1974) she - plausibly - smothers men with her breasts, while in *Double Agent 73* (1974) she is a secret agent with a camera implanted in a boob. Morgan, a stripper off-screen, had an art movie to her credit: *Casanova* (1977), directed by the great Fellini, who has always liked using grotesques. Donald Sutherland plays the great lover, grappling with the deadly weapons.

Finally, let us take a quick, horrified glance at the geek. The term is now merely one of mild abuse, but in the heyday of the American carnivals it signified the most shocking exhibit in the freak show. Usually dressed in skins and billed as a 'wild man', the geek sat in a pit biting the heads off live chickens and devouring them raw. This was a *glomming* geek; an ordinary geek was so drunk or feeble-minded the goodies had to be put into his mouth.

Nightmare Alley starred Tyrone Power as a con man in a cheap carnival, who attains fame and wealth as a crooked medium. Exposed, he ends up in the carnival again, a drunken geek. This being 1947 we don't see the geek's act, but its nature is made clear enough. This, remember, was a major studio production (20th Century Fox) and Power was a romantic star. Female geeks were not unknown, and I think it is high time we had an explicit remake of *Nightmare Alley*. How about Meryl Streep, biting the heads off chickens? ∎

RAISING HELL IN HOLLYWOOD

CLIVE BARKER INTERVIEWED

BY STEPHEN JONES

"I prefer mummy movies to vampire movies for scares - because being seduced isn't as scary as being crushed to death by something that's just smashed through the French windows !"

Since taking the horror fiction field by storm in 1984 with the publication of his visceral short stories in the *Books of Blood*, Clive Barker has become a one-man industry with a bewildering array of novels (*The Damnation Game, Weaveworld, Cabal, The Great and Secret Show*), movies (*Hellraiser, Hellbound: Hellraiser II, Nightbreed*), comic books (*Tapping the Vein, Hellraiser, Nightbreed, Son of Celluloid*) and peripheral items (*The Nightbreed Chronicles, Clive Barker's Nightbreed, Clive Barker Illustrator*) to his name.

The fact that he was born in Liverpool and produced this remarkable body of work while living in Britain is perhaps even more impressive, particularly given the international scope of these projects.

But for those who had hoped that Barker would revitalise the British horror field in a way not seen since the heyday of Hammer Films it came as a shock when he announced that he had decided to emigrate to the United States, buying Robert Culp's Beverly Hills mansion for a reported $1.95 million.

SX: So Clive, was the lure of Hollywood and even bigger bucks something you finally couldn't ignore?

CB: There were many reasons really. In the last three years I've established a lot of good working relationships in America - with two comic book companies, Marvel and Eclipse; a very strong relationship with my publisher HarperCollins in New York; and Universal Pictures. So in those three areas - comic books, books and films - I felt as if I'd begun to build some very useful relationships.

For me, outside the actual items of work, whatever it may be, the prime reason to get up in the morning and deal with people is the people themselves.

There really aren't comic book companies in Britain; there really aren't any film companies in Britain, and I would like to nurture my great relationship with Harper, not just as far as the adult publications are concerned, but also with the children's book side, as I'm also involved in some projects for them.

So finding myself encouraged by my relationships with people, I want to be able to develop them, so that is clearly a good reason to be in the same country as those people.

The comic books with which I'm involved are produced exclusively in America, the movies that I'm involved with from this point on are going to be produced exclusively in America. It gets wearying at six in the evening, when you've finished your working day, and it's ten in the morning in Los Angeles, and people are bright and breezy and ready to talk and do business. And after a while, if you do this night after night because you're involved in some negotiation, you know you're not at your best when you are talking to somebody at midnight and it's only four in the afternoon for them.

And if it happens, as it has for me with many movie projects now, that you do this night after night after night, eventually you realise you can't be giving your best. I think a lot of potential for error and misunderstanding inevitably springs from that.

SX: So what made you move to the West Coast instead of, say, New York?

CB: The passion I had for New York has basically gone. When I was in my mid-twenties I really wanted to live there, I thought that living in Manhattan was just about all one could ever ask from civilised living. Either New York or I have changed, but I suppose both of us have changed. I'm a bit more easily bruised than

Clive Barker enjoys a rubdown at the hands of Peloquin (Oliver Parker) from **Nightbreed.**

(Above right) David Cronenberg and Clive Barker on the set of **Nightbreed.**

(Below right) Andrew Robinson and associate in **Hellraiser.**

I was when I was twenty-five, and New York bruises a bit more readily.

SX: Back around the time of *Hellraiser*, when you were hailed by many to be the Great White Hope of fantasy and horror in the UK, there was a great sense of excitement that you were at the forefront of the dawning of a new age of British horror films. What went wrong?

CB: I was very disappointed, even when we were making *Hellraiser*, that we couldn't raise the money in Britain. It wasn't a lot of money, and I had faith that the movie would at least make that money back with a little bit of profit. I didn't anticipate that it would make so much profit. I was irritated that people seemed to be willing to put money into 'period pastiche', stiff-upper-lip drama, and so on, but couldn't see their way to funding the kind of generic work which has been a cornerstone of British literature and British cinema for as long as books have been written and movies have been made.

This is a terrible cliché, but we have repeatedly exported some of our great talents, and it's *wretched*.

SX: After the success of *Hellraiser*, were you ever approached by a British company to make more films?

CB: No. In a strange way, the fact that the movie was a modest hit in America sort of marked me out as being almost American anyway, and my attitude has repeatedly been seen as Americanised. And that's not just in terms of the movies, but also in terms of the books too.

There is a sense that I'm some kind of wretched

hybrid: he can write reasonably well so that's British, but he talks rather too loudly and has opinions, and that's terribly American. And he goes on chat shows... for fuck's sake, does this guy have no honour, has he no sense of literate decency?

I think there's a lot of that double standard. The British literary establishment and the British cinema tends to look down its nose at the generic and popularism.

SX: Do you have any sense of resentment that you had to leave Britain to pursue your work?

CB: No resentment. I would like to be making movies in the UK, there's no two ways about that. I would like to feel that we could make movies in Britain *à la* Hammer. But there is no commercial appetite.

For example, when we were going to make *Hellbound*, Chris Figg and I were looking around for people to direct the film and we very much wanted to hire a British director.

So we interviewed a lot of people and it was extraordinary how snooty they were. Here was a movie that by that time had made a great deal of money, had some very nice reviews even in Britain, and I remember one man and wife team who worked together came in and basically said, "Well, of course, it's not about anything, is it? There's no subtext. If we were to get involved with the sequel we'd really need to be making a social statement, so we would want complete control."

I thought that this was like a surrealist farce. I don't have an over-inflated sense of my own excellence as a film director, I've made two movies and I'll get better, but they were so high-handed.

The point is whether you think you can use generic convention usefully and interestingly, and feeling high-handed towards it is not the best way to go into that process. That angered me.

SX: Do you think we are about to see a Clive Barker backlash?

CB: I think there's been quite a lot of it already, but it's been sporadic. I think that may be a consequence of doing a number of things: the backlash is happening at different times in different areas.

SX: Obviously, the biggest backlash against your work so far was made apparent in the critical reaction to *Nightbreed*...

CB: I think so.

SX: Do you think the movie deserved the lambasting many people gave it?

CB: The film is the film. It has some neat things in it and there are lots of things I'd now do differently - I'd like a slower movie - but there are things I'd do differently in *Hellbound*. And in the books. You go back and look at this stuff and think, "My God, why did I do that?"

I cannot find it in my make-up to go through my creative life apologising for what I just did. You do what you do. You have your reasons for doing it at the time. And you hopefully change, which means that almost always at the end of writing a book or painting a picture or making a movie I can't remember why I wanted to do it in the first place. That's always a good sign because it means, basically, the process of doing it has taken me to another place with the work. It usually needs somebody else to tell me, "You know what that was about, you know what you're doing there, don't you?"

SX: After the box office failure of *Nightbreed*, particularly in America, did it come as a surprise to be asked to go to Hollywood to make more films?

CB: Not really. I think one of the extraordinary things about movies is that if you have enthusiasm for making them, if you have original ideas, and if you're known to be able to produce original ideas, then there is an appetite for you.

SX: But wasn't Twentieth Century Fox's problem with *Nightbreed* that they couldn't handle a film with so many original ideas?

CB: I wouldn't disagree with that. Take my new book *Imajica* - if I was to take the ideas in that and try to make them into a movie I wouldn't get past the secretary at any of the big studios. I have always said that I want to make modestly scaled pictures, and one of the reasons I want to do that is financially I hope I can eke out a little bit more freedom by doing so.

Take *Die Hard 2* - $70 million worth of movie. And, of course, Renny Harlin, the director, is completely invisible. And yet there are directors in Hollywood, like Joe Dante, who makes movies you know right off are Joe Dante movies, whether you like them or not. I've always liked wit over bombast, and I like the voice of the maker to be in the piece.

SX: But don't you think that Hollywood is likely to place it's own restrictions on the distinctive imagery and imagination of Clive Barker?

CB: Yes, absolutely. And if making movies was my prime objective in life, then I think I'd be much more fretful than I am. I'm not going to Hollywood with the blinkered intention of just making movies. Beverly Hills is somewhere I will live and be involved in movie projects, but I also have a four-book contract which

Clive Barker auditions for the lead in Dr Who...

obliges me to produce a book every eighteen months or thereabouts.

If you want to be a big success then it becomes a dick showing contest, and that's not what it's about. It can't be about "My book sold more copies than your book." It can't be about "More people went to see my movie than went to see your movie." If it is about that, then Danielle Steel must be an extraordinarily wonderful author because she sells so many copies. You can't do the calculations that way.

What interests me is holding to the vision: doing something that is yours and making sure that it can't be like anybody else's.

SX: That's alright for you, the creator, but how can you hope to convince the studios who put up the money that your particular ideology is the correct one?

CB: It doesn't matter because I've got this other career. If I don't make another movie for another three years it's not going to break my heart. And they know that. I'll paint and I'll write books instead.

I come to movie-making as a kind of side-issue, and enjoy it and have fun with it, even take it seriously while I'm doing it, but I don't feel this is the thing that proves whether I exist or not.

What matters are the books.

SX: Having written the opening novels in two trilogies - *Cabal* and the first book of The Art, *The Great and Secret Show* - your new book, *Imajica*, stands alone. Do you enjoy playing with your audience's expectations in this way?

CB: Yes I do. The thing I can never forgive people for is repeating themselves. I find formula creation rather uninteresting, and I got out of horror short

The face that launched a million S&M magazines... Doug Bradley as the Pinhead Cenobite in **Hellraiser.**

story writing when I felt I'd basically said my piece. Which wasn't to say that a couple of ideas wouldn't come along and I didn't want to do them, but I basically said, "Okay, I've done the things I really wanted to do, and I've now said what I wanted to say." When I wrote *Weaveworld* that was all I wanted to say in that area. Now I've finished *Imajica* it's the same thing.

The *Nightbreed* stuff came out of the way The Art came about - I haven't finished, but I wasn't exactly sure how I wanted it to go. I thought, "Well, I can go away and write another big book (which *Imajica* is), and then I'd go on in the fullness of time to do The Art 2."

But I've got to challenge myself, I've got to be doing stuff that is an adventure for me, and I have a very low boredom threshold. Particularly with myself.

SX: What's happening with *Hellraiser III* and *Nightbreed II*, both of which have been mooted in the past?

CB: As far as *Hellraiser III* is concerned, I have withdrawn myself from that whole area of endeavour completely. I don't feel I can police everything all the time, and if you have a life that is full of other things - which mine is - there's only so much you can do. There comes a point where you say, "How many hours do I have in the day and can I look over my shoulder all the time wondering if this is going right or not?" And there comes a point where you have to say, "No, actually, I can't. There isn't enough time."

I still think we'll see a *Nightbreed* sequel...

SX: From Morgan Creek?

CB: I wouldn't have thought so. They read the novel, they liked the script, but they still wanted a much more on-the-nose horror movie than they got. I wasn't born into this world to make movie producers happy, and I don't see it happening with them. However, there are several companies who have shown an interest in doing a *Nightbreed* sequel.

If I sound unfocussed it's because I am. Like I said before, if it happens then it happens. I don't sit around thinking, "This is what I should do, this is the next step." I think my movie career is just a series of loose ends. And I don't mind that.

SX: What about all the other film projects we've heard about off and on over the past couple of years?

CB: Well, *Son of Celluloid* is still being talked about. Some people are showing interest in the screenplay for *In the Flesh. The Forbidden* is being done with Propaganda Films, with a very good script written by Bernard Rose, who will also direct it in Chicago sometime later this year. There's a Harry d'Amour screenplay, called *The Last Illusion*, which exists in a very good first draft. Mick Garris is working on a second draft of *The Mummy*, and Cynthia Williams is doing a screenplay for me based on a science fiction treatment.

SX: So what's the first project you are working on in Hollywood?

CB: Well, I'll begin with joint writing with Cynthia on this science fiction treatment for Universal, and joint writing with Mick on *The Mummy.*

SX: Are you basing your mummy movie on any of the earlier versions?

CB: No. There is nothing whatsoever in the 'Egyptian Project' as we call it - because it may not even be called *The Mummy* - which resembles any Universal or Hammer mummy movie.

Universal came to me and said, "Is there anything you'd like to remake?", and I said, "The only thing I'm really interested in is *The Mummy*." But I'm interested

(Above left) Everyone's favourite femme fatale, Clare Higgins, with a partially clad Frank in **Hellraiser.**

(Below left) Frank proves that it is possible to take too much Ecstasy...

in *The Mummy* for reasons which are not really explored in the original movie.

Egyptology itself fascinates me and has always fascinated me, and its mythological structures are very interesting. One of the reasons they are interesting is because they are so unchanging. This is a theology that remained fundamentally unchanged for millennia. But I told them I'm not real interested in guys in bandages.

So instead I came up with an idea for a science fiction project which I took back to them, and they said, "Great, we want to develop this with you - and by the way, have you had any more thoughts about *The Mummy!*"

Lonesome Cowboy Burt (aka Steve Gallagher), Anne Bobby and Clive Barker try to get extra work in **Twin Peaks.**

And I had. At that point I pitched them an idea and they said, "Great, we'll develop both with you, side-by-side." I just wrote forty page treatments for both movies and then we got in other writers and we're doing them together.

SX: I didn't realise you had much interest in science fiction.

CB: I love science fiction, but not hard science fiction at all. This is an old soapbox of mine, but there are plenty of overlaps between fantasy and horror and science fiction. The reason why I dragged the term *fantastique* kicking and screaming into the collective vocabulary was to try and ease off the definitions, which I think are sometimes reductive.

There are areas of the theological and metaphysical underpinning of the *fantastique* which manifest themselves in very different ways. Yet I very strongly believe that the underlying necessity to address metaphysics in fictional form is the thing that brings people to this area as opposed to other areas of fiction.

The whole point about science fiction as high-tech, hard-edged, phallic forms being blasted into outer space has no call on my imagination whatsoever. I'll line up for *Star Wars IV* when it comes out, and I'll have a great time, but that's not the kind of movie I want to make. There's a kind of humanistic side to science fiction which fascinates me, where you basically use something which is only just plausible.

So where we stand is there are actually three screenplays being developed - *The Mummy*, *The Last Illusion* and the science fiction project - all of which I have first right of refusal on as director.

I'll go on writing with Cynthia and Mick, and I'll also write for Harper a relatively small children's book - about 200 pages - which I'm halfway through in first draft form and have enjoyed doing immensely. It's an idea I've wanted to do for an incredibly long time, and like *Weaveworld* it's an idea that percolated.

SX: Is Clive Barker mellowing in his old age?

CB: I think I already have. The tough, hard, *Books of Blood* Clive Barker was not the young Clive Barker, it was the thirty year-old Clive Barker. Just in terms of the numbers of books sold, *Weaveworld* and *The Great and Secret Show* outsell the *Books of Blood* many, many times over. The figures are huge by comparison.

SX: How do you see your future as an author?

CB: I would like to continue to write personal books which appeal to a large audience. I write books that matter to me, that answer some particular need in me at a given time, and I've been lucky enough to find that what I'm writing is actually answering something in the audience too.

The fact that they came with me in such numbers to *Weaveworld* surprised me. The places I want to go are some damn strange places, but I want to believe the audience will follow me. I think I *am* a hybrid; I do have a lot of things about the way I write which are American. I like many things about American writing, and when I look to the Masters, I usually look to Americans.

If I had to name one single horror novel that really convinced me to just get on and do this, it would absolutely be Peter Straub's *Ghost Story*. It seemed to me here was a man of immense intelligence and insight writing at the top of his talent and scaring the bejabers out of me. That's a book which I still go back to with immense pleasure.

I think a lot of horror writing is very ugly, careless, purposeless writing - writing without any point of view. There's got to be a reason to tell a story, there's got to be a place you are taking the reader to. You're saying to the reader, "At the end of this journey you will be different."

Why does the writer go to the desk in the morning? First to tell a story, second because the story has got to constitute something more than momentum. Because if it doesn't constitute anything more than momentum, it doesn't constitute anything at all.

SX: What about your movie career?

CB: As a viewer, film for me is an entertainment medium. I don't go to movies expecting to be enlightened and I don't think people should look to my movies the same way they look to my books. As far as my movie career is concerned, I'd just like to *survive!* ∎

SEX, DEATH, ANIMAL PORNO AND LESBIAN VAMPIRES

CENSORSHIP AND THE CINEMA IN GERMANY: ONE STORY

BY JACK STEVENSON

Munich. Germany's most conservative major city: capital of thoroughly Catholic Bavaria, home of the Oktoberfest, German folk arts and well-spring of the Nazi party. Bombed into ruins during World War Two, today it is a city of clean modern buildings. It is the most prosperous city in Germany's most prosperous province, home to a serious young class of Mercedes-driving professionals.

One would hardly suspect it's the capital of European underground cinema, and in fact it hardly is. And yet down Fraunhofer Strasse near

The projection room in the Werkstattkino.

TODESFILME

In Zusammenarbeit mit dem Kulturreferat der Landeshauptstadt München

„Was ist wichtig? Das Leben? Wir wissen's nicht. Das Unwichtigste halten wir für wichtig. Und das Wichtigste sehen wir garnicht. Vielleicht ist der Tod das einzige Ereignis im Leben." (aus MORGENROT)

(Above right) *Leatherface up to no good in* **The Texas Chain Saw Massacre.**

the city centre one turns into an arched passageway of moldy stone and proceeds to an inner courtyard to address number nine. Down a flight of stone steps at the right rear corner, under a tavern, one enters a tiny red-painted lobby which in turn to the right opens onto a small fifty seat cinema. Up on screen radiate images of fucking, sucking, dissected cadavers, Nazis from Hollywood, wasp women, tits, rock'n'roll, zombies, Idi Amin, sword-wielding skeletons, flexing musclemen, careening spaceships, concentration camps, Batman, bestial sodomy, sea serpents, women in prison, men at war and Lydia Lunch being raped by a hand gun.

Welcome to the Werkstattkino. Take a seat.

In November 1974 a nineteen year-old local lad and film fanatic, Erich 'Waco' Wagner, joined with a group of friends to open the small cinema, converting it from a cramped one-lane basement bowling alley. They painted the walls black, built a projection room, hung a screen and installed fifty cushioned movie the-

atre seats on an incline. Erich credits the skills of the electrician who wired the room as essential to the opening of the cinema. For two years, while Erich fulfilled his compulsory service in the German Army, the Werkstattkino ('Workshop cinema') operated on a part-time basis. Then, in April 1976, regular shows began at nine and eleven nightly.

The attrition rate among the staff was high. Eleven people were involved in the opening of the cinema. Three months later two remained: Erich and the owner of the projection facilities who checked out a year later. The cinema now had two 35mm projectors and also showed super-8 and 16mm film prints.

At that point Erich was joined by Wolfgang and Gisela, whom he later would marry. Gisela checked out as a regular staffer in 1981 and since February 1982 the staff has consisted of Erich, Wolfgang, Anatole and Dolly - all paid. Both Erich and Gisela work as projectionists at the nearby German film museum to supplement their income. They dislike video and have no TV in their house, although on rare occasions the Werkstattkino has beam-projected big screen video - for example a night of SRL (Survival Research Labs) videos and a night of Manson videos. Over the span of fifteen years since the inception of the theatre, programming has been all over the road. In addition to screening trash, gore and exploitation films back in the mid-70s (even before these films attained cult status in the US), they've programmed frequent screenings of the American underground, including the works of Kuchar, Brakhage, Anger, Morrissey and obscure early Warhol films. They also fed the good citizens of Munich on a steady diet of Vienna Acktionist perversion/porn/coprophilia via the films of Otto Muehl, Gunter Brus and Otmar Bauer.

More recently the Werkstattkino has become a main stop on the schedules of touring American film-makers, geeks and fanatics. Joe and Nancy Coleman have shown films there, as have Michael Weldon (he calls it "the most Psychotronic cinema in the world"), Richard Kern, Alyce Wittenstein, myself and others.

Im Gegensatz zum deutschen Film, der zwar indirekt zu patriotischen Opfern, zum Durchhalten aufforderte, die Existenz des Krieges aber nie zum Bestandteil der Handlung machte, war der Kriegszustand in hunderten von amerikanischen Spielfilmen der Zeit wichtigstes Handlungselement.

Auch im Trickfilm brach der Krieg aus. Donald Duck und andere beliebte Trickfiguren wurden in die Schlachten des Zweiten Weltkriegs und hinter die feindlichen Linien geschickt.

DONALD und die nazis

Originalfassung ohne Untertitel
vom 25.12. - 12.1. um 20.30 Uhr

Most foreign films in Germany are shown dubbed into German and are routinely cut by German censors. *Walking Tall*, for example, has twenty minutes cut out of it. The Werkstattkino, however, always seeks out original, uncut, undubbed prints and even shows Japanese films in original language versions. They show a lot of Japanese, Italian and English films and are not unduly dependent on American items, although they are plugged into a lot of what's going on in the US. Erich occasionally laments that classic American films are the only ones that bring out the crowds on a dependable basis, and yet his prejudice runs deep against "typical Hollywood shit."

No subject is taboo at the cinema - although they might draw the line at something like *Three Men and a Baby*. Even films from the Nazi era have figured prominently in many of their retrospectives and festivals - those that aren't still suppressed. Prevailing wisdom dictates that the Nazi period was an artistically dead period in German cinema, although Erich claims it was the Golden Age.

Nevertheless, in dealing with films from the Nazi era they approach it from all directions. Concentration camp documentaries have been featured in their Death Film Festival(s), while in a festival entitled 'Hollywood Nazis' they examined the ways other nations typecast Germans during the war, and even screened a compilation of anti-Nazi Disney cartoons. Some of the other films featured at the 'Hollywood Nazis' festival included *Desperate Journey, Passage to Marseille, The Secret Life of Adolf Hitler* and *After Mein Kampf*.

Some programmes have naturally attracted controversy, something Erich welcomes but does not seek out. They were twice raided by the *Sittenpolizei* (Vice Squad) after screenings of Otto Muehl films, and the Vice Squad returned when the Belgian film *Vase de Noces* (bestial pornography, aka *The Pig Fucking Movie*) hit the screen and for the showing of the US horror film *Mother's Day* (glorification of violence). Some shows, in fact, they do no promotion at all for to avoid the inevitable busts.

They are treated as something of a hot potato by the local press, often completely ignored. State's Attorneys have attempted to silence them because they were 'anarchists', Red Army Faction sympathisers because they are 'fascists', and feminists because they are 'pornographers'. Left-wing film writers are disturbed because they are everything and nothing - something journalists-with-agendas find most troubling of all. Even old friends of the cinema have occasionally been alienated at some juncture by this concept of 'programming without limits'.

Politically, Erich votes (and says he always will) for the Greens, a party which he describes as "struggling for a new ecological view of life." But he is of two minds on this subject as the cinema feels heat even from this source. "Some of them fuckers not only want to clean the polluted landscape but also our dirty minds. They fight porno as well as atomics. Germany had enough of these do-gooders in the past," he states, alluding to artistic thought-control in the name of a higher 'com-

(Above left) Leatherface up to further no good in **The Texas Chainsaw Massacre 2.**

Anatole (left) and Erich (right) in Göteburg, Sweden, February 1989. They look harmless enough...

abrupt demystification of a subject that has long been banished from the realm of honest discussion and examination. It was, of course, horrifying.

Nothing close to the Werkstattkino's festival has ever been attempted in America. One of the films they programmed, the Belgian documentary *Des Morts/Of the Dead*, was hailed by *Sleazoid Express* editor Bill Landis as his top film of 1980 - 'a powerful, disturbing, stomach-turning documentary on death in various cultures.' Landis had to travel up to the Museum of Modern Art to see this film, indicative of the cloistered, sterile venues - a type of ghettoisation - such confrontational films are relegated to. Other films featured at the festival included: Rosa Von Praunheim's *Death Magazine or How to Become a Flowerpot, Harakiri, Kampuchea 3 & 4* and films about the Warsaw ghetto, concentration camps and so on. *The Act of Seeing With One's Own Eyes*, a 1972 autopsy documentation by Stan Brakhage (*see reviews section. Ed.*), was also in the programme, the Werkstattkino having purchased a 35mm copy direct from Brakhage himself.

But such extreme, confrontational programming is only one aspect of the Werkstattkino's approach to film, and the next night you're just as likely to see *The Blob, Batman, Jesse James Meets Frankenstein's Daughter* or Chesty Morgan in *Deadly Weapons*. Other special events have included retrospectives of David Cronenberg, George Romero, Sterling Hayden, Sam Peckinpah, Sam Fuller, Douglas Sirk and Monte Hellman, to name but a few. Specialised thematic programmes have run the gamut from 'Around the World Mondo Sex Films' and '8mm Amateur Pornography Festival' to 'The Wizards of Gore' and 'Bikers and Gangs' shows.

While poor gate receipts could never fail to be of some concern, the cinema functions above all as a showcase for films the staffers have a personal enthusiasm and conviction for. This gives the programming force, originality and boldness.

By the same token they refuse to book films they have no enthusiasm for. Erich has expressed a longstanding disinterest in the films of both Fassbinder and John Waters and won't book them... (Although he did recently run *Mondo Trasho* to a full house, as it was touring the German off-cinema circuit.)

Erich has also expressed an aversion to Tennessee Williams and turned cold when the Munich film museum programmed a festival of 'Old South Classics,' focussing on "Tennessee Williams-Vivien Leigh fine art soap operas," as Erich disdainfully reports. "The fuckers!" he rages. "No swamp trash or even one good chunk of grits 'n' sowbelly in it. I'm mad. I always wanted to do an Old South series myself at the Werkstattkino, but certainly not the Vivien Leigh kind. The fuckers spoil the whole idea." Spurred on by such effrontery, Erich has since redoubled his efforts and purchased 35mm prints of *Poor White Trash, Wild Harvest* and *Walking Tall*.

The four current staffers have different tastes, naturally, but seem to agree on certain common ground. They are all prejudiced, opinionated and fanatical about films they like and dislike, and that's all to the benefit of the cinema. While the Werkstattkino has survived to see its fifteenth anniversary and has been influential throughout the European underground, it hasn't exactly flourished. Still financially self-sufficient, it sometimes seems barely so and remains an effort of personal dedication for those involved. Erich complains that there was always too little of every-

mon good' that reached its apex under the Nazis.

Even though the cinema is an independent capitalist enterprise, receiving no funds or endowments from the state, they did once become embroiled in the classic 'you-mean-public-funded-grant-money-paid-for-THIS!!?' outrage that is central in our own current art/censorship debate. In the case of the Werkstattkino they organised a three week festival of films dealing with the subject of death, and uproar resulted when it was revealed that some state money had been allocated for the festival. In dramatic fashion several journalists waited outside the doors to catch fleeing patrons and ask them what they thought of state money contributing to such gut wrenching atrocity. Scandal ensued.

The international line-up of obscure and brutally effective films assembled for this landmark festival reveals an exhaustive knowledge of and research into the subject on the part of the staff. The films were for the most part shocking, but could they have had any other effect in an affluent Western society (like our own) where the subject of death has been ruled off-limits? It was forced confrontation with the taboo,

thing: seats, publicity, customers and money. "We always had a good underground reputation," he says, "nationally and internationally, which means, of course, no money but lots of friends."

Yet among the network of some twenty-five to thirty other German 'off-cinemas' that they helped to inspire, the Werkstattkino of Munich remains unique in its absolute range and freedom of programming, unshackled by the collectivist committee mentality that hinders booking policy at other cinemas, and unbeholden to any artistic or political agenda.

There is no equivalent in America to this circuit of off-cinemas in Germany, and in the entire country there is no equivalent to the Werkstattkino (*nor in Britain! Ed.*).

1989 turned out to be an unusually poor year for gate receipts, and personal difficulties between Anatole and the others (which may or may not have been rectified by the time you read this) have further clouded the future of the cinema.

In the recent hard financial times the Werkstattkino came to depend on rental fees from its film archive. Erich credits this supplemental source of income for keeping the cinema afloat. Totalling 170 feature films and documentaries - mostly 35mm prints - the archive was founded in 1985 and today contains many extremely rare films that would be the envy of many a national cinema.

Most of the films are available for rental. During autumn 1989, for example, they were getting good returns on their porno films playing in Vienna, which compensated for the losses they were taking at the cinema where films about Auschwitz were being screened.

In February 1989 the Werkstattkino was invited to Göteborg, Sweden to present a week-long assortment of films. Organised by Radium Records as an annual antidote to the major Swedish festival then underway in Göteborg, this underground event was bent on sucking off some of the publicity and crowds from the main show and spiking the balloon with a few holes along the way.

Erich and Anatole arrived in Göteborg with a programme of extreme films that included early Nazi propaganda, Otto Muehl Acktionist films, the Brakhage autopsy film and the Bodil Joenen animal-porno flick (*A Day in June*), as well as other items sure

Mother's Day:
Glorification of violence.
It's official.

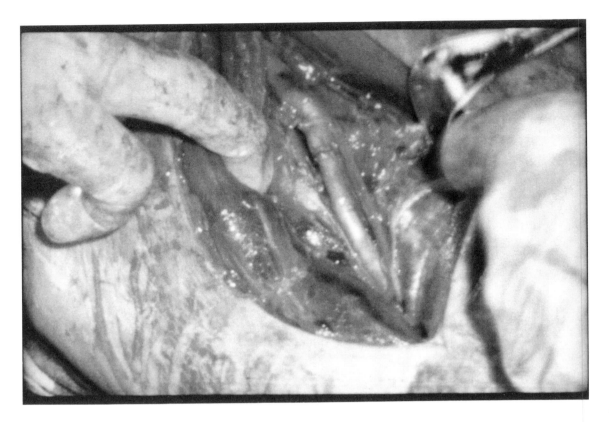

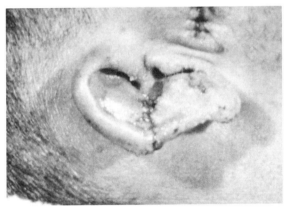

(Both pages) **Army Medicine in Vietnam...** *What else?*

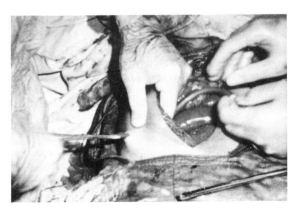

to strain the tolerance of Swedish audiences. Indeed, the shows caused a scandal and touched off a geyser of damnation in the Swedish press. The Swedish organiser received outraged phone calls from his own relatives and his wife almost divorced him. Functionaries of the main festival vowed to bar any further publicity for Radium-sponsored screenings and the underground festival for 1990 was scrapped and replaced by a debate on censorship in the arts.

Supplemented by such tours and rental fees from the archive, Erich predicts the Werkstattkino will survive another ten years. He's also able to make some money by buying and selling film prints through his large network of contacts. The summer of 1990, however, saw a dramatic increase in film censorship throughout Bavaria, injecting a new hysteria into the issue and resulting in a wave of police actions and film seizures.

Things came to a head at the Munich Fantastic Film Festival when a hot-blooded young District Attorney looking to make political hay personally spearheaded a crackdown on splatter films. A 35mm print of *Texas*

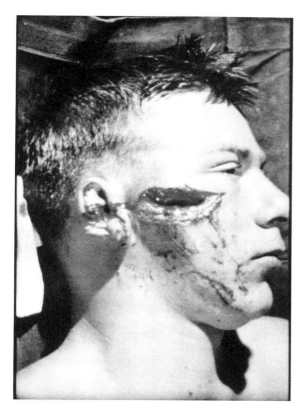

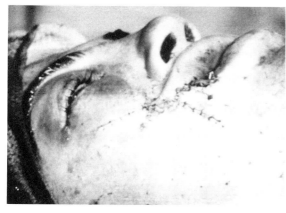

Chainsaw Massacre 2 ordered by air mail was seized at the airport customs by police. It is illegal to show any of the three *Chainsaw* films in Germany. Censorship in Germany often takes the form of raids or film seizures, while in America it is more insidiously applied by economic means such as rating codes, grant money stoppages or pressures brought to bear on offending cinemas by local government or real estate interests. Wholesale theatre shutdowns in inner city New York and Boston illustrate this more publicity conscious form of censorship.

Two days later, back in Munich, "this young rosy asshole of a DA," as Erich puts it, "struck again, at the show place this time where he ripped out a film from the projector and confiscated a couple more prints." Some weeks later the Werkstattkino was itself the target of a police raid, headed by the same DA. Every print they could lay hands on was impounded and documents, business papers and files were carted off as well. "They raged until four in the morning," reports Erich, "but the main thing, the print of Lustig's *Maniac*

which motivated the entire raid, they didn't get, as we'd swapped cans."

Prints and papers were eventually returned to the cinema and Erich now prepares a defence to the charges of 'Glorification of Violence,' enshrined in the German dictionary as *Gewaltverherrlichung*.

In the meantime, programming continues in its usual fashion at the Werkstattkino, and tours are also still on the agenda. A recent week-long festival in Budapest, Hungary met with good success. Four American films were among the items presented to long-deprived Hungarian cinéastes. *Assembly Line* and *Ulcer at Work* opened the festival, while the incomparable true-gore double bill of *The Act of Seeing with One's Own Eyes* and *Army Medicine in Vietnam* closed the festival in convincing if bloody fashion - chasing out over half the 300 audience members from the theatre.

Erich found the audience reaction most heartening and his voice fills with awe as he describes it: "They left but didn't go home - they stayed outside the theatre pacing and chain-smoking cigarettes."

(The following is an excerpt from one of Jack's letters which serves as the ideal conclusion to his feature. Ed.)

Regarding *The Act of Seeing With One's Own Eyes*, they bought that print direct from Brakhage and it's the only one (supposedly) on the Continent. They show it a lot. Also...they are *most definitely* the only ones outside the military to own a copy of *Army Medicine in Vietnam* - I know since I sent them the print. Waco (Erich) was in the German medics corps in 1975 and saw it then, later founding the cinema and seeking that film but unable to find it until I tracked it down for them over here two years ago. He told me about it and upon my return to the US I began the detective work. In light of the present Middle-East war the film is ultra-topical. To help you out I'm enclosing stills from that film, and I'm sending them to you to use only for the book project and in connection with the Werkstattkino article. The stills apply directly to the article since, as I say, Erich in effect 'found' the film, is responsible for it now being shown in the US and Germany, and they remain possessors of Europe's only print of that bloody pearl of a film. I have a print I show over here, and again it's all due to Erich I even know about the film. It's a film everyone should see. It naturally attracts the gore crowds, but nobody can leave a showing in anything but a profound depression, as in fact Richard Kern and others who have seen it state. It is not on video - we intend to keep it that way. I've been asked to show it as a backdrop for bands but utterly refuse to ever do so as I don't wish to see it rendered into an industrial band video backdrop decoration *à la* Butthole Surfers. The thing must be seen intact, unto itself. It's very existence is a political act. And I don't say such things often as I'm usually totally apolitical. As someone commented, "If they showed that on TV, the war would have ended five years earlier."

The legal difficulties the Werkstattkino experiences continue without clear resolution, so I doubt any last minute update will be necessary before publication. Most recently it was occupied by fifteen German cops who cordoned off the cinema and emerged with one lesbian art video, earning them the ridicule and low-grade disgust of all in attendance of said ludicrous event - leading at least one present to draw the Nazi analogy they so readily invite with their over-zealous cultural repression... ■

DOCTOR BENWAY RIDES AGAIN!

DAVID CRONENBERG INTERVIEWED

BY DAMON WISE

Some eight years in pre-production, David Cronenberg's adaptation of William S. Burroughs' seminal novel *The Naked Lunch* finally began filming on 21 January 1991. Produced by Jeremy Thomas, it stars Roy Scheider, Peter Weller, Judy Davis (in a dual role), Julian Sands, Elias Koteas, Michael Zelnicker and Monique Mercoure. Director of photography is Peter Suschitzky from *Dead Ringers*, and special make-up effects are being handled by CWI, who worked with Cronenberg on *The Fly*. Filming will now take place entirely in Toronto studios, where the interiors and the Interzone

Gratuitous hat photo: Peter Weller, David Cronenberg and William Burroughs.

(Burroughs' fictionalised, futuristic vision of Tangiers) exteriors will be constructed. The plans for location shooting in Tangiers have now been abandoned. The following conversation took place a few months prior to the UK release of Clive Barker's *Nightbreed*, with Cronenberg speaking from his Toronto production office.

SX: How faithful have you stayed to the novel?

DC: Not very. It really is impossible to make that book, literally, into a movie. But I think it's impossible to make any book, literally, into a movie. I certainly couldn't do it with *The Dead Zone*, and *The Naked Lunch* is a more difficult case. What I've done is...the movie is really about writing and creativity - and a lot of other things - but it's a lot about the writing of that book. So in a way the focus is quite different. People who've read it, though - including Burroughs - feel that it's somehow very faithful to the book without *being* the book. And I think - if they're right, and I feel very good about this script - then I've done it, y'know? Because that's the only way you could do it, I think.

SX: Have you met with Burroughs?

DC: Oh yes, many times. In fact we went to Tangiers together in about 1985 - he and I and Jeremy Thomas. He hadn't been there since the '60s, Burroughs, and we sort of walked through the streets and, God, there were people, local people, who still recognised him from the '50s. We met with Paul Bowles, who Burroughs hadn't seen for about twenty years and who was an old friend, of course, and, um, it was pretty exciting to be there with him. (*Thomas went on to produce Bertolucci's adaptation of Bowles'* The Sheltering Sky. *Ed.*) So we've been talking to Burroughs, Jeremy and I, for about eight years.

SX: Even if you abstracted some of the themes, you're still left with some very noxious sex scenes; also there's use of heroin as a stabilising factor. How will you deal with that?

DC: Well, I didn't really want it to be a drug movie. I mean, it may sound strange (*laughs*), but I never really felt that *The Naked Lunch* - the book, as opposed to the sort of preface in the publicity around it - was really about drugs. I mean, it's about control and about addiction and manipulation and hunger. But it's not, you know, it's not a drug book in the same way that *Junky* was, for instance. *Junky* was Burroughs' sort of autobiographical book about being a junkie.

But *The Naked Lunch* is really quite something else. I mean, its social implications are vast and it has a lot more to do with the nasty side of human nature than just taking drugs. Also, so much of what Burroughs has written about has been completely assimilated by Western culture, particularly North America. I mean, you can see Burroughs-type sketches, stand-up routines, every week on *Saturday Night Live*. So if you did it straight it would have a certain passé feel about it, only because of the success of Burroughs' insights. So it really required a kind of re-thinking of all that to get to the essence of what was really powerful about the book, which, as I say, was, to me, not about drugs. Although there *is* a lot about drug-taking in the movie, a lot of it is invented drugs. I'm not really into the symptoms of being a heroin addict, you know, that's not really the point. And he, also, used a lot of invented drugs because so much of his imagery was taken from science fiction. That's really, then, what I've kind of concentrated on. So it's really kind of fantasist, 'fantastic' drugs rather than, sort of, natural street drugs.

SX: Will you be keeping that kind of ambiguity about the time scale? What must have seemed futuristic in '58 now seems almost everyday.

DC: It certainly has a period feel. Technically, I'm setting it in 1953, but it's true that most of it takes place in Interzone, which is really an invented place, loosely based on Tangiers, but not really. I don't know how that's gonna work. It felt really right to me. I mean, I wanted to get a feel for what was happening then, when Burroughs was, you know, sort of the first to come up with this stuff, but I didn't want it to be a period piece either, with cute '40s clothes or something. So a lot of this is gonna come through the production design.

SX: Where are you shooting? New Mexico?

DC: No, we'll be shooting in Tangiers for a lot of it, and then we'll be shooting in Toronto for the interiors. The sets and the special effects will all be done in Toronto.

SX: Have you ever been attracted to any of his other novels?

DC: Well, in a way, there's stuff from other writings of his in my script. As far as Burroughs is concerned, all his work is one work and he doesn't really divide it up. I guess you can sort of feel that when you read his stuff, it's like little discrete bundles, and William Lee is the protagonist in a lot of his writing, not just one book.

There's a lot of stuff from all over the place and then there's a lot of *me* in it too. I mean, it really, in a way, is a kind of telepod fusion between me and Bill. That was understood from the outset, you know? For me to just be a kind of translator of him - well, I don't think

that would work. I actually think that to be a good translator you have to be very creative because certain things will not translate correctly. And then what do you do? So there's a lot of me in it as well.

SX: Ted Morgan, Burroughs' biographer, has said that *The Naked Lunch* bears as much resemblance to the conventional novel as videotape does to the Bayeux tapestry. Are you daunted? Will you try to make the film different from other narrative films? Or will you be paring down the episodic structure and keeping to something more linear?

DC: Well, it's not...it certainly does not have a traditional structure. But it's not as fragmented as the book. I mean, it does have some characters. The book really doesn't have characters, it really doesn't have narrative, it kind of has themes and continuing images. So I would say that the movie is a little more conservative than that. But having said that, it seems from the reaction that I get that it's not a particularly conservative movie (*laughs*)... So, you know, it's kind of a balancing act I guess you have to do.

But it came to me...I mean, I must say it felt very organic. When I started to work on it, I was worried about how different it might be because I'd been thinking about it for eight years before I started to write it. In fact, I started to write in London when I was acting in *Nightbreed*. I felt that that sort of isolation from Toronto and my family - and having more time on my hands, certainly, than I do when I'm directing - was the right time to start writing it. And to my surprise, it just started to flow. I had no trouble writing it at all, it just kind of was there. I did it

(Above) William Lee (Peter Weller) gets to grips with modern word-processing technology.

(Left) David Cronenberg demonstrates how to deal with pests when the Roach Motel fills up.

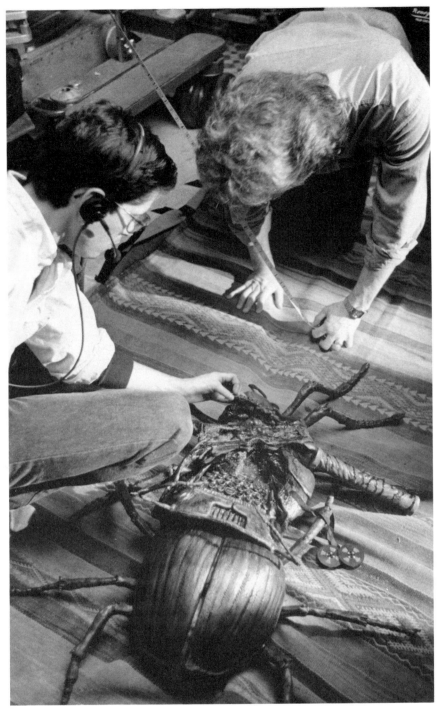

(Above) *Technical stuff.*

(Above right) *The boys do some PR.*

(Opposite below left) *Peter Weller and Thing.*

(Opposite below right) *Monique Mercoure experiences an identity crisis.*

more. I mean, it was much more advanced than my thinking on the subject. He'd just been doing it longer. But there was an immediate affinity, yes.

And there were other things that were quite different. I mean, one of the things we talked about was sexuality and I said, "Bill, I'm not gay, I don't know how that stuff is gonna translate. I don't know what I'm going to want to do and what I can't do. So it's going to have to be from my point of view, from that extent." And he said, "That's fine." He was totally cool about it. He was just very curious to see what I would come up with. And he seemed very satisfied with what there is.

SX: Is there any kind of furtherance of these themes? Will *The Naked Lunch* see all the ideas that are in your other films coming together in one organic heap?

DC: I don't think so. I really don't think so. It's possibly closest to the tone of *Videodrome*, maybe. But there are other things. There's a certain tone in *Dead Ringers* which I don't think will be in this film at all. I'm not sure though. If they're working, they really do surprise you. They take on their own life. Not just when you write them, but when you're shooting them and editing them, they suddenly become something, maybe, that you didn't expect. You kind of want that to happen, really. Only time will tell. But it's not really a compendium, no. It's a very specific project, it really is.

SX: Will Burroughs be making an appearance?

DC: No. I think he was really good in *Drugstore Cowboy* (laughs). But, in the sense that Bill Lee *is* Burroughs' persona, I think it would unbalance the film to also have the real Burroughs in it. I mean, it just doesn't feel right to me to do that. Although, God knows, he certainly has an amazing onscreen presence.

SX: Does it bother you that *The Naked Lunch* has been attempted so many times? Antony Balch almost succeeded, using Mick Jagger.

DC: No, because I really think that those were kind of half-hearted attempts. I know that Brion Gysin also wrote a script but it was done in the style of English music hall and there were songs and dances. No, it really doesn't bother me at all. Everything is different now, the times are different and the scale of what we're trying to do...I don't think those people were seriously trying to do a legitimate commercial movie. It was fairly underground, I think, what everyone was talking about then. And this is not.

SX: Does Burroughs talk much about those original drafts?

DC: No. No. We haven't really talked about it at all. I really didn't want to know. I mean, I wasn't particularly interested in them, especially before I started to write it. Not that it would influence me at all, I just didn't want to know. I mean, there were ways you could do this book, most of them wrong. As it always is, there are only a couple of really good ways, and I hadn't found my own, and once I started to write mine I was interested only in that.

SX: Had Burroughs seen your earlier movies? Or did you have to screen them for him?

DC: Yes, yes, he's seen quite a few of them. When we first met, I don't think he had seen anything. But that was quite a long time ago and as the project developed and we got to know each other then he got to be very curious about what I did, *then* he started to see things. And, of course, once we'd met, as my

myself. And so I didn't fight it. I wasn't thinking - I couldn't afford, really, to think - "What will Burroughs fans think and what will Burroughs himself think?" And so on. I just had to do what I felt right at the time. It was such a good groove. It felt really strong.

SX: In some ways, your work is fairly similar to Burroughs', basically as regards his attitudes to viruses and - you say it was an organic process - his obsession with organisms. Have you always felt that affinity?

DC: Yeah. I think, you know, when I discovered Burroughs I was finding someone who was thinking a lot of the things that I was thinking but from a completely different perspective and who had done it a lot

movies came out - *The Dead Zone*, I think, then *The Fly* and *Dead Ringers* - he was very curious to see whatever I was doing as it came out. So, certainly, he's familiar with more recent stuff.

SX: Did he approve? I'm sure he'd approve of *Shivers*.

DC: Yeah, well, I think he loved *Videodrome* too.

SX: What do you take from Burroughs as he is today? I mean, I'm kind of struck by the fact that you can get to that age and still be unorthodox, original and all-round inspirational. Did you get that from him?

DC: Yes. I mean, he's...yeah. We spent a lot of time in his house in Lawrence, Kansas City, just talking. I would ask him things, some of them fairly major and heavy, like life after death and that kind of thing. And some of them may be kind of offbeat, but very to-the-point in terms of my script. Like his attitude to centipedes and insects. He usually talks about insects in extremely negative terms. You know, "insect eyes" or "dead insect eyes", that kind of thing. And he has a total abhorrence of centipedes, which are not insects but are still, you know, creepy-crawly kind of stuff.

Now, I'm very interested in insects and they have a lot to do with my script, so I really wanted to talk to him about quirky aspects of that stuff. And he's always got a...you just can't anticipate what his point of view is going to be on anything. Because his thinking is so original. It's very honest, too. I mean, it's very direct. And it's really him (*laughs*).

SX: How are you influenced by insects - apart from *The Fly*, obviously?

Monique Mercoure administers some discipline to a sex-beastie.

DC: Well, they *are* fascinating. Interestingly enough, the two writers that always, I felt, were my major influences were Nabokov and Burroughs, and insects play a major part in both their writings. No, I hadn't always thought of that connection before, but it's true. But I was always, as a child, sort of an amateur entomologist and enthusiast.

It's just such a potent life force on this planet - and it is a life form - and yet it seems so alien to us. And also, I think, I'm fascinated by it because of the element of transformation that is, really, a major part of almost any insect's life. They don't start small and grow bigger. Some of them do. Incomplete metamorphosis - you know, they start, like, small crickets and then they get to be bigger crickets. But there are other insects that really transform from one kind of life to another - the caterpillar to butterfly, I suppose, is the common example.

And that kind of metamorphosis is really quite fascinating for me and it seems to have a great potency. And the personality of an insect does not seem to be an individual thing, it seems to be a sort of species thing. I mean insects *do* have personalities, but not as individuals, more as a species. I mean, there are certain types of butterfly that are...*funny*. You know, they're very amusing the way they fly and they're very eccentric. But it's all this particular kind of butterfly, which is called an Angle Wing and it's really noticeable if you're out there trying to catch them with a net or something. These are the ones that sort of land on your head and on your net and it's quite odd...

Anyway, it all seems to have resonances and seems to illuminate human life, somehow. That's part of my fascination. I mean, in the same way that some people are totally obsessed with the possibility of life on other planets, in outer space and so on. We have life forms more alien than you could ever imagine, right here on Earth, it's just that people tend not to notice them.

SX: I read someone quoted as saying you were fascinated with the idea of how long you can love someone who's changing. Is there a change in *The Naked Lunch*? How will you deal with that? Or won't you?

DC: Well, I was talking specifically about *The Fly*, I think, then. But, once again, that really is just another way of talking about identity and transformation. When an insect transforms, is it really the same insect or is it really...something else? Is there some core of identity that still remains, from the egg to the caterpillar, to the pupa, the butterfly itself? Is it really the same, or has something died and something else been created? I'm pretty sure that you'll find that somewhere in *The Naked Lunch*.

I haven't really... See, the process of analysis after the fact, of course, is something I haven't gone through with *The Naked Lunch*, since I haven't made the movie yet. And I really don't work on that plane, except that I do think it's a valid plane and that's one of the reasons why I don't like publicity for the film afterwards, because then you are forced, really, to be analytical about something that you did on a more visceral and intuitive level. And I kind of like that game. But I can't do it right now.

SX: Are you still intrigued by internal beauty? Is that a factor that attracted you to *The Naked Lunch*? There's a passage which features someone being fucked in the brain through the eye socket, for instance...

DC: Yeah, yeah. Well, I think, yes, it will be addressed. Certainly in an indirect way, definitely. I think it will be addressed. It might not be a major theme, I'm not sure, but it is dealt with on one level or another. I think you'll see that. ■

STEPHEN GALLAGHER'S TOP TEN
GENRE MOVIES (THIS WEEK)

This is the pits. I mean, it's great to be asked to pick out a personal top ten, but then what happens? You look through all the back issues of *SX* and find that all the best movies have already gone. *King Kong*? Nope, Ramsey's had it, and ditto with *Night of the Demon. Halloween*? Nah, Hutson grabbed that one. And Clive Barker leaped in and made off with *Orphée* almost before the staff had got the doors pinned back on the morning of the sale. Now, you may feel inclined to say that this isn't the point; it's not supposed to be like a dive into a heap of football jerseys to sort out the best of what's left. A personal top ten ought to be something definitive. Well, I'd agree up to a point...the point being that the sample's going to change

Foiled again. Steve Gallagher is unable to trade his rare unsigned hardcovers for a copy of Gorgo.

depending on the mood of the sampler when making the choice and, given the scope of the field, it would be a damned dull series of articles that simply reiterated the same core group of classics again and again. Having said that, I'd be happy to stand by the selection that follows. It's based entirely on grounds of high artistic achievement and quality of execution, as you'll see when we begin the countdown with...

The Trollenberg Terror (1958).

A quintessential '50s British B-movie, with no visible budget and an imported American star (Forrest Tucker). A deadly mist with deadly thingies in it descends on a Swiss mountain village, cornering and isolating the usual group of squabblers. Those who display the ideologically correct attitude come through, whilst those who obviously haven't seen many horror movies pooh-pooh the danger and make a fast and well-deserved trip to snuff city. I remember being curious about this one because everyone used to say Forrest Tucker looked like my dad, although on the whole I think my dad's a better actor. So, why the top ten placing? I'd have to say that it's a purely personal thing because these things linger...particularly when, as in this case, there's something timeless and classic in the concept. The makers of this film could really have screwed it up by thinking too hard; fortunately they just got on with the job so that something of the mythic quality of the story-beneath-the-story was able to shine through. If the film's famous for anything, it's for the special effect in which a piece of cotton wool pinned to a photograph of a mountain stands in for the mist-cloud. Which is a pity.

Martin (1977).

I knew that something good was coming when I handed the case to the video shop's owner and he said, "I wouldn't bother with this, I've seen it and it's rubbish." This from a man whose shelves groaned with kung fu and Nazi-atrocity rubbish, and whose idea of high culture was a Burt Reynolds movie with no car crashes. John Amplas plays Romero's totally

Martin: your average adolescent. We know this to be true.

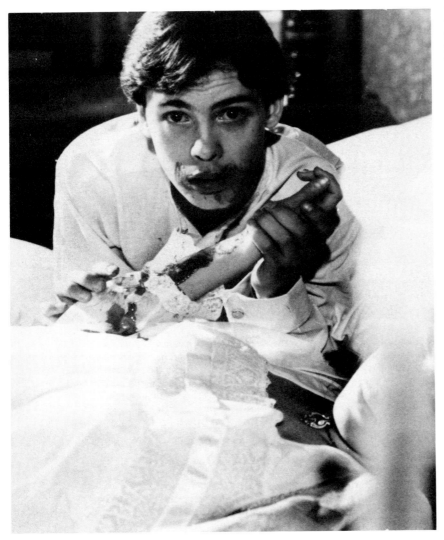

credible, demythologised vampire who doesn't spout fangs but carries a hypodermic syringe and a razor blade. At first glance he's your average adolescent; sullen, silent, retarded-looking, socially awkward but inwardly bursting with dark and vivid fantasies. It's a film that comes over with the same non-Hollywood freshness as early Cronenberg, speaking of which...

Videodrome (1982).

I was forewarned that *Videodrome* was incoherent. Sure it is. It's as incoherent as poetry, or music. (*Shall we tell him Les Daniels had it? Ed.*)

The Omen (1976).

A highly efficient and commercial movie, but I'm not about to run it down just because of that...I liked it better than *The Exorcist* when it came out, and still do. I like the way that it grabs the ball in reel one and then charges relentlessly toward the touchdown, trampling any opponents, forests and small cities that may happen to get in its way. It spawned two sequel films and four spinoff books, not one of which is worth a damn.

Metropolis (1926) or Nosferatu (1922) or The Thief of Bagdad (1924) or The Phantom of the Opera (1925)...

I dunno, I just wanted to give the number six spot to one of the silents and now I don't know which one to choose. There's stuff in *Metropolis* that involves some of the most memorable imagery ever put on film...I'm thinking now of the cityscapes and the factory scenes, of hooded death stalking the land with a scythe and, of course, Rotwang's robot Maria. Unfortunately it also has a dork-brained scenario about hands and hearts and heads working together, and two hours is an awful lot to sit through for such a banal conclusion. Rather like winning the Nobel Prize and finding it's actually a subscription to *The Reader's Digest*. Similarly you can throw out everything in *Phantom* when Chaney isn't on screen and not miss very much. *Nosferatu* is more of a piece. *Thief* is buoyed up by the breezy presence of Douglas Fairbanks, the downside being that you can never quite believe in the dark side of the story with Fairbanks around. Tell you what. Scrub the silents, and I'll have the 1940 Korda remake of *The Thief of Bagdad* instead. That self-assembly flying horse haunted me for years.

Cat People (1942).

I like this, and yet...I feel I ought to like it more than I do. The name of Val Lewton has become a byword for quiet, understated, non-explicit, character-driven horror, and this film is a near-perfect expression of his approach; it's just that I'm left with a lingering feeling that it lacks a certain pizazz, that the emphasis is a little *too* much on the cerebral and that the crocodile half of the viewer's brain is being left to go hungry. The Paul Schrader remake was a mess. The crocodiles got to see Nastassia Kinski go naked, and that was about it.

Solaris (1972).

This is my stubborn-bastard entry. Actually, it was going to be either this or *Gorgo*. Tarkovsky's films always make me feel brighter than I really am, and yet more stupid than I ought to be. *Solaris* is probably his most accessible, although it's reckoned to be the one

that he liked least of all his own works. I know people who've claimed that they could really only enjoy it by sitting with the tape in almost permanent fast-forward. I like the theme of the relationship between the conscious and the subconscious. I like the pervading sense of loss. I love the ending.

Jason and the Argonauts (1963).

The second film I ever saw. The first was *Whistle Down the Wind* with Hayley Mills, which I think we can all agree has no real place in this list. I can't help feeling that Ray Harryhausen inadvertently ended his own career with the terrific job that he did on this movie; everything that he's done since has had the look of a retread, either of this (here I'm thinking of *Clash of the Titans*) or of the earlier *The 7th Voyage of Sinbad* (and here I'm thinking of everything else). *Jason* was the better of the two; it had more skeletons, and it didn't have Kerwin Matthews. Instead it had the macho voice of Tim Turner issuing from the wimpo frame of Todd Armstrong. I wonder what happened to

old Todd? I've never heard of him before, and I've never heard of him since. Maybe he reverted to some other name and accent and went home...or back into a cupboard in Harryhausen's workshop.

La Belle et La Bête (1946).

I don't know exactly how it works, but this film seems to bypass various levels of awareness and strike deep, resonant chords in the unconscious. It's like the older kind of fairytale; not the childish entertainment that the Victorians tried to make of it, but something darker and fiercer and charged with sexual metaphor. Jean Marais' Beast is a truly romantic, tragic figure who goes through hell to gain humanity. The producers of *Beauty and the Beast* TV series should be made to sit through the original and then be led, reflecting on their crimes, into a sparsely furnished room where various implements of suicide lie waiting.

And finally, in the number one slot, to end all the suspense...

*"Shit, it's full of sequels,"
says Gregory Peck.*

(Above and right)
Carnival of Souls.

Carnival of Souls (1962).

Actually, I can forgive you for looking blank. For years I seem to have been the only person in UK fandom to have seen this movie. It came to my home town as half of a Sunday double-bill sometime around the early '70s, and then seemed to vanish off the face of the earth. A low budget independent feature shot in Kansas with a finale at a deserted pavilion near Salt Lake City, its making parallels that of *Night of the Living Dead* in a number of ways; a documentary/industrial background for its makers, a cast filled out with non-professionals that included some of the backers and crew, a first venture for all concerned, horrendous distribution problems, and finally cult status. Also, no money for those involved.

Put simply, it's the story of a woman who survives drowning after her car goes off a bridge, only to find that she's losing touch with reality and haunted by a spectral figure. The figure finally draws her off to the Carnival of Souls, where the dead dance in the old pavilion as if it were a zombie Roseland. When she attempts to escape, they pursue her down the beach; her footsteps and a single handprint are found the next morning, ending right in the middle of nowhere with no trace of how she might have vanished. At the same time, the people back home are finally dredging up her car from the river; and there she is, still inside it, several days dead.

I'll be the first to admit that it's all more than a little rough around the edges. Some of the cutting betrays a lack of coverage, some of the performances are less than adequate (and it's a pity that one of the best, from Sidney Berger as a would-be seducer, appears in an unfortunately slack patch in the central section of the story), and some of the dialogue can get a bit heavy-handed; but the Carnival of Souls itself is a wonderful, compelling conceit, and the overall story and its execution bit deeply into me and changed the internal geography of my imagination forever. I only realised how when I saw it again, on a US video; not available in the UK and, as far as I can tell, no prospect of it. But then, what can you expect? The US is another country. The video industry does things differently there...

Well, what can I say? My thunder's been stolen. I first saw this haunting and highly effective low-budget creeper on a Sunday double-bill in the early '70s, and have been talking about it to anyone who'd listen ever since.

For so long I seemed to have cornered the movie and made it my own; almost nobody else seemed to have heard of it and of those who had, no one had seen it. After nearly twenty years it had begun to feel like exclusive property. Then I managed to get hold of a NTSC copy from the States and had it standards-converted at enormous expense - well, sixty quid - and lo! Those flickering shadows lived again, even if in places the copy *did* resemble one of those terrible *E.T.* bootlegs that went the rounds (you know the ones I mean - the ones that you watched for about fifteen minutes and then turned bewildered to the person beside you and said, "Has it started yet?"). Now, at last, I realised why so many of my stories featured people drowning in or out of cars. I'd rediscovered a key influence. *I'd pinpointed one of the actual moments in which I'd been warped forever.*

Of course, my zeal was redoubled. Now I didn't just talk about it, I wondered aloud about the chance of a UK release. I was all set for another twenty years. And what happened then?

Palace released it.

In a new print; first at the ICA, then various festivals and regional film theatres, and finally onto video. I was dumbstruck.

I mean, now just anybody could get to see it!

It was a near-mortal blow, and I'm not sure that I'll ever recover. They let me do the video sleeve notes - I suppose they decided that they could only take so much snivelling and pleading, and it must have been a bore having to step over me on the way into work every morning - but I don't know, I still feel like someone with a warehouseful of 'Maggie Out' T-shirts. I suppose I'll get over it eventually.

Ah, well, still number one. But has anybody out there ever seen a film called *La Jetée*...?

Last minute news: Palace now tell me they've had to drop the sleeve notes to make way for ads. Back to the doorstep... ∎

(Absolutely the last Last Minute News: Carnival of Souls *just made it onto nationwide television. Sorry Steve... Ed.)*

Born in Salford, Lancashire in 1954, Stephen Gallagher first worked as researcher for Yorkshire TV's documentaries department after graduating from Hull University. 1978 saw his first professional sale and he became a full-time writer in 1980. His novels include Chimera, Follower, Valley of Lights, Oktober, Down River, Rain *and* The Boat House, *five of which he has adapted for TV or cinema. He is currently researching* Nightmare, With Angel, *his next novel, and working on no less than five screenplay, adaptation and direction projects for cinema and TV. He has also written much short fiction and criticism.*

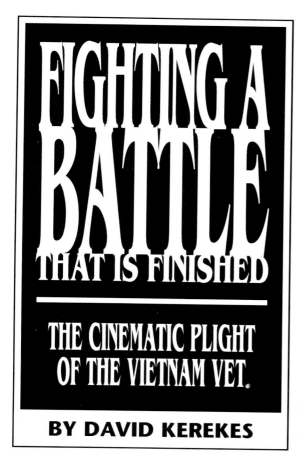

FIGHTING A BATTLE THAT IS FINISHED

THE CINEMATIC PLIGHT OF THE VIETNAM VET.

BY DAVID KEREKES

In *Head* - The Monkees' only feature length movie - among its crazy succession of broken and unrelated sketches, there is one sequence in particular which seems to hit the spot in encapsulating the mixed-up, apocalyptic attitude of those 1968 pre-Woodstock times.

In what is basically a last-ditch attempt to rake in a couple of more bucks from the fans, *Head* has The Monkees destroying their old teeny-bopper TV show image. The Monkees try to get with it by making references to their old selves as corporate pawns, as well as by smoking dope; by utilising lots of

*In an attempt to avert Mickey Dolenz dreaming up **Metal Mickey**, the government sends him to Vietnam. He is shot. He dies. The future is safe. Peter Tork (right) decides to change his name to Kurtz and head up-river.*

(Previous page) The representative from the Vietnam Veterans Benevolent Fund.

psychedelic images; by having anti-establishment guest stars like Frank Zappa, and by playing some pretty groovy now sounds.

When a sequence of The Monkees singing "The money's in/we're made of tin/we're here to give you more" is played to an accompanying barrage of slapstick TV images, the sound of a single gunshot abruptly cuts the song dead. The slapstick TV images then cut to the infamous news footage of Police Chief Nguyen Ngoc Loan executing a Vietcong suspect point blank to the head. A girl's screams ring out, but it's soon made clear that the screams are not those of horror or outrage, but of ecstasy; the screams come from a Monkees fan at a Monkees concert.

What follows is typical of the movie, but nowhere else is *Head* quite as poignant. The band, in the true tradition of teen-generation gurus (waning though they may have been), act as cheerleaders at the concert and get their audience to spell out W-A-R! In the next instant, the group find themselves on a battlefield in combat dress, debating among themselves as to whether wearing a helmet is cool or not. Mickey Dolenz is shot dead, but is alright in the end, and the group mount an attack...running straight out of combat onto stage and into song. Shots of the band are intercut with those of the screaming girls in the audience, and of screaming Korean women and children.

Manufactured though they may have been, (undoubtedly so in their movie as much as in their TV shows) in *Head* The Monkees managed to capture the spirit of the times. Here, after all, was an America torn between the love generation and the war that was raging in Vietnam.

"I still dream about it. My wife hears me screaming in the middle of the night. I swear to God, it's so real sometimes...I'm standing by myself and I don't have nothing and these fucking gooks are coming at me. I wake up and my stomach will be funny-feeling. I get headaches and things."
Anonymous Vietnam veteran

"My life has taken another turn again. The days move along with regularity, over and over, one day indistinguishable from the next. A long continuous chain. And suddenly, there is change..."
Robert De Niro, *Taxi Driver*.

"You wanna go to 'Nam? I'll take you to 'Nam."
Dennis Hopper, *Tracks*.

There has been internal military unrest in Southeast Asia for several decades, since the Japanese occupation in the '40s.

In 1955 South Vietnam refused to take part in the all-Vietnam elections, stating that free elections are impossible in the Communist North. That same year, South Vietnam formally requested US instructors for its armed forces. Conflicts escalated between North and South Vietnam. In 1961 the United States decided to increase military aid to South Vietnam. By the beginning of 1962 the number of American troops in South Vietnam had reached 4,000. By the end of the '60s total US strength had reached 536,100.

Vietnam was the soap opera war. It was the weird war. At its height, Vietnam was broadcast on the television news every day. And, as with all soap operas, each news report from Vietnam took an already convoluted story into yet wilder territories. American teenagers seemed to be really freakin' out over there, doing stuff like wearing necklaces made from the ears of dead North Vietnamese; taking tabs of acid that had been distributed, not by the Ruskies as a means of breaking the Americans, but by the US Government itself to keep their boys happy; some of the troops, meanwhile, were getting their 'high' in wiping out whole villages, and other troops were gunning down their own men for doing so.

Before too long, as well as having to come to terms with the fact that he was fighting a losing battle, the American soldier in Vietnam was being hounded by widespread anti-war demonstrations back home. He was also rapidly becoming an embarrassment for the American Government.

When the last American combat troops left Vietnam in March 1973, it wasn't to any conquering heroes' welcome; those who survived came home empty handed and alone. All they had to show was the war which continued to rage on hard, deep behind those confused and weary eyes.

Without doubt, Vietnam is now as American as Mom's Apple Pie.

Quite understandably, very few American movies of the last two decades exist without some reference to the Vietnam War. And because it is within earshot of both those magical nowhere lands of 'the Summer of Love' and Woodstock, Vietnam is often spoken of with that same accent of sickly sweet nostalgia. The Vietnam War is awash with the emblems of peace and the colours of psychedelia.

For all of those who went into Vietnam and made it back to tell the tale, life has become a barrage of dissolves and overlapping sequences from the movies: the firefights of *Platoon*, the brutalities in *Physical Assault*, the Mickey Mouse theme song from *Full Metal Jacket*. Life for the Vietnam veteran is an incessant rerun of *Chrome and Hot Leather*, *Armed Response*, *The No Mercy Man*, *Cease Fire*, *Exterminator 2*, *Trained to Kill*, *Rolling Thunder*, *Forced Vengeance*, *Search & Destroy*, *The Deer Hunter*, *Uncommon Valor*, *Coming Home*, *Revenge is My Destiny*, *Good Guys Wear Black*, *Black Sunday*, *Street Trash*, ad nauseam.

Yes, the genre of the Vietnam veteran cinema is just as mixed up as the logistics which kept the boys over there in the first place, and what's more, the genre makes no bones about where its sympathies lie. With barely a handful of exceptions, the cinema holds the Vietnam veteran responsible for a multitude of sins. When the police reach a dead end in their search for a sex killer in *Don't Answer the Phone*, for instance, they naturally surmise, "Maybe we're looking for a Vietnam veteran."

The Vietnam era has become the great contemporary pseudonym for rampaging psychosis. This is because in the general order of the movies, it is far easier to impress upon the audience the fact that the ex-soldier has *no social conscience or social commitment* whatsoever, and that he is quite capable of maiming, raping and killing with barely a pause for thought.

But if the truth be known - and known it is in movies like *Combat Shock* - the Vietnam veteran is not really killing aimlessly or wandering in a void, he is in all actuality engaged in a constant search for that war back in Southeast Asia.

Frankie (Ricky Giovinazzo) wanders the dilapidated streets of his home town in *Combat Shock*. A typical day for him starts with flashbacks of the 'Nam and waking to the voice of his nagging wife; "You don't want a job, you're waiting for the world to end," she

Nicholas Worth inspires a typical reaction in **Don't Answer the Phone.**

tells him. Before he gets dressed, Frankie has to first contend with his bawling mutant baby; trying to find his missing shoe; putting up with a shoelace breaking; fixing the toilet which suddenly won't flush, and written notice from the landlord that his family has to vacate the apartment later that day. He has no job, the house has no food and his baby is starving.

As he makes his daily journey across town to the unemployment office, Frankie passes boarded-up shop fronts, overturned dustbins and an array of peculiar people; no one in *Combat Shock* has any redeeming qualities whatsoever.

Through what appears an almost independent series of episodes - episodes in which Frankie finds a friend dead after shooting up with a rusted wire coathanger, or that in which he is disowned by his father, or that in which, out of sheer desperation, he steals a handbag - Frankie finds himself with a revolver and shoots down the gang of hoods that has been on his back.

This last episode takes Frankie over the precipice. He returns home and stands in the kitchen as scenes from the Vietnam War are projected onto his face. He shoots his wife and baby son, puts the baby in the oven, and takes from the fridge a carton of milk. Disturbing though it may be, it isn't so much the killing of his wife and child that accentuate Frankie's dementia, but more the fact that he then sits down and, without as much as a wince, drinks a glass of the now lumpy milk which has been festering since the beginning of the picture.

When it comes to post-war 'Nam movies, *Combat Shock* pretty much stands up there with the select. Director Buddy Giovinazzo has managed to piece together the most harrowing and sensitive features of all the screen veterans, and come up with, in Frankie, the epitome of the vacuous soul-searching loner. When Frankie comes home in *Combat Shock*, he is totally oblivious to the atrocities which surround him, he is oblivious to everything but his own permanent

(Below) Ricky G. attempts to avoid sequels to **Combat Shock.**

state of confusion.

Gene (Greg Mullavey) is another Vietnam veteran trying to salve his own conscience in *My Friends Need Killing*. Greg needs to erase the ever-recurring nightmares he has of burning villages and screaming Vietnamese children. This he does by waking one morning and deciding that he will kill all of his ex-army buddies. There isn't much more to *My Friends Need Killing*. Of course there are the killings, which are preluded by Gene's schizoid rantings; for instance, when in a room with one of his old buddies, Gene begins to bark orders to non-existent troops standing outside the door. Similarly, Gene barks orders with every one of the old buddies that he meets. Then he kills them (or has them kill themselves) after remonstrating all of those atrocities, all of those burning villages, and all of those dead children.

Despite having a truly unexpected ending, *My Friends Need Killing* is pretty bland. There is no psychological foreplay involved, Gene simply goes out and kills. In fact, the only depth the character of Gene is given is that he has a wife - but this in itself seems to be for no other reason than that of having someone to discover Gene in the unexpected ending.

As is typical of both Frankie and those movies to follow, Greg is a Vietnam veteran haunted by the past. It is this past which drives Greg - and the veter-

an in general - on to shape the future. And if he can't shape the future, the veteran is going to have to kill it in order to save himself.

With the hardcore porn flick *Forced Entry* comes another veteran; a shell of a character - a mere ruse in which to carry out the meagre plot. This veteran, however, is driven by the generic nature of the movie not to kill, but to rape. What begins with grainy Vietnam stock footage, soon leads into the grainy photography of the actual movie itself, as a narrator decides that the legacy of Vietnam - the confusion, fear and rage - can only culminate in the veteran's "desperate need to find a victim."

Armed with this philosophy, it isn't too difficult to anticipate what manner of desperate needs the nameless veteran of *Forced Entry* harbours. And, after carrying out a series of sexual assaults and rape, our veteran kills himself.

This is what happens when the Vietnam veteran sees no way of changing the future or saving himself, he is left with no other choice but suicide.

Greg does it. The loner of *Forced Entry* does it. Frankie does it in *Combat Shock* (as the blood of his baby son dribbles from the oven door, he puts a gun to his head and blows his brains out). After Vietnam there seems to be something very deep and very basic that is missing from the veteran's life; something which is much more primal than love or hate.

What this primordial quality boils down to, and what seems to be now missing from life, is the *gratification from survival*. As one of the veterans speaking in Mark Baker's book, *Nam*, says, "It wasn't going over there and saving the world from communism or defending the country. The matter of survival was the only thing you could get any gratification from."

With Vietnam over, and the gratification from survival somewhat eradicated, the ex-soldier finds that he must live out his life forever seeking a substitute.

Travis Bickle finds it when he wipes out the child prostitution racket in *Taxi Driver*. And we know that he has achieved that elusive plane of self-gratification when, in *Taxi Driver*'s closing frames, Travis looks into his rearview mirror and sees 'himself' (a revelation of his true self, or the nature of the beast) for the first time.

Travis is driven to wipe out the prostitution ring so that he can change the future, so that he can do some good in his life, so that he can at least come close to capturing that same gratification he once attained through that pure, unadulterated instinct of survival: that which necessitates the will to live. It is this elusive something the veteran is searching for when he wanders the streets of *Taxi Driver*; or when he decides to take the law into his own hands in *Cutter's Way*; or when he takes on the position of a psychiatrist in *The Ninth Configuration*.

But the film vet can't put a finger on what is suddenly missing from life - the fear of imminent death; in fact, he doesn't really know what it is he wants. He is merely searching for something he may or may not have once seen. As war veteran Dennis Hopper remarks to his new girlfriend in *Tracks*, "I've not seen anything like you since I was sixteen...I'm not even sure I saw it then." You can't hold onto gratification from survival; it can only be squeezed out under pressure. When the fear of getting your balls blown off has been taken away, so goes with it that gratification; there remains a void. Something has to take its place in order for you to survive.

There is little to fill the emptiness after Vietnam. Nobody wants to be there, but nobody knows what to do after it's over. As Martin Sheen contemplates in *Apocalypse Now*, sitting in a Saigon hotel room and thinking of being back home with his wife, "When I was here I wanted to be there. When I was there all I could think of was getting back into the jungle."

Director Luis San Andres in his movie *Night Flowers* suggests that the Vietnam veteran's 'elusive something' is to be found on the trail where *The Deer Hunter* and *Apocalypse Now* left off.

Tom and Luis are two army buddies who have drifted to New York. As the video box copy has it, they 'suffer psychotic revolutions that force them to rape and murder unconsciously.' They wander the streets, exchanging monumental dialogue like: "I'm going to get some foot powder. Want anything?"

Tom (Gabriel Walsh) is unable to hold down a steady job because he keeps "forgetting things", while buddy Luis (Jose Perez) is half crazy because of his uncontrollable sexual frustration. Luis is prone to sidling up to female students in bookstores and trying to win them over with introductions like "Don't I know you from somewhere?" Luis later confides in Tom, "Why do women always have to play games?"

Despite Tom's stumbling through several reconcilia-

DON'T MUCK AROUND WITH A GREEN BERET'S MAMA!

...He'll take his chopper and ram it down your throat!

introducing
MARVIN GAYE
as Sgt. Jim

CHROME AND HOT LEATHER

WES BISHOP and LEE FROST present "CHROME and HOT LEATHER" starring WILLIAM SMITH
TONY YOUNG · MICHAEL HAYNES · PETER BROWN · MARVIN GAYE
MICHAEL STEARNS introducing KATHY BAUMANN with LARRY BISHOP as 'Gabe'
Produced by WES BISHOP · Photographed and Directed by LEE FROST · COLOR by MOVIELAB GP
Screenplay by MICHAEL ALLEN HAYNES & DAVID NEIBEL and DON TAIT
Story by MICHAEL ALLEN HAYNES & DAVID NEIBEL · Music by PORTER JORDAN · An AMERICAN INTERNATIONAL Release

©1971 American International Pictures, Inc.

tory meetings with an old girlfriend and then his father, it is really both Tom's and Luis's non-adventures round town together that catch *Night Flowers* at its best. In one of his continuing attempts at trying to pick up a girl for both himself and Tom, Luis puts an ad in a supermarket window, which reads:

APARTMENT FOR RENT
YOUNG GIRLS ONLY

Amazing as it seems, a number of girls are stupid enough - or post-Vietnam liberated enough - to reply to the ad. It is one such caller to the flat that provides *Night Flowers* with its most inspired and potent moment. Tom sits on the bed with a vacant stare as Luis shows a young girl around the flat. This encounter between the two buddies and the girl establishes a genuine attempt by *Night Flowers* to dig beneath the surface of the Vietnam legacy; that there are indeed two generations of Vietnam vets: those who went to Vietnam and those who didn't.

The girl falls in love with the apartment, but doesn't seem to grasp the fact that Tom and Luis have no intention of moving out. There is suddenly an awkward conflict of priorities within the apartment. The viewer realises that *Night Flowers* has set this girl up as *The Person Who Has Never Been To War But Has The Audacity To Say To Someone Who Has* something as insignificant as "I'm into Indian poetry now", with which Luis agrees, naturally. In fact, Luis agrees with everything the girl says, wanting nothing more than to get inside her pants. Regardless of the girl's declaration to Luis that "we are all cosmic childs", all the girl is really advocating is her own narrow-mindedness, her self-image, not peace or love or Indian poetry; the closest this 'cosmic child' has got to the war in Vietnam is listening to Buffalo Springfield.

When Luis does make a pass at the girl and is rejected, the encounter ends in rape and murder. But because of the universal order of 'Nam, Tom stays with his buddy Luis to try and help him out of the mess he's got himself into.

With all the Vietnam veteran movies discussed so far, there can be drawn some very obvious parallels. Though it wouldn't be correct to assume that all Vietnam veteran movies are intrinsically the same, they do, however, push the Vietnam veteran into one of three bags. These three being those movies which:
- bring the 'Nam buddy on home, whether he be dead or a prisoner of war
- utilise the 'Nam veteran as a mystical figure, capable of the most dazzling feats of strength or ingenuity (that's what comes of living on your wits, brawn, etc)
- can't shake that Vietnam guilt trip (with the veteran's guilt manifesting itself ultimately as a detriment or as a benefit to society).

This last sub-genre of Vietnam veteran cinema - that of the 'guilt trip' - is the more common, and has been typical of all those movies covered so far. As seen in *My Friends Need Killing* and *Night Flowers*, the veteran's guilt trip is synonymous with the difficulties he experiences in trying to recover his social standing and adjust back into everyday life. On the other hand, some movies may play out *society's* 'guilt trip' toward the veteran, in that it was society which cheered the soldier off to Vietnam, and it was society which shunned the veteran on his return. *Cutter's Way* is one such guilt trip.

Cutter, the embittered crippled veteran of *Cutter's Way*, is one of the many who find it difficult to adjust back into civilian life upon leaving the 'Nam. Cutter finds himself wandering from day to day, doing nothing more than trying to stomach his inner emptiness. Cutter does eventually manage to put some perspective on his life, however, when his friend Bone thinks he has been witness to a murder: Cutter goes all out to try and unmask the murderer.

Cutter's Way shows its veteran to be as aesthetically tormented as the next ex-soldier, as Frankie in *Combat Shock* or Travis Bickle in *Taxi Driver*. Cutter is on a one-way path to self-destruction unless he can purge himself of his hollowness, unless he can once again find the gratification that was staying alive in the 'Nam. But *Cutter's Way* is worthy of note in that it insists that it isn't the crippled veteran who is at fault with society, but it is really society which is at fault with itself: if this was such a righteous and God-fearing place, why does it take a physical wreck like Cutter to be the one to stand up and try to put a murderer behind bars?

One movie which certainly makes no attempt to fabricate any theories on its rampaging, unable-to-adjust Vietnam veteran, is the Peter Maris movie *Delirium*.

In *Delirium* we have Charlie (Nick Panouzis), a Vietnam vet who is hired as an assassin by a vigilante group. Charlie is sent out to kill those who have done wrong and managed to escape the scales of justice. But, compelled as he is by flashbacks of the war, Charlie soon goes out of control and begins to kill at random anyone he meets...particularly if they're young girls in hotpants.

Despite its initial twist on the old formula, in that this killer veteran is a pawn to others and not himself, *Delirium* makes no attempt to elaborate, and opts instead to have Charlie simply stalk and slash his way through several beautiful women - with one particular slaying being shown no less than three times. In the prelude to one murder - in which Charlie picks up a hitch-hiking girl only to drive like crazy and crash the car near a beach - Charlie is confronted with the immortal lines, "Do you realise you almost got us killed back there? Are you okay? I'm going for a swim."

Without doubt, Charlie and *Delirium* must stand as being one of the worst examples of Vietnam veteran cinema. That Charlie carries out his lunatic attacks without uttering a single word of dialogue might be levelled as a major contributing factor to the movie's downfall, but the fact is that Charlie is so boring anyway. The movie kills him off about two-thirds of the way through (though to be fair and to avoid any disappointed vet fans in the audience, *Delirium* subsequently reveals that Stern, the head of the vigilante group, is himself a Vietnam veteran).

Contrary to all those soldiers we have seen come from Vietnam as hollow men - the rampaging Charlies or the confused Genes of this world - there are those few, the movies would have it, who came back infused with a special kind of magic. The jungle, it would appear, leaves its mark in mysterious ways. And, if only for a handful of troops, this mark is not necessarily a damning one.

For instance, there are those veterans who manage, in an almost superhuman capacity, to defy all odds

and avenge the death of a loved one; Richard Harrison in *Fireback*, Robert Ginty in *The Exterminator*, Jim Brown in *Slaughter*.

Similarly, there are those veterans who manage to bring together poor, downtrodden neighbours and lead the revolt against a tyrannical landlord or neighbourhood gang: Richard Hatch in *The Ghetto Blaster* Kris Kristofferson in *Vigilante Force*, Stephen Lang in *Band of the Hand*.

Or indeed, there are those veterans who find that they have acquired a skill for killing people, in spite of having to overcome appalling disabilities to do so: Rutger Hauer in *Blind Fury*.

The very exploitative nature of this 'mystical figure' sub-genre of the veteran cycle would seem to decree that the majority of the above movies are in themselves instantly forgettable. Yet, despite all of their

JOHN SAXON in CANNIBAL APOCALYPSE

POW's in Vietnam...starved in captivity... released with a taste for human flesh.

self, and pretty soon he is out there with them, running wild, killing and feeding.

Just as difficult to stomach as *Cannibal Apocalypse* is Sylvester Stallone's Rambo.

After demolishing a town of rednecks in *First Blood*, Stallone's mumbling, one-dimensional Rambo character went on to become something of a Vietnam veteran superman. In the sequel, *Rambo: First Blood Part II*, Rambo manages to flatten a country by himself in an attempt to rescue POWs held by the Vietcong. In a spark of originality, however, *Rambo III* has the scenario change from Vietnam to Russian-occupied Afghanistan, while the POWs have become a former superior who needs to be rescued.

Hardly surprisingly, the most interesting aspect of the Rambo movies is not the movies themselves but the children's animated feature which they spawned, *Rambo: The Rescue*. *Rambo: The Rescue* gives credence to a whole new generation that Vietnam is, in actuality, this neverwhere land in which supermen of one form or another are born.

The superman of *Born on the Fourth of July* is not a giant of a man, but rather a man who would stand for president.

Patriotic Ron Kovic (Tom Cruise) comes back from Vietnam paralysed from the waist down and in a wheelchair. Understandably, the waters of doubt begin to erode Kovic's all-American conviction and he starts to question just what has been gained by the loss of his legs, or indeed what has been gained by the loss of all those lives in a war being fought 13,000 miles away. Pretty soon, Kovic is the voice of a whole generation, speaking out against Vietnam on a trail which he hopes will take him to the White House.

Unfortunately, *Born on the Fourth of July* falls short of facing any real issues, preferring instead to substitute them with cheap attempts at heart-tugging melodrama. There is little other reason for scenes of the wheelchair ridden Kovic reliving his running, jumping, pre-Vietnam days of youth, or indeed, scenes of the crippled veteran trying his damndest to walk again.

It is somewhat ironic that *Born on the Fourth of July*'s most touching moment should come, therefore, not when the flaccid John Williams score cranks up, but on a more sombre note. During a late night argument with his mother, a drunken Kovic finally opens himself and his heartaches up to the world. He doesn't want to be a cripple for the rest of his life, he can't even get a hard-on. It is when Kovic grabs a crucifix while laying the blame for his paralysed penis on God, that Kovic's mother goes on to top the sequence with the line, "Don't say penis in this house!"

Given illustration of this truly disturbing set of values, the viewer's heart can only bleed for Kovic.

Stacy Keach has appeared in more that his fair share of Vietnam veteran movies. Keach appears in *Intimate Strangers*, in which a husband and wife medical team become separated in Saigon, finally getting to meet up again ten years later. While in *The Forgotten*, Keach is among a group of former POWs who return to the USA, only to find that they're on the receiving end of a sinister Government plan.

In the scope of 'Nam vet movies, both *Intimate Strangers* and *The Forgotten* are to be found struggling near the back. Fortunately for Keach, however, there is another 'Nam vet title of his which does manage to pack a fair punch. In fact, *The Ninth Configuration* is so

shortcomings, these movies are important if only for the simple reason that, together, they have played a major part in the evolution of the mystique - a very real mystique - which now surrounds Vietnam and its veterans.

In turn, this mystique could bring about something as improbable as a dead soldier returning to his home town as a veteran corpse (*Dead of Night*), or something as odd as a post-'Nam news reporter determined to make the ultimate autopsy movie (*Autopsia*).

In *Cannibal Apocalypse*, John Saxon's army buddies (John Morghen and Tony King), kept prisoner by the Vietcong, are 'forced' to feed on human flesh. When Saxon arrives to rescue them they take a bite out of his arm... On their return to 'civilisation' King and Morghen discover that old 'Nam habits die hard and before long are on the rampage for tasty morsels.

Saxon, 'infected' by their bite, just can't help him-

good a movie that it puts Keach's veteran within shouting distance of both Giovinazzo and De Niro.

The Ninth Configuration utilises all of the familiar motifs from the vet genre; it has a psychopathic vet, flashback sequences, comradeship and sociopathic monologues. But it isn't simply the use of all these familiar generic motifs that makes *The Ninth Configuration* interesting; it just so happens that *The Ninth Configuration* is very possibly the first existential Vietnam veteran movie.

Keach plays ex-Marine Colonel Kane, a brilliant and unorthodox psychiatrist, back from the 'Nam. Kane has been brought to a secluded mansion in an attempt to analyse a group of high ranking military officers, all of whom seem to be suffering from mental breakdowns. Kane has to discover whether or not the men are faking it. The movie revolves around set pieces in which Colonel Kane addresses each of the officers in turn, with each address becoming increasingly eclectic. For instance, throughout *The Ninth Configuration* Kane pursues the argument that it is possible for one man to give up his life for the love of his fellow man; that such an act need not necessarily be a mere reflex action or an act of suicide.

Colonel Kane gets to prove his theory in the end, but not before he has had the time to chew over other

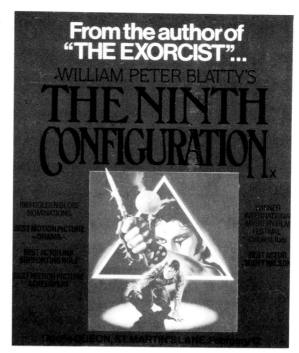

(Below) A couple of swell guys lookin' for a party - Willem Dafoe and Tom Cruise in **Born on the Fourth of July.**

Clueless individuals with large weapons dept: Sylvester Stallone in **Rambo: First Blood Part II** *(right) and Charlie Sheen in* **Platoon** *(below) perfect their psychotic glares.*

philosophical issues *en route*. One such issue, that of religion, provides Kane with the movie's title:

"In order for life to have appeared spontaneously on Earth," he begins, "there first had to be hundreds of millions of protein molecules of the ninth configuration. But given the size of the planet Earth, do you know how long it would take for just one of these protein molecules to appear entirely by chance? Roughly ten to the 243rd power billions of years. And I find that far, far more fantastic than simply believing in a god."

Before long it becomes unclear as to who exactly is addressing whom in *The Ninth Configuration*'s sanatorium. After all, where are these philosophical debates leading? Why does Colonel Kane's mind keep wandering? What *is* he talking about? Indeed, is Colonel Kane really the psychiatrist he first seemed, or is it a case of the lunatic having taken over the asylum? Could it be that this Colonel Kane is in actual fact the legendary Killer Kane of Vietnam, the Marine who flipped his wig back there after slaughtering half of the enemy with his bare hands?

Refreshing though *The Ninth Configuration*'s didacticism proves to be, it rarely gives up. And if one criticism can be be levelled at the movie, it would be that it only once shifts out of its thought-provoking, yet ponderous, low gear. In contrast to the brainlessly violent *Delirium*, it seems almost sacrilegious to suggest that, when *The Ninth Configuration* does finally get to kick ass, it provides the whole Vietnam genre with one of its most warped, twisted and finest moments.

When Kane goes to rescue one of his patients from a barroom full of Hell's Angels in the movie's closing minutes, he finds himself and his patient on the receiving end of a barrage of degradations. Kane remains calm throughout the humiliation of having to denounce the Marines, of having to lick beer off the floor and having to see his patient submit to sucking the dick of one of the bikers. When Kane's pacifity does crumble and he goes berserk, as the viewer knows he will do, it brings the same cathartic rush as *Taxi Driver*'s climactic shoot-out: Kane levels the bar, methodically ploughing through each of the Hell's Angels in turn with his bare hands. Before long there isn't an arm that hasn't been pulled from its socket, a head that hasn't been splashed against a wall, or a back that hasn't been snapped by the ex-Marine - no man or woman is spared by Killer Kane.

It seems natural that Kane should, without hesitation, go and rescue one of his patients from the clutches of imminent danger. That Kane is also one of the mystical supermen of the 'Nam is peripheral to the reason behind him putting his own life in danger to save that of another. Vietnam veterans are always saving lives. It stems from the 'gratification from survival' and the need for fulfilment.

This display of personal duty towards his friends and fellow man is to be found in abundance in the Vietnam veteran cinema, and it goes on to form the third sub-generic type. As is to be expected, however, the duty displayed by the screen veteran often transcends that of all credibility. Crack teams, the movies would have us understand, are often called out to extract POWs back from the 'Nam. Some of these teams have Chuck Norris leading the way, as in *Missing in Action*, or they might carry an unusual slant, like that of the *Ultimax Force*.

Ultimax Force are an elite group of US Commandos,

Stacy Keach 'corrects' a biker in **The Ninth Configuration.**

all trained in the skills of the Ninja warrior. Their mission is to go to Vietnam and liberate a POW camp run by a sadistic colonel. But the road to Vietnam is not an easy one, and the journey is peppered with such ludicrous statements as: "As soon as we're in 'Nam we won't get a minute's rest."

As if the script itself isn't enough to put the Ultimax team off their mission to Vietnam, the group's personal battle for Macho of the Month - strutting and posing at every given opportunity - should have been enough to ensure that they wouldn't have made it as far as San Diego.

Unfortunately, the crass gung-ho tactics of teams like the *Ultimax Force* seem to dominate the 'bringing the buddy home' sub-genre of the Vietnam movie. They all seem to want to get together and plough through an alien landscape; a landscape in which Vietnam becomes nothing more than a place to kill nameless, faceless people with no recompense, and usually with big guns. Contrary to one man's suggestion in *Ultimax Force* that, "Nothing's ever simple in 'Nam," if the majority of this type of movie is to be believed, it would appear that everything in the 'Nam is in actual fact dead simple...just send in more troops and bigger guns.

One of this sub-genre's few detours away from the simplistic muscle-headed likes of *Ultimax Force* comes with a semi-delirious tale of one man and a coffin.

Tracks takes place almost entirely on a train journey with veteran Jack (Dennis Hopper) escorting his dead buddy across country. The movie opens with President Nixon's speech announcing the end of the conflict in Southeast Asia.

As Jack's journey progresses, so too does his relationship with the other passengers on board the train. Particularly with the real estate agent, whose line of conversation always leads to land and the selling of it; the psychologist who insists that a relationship exists between playing chess and anal-masochism; a sweet-talker who is continually trying to woo the ladies; and Stephanie, the beautiful young girl whom Jack falls in love with. But Jack can't hold down any one conversation for too long without becoming restless, and one passenger remarks of him, "He seems like...disconnected."

When Jack tries to kiss Stephanie, she has to keep telling him to be more gentle and put his tongue away. Jack has no idea of how to make love to anyone but Vietnamese prostitutes. Jack's only reality is a radio he keeps by his ear, always tuned to a station playing sugary tunes like 'These Foolish Things' and 'Don't Sit Under the Appletree'. These songs are the only reality that Jack has because they remind him of the 'Nam.

Before long, plagued by a journey of both hope and rejection, Jack begins to have daydreams in which the beautiful Stephanie is being gang-raped by the other passengers. He pulls his gun, and the daydreams seem suddenly very real. In another sequence Jack hears the passengers whispering behind his back about Vietnam; the stewards drag one old lady away because of this, he thinks.

All Jack wants to do is get his dead buddy back to his home town and the hero's welcome he deserves. But this is no longer the 1967 of *Born on the Fourth of July*, the war is no longer at its height in Vietnam; the war is over and nobody wants to even remember it, let alone celebrate its dead.

When the train journey ends and Jack finally gets his buddy home, there is no parade or bandstand for "the biggest hero this town ever had", there is no hero's welcome. The coffin is met by two undertakers and no one else shows up for the funeral.

Tracks ends with Jack breaking open the coffin, and donning his dead buddy's combat gear and arms. "Because I love I hate," Jack screams as he charges toward town in the movie's closing freeze frame.

With his proclamation of "Because I love I hate" (in which Hopper can be seen at his improvisatory, psychotic best), Jack has managed to clamp his own naive philosophy around the '60s. The '60s certainly seemed to be happening, but all too often in opposing directions; that long lost Summer of Love wasn't simply a time for peace and love and dropping-out, it was designed to give a whole generation an identity other than that of the war. It was designed to give a uniformity to those out of uniform, and it was a uniform that shunned the khaki of Vietnam.

Along with those fond images of dancing naked wearing face-paint, so too must come images of screaming soldiers and napalm. Like The Monkees' *Head*, the rock concert has to be interrupted by Colonel Loan putting a bullet through the head of a Vietcong suspect, if only to illustrate the conflict facing the veteran on his return to society. Suddenly, for the veteran returning from Vietnam, the world was a whole different place. It wasn't Indian poetry and it wasn't firefights.

If we are to come anywhere near close to the paradox of the 'I love I hate' era of Vietnam, or indeed, come anywhere close to seeing what lies behind those 'disconnected' eyes of Jack and the other veterans, then it's necessary to go back to the movies.

Even though the movie *Physical Assault* doesn't at any time specify names or locations, it is undoubtedly an anti-war movie set in Vietnam. This often obtrusive, Kafkaesque absence of actual names or places becomes quite rational, however, when one realises that *Physical Assault* was made before the war in Vietnam had come to its sticky end.

Physical Assault is set almost entirely within the confines of one room, in which a group of US soldiers are put under lock and key in order to interrogate a Vietcong suspect. The strain of the confinement, and indeed interrogation, results in a series of conflicts between soldier and suspect, and soldier and soldier.

The soldiers subject their prisoner to brain-washing techniques in order to try and extract information. One torture inflicted is the repetition of a solitary question ("Where did you get the medicine and grenades?"), over and over again, in the same monochromatic voice, to which the suspect always replies with the same answer of non-commitment.

There can be no truthful answer to the question in *Physical Assault*. The suspect is so tired and so disorientated that he is answering on a motor instinct. Before

What did they do to the nicest town in the county to make it erupt in revenge?

What did they do to the All-American boy to make him explode into

THE NO MERCY MAN

IT IS EXACTLY ·03 SECONDS TO THE GREATEST ADVENTURE OF REVENGE IN SCREEN HISTORY!

long it becomes obvious that the interrogators don't even *want* the truth, but a confession; or better still, the name of a village to bomb.

The whole of the Vietnam conflict is represented by the men locked in *Physical Assault*. The war is one of futility; it is the unsatisfactory reply to a pointless question, looping endlessly. As for the soldier stuck out in the hell of 'Nam - bombarded by bullets, bombarded by protests back home - this reply, this conflict was becoming increasingly hazy. And of the question itself, nothing remained but a ringing assonance in the soldier's ear.

It takes a movie like *Physical Assault* to really dig the dirt and tell it like it is.

For the vacuous loners, the disorientation of *Physical Assault* is the Vietnam Era. It is *Physical Assault* that Travis sees as he stares beyond the windscreen of his cab in *Taxi Driver*, and it is *Physical Assault* that Gene hears when he barks orders to non-existent troops in *My Friends Need Killing*. Cinema's Vietnam veteran stands alone, whichever way he turns. If he finds acceptance back into society, it is because he is the spokesperson of *Born on the Fourth of July*, or leading the revolution in *The Ghetto Blaster*; he is that special, mystical person. If the Vietnam veteran doesn't find it easy to rehabilitate back into society, as is often the case, he is the sexual offender of *Forced Entry*, or the psycho killer of *Don't Answer the Phone*; he is the madman still parading in his combat jacket.

But, if it is madness that, say, Frankie can be

accused of when he pushes his own baby son into the *Combat Shock* oven, then it is symptomatic of the madness that had Frankie sent to Vietnam and caused his son to be born a mutation in the first place: all that fighting, all those untested chemicals, all that protest, all of that peace and love and shit, made him the way he is.

Movies like *Physical Assault* and *The Ninth Configuration* may seem a wildly alienating and abstract interpretation of the Vietnam conflict, but if madness doesn't make much sense, then the Vietnam War positively revelled in it with a big stupid grin.

And Vietnam grins for the Vietnam veteran like an obese Cheshire Cat; it curls back its teeth and sneers "Because I love I hate" in bitter defiance.

Not only was Vietnam the war with no front line, or the rock 'n' roll war, or the war that made prime time TV, it was also the war that makes less sense now than it did then. Vietnam is still raking in casualties with *Jacob's Ladder* and *Casualties of War*.

It's like Frankie says in *Combat Shock*: "The battlefield may have changed, but the war is not yet over." ∎

Selected filmography

BORN ON THE FOURTH OF JULY.
USA 1990.
Dir: Oliver Stone. Scr: Stone & Ron Kovic. Based on the book by Kovic. With: Tom Cruise, Willem Dafoe, Kyra Sedgwick, Raymond J. Barry.

CANNIBAL APOCALYPSE
(aka APOCALYSSE DOMANI).
Italy 1980.
Dir: Anthony Dawson (aka Antonio Margheriti). With: John Saxon, Tony King, John Morghen, Cindy Hamilton, Giovanni Lombardo Radice.

COMBAT SHOCK
(aka AMERICAN NIGHTMARES).
USA 1986.
Dir, Scr & P: Buddy Giovinazzo. With: Ricky Giovinazzo, Veronica Stork, Mitch Maglio, Asaph Livni.

CUTTER'S WAY
(aka CUTTER AND BONE).
USA 1981.
Dir: Ivan Passer. With: Jeff Bridges, John Heard, Lisa Eichhorn, Valerie Duran, Stephen Elliott.

DELIRIUM.
USA 1977.
Dir: Peter Maris. With: Turk Cekovsky, Terry Ten Broak, Barron Winchester. Thanks to 'The World War II Historical Re-Enactment Society.'

DON'T ANSWER THE PHONE.
USA 1980.
Dir, Co-Scr & Co-P: Robert Hammer. With: James Westmoreland, Flo Gerrish, Ben Frank, Nicholas Worth, Pamela Bryant.

FORCED ENTRY.
USA 19??.
Dir & Scr: Helmuth Richter. With: Laura Cannon, Tim Long, Ruby Runhouse, Nina Fawcett, Helmuth Richter.

HEAD.
USA 1968.
Dir: Bob Rafelson. Scr: Rafelson & Jack Nicholson. With: The Monkees, Victor Mature, Sonny Liston, Frank Zappa, Teri Garr, Tor Johnson.

MY FRIENDS NEED KILLING.
USA 1976.
Dir, Scr & Ed: Paul Leder. With: Greg Mullavey, Meredith MacRae, Clayton Wilcox, Carolyn Ames.

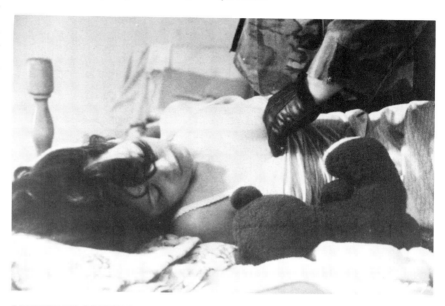

Nicholas Worth's home help service in **Don't Answer the Phone.**

NIGHT FLOWERS
(aka NIGHT ANGELS).
USA 1979.
Dir: Luis San Andres. Scr: Gabriel Walsh. With: Jose Perez, Gabriel Walsh, Angel Lindbergh, Sabra Jones, Lazaro Perez as Dancing Danny.

THE NINTH CONFIGURATION.
USA 1980.
Dir & Scr: William Peter Blatty. With: Stacy Keach, Scott Wilson, Jason Miller, Ed Flanders, Neville Brand, Joe Spinell, Moses Gunn.

PHYSICAL ASSAULT.
USA 1973.
Dir & Co-Scr: William H. Bushnell Jr. Based on the novel *The Prisoners of Quai Dong* by Victor Kolpacoff. With: Mako, Peter Hooten, David Moody, Jesse Dixon, Robert Glen Reece, Mark Bramhall.

TAXI DRIVER.
USA 1976.
Dir: Martin Scorsese. Scr: Paul Schrader. With: Robert De Niro, Jodie Foster, Cybill Shepherd, Harvey Keitel, Albert Brooks.

TRACKS.
USA 1977.
Dir & Scr: Henry Jaglom. With: Dennis Hopper, Taryn Power, Dean Stockwell, Topo Swope, Alfred Ryder.

ULTIMAX FORCE.
USA 1986.
Dir: Wilfred Milan. With: Arnold Nicholas, Jeremy Ladd, Patrick Scott, Vincent Giffin, Vivian Cheung.

ONE STEP AWAY FROM THE COUNTY LINE

HARRY ALAN TOWERS INTERVIEWED

BY ALLAN BRYCE

Veteran British born producer Harry Alan Towers is perhaps best known to genre buffs for his colourful mid-'60s series of Christopher Lee Fu Manchu pictures. But his credits also include a number of Jess Franco abominations, and more versions of *Ten Little Indians* than one would care to remember (usually freely adapted by Towers under his regular pseudonym of Peter Welbeck).

The irrepressible Harry.

He explained that he keeps returning to this old Agatha Christie warhorse because, "I love the idea of having a number of people trapped in a desperate situation where they can't get away, if you see what I mean." If you've ever sat through one of these movies you will know *exactly* what Harry means...

Some producers favour the hands-on approach, but not our Harry. Says Jess Franco, "He is a very clever man, who has some brilliant ideas as a scriptwriter. But when shooting begins, he disappears and you never see him again. You will be shooting and get no news from him. That would be nice, but there is also no news of the money. It is mad, completely mad!" This is a typical comment from someone who has had a *good* working relationship with Towers!

To say that Harry has a reputation for sailing rather close to the wind would be an understatement akin to suggesting Richard Nixon might have made a few wayward decisions. Towers once boasted that he could

step off an airplane in any country in the world and have a film in production within twenty-four hours. He neglected to mention how quickly he would be compelled to take the return flight.

"I always like to take advantage of the economy instead of having it work against me," he says. His skill at having done this over the years is legendary, and the apocryphal reports of his shadowy involvement in everything from a number of labyrinthine tax shelter deals to a certain well known '60s scandal would certainly make a better screen story than most of the celluloid atrocities instigated by the pen of Peter Welbeck...

The sanitised version of Harry's career runs like this. He was born in London in October 1920, started out as a child actor, became a prolific radio writer during World War Two, and was appointed head of the Overseas Broadcasting Services. After the war he went on to form his Towers of London organisation, which pioneered the international syndication of transcribed radio programmes. Then, with the coming of commercial television, Towers headed the British ATV company and was the Programme Director of the first company to supply London Weekend Television. He went on to enter the field of independent TV production, where he was responsible for such successful

Liza (Diane Bond) becomes 'a plaything of vice' in **House of 1000 Dolls.**

She Rules a Palace of Pleasure ...for WOMEN!
where men are used in a diabolical plot to destroy civilization!

AMERICAN INTERNATIONAL presents

THE MILLION EYES OF SU·MURU

in TECHNICOLOR® and TECHNISCOPE®

STARRING FRANKIE AVALON · GEORGE NADER and SHIRLEY EATON and Special Guest Star WILFRID HYDE-WHITE as SU-MURU

Directed by LINDSAY SHONTEFF · Produced by HARRY ALAN TOWERS · Screenplay by KEVIN KAVANAGH · Original Story by PETER WELBECK · an AMERICAN INTERNATIONAL Picture

shows as *Dial 999*, *The Scarlet Pimpernel* and *Tales From Dickens*. Then in 1962 he became a film producer with a minor B-feature entitled *Invitation to Murder*. Since then he has produced countless other pictures, often scripting them himself. Towers' extensive credits in the horror/exploitation field include *Psycho-Circus*, the Chris Lee Fu Manchu series, *Five Golden Dragons*, *The Million Eyes of Su-Muru*, *House of 1000 Dolls*, *Venus in Furs*, *Count Dracula*, *The Shape of Things to Come*, *Fanny Hill*, *Gor*, *Edge of Sanity* and *Howling IV*.

In recent years he tied his wagon to the Menahem Golan 21st Century gravy train, producing a new version of *The Phantom of the Opera* starring Robert Englund, as well as a number of movies based on Edgar Allan Poe stories. (Harry is always interested in writers whose works happen to be in the public domain.) Predictably, the Towers versions of *The Raven*, *The House of Usher* and *The Masque of the Red Death* are not a patch on the '60s Corman adaptations, but at least they look good, thanks to Towers' ability to stretch a buck. "Harry insisted we recycle all the sets," explained *Usher* director Alan Birkenshaw. "He's one of the most environmentally conscious producers around..."

Towers has rarely been interviewed over the years, except perhaps by the authorities (in fact I believe he uses the same press agent as Lord Lucan). When not jetting around the world making movies, he apparently spends most of his time in Canada. But I managed to catch up with him at his London apartment, which is located just around the corner from Broadcasting House. The place is a cleaning lady's nightmare, a treasure trove of musty old books and press clippings. Edgar Allan Poe would approve. A plaque reveals

(Below right) *"You'll catch your death of cold in that little number,"* says Richard Todd to Helmut Berger in **Dorian Gray**.

George Orwell died on the same site - possibly of claustrophobia!

The man himself is not what you might expect. A portly old fellow with pouches under his eyes, he certainly doesn't project the image of a fast-talking wheeler dealer who is so tricky he could hide behind a spiral staircase. When he speaks it's with authority, in a rich, deep, well-educated fashion. Yes, I probably *would* buy a used car from this man...

It was early in the evening when I arrived at his apartment, and he was dressed in pyjamas and sipping a glass of port, saying, "I find it helps me to relax during interviews." I suppose with his background he has earned the right to be just a little bit eccentric...

SX: Let's start by talking about your Fu Manchu pictures, which marked your entry into the horror genre.

HAT: Yes, I seem to remember I did quite well out of them, although despite the presence of Christopher Lee they were never really horror pictures. The first three in the series were very successful, but the fourth and fifth were not. That was because one was directed by a little Spaniard called Jess Franco. When I looked at that I said, "Jess, you've done something there that nobody else has achieved." "What's that?" he asked. "Killing Fu Manchu," I said. Franco is, of course, still directing movies. Gerard Kikoine, who made *Edge of Sanity* for me (a recent Towers remake of the Jekyll and Hyde story), started as an editor for Jess Franco. I tend to pick up these rather weird characters and exaggerate the depths of their talent. Franco was a terribly nice man, but he shouldn't have been allowed to direct traffic. He was a jazz musician who played the trombone until he discovered the zoom lens...

SX: Nevertheless, Franco has actually become something of a cult figure...

HAT: Goodness knows why! I saw one of his movies recently and he's still got that annoying habit of zooming in and out with the camera for no discernible reason. Franco has many different names, but he always delivers the same film. He made one big hit movie for me, called *99 Women*. I must tell you how that came about. I had a picture called *The Million Eyes of Su-Muru*, which was about a female Fu Manchu character played by Shirley Eaton. This was reasonably successful, so I did a deal to make a sequel. I had Franco in Brazil at that time, so we set the sequel there and planned to finish up with the footage from the carnival in Rio. Now, Jess, with all his zooming about, always finished very quickly - usually in time to have lunch. Anyway, on this occasion he actually finished filming a whole week before the carnival, so all the cast and crew were just sitting around. I couldn't stand to see this, so, literally over the weekend, I wrote a script called *99 Women*, a sexy women's prison picture. There were actually only three women in it, but we hoped that people wouldn't notice!

The story was that these three girls were escaping through the jungle. We cast my wife (actress Maria Rohm) and two other actresses and we went back to a botanical park about thirty minutes from Copacabana beach and shot for six days. We came home with one third of a movie, which I showed to some producer friends of mine who agreed to put up the money to finish the film off in Alicante with my old friends Herbert Lom, Maria Schell and Mercedes McCambridge - who played the sadistic woman governess. We shot for three weeks in Alicante and had a movie. I remember coming out of a projection theatre on the Champs Elysée with a distributor friend who said, "I smell money." He was right. That picture - which cost less than a quarter of a million dollars - went into distribution in the United States and became the biggest grossing picture in America for three weeks. Unfortunately the company for which I made it, Commonwealth United, had got into all sorts of stupid adventures and went bankrupt. But that was Jess Franco at his best, his moment of greatness. I still like him a lot as a person. He's a nice little man.

While we're on the subject of Franco, he made quite a good erotic picture for me based on the Marquis de

If Harry achieved nothing else he at least got to marry Maria Rohm (below, in **Count Dracula**).

Sade's *Justine*, with Maria Power, who was Tyrone Power's daughter, and a very good cast - Jack Palance, Mercedes McCambridge again, Akim Tamiroff, Sylvia Koscina and Klaus Kinski. Kinski never forgave me for that picture. He's made many films for me since of course. I mean, he was rather hot stuff in Italy at the time. I only needed him for one day's shooting, but he haggled with me through his agent. I finally agreed to pay him his asking price, but for only half a day. In the morning we picked him up in Barcelona and drove him to the castle where we had constructed a set with naked girls hanging from chains. All Kinski had to do was sit in the middle of this set, writing away with a quill pen - never saying a word! We shot a great deal of footage of this, with Franco zooming in and out, and used this not only at the beginning and the end of the picture, but all through it as well, where we kept cutting back to Kinski, putting the Marquis de Sade's words over the top, dubbed by an actor who sounded like Klaus Kinski. The picture opened all over Germany billed as 'Starring Klaus Kinski' - and he was furious because he had only been paid for half a day!

SX: Is Kinski as temperamental as everyone says?

HAT: Klaus at the moment is unemployable, not because I wouldn't employ him, but because he wants to direct, and that is something that even in my madness I wouldn't agree to. He got into a deal with some Italians in which he agreed to do a picture in Africa playing Paganini, but as far as I know that turned out to be an utter disaster. I did a version of *Count Dracula* in 1970 which was directed by Jess Franco and starred Christopher Lee. I wanted Kinski to play Renfield in this, the guy who eats the flies. He wouldn't do it, so I did the deal with his agents and persuaded them not to tell him the name of the picture he would be working on. He turned up for the first day's shooting and went straight onto a scene where he had to strangle a girl, who was played by my wife. After the cameras stopped turning, he looked at me and said, "Why do I feel I am in a Dracula picture?"

Klaus Kinski and Maria Rohm discuss starting a Jesus Franco fan club in **Venus in Furs.**

I remember another time when he came over here to do a film for me in the '60s (*Psycho-Circus*), and he had a scene where he got shot, fell to the floor and died. When the time came to film this, Kinski pirouetted, fell down, coughed blood, got up, pirouetted again, died a third time, got up and pirouetted again before finally collapsing. And the English director - a fellow named John Moxey - said, "Thank you very much, Mr Kinski. Would you mind doing a second take, perhaps a little shorter?" And Kinski pulled himself up to all his five foot nothing and said, "Yes, I would. I've died in more fucking movies than you've directed!" He was right of course.

SX: You seem to have a particular fondness for producing horror movies.

HAT: The good thing about a horror film is that if you do it well then nobody bothers about how much it costs. Most of the horror films I have been associated with have made quite a lot of money. Erotic movies are the same, though you can get into censorship troubles there.

SX: I believe you often get round this by shooting stronger 'Continental' versions of your films for the foreign market.

HAT: That's unnecessary today. It's not worth the trouble. Back in the '60s I did that with films like *The Brides of Fu Manchu*. The girls took their tops off in the version that played on the Continent. The Fu Manchu films were always very popular. The rights are back

with us now, so maybe we will bring Fu Manchu back for television. The real problem about Fu Manchu first of all is that he is a villain, an archetype villain, and it's very difficult to do a television series with a villain as a leading man. Second, I personally believe that you have to do Fu Manchu in period. You can't have a Chinaman like him with those long nails flapping around in a contemporary world.

SX: How did you come to adopt the *nom-de-plume* of Peter Welbeck?

HAT: I was a prolific radio writer when I was young and used to write two or three shows a week for the BBC. Some of the higher-ups said, "Stop this young man writing everything." I've always lived in this area near Broadcasting House, and before they had numbers the telephone exchange code was Welbeck, so I adopted Welbeck as my pseudonym. Peter Welbeck has now more or less retired. He writes the treatments rather than the scripts. He likes the good life too much.

SX: Do you have any favourites among your own movies?

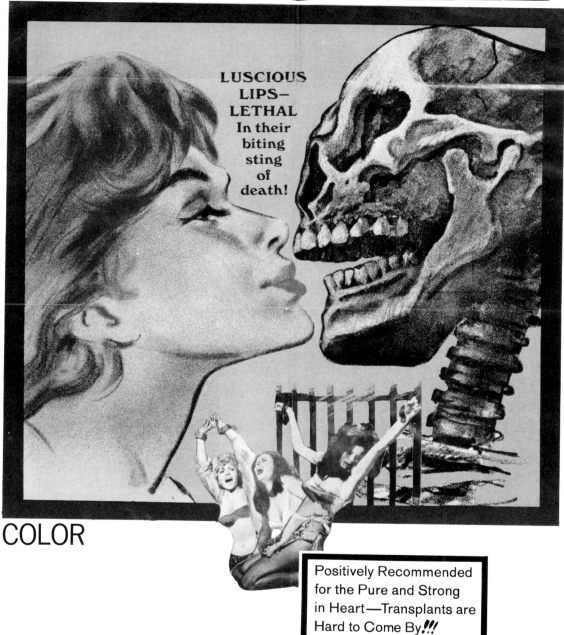

KISS & KILL

LUSCIOUS LIPS—
LETHAL
In their
biting
sting
of
death!

COLOR

Positively Recommended for the Pure and Strong in Heart—Transplants are Hard to Come By*!!!*

A Commonwealth United Corporation Presentation
STARRING
CHRISTOPHER LEE · RICHARD GREENE · SHIRLEY EATON

Screenplay by PETER WELBECK from a story by SAX ROHMER · Directed by JESS FRANCO · Produced by HARRY ALAN TOWERS
A Commonwealth United Entertainment, Inc. and Towers of London (Films) Limited Productions
Released by Commonwealth United Entertainment, Inc.

Copyright © 1968 Commonwealth United Corp.   69/41

HAT: The ones I made most money on! The early Fu Manchu films, particularly the very first one, *The Face of Fu Manchu*. In more recent times I was very pleased with *Phantom of the Opera*. Dwight Little did a good job of directing that one. I also have a particular fondness for *Ten Little Indians*. I've done *Ten Little Indians* three times now. I've just done it again in Africa with Donald Pleasence, Herbert Lom - the whole repertory company. Same script - different locations. You always kill off the most expensive stars first!

SX: How many films do you think you've been involved in over the years?

HAT: I couldn't even hazard a guess. I don't have a complete list of my films any more. I used to, but it got thrown out. I don't expect there would be as many films on it as there would be on Jess Franco's list! Actually I've just thought of another funny Franco story. He has a cousin or a nephew who is now quite a successful member of the French avant garde movement - Ricardo Franco. I remember that Jess was once making a picture for me on which Ricardo was his assistant. I heard Ricardo talking one day, saying that he had just made his first feature movie, and when I congratulated him and asked who had provided the finance, he said, "It was very difficult - Jess could only give me the camera and the crew for two hours a day." It turned out he had made his picture on my time and my negative!

SX: Tell us about some of your recent projects. Let's start with *Edge of Sanity*, the Jekyll and Hyde picture you did with Anthony Perkins.

HAT: We shot a weekend in Clapham, and the rest in Budapest, with a French director (ex-porno director Gerard Kikoine). I had high hopes for that picture, but it didn't work out quite as I thought it would. I personally would have preferred to have made the whole movie in England, but of course it's another million dollars on the budget to make a picture in England nowadays. So we chose the compromise. We had a very imaginative French art director - I don't think he had a very good sense of period (*chuckles*). Many people have brought up the fact that the film is supposed to be set in Victorian times and yet some of the characters are dressed in a contemporary fashion and use pound coins! But ninety per cent of video sales are in places where it wouldn't matter at all if they had five pound notes made of toilet paper!

SX: Did you enjoy working with Anthony Perkins?

HAT: Perkins is great fun. I'm hoping to do another picture with him. What am I saying? I *am* doing another picture with him! We're doing a picture together in Israel, which Ken Russell is directing. Ken and I have had various schemes through the years, but none of them has ever got made. This one will get made because it's a mummy picture and Perkins has always wanted to do a mummy picture. It has rather a good script written by Nelson Giddings, who wrote *The Haunting*, and I've done a deal with Cannon or Pathé or whatever they call themselves to shoot it in Israel, which is rather good because there are a lot of Egyptians over there! Giddings has taken the Tutankhamen situation, with Carter and everybody else getting their comeuppance for digging up the tomb. It has a certain amount of sex in it. Well, it would have to have with Russell and Perkins both involved! Did you know that Russell gave an interview after he made *Crimes of Passion*, in which he said that all the basic ideas he had in the film had come from a long reconnaissance of the fleshpots of Europe he had done with me for another film?

SX: What about the series of Edgar Allan Poe films you've recently been involved in?

HAT: I didn't want to compete with the Corman-Poe films of the '60s. My idea was to make them gothic in their look, but contemporary as well. We made *The House of Usher*, *The Masque of the Red Death* and we're finishing up with *The Raven*, with Donald Pleasence again. I also did something called *Buried Alive*, which is based on Poe (*whose name is misspelled in the credits! Ed.*). It has elements of *The Black Cat* and *The Tell-Tale Heart*. We shot that in South Africa and it was the last film in which dear old John Carradine appeared. He died shortly after completing his role. The thing about Poe is that most of the stories are really only short anecdotes, and just provide the starting points for movies. He wrote very few pieces - with the possible exception of *The Murders in the Rue Morgue* - that contain a full plot. I must say that I think I've done my Poe bit, I'm not a particular fan so I'm not going to do any more. I have done a number of other horror things lately as well. I made *Phantom of the Opera* of course, which was quite a big production with Robert Englund. We made that last year, partly in Budapest, but also with some shooting in the USA. We got good reviews in America but it didn't do as well as we all hoped. I realise now that though the Andrew Lloyd Webber *Phantom* has brought the story a lot of popularity, most people still tend to be discouraged by the word 'Opera' in the title. We were going to make a sequel called *Phantom of Manhattan*, and may now do it as *Terror in Manhattan*, once more with Robert Englund.

SX: You once apparently boasted that you could get off a plane in any country in the world and have a film under way within twenty-four hours.

HAT: There was a period in my life when I relished that challenge. My dear wife says I'm only really happy when I'm attempting the impossible. Yes, I think I probably did say that, and I would stand by it still. ∎

(Above left) Robert Englund emotes in **Phantom of the Opera**.

(Below left) Jack Palance does the 'funky robot' in **The Shape of Things to Come**.

(Below) Another 'write your own caption' shot (from **House of 1000 Dolls**).

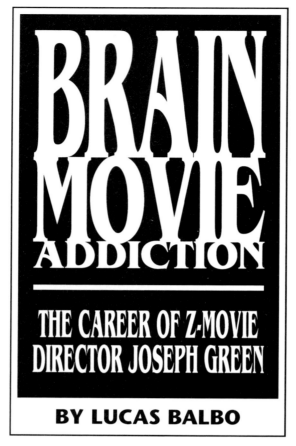

BRAIN MOVIE ADDICTION

THE CAREER OF Z-MOVIE DIRECTOR JOSEPH GREEN

BY LUCAS BALBO

I've always been fascinated by mad scientist films - that is, films where a sadistic doctor tortures poor, helpless souls (which is often the case with 'normal' doctors as well...). *Les Yeux Sans Visage* (aka *The Horror Chamber of Dr Faustus*, aka *Eyes Without a Face*) and its twin brother, Jesus Franco's *The Awful Dr Orloff* (aka *The Demon Doctor*, aka *Gritos en la Noche*, etc, etc) are two of my favourites. So when I discovered their American equivalent, *The Brain That Wouldn't Die* (aka *The Head That Wouldn't Die*), I was really thrilled. It has recently resurfaced on the US video market in a

(Below right)
Joseph Green at work.

complete version (although the film was originally released intact, it was censored for subsequent TV showings). Joseph Green wrote the screenplay in about three days (!) and directed the film under the very limited production (interiors shot in a hotel basement, exteriors in a New York suburb) of B-picture veteran Rex Carlton. Carlton also wrote and/or produced such

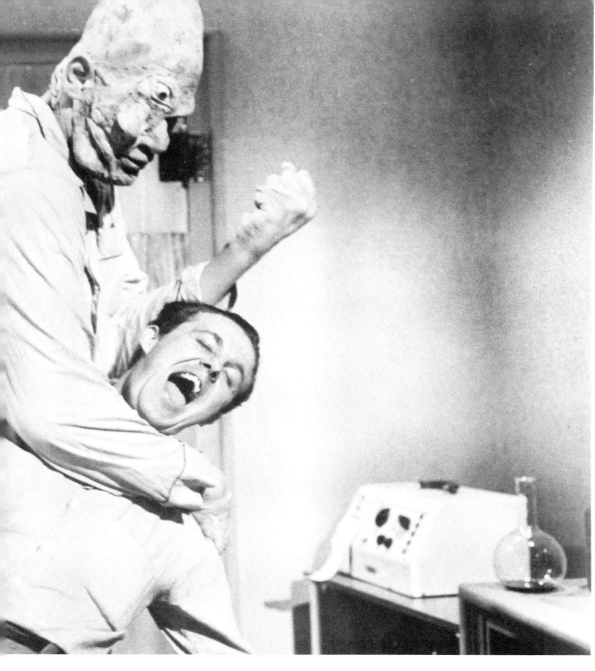

*After he's come out of the closet, **Brain**'s giant pinhead makes short work of the cast and cardboard sets. Note the Rossellini-style neo-realism of the action.*

classics as Al Adamson's *Blood of Dracula's Castle* and Bud Townsend's *Nightmare in Wax*.

The film begins with a documentary-style heart transplant performed by a rather talkative, handsome doctor. He decides to take his fiancée to a cottage (where he performs twisted experiments) for the weekend. Unfortunately they have an accident on the way and she is decapitated. So what does he do? Does he cry? Curse the car/road/God for the death of his woman? No, he picks up her head and runs off to his mad lab for a quick experiment in head transplantation...

Dissatisfied with his mate's ex-body, he investigates the more abundant charms of young strippers and decides on a disfigured model (who wears a tigerskin bikini) for his talking head fiancée's body. Meanwhile the head has made a psychic link with an unfinished human experiment kept in a closet (Eddie Carmel, an ex-Israeli wrestling champion known as The Happy Giant Clown on US TV). He/it is going to help her rest in peace (she's already in pieces) and there follows a gory apocalyptic finale.

While *Dr Orloff* made its impression through its superb photography and Gothic atmosphere, *Les Yeux* through its gloomy, macabre realism, *The Brain* struck me with its sleazy delirium. It is like seeing your nightmares on screen: everything looks real, but as soon as you start to think about it it's totally unbelievable. Add to that the minimalist dialogue ("Hey, you out there in the closet, get out and free me!") and the tongue-in-cheek humour and you have a genuine classic of weirdness. So when I had the opportunity to interview Joseph Green in his rather peculiar distributor's office I jumped at the chance.

SX: What did you do before *The Brain That Wouldn't Die?*

JG: That was the first picture, and I wrote the screenplay and directed it. Before that I had been in the US Air Force. I made some documentary pictures when I was in the service, but that was my first professional movie.

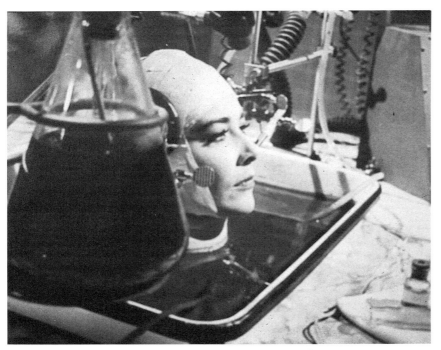

SX: Were you a fan of horror movies at the time you wrote the screenplay?

JG: Oh yes. I always enjoyed horror movies as a kid. The scariest movie I ever saw was *The Invisible Man*. It took me years to get over being scared by that. I saw it when I was very young and the idea of a person becoming invisible and unwrapping the veils from around his head was very visual and very horrific at the time. I'd seen other horror movies - the original *Frankenstein*...

SX: Have you ever seen *Les Yeux Sans Visage*?

JG: No, I've never seen it, why? Does it remind you of *The Invisible Man*?

SX: No, rather of your film.

JG: (*Laughs.*)

SX: In the film, the doctor goes to a cabaret to find an attractive female body for his plans. Were there two versions shot, one more 'sexy' than the other?

JG: When the film was produced it was rather difficult to have a lot of nudity in American pictures, so actually, there wasn't much nudity; it was suggestive dancing, she was in a fairly skimpy costume, but there weren't two versions. Maybe there were some publicity pictures that you've seen, but they weren't in the film. When the picture was shot it was strictly with one version of the dance scene.

Later in the film the doctor goes to a girl's studio where she is modelling for 'thrills' photographers. In that sequence she was in a skimpy bikini, and there was one brief scene of her partially nude for a still shot only.

SX: Most of the characters in *The Brain* are very dark - was it intended as a joke or seriously?

JG: It was intended as a dark movie, no humour intended, though it may seem that way. The hero was really an anti-hero; he looks nice, a handsome man, a young doctor who was always exploring the unknown, with freaky monsters in his country estate - in captivity in his closet. But the villain, if you want to call him a villain, was a good leading man type, yet he is really dark-hearted. He wanted to reach out into worlds he should have left alone. He had the crazy idea of bringing his girlfriend back to life after she had

her last kiss ...
a horror worse
than dying

Kiss me
MONSTER

(Top) The Head in **The Brain**...

been decapitated...but to put her head back onto another body was really black - a part of medicine we can't touch.

SX: How was the film received at the time of its release?

JG: It was released by American International, and was rather well received and did fairly well at the US box office. After it had been sold in a TV package by AIP it has played over and over again. In fact, in New York right now it's in the library of Channel 11, WPAX, and it's still playing maybe once a year. I regularly get phone calls from friends of mine saying, "Hey, *The Brain* is on TV."

SX: What did you do after *The Brain*?

JG: In 1968 I bought a picture called *Daydream* by the Japanese erotic novelist Tomasaki. I wanted to enter into distribution - it was a very controversial picture, it had been picked up by another distribution company and I bought it because I heard that they had had a very difficult time with it. It was not accepted in San Francisco and other cities because of its nature. I liked it and bought it from the Sakiku Company in Japan with the proviso that I had the right to incorporate new dream sequences. The reason I chose a Japanese picture was that I was stationed in Japan and had become very familiar with Japanese culture, face masks, the pushing back of your inner feelings which is typical of Japan, China and other Oriental cultures. That was the first picture that I plugged in when I went into distribution, and I put on the credits 'dream sequences directed by and produced by Joseph Green.' From that time, nearly 1970, I pushed my directing aside and became very involved in distribution, and accumulated a good number of films, about twenty-five of which came from France.

SX: Do you prefer directing or distributing?

JG: I did prefer directing but while I became very involved with distribution after *Daydream* I still wanted to go back to directing. Finally in 1988 I directed *The Perils of P.K.* which should be out soon. It stars Sammy Davis Jr, Anne Mirror and a lot of movie and TV names, about eight of them, all very well known in the US. I'm now involved in another picture called *The Psychedelic Generation* which is three-quarters finished. I expect to have it released by the end of 1990. It's strictly a drama. It's about a young teacher and how he drops out of society during the so-called hippie revolution in the US, which begins about 1965 and takes him through college up to the present time. Against the background of his misadventures we have the great events of the last twenty-five years: the Congo, the Middle East, civil unrest in the US, Vietnam, Algeria, all these events or happenings which colour his interpretation of how he feels about himself and the world.

SX: Is it an allegory of your life?

JG: No, I don't believe in dropping out. My point of view is if you want to change the world you will roll up your sleeves, go to work and try to do something. You don't drop out, drop acid and blow your brain up with coke and things like that, that's suicide. The lesson, if there is any lesson, that is specified in the story is exactly what I just said: if you want to make the world a better place, you drop out...oh, sorry...(*laughs*)...no, you don't drop out, you work towards bettering society. That's what the hero finds out after about twenty years of just drifting. He sees the world not being what he hoped it to be, a place of love and beauty; it's a hard place and, in order to change mankind, to change society, you have to work at it. But he finds out too late as he is falling to his death. His whole life is flashing through his mind. That's the moral to be painted by *The Psychedelic Generation.*

SX: You totally left the horror field...

JG: Yes, I did. I have two scripts that I hope to get to in the next year or so. They aren't horror films, I would call them more science fiction chase thrillers. I would not say that I left totally, I also have an idea for what would be a comedy take on a horror idea I had. It would be a horror movie satire because I think that today there have been so many horror movies - and they are more explicit and more graphic, each one more so than before. I mean bodies blowing up and special effects, you know...I want to try to get inside people's minds and if I can't do that, why not kid the horror movie. But that isn't written yet, but hopefully I'll get around to it after the next couple of projects.

SX: You distributed two Jesus Franco movies...

JG: Yes, *Sadisterotica* and *Kiss Me, Monster.* Franco is very well known in Europe, he is pretty much of a cult item there. I was very impressed with the photography and the production. You can tell that the films were being made very fast but the photography was excellent. I bought those from Atlas Distributors in Germany and they were probably the only horror films I've distributed...oh no, I also acquired later on a film that had been previously released as *What!* with Christopher Lee and Daliah Lavi (*Mario Bava's* La Frusta e il Corpo, *aka* The Whip and the Body, *aka* Night is the Phantom). That is in my library. I guess I have to go and make more horror movies and release them.

SX: Yes, the horror market is waiting for your return!

JG: As I said, I've got those two science fiction films and the satire (which doesn't mean it can't be exciting and scary). It would probably have a lot of comedy relief at very crucial moments. Otherwise, what are you going to do - the person has to blow up or the head has to turn around. I don't denigrate the special effects movie, I'm very impressed when I see a good one.

A Green-directed insert from **Daydream.**

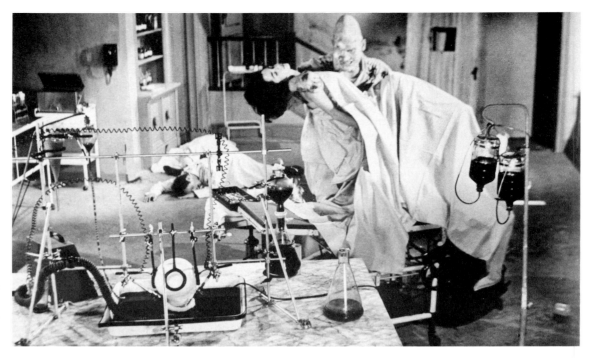

(Right) Pinhead amuck!

(Below) Hi-tech mad lab equipment gives **Brain** its 'unique' flavour.

SX: *The Brain* **was a sort of special effects movie for the '60s...**

JG: The budget was miniscule, very small, it was a black and white movie. If I had had a few dollars more I could have done a better job. It was shot in about thirteen days, and that isn't a shooting schedule, it's a race. In your screenplay you may have five different set-ups and you have to combine them in maybe two set-ups so you don't waste time. You have to move, it's always running, running. That's not a way to make a movie.

SX: Do you still have any contact with the people who acted in *The Brain***?**

JG: No. The only one I had any contact with was Jason Evers (*also known as Herb Evers*). He went to Hollywood and was successful in a western TV series

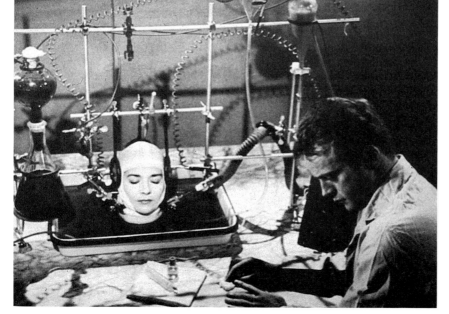

called *The Wrangler* that was the first series in Hollywood to be made on tape. He was also in other pictures like *The Green Berets* and I see him every once in a while starring in a TV movie (*he also recently appeared in* Basket Case 2*! LB*). The rest have all gone their separate ways and, again, it was some years ago!

SX: Did you know that Frank Henenlotter, a new young director, had a vague idea of making *The Brain, Part II***?**

JG: (*Laughs.*) I appreciate that he liked it, although I don't know him. Actually, it seems there is a renewed interest in the movie. Just a few months ago I was interviewed by one horror magazine (*Filmfax*) and they did a very long and nice article.

Let me tell you something interesting about the recent movie *Heartburn* with Jack Nicholson and Meryl Streep, two struggling actors. I'm sitting in the cinema with a lady friend and we're watching it. In one of the early scenes they're sitting in bed, talking, eating Chinese food and watching TV across the room...and on comes *The Brain* as a background! So I give my girlfriend a poke in the ribs, "Hey, this movie there, you see, it's mine!"(*laughs*).

When I saw *Heartburn* again on TV, just to check if they had used it again, I was wondering why the director Mike Nichols used my movie. I'm a little flattered. Some day I'll meet him and ask him.

SX: Well, it's got a cult following in the US.

JG: I'm flattered, I really am. It's not a movie I would like to have done, I would have liked to have had more of a budget. I had a lot more ideas and I had to leave a lot out. Who knows, maybe you're right, maybe I will make *The Brain, Part II...* ∎

THE BRAIN THAT WOULDN'T DIE.

USA 1959, released 1962.

Dir, Scr & Co-Story: Joseph Green. P & Co-Story: Rex Carlton. Ph: Stephen Hajnal. Sp Eff: Byron Baer. Make-up: George Fiala. With: Virginia Leith, Herb Evers, Adele Lamont, Bruce Brighton, Doris Brent, Leslie Daniel, Bonnie Shari.

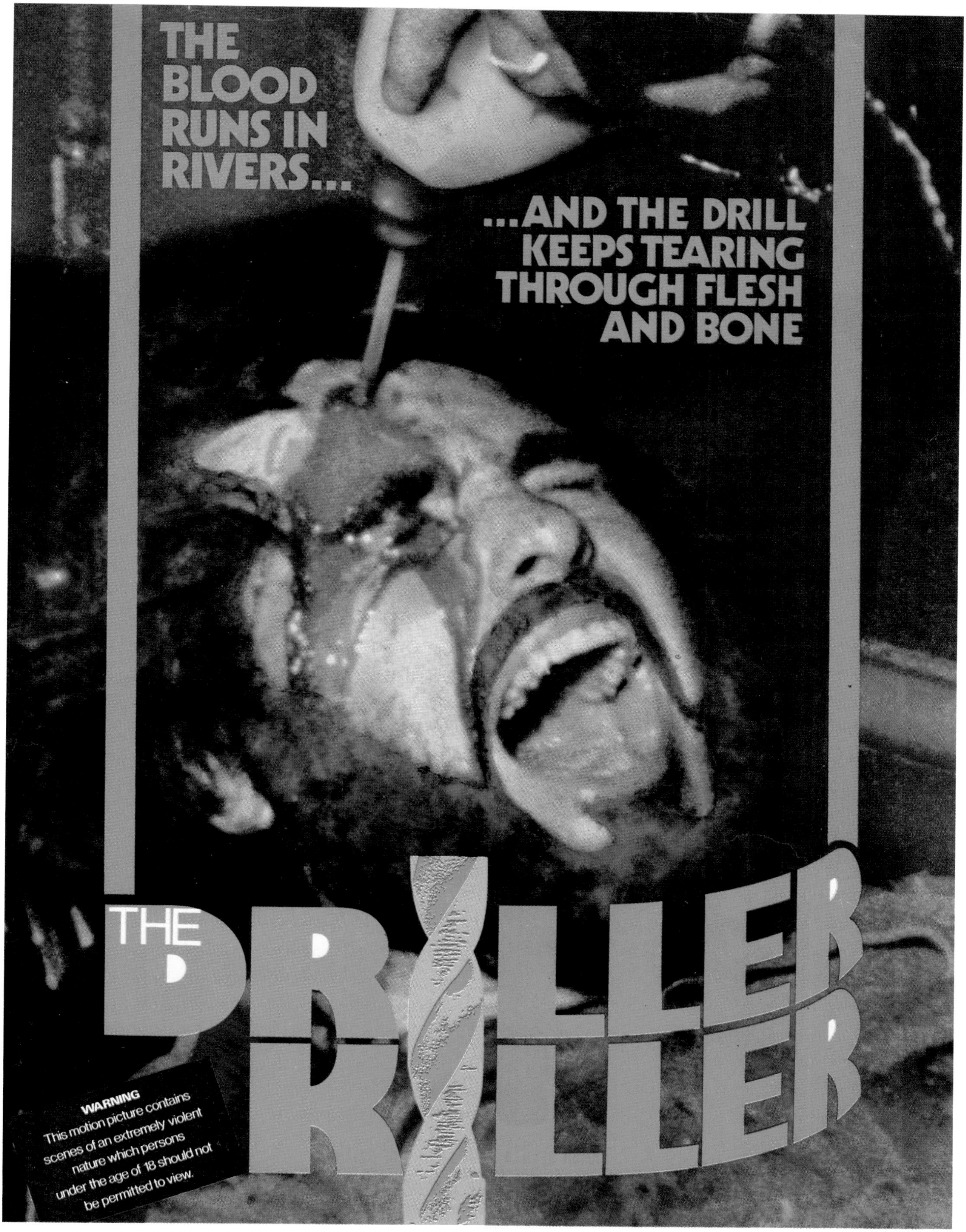
THE BLOOD RUNS IN RIVERS...
...AND THE DRILL KEEPS TEARING THROUGH FLESH AND BONE
THE DRILLER KILLER
WARNING
This motion picture contains scenes of an extremely violent nature which persons under the age of 18 should not be permitted to view.

WHAT POWER
SHOULD A MAN
POSSESS TO
CHALLENGE
THE PRINCE OF
DARKNESS?

THE KILLING OF
SATAN

CINEX FILMS, INC. PRESENTS
RAMON REVILLA IN THE KILLING OF SATAN
ALSO STARRING ELIZABETH OROPESA GEORGE ESTREGAN PAQUITO DIAZ CECILE CASTILLO AND CHARLIE DAVAO
ASSOCIATE PRODUCER FRANCISCO C. PUZON, JR. EXECUTIVE PRODUCER CONRADO C. PUZON PRODUCED BY PIO C. LEE
WRITTEN BY JOSE MARI AVELLANA MUSIC BY ERNANI CUENCO DIRECTOR OF PHOTOGRAPHY RICARDO HERRERA DIRECTED BY EFREN C. PINON

Lloyd Kaufman and Michael Herz present a Troma Team Release

COMBAT SHOCK

Direct from theatrical release to home video!

"...breathtaking primitivism."
—VINCENT CANBY, THE NEW YORK TIMES

PRISM
ENTERTAINMENT

PRE-ORDER DATE: MARCH 11, 1987 NATIONAL RELEASE DATE: MARCH 24, 1987

(Right) *A scene cut from* **Blood of Fu Manchu,** *aka* **Kiss and Kill.**

(Below) *Medical madness in* **The Sect.**

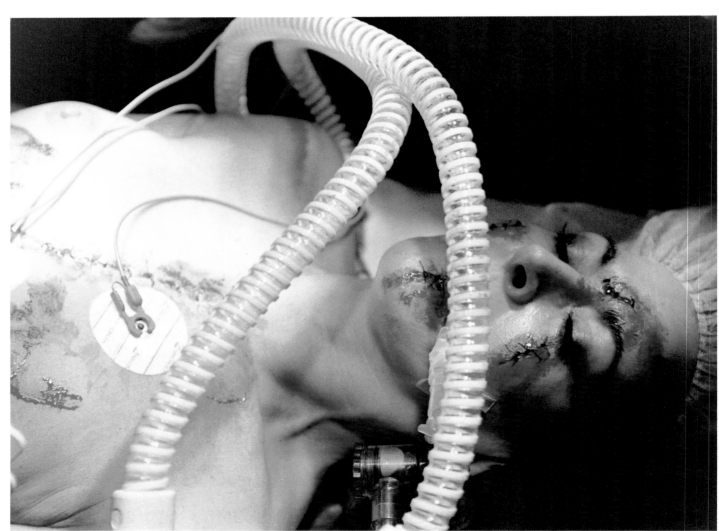

(Above) Some freaks from **Freak Orlando**, *a film you'll never see...*

(Left) *Joe Spinell gets hacked to bits by scalped, dead women in* **Maniac.**

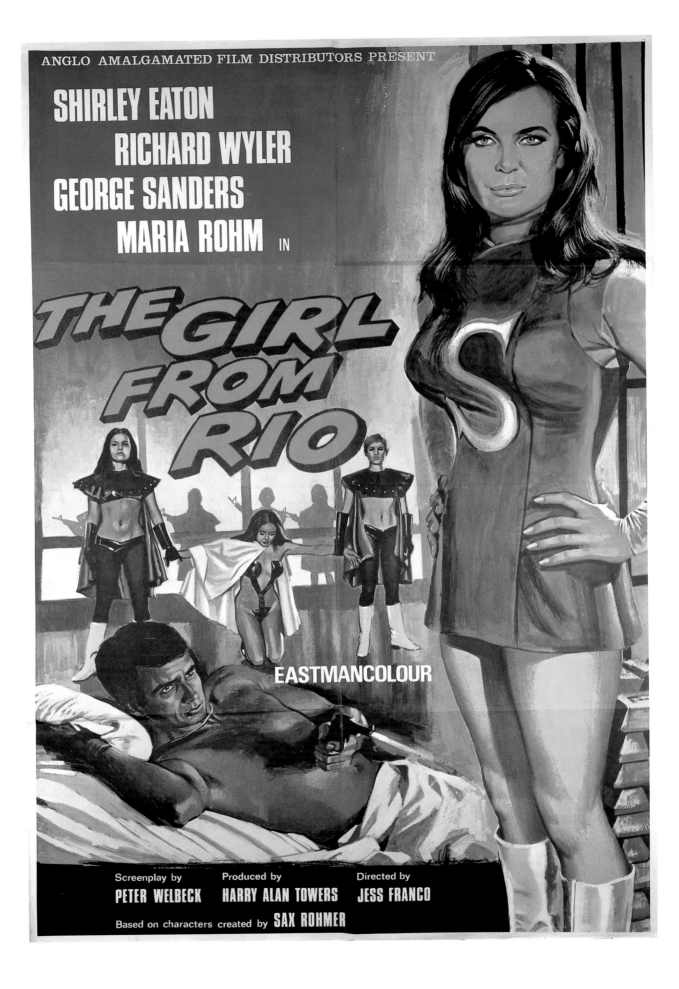

All the HORRIFYING NIGHTMARES of a THOUSAND FRIGHTENING DREAMS in one PANIC-PACKED SHOW

MAD DOCTOR OF BLOOD ISLAND

IN BLOOD CURDLING COLOR

Starring

JOHN ASHLEY • ANGELIQUE PETTYJOHN

AND

BLOOD DEMON

IN BLOOD DRIPPING COLOR

Starring

CHRISTOPHER LEE   LEX BARKER   KARIN DOR

The DEAD RETURN TO LIFE—
LIVING and LUSTING
for BIZARRE PLEASURES!

HEMISPHERE PICTURES, INC.
The House of Horror
165 West 46th Street, New York City, Phone (212) 245-6874

Printed in U.S.A.

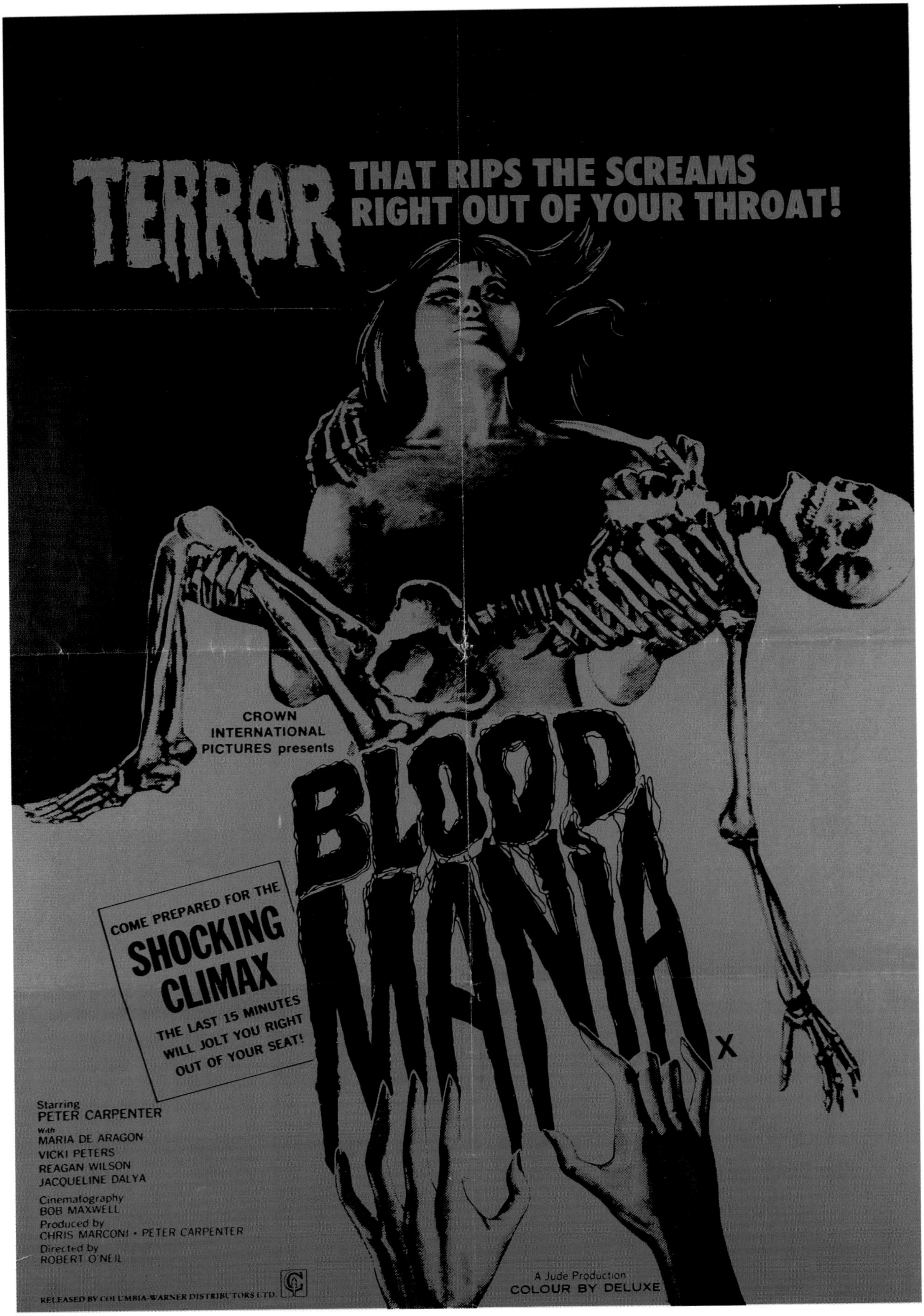
TERROR THAT RIPS THE SCREAMS RIGHT OUT OF YOUR THROAT!
CROWN INTERNATIONAL PICTURES presents
BLOOD MANIA
X
COME PREPARED FOR THE
SHOCKING CLIMAX
THE LAST 15 MINUTES WILL JOLT YOU RIGHT OUT OF YOUR SEAT!
Starring
PETER CARPENTER
with
MARIA DE ARAGON
VICKI PETERS
REAGAN WILSON
JACQUELINE DALYA
Cinematography
BOB MAXWELL
Produced by
CHRIS MARCONI • PETER CARPENTER
Directed by
ROBERT O'NEIL
RELEASED BY COLUMBIA-WARNER DISTRIBUTORS LTD.
A Jude Production
COLOUR BY DELUXE

BY GREG GOODSELL

Blood Mania and *Point of Terror* are two extremely odd genre entries. Both are bids by screenwriter and star Peter Carpenter to showcase his acting and singing talents to the public and potential producers for further film roles. Carpenter's main claim to fame prior to these projects was a brief bit as a Royal Canadian Mountie who scratches Erica Gavin's insatiable itch in the first five minutes of Russ Meyer's *Vixen*. While the tantalising ad mats for these pictures promise all

sorts of chills and *frissons*, their audiences more than likely walked away with a confused "what the hell was that about?" Both are borderline entries, edging just slightly into the horror genre. Doubtless seeking a return on his investment, Carpenter made fright films in a bid to get to 'that type of audience'. Suspense and scenes of fright take a back-seat to shots of Carpenter singing, showing off his muscular bod and seducing women.

Blood Mania was still making the rounds at New York City's Times Square as late as 1983. Oddly fascinating and dream-like, it sucks the viewer into a trance state while not being any good at all. Carpenter plays Dr Craig Cooper, a swinging Southern Californian physician fingered by a blackmailer for illegal abortions performed while a struggling medical student. An elderly millionaire with a heart condition (Eric Allison) enlists his services. Victoria (Maria de Aragon), his brunette bitch daughter, looks after him in their gloomy mansion when she's not busy flashing her breasts at the the pool boy. Carpenter begins to check Victoria's oil in addition to the blonde bimbo he keeps stashed at his bachelor pad. Sure to inherit her father's fortune once the old man dies, Carpenter sees Victoria as a solid meal ticket and a short term solution to his 'tax problem'. Victoria turns Carpenter onto the joys of amyl nitrate after a bout of love making where he tells her "those things can be fatal, you know...to people with heart conditions." With that timely suggestion in mind, she pops a tube under her daddy's nose while he sleeps.

After the funeral, Victoria's estranged blonde sister Gail (Vicki Peters) returns to the household for the reading of the will. Victoria is to be bequeathed the house with a measly allowance to live on while Gail, gone for over seven years, is to inherit dear dead Daddy's millions. Going even further over the deep end when Carpenter begins to turn his attentions to Gail, Victoria bashes her head in with an ornate candlestick.

Stumbling into the murder scene, Carpenter embraces the demented Victoria and tells her that he will dispose of the body. Putting Gail's corpse in the backseat of his sportscar, he returns to the bloody bedroom to reassure Victoria when the scummy blackmailer enters with Gail's nude, battered body. Carpenter will not only be held for a few scrape jobs he did in med school but as an accomplice to murder as well! Carpenter flashes a 'life stinks' grin as the camera freeze frames and the background music reverbs over and out.

Blood Mania is a bizarre experience, the cumulative efforts of artfulness and ineptitude. Robert O'Neil's direction recalls Jean-Luc Godard and department store security cameras. One shot will show a character from thighs to neck without close-up reaction shots. The camera just happens to be pointed in that direction at that moment. Producing on a shoestring, the film-makers pad out the minimal plot with actors delivering their lines in a slow, hesitant manner. People will speak, count silently for fifteen seconds for the other actor to say their lines. "What will we do with the money?" (Pause...thirteen, fourteen, fifteen.) "I don't know." (Pause...thirteen, fourteen, fifteen.) "Maybe...(pause...thirteen, fourteen, fifteen) liquidate certain assets."

(Right) A groovy beach scene from **Point of Terror.**

(Above) Carpenter canoodles in **Point of Terror.** *Note the gratuitous bongos.*

Blood Mania has an inordinately high skin quotient. Female characters doff their tops every fifteen minutes. After killing her father, Victoria has time to narcissistically massage her breasts in a mirror. This posed a problem when *Mania*, essentially a softcore skin item with gore inserts, was sold to TV, so a special edition was filmed. All scenes of nudity were excised in favour of hastily assembled post-production shots of Carpenter favourite Leslie Simms as Nurse Turner at home alone feeding potato chips to her dog. Even more disjointed and incongruous than in its original version, *Blood Mania* on late night TV was highly likely to be brushed off as a dimly remembered nightmare by most viewers.

Point of Terror is in every way a superior film. It has the added bonus of Dyanne Thorne in her pre-Ilsa days of S&M iconhood. Thorne referred to her character in an interview as "a housewife, but still a very Ilsa-type character."

Carpenter plays Tony Trelos, a Vegas-styled Tom Jones-type crooner who performs in a tinfoil-lined nightclub on the Santa Monica pier. His biggest fans are the blue-haired lady set, who flock to his performances to ogle his hairy chest and hear songs of wayward love. (In keeping with Carpenter's obsession with early '70s tack, all his lyrics end with "babe" and feature lush string arrangements.) He catches the eye of Andrea (Thorne), the frustrated wife of a wheelchair-bound industrialist (Joel Marston). They begin to meet clandestinely, with Andrea promising to front the money necessary for Tony's album. Instrumental in the murder of her husband's previous wife, Andrea drowns her crippled hubby in the backyard swimming pool in an impromptu game of 'Ferdinand the Bull'. Dressed in a blood-red toreador outfit, Thorne waves her cloak at her enraged husband as he blindly plunges into the water. Thorne glows in a superb example of pre-Ilsa triumph.

As in *Mania*, a younger and more innocent blonde, this time Andrea's stepdaughter Helayne (Lory Hansen) catches Tony/Carpenter's eye and he is once again torn between two voluptuous women. Carpenter throws Thorne off a cliff, only to be gunned down by a spurned barmaid who is carrying his child. Tony screams, wakes up, and finds out it's all been a dream. Now where have we seen that kind of ending before?

Carpenter was to appear in mostly softcore fluff such as *The Erotic Adventures of Pinocchio* and *Love Me Like I Love You* (again with Dyanne Thorne). All further research came to a dead end. A few terse phone calls to Crown International gave me no clues to his current whereabouts, the rubber stamp quality of his professional name further burying attempts to contact him. Considering the quality of his films, sleazy melodramas served up in the guise of horror, this writer didn't really relish talking to Carpenter in the first place.

In a way, Carpenter's movies are as frank and candidly revealing as anything presented to the public. He gets us to see his films in theatres, rent them on video, or catch them on late night TV in ghoulish expectation of gore and fright, and we are disappointed by the rather shock-less product but are treated to a unique screen persona. Perhaps as the screenplays suggest, Carpenter is one scummy, conniving SOB, not only in his self-penned stories but in the act of getting our attention in order to watch them. Suckered again!

Carpenter presumably failed to generate interest with these pictures, drifting into obscurity shortly after. (*Unless he mutated into the writer of such TV themes as* Hill Street Blues! *Ed.*) These vanity productions did little to achieve the stardom he so desperately strived for. As the nouveau-folk singer with buckwheat braids sings it, we all have to "Be someone, be someone." *Blood Mania* and *Point of Terror* are intriguing cinematic displays in the Modern Museum of Egomania. ∎

BLOOD MANIA.
USA 1970.
Dir: Robert O'Neil. P: Chris Marconi, Peter Carpenter. Story: Peter Carpenter. With: Peter Carpenter, Maria de Aragon, Vicki Peters, Reagan Wilson, Leslie Simms, Eric Allison. 88 mins, cut to 81 mins in UK.

POINT OF TERROR.
USA 1971.
Dir: Alex Nicol. P & Story: Chris Marconi, Peter Carpenter. With: Peter Carpenter, Dyanne Thorne, Lory Hansen, Paula Mitchgell, Leslie Simms, Joel Marston. 88 mins.

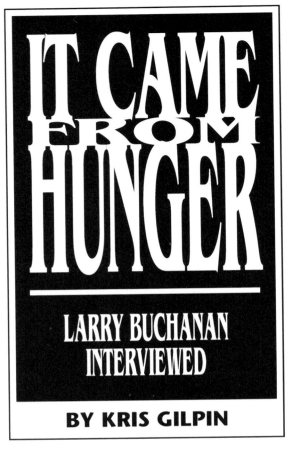

IT CAME FROM HUNGER

LARRY BUCHANAN INTERVIEWED

BY KRIS GILPIN

I first discovered the films of Larry Buchanan on late-night TV as a teenager, on Channel 6 in Miami and Channel 12's (from neighbouring West Palm Beach) 'Creature Feature' programme, and I was delighted by their low-budget antics. Later I was to see *Goodbye, Norma Jean* **and** *Hughes and Harlow: Angels in Hell* **theatrically in South Florida and, on 6 August 1984, finally got the chance to interview Larry Buchanan over the phone in Los Angeles. He is an extremely nice fellow, and spoke with me for seventy minutes.**

Larry Buchanan 'today'.

SX: I thought we might start with a general history of how you got started in the film business.

LB: I grew up in an orphanage in Texas and was adopted by the Variety Clubs of America, which is a national organisation made up of people in the motion picture business who take care of the Will Rogers home in Oklahoma and the Woodland Hills home here in California for old actors. I was kind of unofficially adopted by them and, eventually, got a job here at Fox in the prop department; this was 1942 and I was eighteen. I was doing acting work at Fox - bit pieces with Greg Peck in *The Gunfighter* and things like that - and grew up more or less as a Fox contract player in about two years, fast, but I really wanted to make films; I wanted to be a director and producer and writer but, in the early '40s the union wouldn't let you get on a crew, or get through the gates. You couldn't get on a crew, or even learn to direct; but Woody Van Dyke (*W.S. Van Dyke, 1889-1943*), who was one of the great directors of all time, cut in the mold of John Huston and Wellman, had classes in his Beverly Hills home in editing. There were no cinema degrees being given in Dallas, so that's where we learned our craft. He said, "Get to New York. Go to the Signal Corps Photographic Centre where they'll pay you to direct." So I went to New York and, while acting in the theatre in the evening, I went out to the old Biograph Studios on Long Island, and we made training films for my home town, Dallas, to head up Jameson Studios there; they had invited me down there after they had seen my first feature. I was in a play with Jack Klugman, and I took Jack to the Big Ben country where he played the heavy in a thing called *Apache Gold*, my first feature, a $17,000 black and white western. The leading lady, who was playing a Mexican, was Neile Adams, who later became Steve McQueen's first wife and bore him two sons. Anyway, the Jamesons liked the film and said, "We need a director down here because they're making international commercials,"

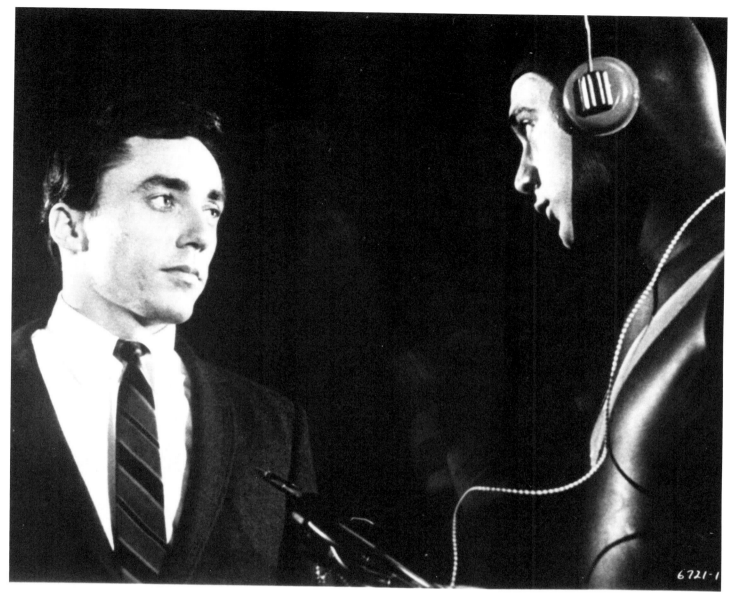

The multi-talented Anthony Houston (left) and Tommy Kirk in **Mars Needs Women.**

and so forth, and that (*film-making*) was the beginning of the big boom out in Texas; we started something down there that's gotten very big now, second only to LA, I think. Jameson gave me a free hand, which meant I could do features in between; they said, "Fine. If you find the time, make your features." So I made a thing called *Free, White and 21*; it was the first of the blaxploitation pictures. I had made other pictures before then, but you can almost forget them - you're talking about *The Naked Witch*, which I made for $8,000 in colour and 16mm (*coincidentally the title of 'genius' Andy Milligan's first film which also features Dallas locations. Small world...Ed.*); I made *Naughty Dallas*, in which we actually used clips of Jack Ruby, who would years later come to shoot Oswald - all kinds of weird things happened down there. But I attribute my first feature with any real clout in the marketplace as *Free, White and 21*. It was in the spring of '63 and our film, which was made for $40,000 in black and white, was in the top grossing pictures in the US for about four months. It was an incredible success for AIP and they said, "Name your ticket; we want half-ass names in them, and we want them now." So

we signed a contract for three at first; this went on to three more, then three more; I did about nine or twelve of those. And between *those* pictures I had a deal between a deal, in which I could do what I call 'my personal pictures.' Things like, for example, *Strawberries Need Rain*, which I defy you to tell apart from a Bergman picture. Now, I know that's a very specious, immodest statement, but I started out to prove something - I love to do these things, Kris. I said, "Look. I can take $50,000 and go into the German Hill country of Texas, where it looks like Sweden, and make a film with three characters, and I can put Ingmar's name on it and they'll accept it." We actually pulled it off. Now, of course later I put my name back on it after we got the distribution...

SX: You actually put Bergman's name on it?

LB: Absolutely, and we opened in an art house in Dallas, and all the SMU students came and raved about it. Of course, the press was in on it; I could not do that, it would be an illegal infringement, so I told them that it was nothing more than an experiment and that I would take it off after that engagement. But anyway, that's beside the point; that's a personal picture. I did

GANGSTER GUNS ARE BLAZING!

A BULLET FOR PRETTY BOY

STARRING FABIAN FORTE AS PRETTY BOY FLOYD
JOCELYN LANE · ASTRID WARNER
and ADAM ROARKE AS THE PREACHER · IN COLOUR

Released by MGM-EMI

(Top) Anthony Houston grasps his communication object (or something) in **Zontar.**

hunchback who could never make it as an actor - screen all of my pictures. They tie me up the way they did Malcolm McDowell in *A Clockwork Orange*, hold my eyes open and make me look at all this crap for four days without sleep. Well, someone took me seriously, so I might actually be doing a few clips from each picture, including *A Bullet for Pretty Boy* with Fabian. I would have *It Came From Hunger* starring Fabian, John Agar, Tommy Kirk, Les Tremayne, Francine York - I could go on and on...

SX: I bet if you released it on video it would sell well...

LB: It's funny you should mention that, because I have a little video playback here, and I went up to get something to show the family the other night - I had them over - I think I was trying to find *Green Mansions* with Audrey Hepburn, and I came across a title I knew very well, but I didn't know that younger people knew it; *Reefer Madness*. That's very interesting, because that goes back to when I first got here. The leading lady, a very attractive blonde girl who was about eight years my senior, kind of took me under her wing - it was not a gigolo relationship, but it was a relationship. Anyway, the guy at the video store said, "We need more of this kind of thing (*camp*). We have this out all the time, even more than things like *A Clockwork Orange*." So, I'm glad to hear your response to that, because I like to get a younger response; after all, I'm crowding sixty now.

SX: It would be terrific fun; I've wanted to get your films on tape for years.

LB: Well, I was thinking of going to New York and going from the original negatives - that's the way to make a tape transfer; you can work from a composite print, but it's not as good quality. I'd go up to a one-inch on everything (*all the films*), then come back and edit it, then go back and only take those sections I like and go up to 35mm negative.

SX: You should release films like *Zontar, Thing from Venus* and *Mars Needs Women* separately; I bet they'd sell.

LB: I honestly believe that...

SX: I do, too.

LB: ...and now that my son, Barry Buchanan, has realised he's not going to make enough acting, he wants to try to learn to edit, so I think I'll put him to work.

There was an article in *TV Guide* that mentioned *Mars Needs Women* twice as being on BBC, and the guy who wrote it talked about England having run the Golden Turkeys, and he said he wound up loving *Mars Needs Women*. And then, of course, along comes *Rolling Stone*, reviewing Peter Wolf's new album, in which the number 'Mars Needs Women' is 'the no. 1 number'. So all of a sudden these things are coming back to haunt me.

SX: What do you think of the Peter Wolf song?

LB: I've heard it, and I had fun listening to it; I think my sons would like it better than I do. I'm a folk musician, and made my living that way for a couple of years. But I love rock - such as Elton John. As a matter of fact, the film we just finished is *Down On Us*, which is the story of the elimination, or silencing, of Janis Joplin, Jimi Hendrix and Jim Morrison; it was all a conspiracy. We have all that on film and it's finished.

SX: You're saying that it's true, that it was a conspiracy?

LB: It's true; we can tell you now it's true. We couldn't tell you last year, but we can tell you now: it's

several personal pictures: one called *High Yellow*. Because I'd done so well with *Free, White and 21*, *High Yellow* was a picture about a young girl passing for white. So all of those pictures: *Creature of Destruction, It's Alive!* - by the way, mine was the first *It's Alive*. Larry Cohen came along later and made a thing called *It's Alive*, which of course did a whole lot better than we did, then he made *It's Alive II*. I don't sue people about anything, but I did have the first *It's Alive!*.

SX: How much did those pictures cost to produce?

LB: They averaged, believe it or not, between $20,000 and $22,000, and that *included* John Agar, say, at $1,500 a week for three weeks. I never spent more than two weeks except on the Agar pictures. On the Tommy Kirk pictures - on *It's Alive!*, for example - we shot in a cave in Arkansas for seven days, for $14,000 or $15,000, using the new fast Ektachrome. I never blew them up; they're in a New York lab right now and I own the theatrical rights, but they did not have theatrical property then, although something is shaping up that might put them in theatres finally. But it would be done in a unique way. Some people saw *It Came From Hollywood*; we got talking at a gathering and very jokingly - I had a drink in my hand, I think - I said, "Well, I think I'm gonna take the best clips from all those pictures and make a film called *It Came From Hunger*." It would be the story of my being abducted by young film-cult kids leaving a theatre where they've been hooked - they're looking for something to replace *Rocky Horror*, and *Mars Needs Women* just might be it, you see. So they take me up to a mansion in the hills and make my projectionist Igor - a

true. The man who worked with us over several years was the same man who helped me on *The Trial of Lee Harvey Oswald*. You see, we knew Oswald, and yet nobody ever came and interrogated us; the Warren Commission didn't ask me about Oswald. We made our film shortly after the murder of Kennedy, and we had stuff in there that is still not in the Warren Commission and, believe it or not - what was it, fifteen years later? - Chuck Fries here picks up and does almost the same thing we do. Now, where he entrapped himself was using stuff that was not public record, but *our* record. The point is, the man who helped us on that was Second in Command of the FBI for thirty-two years. Our children started growing up together in Dallas, although he lived in Washington, and we know a lot of things; we know a whole lot about Wounded Knee we could tell you, but we're not going to do that. But I can tell you that Hendrix and Joplin were silenced by an *ad hoc* of what they call the Plausible Denial Committee, by money washed through Mexico, because of the upcoming '72 election of Nixon. It's all true, and everybody *knows* it in Washington, but no one can put their finger on it. And Morrison beat it! He staged his death in Paris; he didn't die until 1974, instead of '71. Very few people know that; we have the documentation.

SX: Morrison was alive for three years, after staging his own death?

LB: Absolutely; there was no body in the coffin, no doctor and no death certificate. We thought people would put it all together because, on the very day that Morrison died in the south of France, his wife Pamela took her life here. No one was able to put that together, and finally, of course, we decided to go ahead and do the film after a couple of people got out of the act. We had to eliminate Haig from the film - we could tell you a lot of things about Haig - we had to cut that out because he's a living person, and there's only a slight reference to Nixon, very little. So it's mainly a rock story.

SX: Bill Thurman was your Dick Miller, so to speak. What's he doing now, and how did you guys get together?

LB: (*Laughs*) Bill was a professional wrestler in Texas and, I don't remember if it was *The Eye Creatures* or what - maybe it was *Zontar* - but in an early picture I needed a really tough guy to play a cop. And he and John Agar got on very well, and we became close friends; Bill became part of what I call my stock company: good, dependable day-players who could probably never really make it as (*full-fledged*) stars, but certainly can make good cops, truck drivers, waitresses and so forth. They're all down in Dallas; there's a good talent pool down there now. I started using the same people over and over because they were good, and Billy, believe it or not, has a tremendous international reputation; I get all kinds of letters (*about him*). I gave Steve McQueen his first job: when we got back from New York we were doing some looping, and Steve was out with a play, intermittently, with Melvyn Douglas, and Steve was in town to see Neile - I had introduced him to her. He came over to loop for me and said, "This is the first time I've ever done a loop job. I like it." And the rest, as you know, is history. Anyway, the reason I bring Steve up is not my relationship with him, but the fact that he saw Billy Thurman one night on television - and at two or three in the morning he'd watch these things, not major pictures - he called me through somebody and wanted to know who this guy

is and where he could get him. He then started using Billy - he used him right up to *Tom Horn*, even if it was just to have him on set. You know, there's a lot of that going on - John Ford used to do it - where a filmmaker would like a guy so much that, even though he wouldn't have anything for him he'd put him on the payroll just to have him around! Just to be around for talk, and to chew the fat, talk about the old times, or whatever. So, Billy has remained a friend; he works in Texas, he does a lot of commercials, he'll fly out here and do a thing for Disney - they'll pay for him to come out here and do three days. Look at Spielberg, when he was doing *Close Encounters*!

SX: He was looking at the monitor at the beginning of the film!

Yvonne 'Batgirl' Craig (left) in **Mars Needs Women.**

LB: That's right; Billy Thurman. And you realise they could've gotten a million actors for that, right next door. And a lot of people have done that with him; they call him in for one day; they've got ten thousand people here who could do that role, but they like Billy. He has an appeal to audiences; as the cop he took *Zontar* away from John Agar.

SX: How did you learn that your AIP pictures had been dubbed into Yiddish?

LB: I was at the Cannes film festival with *Goodbye, Norma Jean*, which is quite a successful film of mine - I'm still getting money from it, and that was years ago - I was at the Carlton and I got a call from the lobby from a man using broken English who says his crew is there, and they'd like to interview me about *Mars Needs Women*. And I say, "Oh shit. Who is this? Who's kidding me?" and I hung up! I thought it was a friend having fun, or drunk or something. They called right back and I had them come up; I didn't believe it but, sure enough, in come about five guys and a lady with a script in her hand, and they told me that *Mars* had been dubbed into Yiddish and was very successful on Israeli TV and throughout the Yiddish-speaking world. And I thought through the entire hour long conversation that I was being put on, so I was very guarded until it occurred to me that nobody is this good an actor - five or six people cannot walk in here and be that good; these people are *serious*! And so then I relaxed and started helping them, but at first I just kept waiting for the bomb to drop, for someone to say, "Someone put us up to do this." But no, they were quite serious, because (*those films*) *do* have staying power, and I wish I could remember the expression that writer in the *TV Guide* article used to explain these pictures. He said, 'It is not that they are that good - in fact, many of them are very bad - but what we must study is: why do they endure? Mr Buchanan only spent a pittance on these, yet somehow they continue to play.'

I want to go to New York soon about (*my films*), because the marketplace today is so strange; people are looking for some escape theatre, and I think that some people will get just as much enjoyment out of something like *Mistress of the Apes*, which (*chuckles*) was made in ten days in '81! Now, that can't be done by anybody, and it was in 35mm colour. The guy that owns it from Cineworld, who financed it, has done some test dates with it in Europe and they love it, and he's done some test dates in Florida and they love it. I'm talking now about drive-ins and small theatres - we're talking about a picture that cost less than $60,000 in '81.

SX: But these are fun pictures.

LB: That's the key word. I can go out here and do something like *Hughes and Harlow: Angels in Hell* - it's a tax deal. I worked hard on it, for what little money

Larry (right) saves $40.00 by appearing as an extra in **Year 2889.** *(True story...)*

they gave me, but it was no fun because I found out in the second week of principal photography that it was to be a tax shelter; all of a sudden the fun went out of it. I don't play that game, that's not my world; I wanted people to see it, and Nicholas Von Sternberg, Josef Von Sternberg's son, shot the film - he shot several pictures with me - and we love *Hughes and Harlow*; it's at the UCLA Film Library and they do have a lot of requests for it. It's unassuming, it's sincere, it's *cheap* (*chuckles*). Lindsay Bloom has gone on to become the leading lady with Stacy Keach in his new series, and these are nice people; they were enjoyable people to work with and, in thirty years, I have yet to have any actor say he would not go back to work with me for scale. Many of them have moved on up to bigger money, of course; for example, in *A Bullet for Pretty Boy* I gave Morgan Fairchild her first job.

SX: What happened to *The Loch Ness Horror*?

LB: It was bought by Cineworld in Florida, had some test dates, and what happened was that two things were wrong. Number one, the title was wrong - it sounds like a Loch Ness whore. You try to explain to an exhibitor you've got a film called *The Loch Ness Horror*, he says, "*Loch Ness Whore*, what's that?" So it's now just called *Nessie*, and the bloodletting was let out of it - it becomes now more of a Disney thing; it's a good monster, more of an *E.T.* monster now. And the distributor called me recently and his first two test dates were very nice; it was at a drive-in and a couple of hardtops that cater to the family types - we were trying it as a straight horror, it was just not bloody enough. I am not a bloodmaker; I don't do that. Even in *Creature of Destruction* I don't believe in running blood - I don't believe in pulling arms off people and gushing blood. I don't fault the people who do it; after all, one of my protégés is Tobe Hooper. Fine, do that if that's your thing; I never discouraged any of them. I said, "Do what you do well, and if you happen to do, say, camp well, do it - I mean, at least you can work." You see, the important thing in film - and I told the students this when I talked to USC a couple of times - is to make film, and if you can't make *anything* but 8mm porno, do it. Make film! Hollywood is perimeter-bound now, even very fine film-makers can't start a picture because it takes seven years to mount it or finance it; I'd rather see that artist sell his car - and many of them did in the old years. Mortgage your house and go make something you believe in. I think Hollywood as such will be a graveyard in ten years, and I think it'll all be Dallas, New York, the Bahamas, Florida, and so forth. Even the finishing is too expensive here. I can fly to Dallas with all of my material and totally post-produce a film at ten cents on the dollar. And the actors are beautiful, the crews are great - we have IA crews down there, we have non-union crews, we have very fine houses of equipment. And this is true in Colorado or...not just in Texas; I happen to favour that because that's where I started.

SX: Right. You in fact hold a record for directing in 1968, don't you?

LB: Six or seven pictures over a period of twelve to fourteen months. Some of them were the AIP pictures, and I'm pretty sure I did *Comanche Crossing* in that time. I did what was really a feature documentary called *The Other Side of Bonnie and Clyde* with Burl Ives narrating, and that was interesting. Now, because I do cut and score and everything to all my pictures, it's taking longer, but that's not due to me; for example, you take *Down On Us*. I shot it in December, finished it

right before Christmas and, normally, I'd have an answer print in eight weeks - we didn't have an answer print (*the first sound and picture print sent by the lab to the producer for approval*) until May because of the services here; you just can't move them any faster. But next time I'd fly down to Texas and have it out in eight weeks. In *Down On Us* we recreated everything and cast three people in the roles, and the biggest challenge we had in the artwork was: how do we convey to young people that this is not a documentary, it's real, and we have created these people with new music? That, I think, is done in the artwork, but that'd be a question in people's minds until they'd seen the artwork.

SX: I've been waiting for years for someone to put you in a book. What's the chance of that happening soon?

LB: Well, my script/continuity girl who was with me through all of this in Dallas wants to do something, and has asked for pictures; I very rarely retain a company photographer because that's expensive; that's another item you can forget because, in today's market, you just need five or six shots to promote a film, you do not need 3,000 stills the way they shoot on a feature - they all wind up in a warehouse. At the very worst you can go to your negative and reprint, because you need a couple of lobby stills; you can go to outtakes and get actual production stuff; it's a hair

soft but it's still workable. Anyway...my own thing - it was just half in jest, but I may have to do it - is my own autobiography called *'Tis Past*, because I noticed that after we went to Tunisia and broke the ground with the first Hollywood feature to be entirely shot there, that was *The Rebel Jesus*, everyone is going to Tunisia to make religious pictures now; they're using our same liaison people, so they keep me informed. I'd love to do it (*my autobiography*) and now, with my computer, it'd be a lot easier.

SX: How many films have you written and directed, and do you have any favourites?

LB: I'd say I've done twenty to twenty-five features; some of them I've even forgotten. Somebody reminded me of an all-black picture I made in the swamps of East Texas in 1956; it's a 35mm black and white that we're all trying to find, and I can't even remember the name of the picture! Because we were working at a time when we would shoot something and say, "Okay, we've got eight titles we might use." Believe it nor not, one of those titles was *Black Like Me* which, of course, really belonged to my friend John Howard Griffin, who has since died. His book was made into a film starring James Whitmore, but I had the first option on that. He was a very fine writer. Anyway, our black picture, I think, was called *A Taste of Venom*, and it involved voodoo, swamps, all that stuff, and we're trying to find it; it might be in one of those labs down in Texas. So, to answer your question, there might even have been as many features as thirty; the first one was *Apache Gold* in 1952 or '53. A funny thing is, I turned right around and, using some of *Apache*'s outtakes, made another one called *Grubsteak*, but no one understood that title (*it means funds advanced to a prospector in return for a promised share of the profits*), so I had to change that one, too, and I can't remember that title,

either. So there's a little western, a frontier epic, running a round Canada somewhere that used to be called *Grubsteak*, that has outtakes from *Apache Gold*...and Neile Adams and Jack Klugman were in all of them.

SX: What was *Under Age*?

LB: Oh, *Under Age*, 1964! I did that for AIP, but it was not in the other series; it went into theatres. A black and white film and everybody said, "Forget it," and *Under Age* does very well in South America and all the Spanish-speaking countries for the simple reason that the young man in it, who has a relationship with an under age girl, was a Spanish boy in Dallas. The film was based on a real court case, as was *Free, White and 21*. The film was dubbed into Spanish and based on an incredible law in Texas where, if a man has a relationship with an under age girl, the *mother* is charged with rape! Now, that's a hook, isn't it? It was very cheap; we shot it for $45,000. Shortly after that I did *A Bullet for Pretty Boy* for AIP and *finally* they gave me a little more money: a quarter of a million, but that was still nothing in Hollywood in 1970. And yet *Pretty Boy* is very successful; the numbers on TV are even big, and it comes back again and again. The film has Fabian, blood and lots of action; I'm very proud of the machine gun scenes in it. And I still have that one day on every shoot where I film a scene the way *I* want to film it, my personal scene, and that's unheard of on a low budget.

SX: What else, besides *Down On Us*, is coming up?

LB: I'm going to MIFED to present three or four bigger ideas. One of them will be called *The Eighth Day*, a beautiful novel that I'd like to do. Another might be a thing called *The Torture Garden*, in which I will play a lead, an older writer who takes a French girl to an island in the South Pacific, not for hanky-panky but to

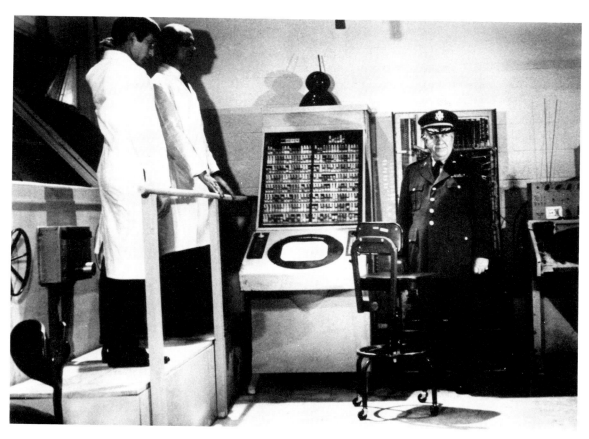

(Above left) Jerry-built packing crates contribute to the futurist 'set' in **Zontar**.

(Below left) The savage ping-pong ball-eyed monster from **It's Alive!** and **Creature of Destruction**, and probably many others...

translate French for me while I work on a screenplay. A young man shows up in a boat, and it becomes a three-way, *Knife in the Water*-type thing. Also, some people want me to continue with my idea of *Who Killed Poor Marilyn?* and use some cuts from *Goodbye, Norma Jean* and redo that night she was killed, of which I could tell you something that would shock you: it's not that she was killed, of course - it's how many *times* she was killed, who did it and why. She was killed three times that night; this is the truth. So, if no one wants any of these ideas in October, I'll go do *Who Killed Poor Marilyn?* (*This project was released in 1988 as* Goodnight, Sweet Marilyn. *Ed.*) And that's a *double entendre* title, because she was no poor girl, my friend; I knew the woman at Fox and I hate to see the crap that's going around about her. Plus, I have a script which is the result of my seeing a snuff film in the early '40s, and the more recent, real snuff film in Rio in which they killed children; the children were bought from their parents and killed and, as an Aquarius, it just boils my blood. It makes me so angry, I have a script called *The Cod Squad* about a group of young ladies, each of whom has been raped who, real-ising the police are doing nothing about the high rate of rape and child abuse, take their knives - one of the girls is a nurse - and castrate the men who get away from the police. It becomes a vengeance thing.

SX: **How often do you hear from fans?**

LB: From fans, it's almost daily. At first it was from people asking, "Where did you shoot *Swamp Creature* or *Creature of Destruction*?" or whatever, and many times trade people call me; they've seen one of my pictures and they ask me, "Where did you get that location?" or whatever. There was a production manager for George Lucas who called before they made *Star Wars* about Tunisia, and I got them in touch with the man who is

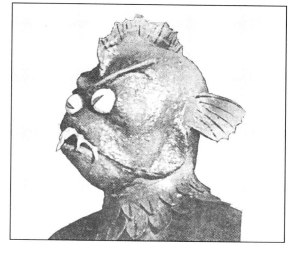

now the liaison between Tunisia and the majors. And we even get called from people who say, "You stole my story", the usual thing, and I say, "Check with the Writers Guild of America, and you'll see that we didn't." And sometimes the fans come up with some really strange questions. And, believe it or not, we got a call in Dallas from Europe about *Strawberries Need Rain* saying that we had confiscated one of Bergman's pic-tures and had retitled it - I loved it!

SX: **That's the same green monster suit in** *It's Alive!* **and** *Swamp Creature* **and others, right?**

LB: Oh, yes; we couldn't afford anything else. We put new ping-pong balls in the eyes - we could afford that - and maybe sprayed it again with paint, or maybe wet it down or something.

SX: **And which films are your favourites?**

Misty Rowe as Norma Jean Baker in **Goodbye, Norma Jean.**

LB: I'd say *Strawberries Need Rain*, without a doubt, and, certainly from a fiscal standpoint as to the mortgage for a number of years, *Free, White and 21* - it was a surprisingly big success for us. I loved *Hughes and Harlow* and I'm going to try something about that one - I'm going to talk to Uncle Sam and see if I can get it and get it back in theatres. *Rebel Jesus* will be fine when I can put a new, contemporary frame on it; it was never really completed. Bob Jessup shot it in Techniscope, and he does the *Dallas* series now; it was his first job and I got him for around $200 a week; he's very expensive now. We wanted to give it the contemporary frame that'd be necessary to make the thing work, but the money-man said, "I like it the way it is, don't change it." And I said, "But it's not completed." So, now I own the picture, and I'm thinking seriously of working on that; *Rebel Jesus* was in 1972 and it only needs a week's work. I grew up in a religious orphanage and we were forced to study the life of Jesus and, although I'm not that religious myself, I am at least an authority on the Nazarene. There are very few things I'm an authority on, but that's one of them.

SX: One final question. Have you any amusing anecdotes which happened during shooting?

LB: Well, let me give you one Billy was involved with. Billy, John Agar and I had gotten to be pretty friendly by the time we did *Curse of the Swamp Creature*. We were out in the swamps and, by that time, John was pretty anxious to get back to LA; he was tired and, even though we're both Aquarius and both born on the same day, we started fighting, arguing with each other; I'm an easy-going character and I don't like to do that. So Billy was trying to keep us apart all day long and John said, "When that sun goes down, I'm going home." My contract said that, if I went passed six

o'clock I had to pay him for another week, so I worked my tail off that day; we probably did ten or fifteen minutes worth of cut screen time in that day. John was really rushing too, and at the very last cut before the sun went down he walked; although we were friends, he walked. The entire day's work was lost in the lab! I had to go and take everything else out and rework the film, because I couldn't bring John back; I didn't have the money. Funny thing is, I brought John Agar back for one more called *Hell Raiders*, which was a little war picture made after *Swamp Creature* - I can't even remember the year - in which John played a typical cigar-chewing lieutenant lead. It worked out pretty well. Another incident happened during *Rebel Jesus*, and it's where I get my title *'Tis Past* from. My Tunisian liaison was just a young boy they assigned to me to interpret. The Government gave me a Mercedes and gave him a Mercedes to work with, and I went to scout locations where there's nothing but nomads, and once in every forty or fifty miles you'd come across a gas station. Well, the liaison, whose name was Hameed, went ahead of me and I stopped at a gas station, and I was still on French francs. He filled up the tank and told me how much it was and, into my next hundred miles into the desert, I figured out in my head that, because I was still on French francs, I had paid $180 to fill the tank. And I was so mad that, when I saw Hameed, I said, "Where were you? I just paid $180 to fill the tank of this Mercedes!" And he said, "Mr Buchanan, 'tis past." And then he proceeded to give me his whole philosophy: 'tis past; it's gone. So that became the watchword in the movie; every time a generator would blow or whatever, everyone'd say, "'Tis past." It became a running joke, so that's why I want to make the name of my book, *'Tis Past, or How I Found Tunisia, Lost God and Got Out of the Motion Picture Business.* ∎

LARRY BUCHANAN: Filmography

1952?:APACHE GOLD.
With: Jack Klugman, Neile Adams.

GRUBSTEAK
(aka ???).
With: Jack Klugman, Neile Adams.

1956: A TASTE OF VENOM (???).

1961?:THE NAKED WITCH.

1963: FREE, WHITE AND 21.
With: Frederick O'Neal, Annalena Lund, George Edgley, Johnny Hicks, George Russell.

1964: UNDER AGE.
With: Anne McAdams, Judy Adler, Tommie Russell, Roland Royter.

THE TRIAL OF LEE HARVEY OSWALD.
With: Charles Mazyrack, Arthur Nations, George Russell.

NAUGHTY DALLAS.
'Documentary'.

1965: THE EYE CREATURES.
With: John Ashley, Shirley McLine, Cynthia Hull, Warren Hammack.

HIGH YELLOW.
With: Cynthia Hull, Warren Hammack, Anne MacAdams, Bob Brown.

1966: ZONTAR, THE THING FROM VENUS.
With: John Agar, Anthony Houston, Susan Bjurman, Warren Hammack, Bill Thurman.

MARS NEEDS WOMEN.
With: Tommy Kirk, Byron Lord, Yvonne Craig, Anthony Houston, Bill Thurman.

CURSE OF THE SWAMP CREATURE.
With: John Agar, Francine York, Shirley McLine, Bill Thurman.

YEAR 2889
(aka IN THE YEAR 2889).
With: Paul Peterson, Charla Doherty, Quinn O'Hara, Neil Fletcher, Bill Thurman.

1967: CREATURE OF DESTRUCTION.
With: Les Tremayne, Pat Delaney, Aron Kincaid, Anne MacAdams.

1968: HELL RAIDERS.
With: John Agar, Richard Webb, Joan Huntington, Bill Thurman.

IT'S ALIVE!
With: Tommy Kirk, Bill Thurman, Shirley Bonne, Carveth Austerhouse.

THE OTHER SIDE OF BONNIE AND CLYDE.
With: Jo Enterentree, Lucky Mosley. Includes documentary footage. Narrated by Burl Ives.

COMANCHE CROSSING.

1969: LOVE AND THE ANIMALS.
Documentary on the mating habits of animals. Narrated by Lorus J. Milne & Margery Milne.

1970: A BULLET FOR PRETTY BOY.
With: Fabian Forte, Jocelyn Lane, Astrid Warner, Michael Haynes.

STRAWBERRIES NEED RAIN.
With: Les Tremayne, Gene Otis Shayne.

1972: THE REBEL JESUS.
(Incomplete?) Dir & Scr: Anthony Houston. P: Buchanan. With: Garth Pillsbury, Roberta Haynes, Howard Rubin, Warren Hammack.

1973: CAMILLE, BABY.
(Incomplete?) With: Anne MacAdams, Robert Glenn, Bill Thurman.

1976: GOODBYE, NORMA JEAN.
With: Misty Rowe, Terence Locke, Patch Mackenzie, Preston Hanson.

1977: HUGHES AND HARLOW: ANGELS IN HELL.
With: Lindsay Bloom, Victor Holchak, Davis McLean.

1981: MISTRESS OF THE APES.
With: Jenny Neumann, Barbara Leigh, Garth Pillsbury, Walt Robin.

Houston (centre) with 'Martians' in **Mars Needs Women.**

1982: THE LOCH NESS HORROR
(aka NESSIE [?]).
With: Barry Buchanan, Sandy Kenyon, Cort Falkenberg, Preston Hanson.

1984: DOWN ON US
(aka BEYOND THE DOORS).
With: Gregory Allen Chatman, Riba Meryl, Brian Wolf, Sandy Kenyon.

1988: GOODNIGHT, SWEET MARILYN
(orig title: WHO KILLED POOR MARILYN?).

"THE END...IS NEAR!"
THE MARK IV PROPHETIC FILM SERIES

BY GREG GOODSELL

The question arises, time and again - why hasn't there been a definitive horror film based on the Book of Revelations? Think of it: the Apocalyptic imagery, the lining up of humanity to receive the irreversible Mark of the Beast (sure to strike a responsive chord in the most cynical unbeliever increasingly dependent on their credit cards), the swirling scenes of death, famine, war, despair...all of it crying out for that Hollywood, Cecil B. DeMille treatment.

Adapting the final part of the Good Book, which has literally scared the hell out of Western man for centuries, has proven an insurmountable task for secular film-makers. Doubtless the religious aspects and variety of interpretations have discouraged mainstream film-makers from attempting such a task. *The Omen* series, in spite of dealing with the machinations of the Antichrist, owed very little to the Bible, being merely an excuse for 'creative death' scenes. *Fear No Evil* included Biblical prophecy in an already crowded *mélange* involving high school angels and devils. 1988's *The Seventh Sign* was the most coherent attempt to adapt the Book of Revelations and weld it to a thriller narrative to date, weaving a reincarnation sub-plot into a Christian religious fantasy, but was saddled with some poor acting and special effects. And even the most noble, well-intentioned films with Christian themes are almost always scorned and persecuted by fundamentalist born-againers - just ask Martin Scorsese.

The Mark IV Prophetic Films series - *A Thief in the Night, A Distant Thunder, Image of the Beast* and *The Prodigal Planet* - stand as chief examples of Christian fundamentalist film-makers adapting the Book of Revelations to a loosely science fictional format. The films maintain the proud tradition of the early exploitation film-makers hawking their wares to isolated rural folk with movies of bathrobe-clad Jesuses rolling away tinfoil boulders from Lazarus' tomb. (Check out related film clips from Diane Keaton's documentary *Heaven* for similar scenes.) Firmly fitting in with the Christian exploitation pictures of Ron and June Ormond (*The Burning Hell*), the series constitutes an entirely different kind of filmic underground - shown in churches, tent revival meetings and the odd theatre in the American Midwest and South with the obligatory altar calls to have the audience come up to accept Christ as their saviour.

Filmed in and around Des Moines, Iowa, these movies adapt the no-budget futuristics of early Roger Corman and Larry Buchanan for soul-winning causes. A couple of actors reprise their roles over the series' ten year period - for example executive producer Russell S. Doughten Jr appears in all four instalments as the liberal preacher turned survivalist Biblical scholar. In *Thief* he is a humanist pastor who finds value in other belief systems, *A Distant Thunder* a repentant old line evangelist preaching to empty pulpits, and in *Image of the Beast* and *The Prodigal Planet* a crusty old mountain hermit who introduces the phases of tribulations in the particular chapters. The only other

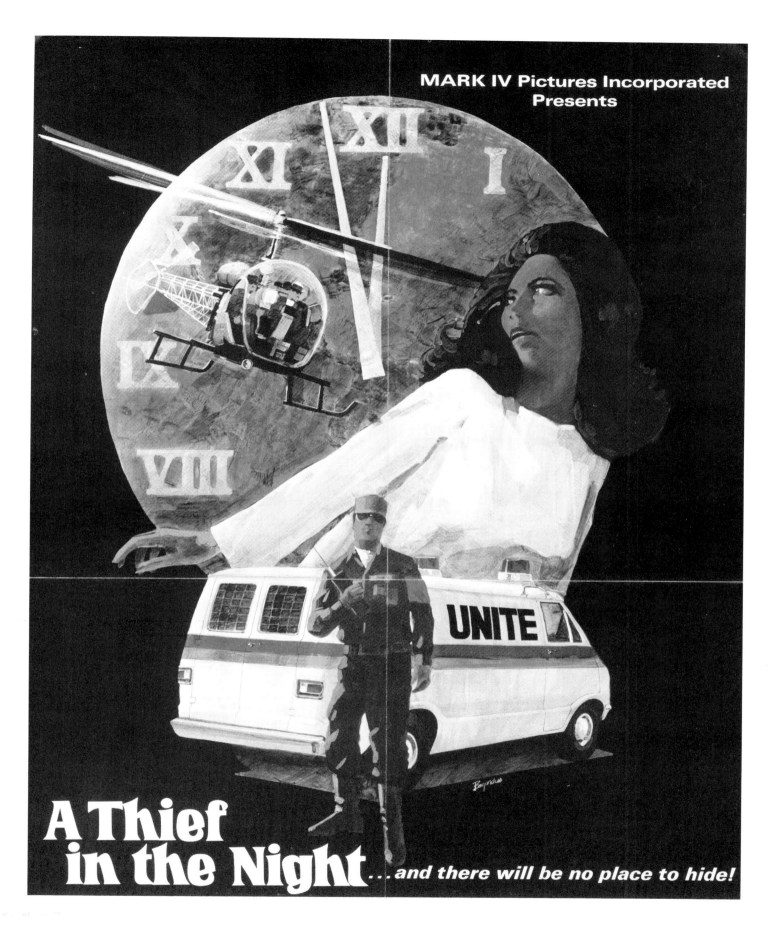

recurring figure in the series is Thom Rachford as the oily next door neighbour who persecutes Patty Dunning in *Thief* and *Thunder*, and appears as a UNITE toadie in *Beast* and *Planet*. Rachford maintains audience identification by wearing the same villainous moustache in all four segments. Unintentional humour abounds in *Beast* when he sports an outrageously phony cookie duster that is positively half off, hanging straight off his upper lip in many shots!

The views expressed in these moving religious tracts are largely at odds with the readers of free-thinking publications such as this. The secular doomsday drama lures bodies into the cinema with the promised titillations of 'what will the end of the world look like?' The Mark IV series, available at Christian bookstores in the USA, offers an even more horrific vision. 'What does a midwestern American acolyte of Jerry Falwell or Jim and Tammy Bakker think the end of the world, or in fact the world, looks like?' You really don't want to know...

The first film in the series, *A Thief in the Night*, is a fever dream of *Red Menace*-style paranoia, home revivalist meetings, *Blood Feast*-like colour photography, dimestore Apocalypse - literally *everything* a viewer expects from a fundamentalist Christian horror/science fiction movie. It's hard to believe that even the most isolated backwoods rustic doesn't fall off his folding chair at the tent revival when *Thief* is screened today. The hideous fashions, stilted acting and garish knick-knacks are truly from some alternate universe.

Thief concentrates on Patty (Patty Dunning), a Christian fence-sitter who is unreceptive to the doomsday talks given by the local pastor at the youth canteen. Spooked by his scare tactics, Patty opts to visit a congregation presided over by a clergyman who blasphemously finds value in other belief systems. Her husband accepts Christ into his heart, and Patty rebukes him. The Rapture takes place, and all the believers disappear from the face of the earth in the twinkling of an eye, like a 'thief in the night'. The Rapture is economically rendered by having the youth pastor pushing a lawn mower across a strip of grass as the camera raggedly pans up into the sky, the shot ending with the mower, *sans* pastor, sputtering on the lawn.

Patty, left alone after her husband is carried away into the clouds, sees the shit really hit the fan as a dreaded one-world government springs into action to cope with the crisis. A spokesperson for UNITE comes over Patty's black and white TV set and says everybody must take tattoos on either the hand or forehead in

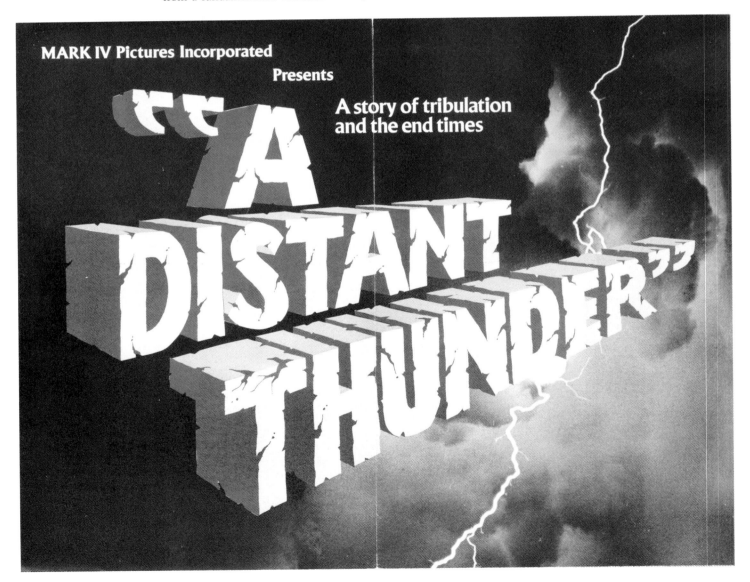

order to trade or barter. Crowds flock to abandoned churches to take the mark of the beast. Patty tries to console herself with shopping, only to be confronted by signs in drugstores saying 'CITIZENS ONLY! 666!'

Patty's secular humanist neighbours turn her name in to the authorities, leading to a long flight through the Iowa countryside. The UNITE goons pursue her by jeep and helicopter to the Red River dam. Her neighbours wave the mark o' the beast tattoo gun as Patty dives over the railing and into oblivion... Nnnooooooo.....! But wait! It was all a dream! Patty wakes up, a voice crackles over her clock radio that Christians all over the world are missing, her husband is gone - nnnooooooo...! The camera settles in on a still of an atrocious yellow enamel clock 'running out of time' as the titles portentously spell out, character by character, 'the end...is near!'

A Thief in the Night was a big success across America partly because, for whatever right or wrong reason, it was entertaining. Producer-director-screenwriter Donald W. Thompson was encouraged by the favourable response and decided to make a series on Bible prophecy for the evangelical market. The series would vary in quality. It took five long years before he got around to filming the sequel, *A Distant Thunder. Thunder* takes place at the exact point where *Thief* ends, with the noticeably older Patty Dunning high-tailing it out to the countryside with neighbours Sally and Sandy (Sally Johnson and Sandy Stevens - the film lists the actors' names without stating who plays what, leading this writer to believe that Thompson lazily has many of his players use their real first names for their roles). *A Distant Thunder* has the look of a bland, polished, made-for-TV feature, but is the absolute dog of the quartet. The three women discuss theology endlessly in a farmhouse devoid of any décor. Apocalyptic imagery is kept to a minimum: a farmhouse is set on fire with horses trapped inside, a white stallion escaping symbolises the 'rider on the white horse' - ie Death. A bogus earthquake with falling bits of styrofoam dropping from the ceiling is meant to suggest geological cataclysms shaking the globe. In one telling scene, Patty receives news of catastrophe and death through the mail. Larry Buchanan would be poleaxed.

The UNITE stooges are out canvassing the countryside for people to stamp tattoos on. A van whisks Patty away to a church-cum-deathcamp where prisoners are offered the choice between accepting the mark o' the beast or execution. Patty is taken to the awaiting guillotine outside where it is revealed that the young, angelic-looking Sandy was the one who shopped Patty to the devil's emissaries. Patty is led kicking and screaming to the blood-caked guillotine as the film cuts to an especially long stretch of black leader where the presiding pastor can then ask the assembled audience, "What choice will it be for *you* this evening?"

A Distant Thunder served as a turning point for the series as Thompson would now eschew the scare tactics of the first two episodes to concentrate on scenes of sincere, long-suffering Christians selflessly sacrificing themselves for the greater good. This move appealed to the audience's nobler side. Still, *Image of the Beast*, the third in the series, contains the quartet's most chilling shot; beginning right where *Thunder* left off, it has Patty strapped face up on the guillotine as the sky turns black and earthquakes rage. "I - I take the mark!" she screams as the blade comes down. Uh-oh, looks like Patty has gone to the Other Place. Snitch

This prophetic series began with "A THIEF IN THE NIGHT" then came "A DISTANT THUNDER"

... and now the MIGHTIEST of them all ...

IMAGE OF THE BEAST

Mark IV Pictures Incorporated OF IOWA

Sandy is seen briefly - after a space of two years between instalments she now resembles a matronly mother of four!

The second-billed Patty Dunning is killed not even five minutes into *Beast*, and we are introduced to the series' new hero, David Michaels (William Wellman Jr), a real Christian soldier working counter to the directives of his UNITE bosses. He meets up with a Christian woman who narrowly escapes execution by the guillotine. *Beast* details the story of believers living underground in the nightmarish, totalitarian state imposed by the Antichrist. We finally meet the evil one in a scene where he addresses his followers in a temple in Jerusalem - a white-haired old man with a forehead tattoo, calculator on a gold chain around his neck, sitting on plywood boxes painted silver, surrounded by plaster of paris statues painted gold on a set with tin Roman columns. Tacky...

Like the others in the series, it is bogged down in talky scenes of preachments and exposition. There are a few scenes of car crashes to liven the pace, but the cumulative effect of watching the series on video has at this point become a mind-numbing, stifling experience. The bright, flat lighting; dull, unimaginative

THE PRODIGAL PLANET

A TRUE STORY THAT IS YET TO HAPPEN.

Mark IV Pictures

clothes that are always clean and ironed as worn by the survivalist Christians; the artless, claustrophobic sets; the banal dialogue... This is one Hellish Tribulation. The overall effect is not unlike the one we experience coming away from Nicholas Meyer's *The Day After* where one favours unilateral disarmament because we've just learned how boring the aftermath of a nuclear war can be.

Beast is prefaced by the reappearance of Doughten's secular humanist preacher first introduced in *Thief*. Here he is a Grizzly Adams-type in a log cabin who introduces the branch of Divine Judgement that is to befall the planet in that instalment. Soldier David Michaels perfects an artificial mark o' the beast to go shopping for groceries with and visits a UNITE church where the service resembles a stockbroker meeting. Tediously, Michaels is captured by the authorities and is led to the guillotine as the balloon of a freshly executed little boy floats off into the sunset.

The conclusion of the series, *The Prodigal Planet,* is a wild and woolly compendium of science fiction movie clichés and low budget spectacle. David Michaels is rescued by a UNITE double agent and is sent on a cross-country search for a renegade group of believers intent on establishing a pirate radio station to interfere with UNITE broadcasts. A nuclear war has broken out, there is no nuclear winter, and radiation levels supposedly 'decay' to humanly acceptable levels in a matter of days. En route to the pirate station, Michaels picks up a nuclear physicist housewife and her spoiled Valley Girl daughter. Stopping in deserted Santa Fe, they pick up a radiation-scarred teenage boy who falls in love with the girl - "It's not the scars on my face that count, it's what I feel inside!" he chastises her.

At two hours and nine minutes, *The Prodigal Planet* ties up the loose ends of the series - the Tribulation period is ending and the bad guys are getting what they deserve. *Prodigal* ends on a triumphant note, with Michaels joining the believers at the clandestine radio station and the promise of UNITE's evil forces finally

being ruined. However, the implied return of Christ is some way off - "Scripturally, we need to cover the Battle of Armageddon before this happens. We have material for an additional three instalments, which are now in the scripting phase," says Mark IV spokesperson Madge Thompson. Writer/director Donald Thompson is no longer with Mark IV Productions. (It's interesting to note that husband and wife acting team Dee Wallace and Christopher Stone appeared in such Mark IV Productions as *The Shepherd* and *All the King's Horses*, both directed by Donald Thompson, early in their careers.)

As an American, I get down on my knees every night and thank God that our glorious leader George Bush's thugs saw to it that Pat Robertson was not made a presidential candidate. The mentality at work behind films such as the Mark IV series is a good deal more sinister than the UNITE goose-steppers on display therein. The only black face we see in the entire series is a young girl set to be executed in *A Distant Thunder*. The sterile, suburban settings make the gloomy dystopian excesses of *Brazil*, *A Clockwork Orange* and *Blade Runner* infinitely better places to live. Even *THX-1138*'s habitats would be an improvement over *Image of the Beast*'s domiciles. Mark IV Productions would fail to see the irony in depicting the fascism of UNITE's minions as they themselves strive to remove Satanic unicorn dolls from the nation's toy shops. The Mark IV series' alternative science fiction universe is one without irony.

At present, fundamentalist Christians hold an unprecedented role in governing America's internal affairs - a single irate letter from a housewife can get a network TV show cancelled and a woman's right to safe abortion is under scrutiny. The fact that these very people insist that a government under the control of Satan is imminent when they presently hold such a vitally important position in American politics is the sole delicious morsel to be gleaned from this sad state of current affairs.

The End...*is near!* ■

A THIEF IN THE NIGHT.
USA 1973.
Dir & P: Donald W. Thompson. Scr: Jim Grant. With: Patty Dunning (aka Patty Dunning Risinger).

Winner of 'Best Film of the Year' - National Evangelical Film Foundation of Valley Forge, Pennsylvania.

'The audience realised as they viewed the film that indeed Christ is getting ready to return very soon and they must be ready.' (Gospel Tract Ministry, West Virginia.)

A DISTANT THUNDER.
USA 1978.
Dir & P: Donald W. Thompson. With: Patty Dunning, Sally Johnson, Sandy Stevens.

'We were thrilled to see a large number of people come forward and accept Christ as their personal Saviour when the invitation was given.' (Pastor Stan Cram, Texas.)

IMAGE OF THE BEAST.
USA 1980.
Dir & P: Donald W. Thompson. With: William Wellman Jr, Susan Plumb, Patty Dunning, Ty Hardin (as The Missionary).

'Even children will understand the Gospel. They will see a little boy facing death with bold new faith in Jesus Christ.* (*This movie is recommended for children when viewed with a Christian adult.)' (Mark IV Productions publicity material.)

THE PRODIGAL PLANET.
USA 1983.
Dir & P: Donald W. Thompson. With: William Wellman Jr, Lynda Beattie, Cathy Wellman, Thom Rachford, Robert Chestnut, Terri Lynn Hall.

'Even a planet that has become a prodigal is not beyond the reach of the love of God. *Prodigal Planet* is a true story that is yet to happen.' (Mark IV Productions publicity material.)

A selection of scenes from **The Prodigal Planet.**

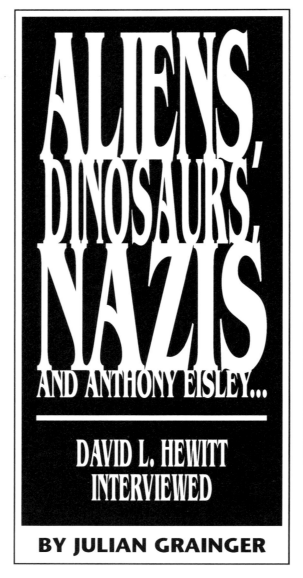

BY JULIAN GRAINGER

The films of David Hewitt span several genres: science-fiction (*The Wizard of Mars* and *Journey to the Center of Time*), horror/fantasy (*Dr Terror's Gallery of Horrors*), biker/JD (*Hell's Chosen Few*), a monster movie (*The Mighty Gorga*) and even a war/science fiction film (*The Lucifer Complex*). All were made with more ingenuity than cash and most suffered the further iniquities of post-production tampering.

He has been active throughout the industry; not only as a director, producer and writer but also as a production manager, film distributor, exhibitor and a (mechanical and optical) special effects man.

Hewitt is an immensely friendly and likeable guy, and it was easy to see why Anthony Eisley (in his interview with Tom Weaver) spoke so very highly of him. Hewitt was happy to talk about his movies and seemed genuinely surprised that people should be interested in his work. After showing me around the optical special effects company that he owns and works in, we settled down to a chat that ploughed through his lunch-break and which eventually lasted several hours. He has great affection for the people with whom he has worked and thinks carefully before answering some of my questions.

Mr Hewitt is just past his half century, with a distinguished-looking grey beard and relaxed demeanour. He now looks back at his directorial work with affectionate self-depreciation, making comments like, "I made those pictures when I didn't know any better" and "I was a young man then." There is much laughter and considerable twinkling in his eyes.

SX: **How did you get started in the movie industry?**

DLH: I used to be a magician. I ran away from home when I was a kid and travelled with a magic outfit called 'Doctor Jekyll and the Weird Show' - one night stands in theatres. Forrest J Ackerman came to see the show in Nevada and when I arrived in California he introduced me to Ib Melchior. Melchior said, "Why don't you make a promo reel with some special effects, using illusions instead of opticals." We shot one day in a little religious film studio in Glendale (that is now a parking lot) called Alpha Omega and showed it to Bill Redlin. He went to AIP and they financed the film and we did the picture. That was *The Time Travelers*. We shot that for a month or so.

SX: **What next?**

DLH: After that I did something called *Monsters Crash the Pyjama Party*. It was always shown at midnight; 'A thousand and one thrills' ran the ad. It's thirty-three minutes long and at the end of the movie, monsters come out, go into the audience and carry a girl back into the screen. I got the idea from a magic show. I built the sets at Carthay Studios by hand. It was a lot of fun.

SX: Is it available?

DLH: I found a print and I've got the old negatives to it so I'm going to showcase it in an old theatre. I have run into a lot of adults that say, "I saw that when I was a kid and loved it." We are (*also*) going to have a guy interview these people, interview the mad doctor (*he's still alive*) and run the film with another short movie on videocassette - just for the fun of it.

SX: What came next?

DLH: The first film was *The Wizard of Mars*. Originally, in the sketches, we had these great roads stretching across Mars and when we got down to doing it, we had enough money to buy about eight tiles which we sprayed gold and put them in the sand! It was supposed to be a very aesthetic film.

SX: I thought that some of the matte work, for its time, was excellent.

DLH: We built that (*Martian*) city out of celetext. A guy named Armando Busick sculpted and built the city. I built the spaceship, made the model and then Austin McKinney shot it on the sound stage. I was real unhappy with it. I was young and hadn't thought the whole thing through. When it was over I realised that it wasn't paced properly - there was no conflict in the script. I was in my early twenties when I made it and didn't know any better! (*Laughs*.) It was supposed to be a great artistic endeavour.

SX: How long did it take to shoot?

DLH: About a month. John Carradine was superimposed over starfields. He came in and worked one day. He memorised the entire speech - it's over ten minutes long - sat down and did it the very first time.

Originally Hewitt chose to utilise his magician's talents by touring with the film and presenting live special effects, such as fireballs, at the screenings. Unfortunately Hewitt was forced to admit that this method of personal exhibition simply wasn't cost effective. The film was eventually handed over for release to American General Pictures, a distribution outfit for which Hewitt worked. (The film is now available on videocassette in the US under the titles *Alien Massacre* and *Horrors of the Red Planet*. This latter title erroneously credits Lon Chaney Jr as a co-star!) A couple of years later, when American General was looking for filmed product to release, Hewitt tracked down a film made by his friend Jack Hill that had been foreclosed on and was languishing in a laboratory. The title was *Cannibal Orgy*, but American General retitled it *Spider Baby* to cash in on the success of Polanski's *Rosemary's Baby*.

DLH: I was involved in film distribution with American General Pictures. Al Adamson had made a picture called *Psycho a Go-Go!* New scenes were filmed with John Carradine and that welder's hat with wires sticking out! That was released as *Fiend with the Electronic Brain*. It didn't do a lot of business, it wasn't really a psycho a go-go story but a diamond robbery story.

SX: So tell me about Al Adamson...

DLH: He's a super-nice guy. A business man. He felt he turned out the best picture for the least money, better than anyone else in the business at that time. He

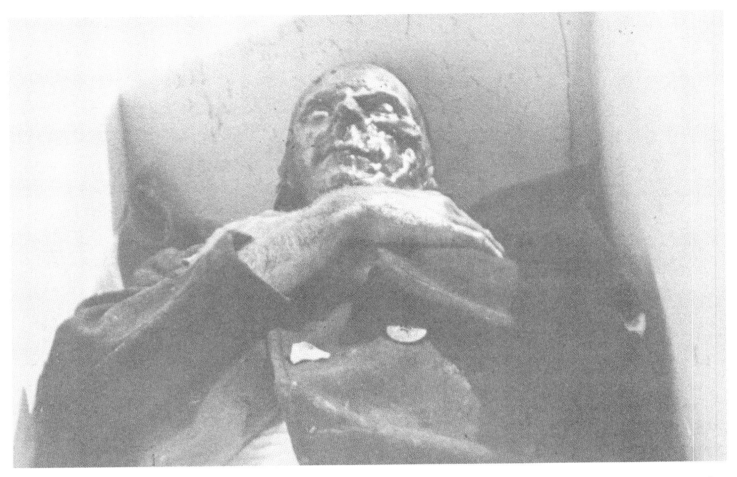

(Above) Ron Doyle wisely stays horizontal in **Dr Terror's Gallery of Horrors.**

(Previous page) Great idiotic retitles of our time dept: **The Blood Suckers** *is* **Dr Terror's Gallery of Horrors. The Liver Eaters** *is* **Cannibal Orgy** *or* **Spider Baby**, *etc, etc... Where will it end?*

sure got his money's worth. I have a lot of respect for Al Adamson. He would drive a hard bargain but you always knew you were going to get your money with Al. Al borrowed costumes from *The Time Travelers* for his *Horror of the Blood Monsters* and it was part of my *Wizard of Mars* set that he shot on. He also used the Gorga gorilla suit in *Dracula vs Frankenstein*.

SX: You worked with John Carradine again on *Dr Terror's Gallery of Horrors*.

DLH: That movie was supposed to be a comic book and if you noticed, there were page turns from Carradine's scenes. There were supposed to be all sorts of blood-dripping wipes and 'Aarghs' and 'Aaeees' printed on the screen, plus the legend, 'Meanwhile back at the graveyard'. It was all campy. We had a little problem in post-production and they wouldn't let me finish it the way I wanted. That's one of my least-liked films. I wanted to buy some comic book stories from James Warren (*publisher of* Famous Monsters of Filmland *magazine*) from 'Uncle Creepy', but he said, "I want $5,000 per story", and I couldn't afford that. He was one of the most obnoxious people I ever talked to. He said, "Well, if you don't buy them from me, I'll sue you if you ever make a movie with those comic book devices." So I found another comic book by Russ Jones (*who was the editor of* Monster Mania *magazine*) and bought the stories from him. We shot the whole thing in six days at the Hollywood Stage studios. We would build the sets at night, go out and get the costumes and everything the next morning, and shoot that day!

SX: Tell me about John Carradine.

DLH: John was a very nice man. Al Adamson and I

were both shooting at the Hollywood Stage at that time and we each hired John Carradine (*Adamson was filming* Blood of Dracula's Castle). We used to go to a restaurant near there called The Shack. My crew was done working and John was working for Al but he didn't know he had to go back to the studio. He was, errr (*mimes putting a glass to his lips*), relaxing there at the table with us. He was telling this funny story that David Niven had told him about World War Two and then, in the loudest voice, delivered the punchline "BECAUSE I'VE NEVER FUCKED A MAJOR BEFORE!" John didn't realise that the restaurant was full of families and kids all eating away. Well, everyone looked up, and he did the line again because he thought it was so funny!

SX: Was *Dr Terror's Gallery of Horrors* successful in financial terms?

DLH: In those days the motivation for doing a picture was that I knew I could go right to television with them and get my money back. You would get an advance for them. That was the case for *Dr Terror's Gallery of Horrors* and *Journey to the Center of Time*. Both cost under $100,000 and we got our money back.

SX: I have been unable to find your 1966 film *The Girls from Thunder Strip* anywhere. Is it available?

DLH: Apparently the negative got lost. American General Pictures had that and they sold it to another company for shipment overseas. It never got there. I believe it really was lost because it has never surfaced again.

SX: What was next?

DLH: Next was *Hell's Chosen Few*. A guy named

Titus Moody owned a documentary called *Outlaw Motorcyclists* and someone else had a documentary with the Miss America of that year in it. I said, "If you give me your *Outlaw Motorcyclists* footage, I'll give you 25% of the movie. If you give me your teenage bride religious film, I'll give you 25% of the movie." I wrote together sequences that tied this stuff together and shot it. The father in *Hell's Chosen Few* (*Joe Folino Jr*) was a plumber in the original story! I got him back for one day and made him the sheriff. I think the footage behind the main titles is the only motorcycle footage in it. We shot it in 16mm, blew it up and it looked terrible. Ken Hartford sold it....

SX: What about *The Mighty Gorga*?

DLH: That was a five day film that ran out of money. After we cut it, it ran fifty-nine minutes! So Tony Eisley, Gary Graver and I bought round trip air tickets to the San Diego Zoo. (*Laughs.*) Graver had this little satchel with his Arriflex (*camera*) in it and as soon as we were airborne I said to Tony, "Now sit there, light a cigarette and read a magazine" and we filmed that. We just started padding the picture. We were shooting clouds out of the window when the stewardess said, "You can't do that in here", so we had to stop. Graver ran off the airplane first and filmed Tony coming out, with me followed by my first wife. Then we shot in the airport and at San Diego Zoo. There are minutes of animals! A sequence where the witch-doctors hear Gorga coming we shot in a parking lot at night beside our editing room. For the gorilla suit we got a car coat suit and glued hair on it. We got a solid rubber gorilla head and tore the foam out to put in glass eyes that never blinked. That was The Mighty Gorga! Anyway, when it was finished it was just horrible, it was terrible. I couldn't get rid of it except to the foreign market. A few years ago, when I paid off the lab bill and got my money out of it, I sold it to Elvira.

I worked with John Carradine on other shows too; one that Ken Hartford did out in the desert that was never completed called *1,000,000 AD*.

THE GREATEST HORROR MONSTER ALIVE!

SX: I wasn't aware that you worked on that project.

DLH: I was production manager on that. The idea was to shoot for one week - it was to be a big part of the picture. We went out to the desert, outside of Barstow, and the director, Joe Mazuka, said to us, "We're here to make a big promo reel and we're just going to throw away the script and we're going to wing it." They got a Greyhound bus-load or two of cavemen extras, trucks, generators, props - I mean a lot of stuff. No one knew what anyone was to be doing and he (*Mazuka*) changed everything. From then on it was like a roller-coaster ride down hill. We had generators to shoot in caves we never shot in.

Russ Jones, editor of **Monster Mania,** *in the only 'action' scene from* **Dr Terror's Gallery of Horrors.** *The 'real' actor is Vic McGee.*

Instead he wanted us to make an artificial penis and testicles for the Queen of the Cavemen (*played by Jo Morrow*) to hold up after they had cut it off, and then cook that and eat it. We were calling ourselves Junior Film-makers of America! (*Much laughter.*) I remember that when they screened it the director came to see it and he walked out, wouldn't speak to anybody. Ken Hartford threw it into the garbage can and the negative was thrown out also.

Hartford took the film to the Cannes Film Festival in 1973 seeking completion money but clearly none was forthcoming.

I mentioned an almost creditless biker movie released to video both in England and the USA in 1986 called *The Tormentors* starring James Craig and frequent Hewitt colleague Anthony Eisley. To my amazement Hewitt revealed that he was the film's original director.

DLH: Originally it was called *The Day the Adults Died* - we filmed that about twenty-two years ago for under $40,000. James Gordon White and I were the producers on that. We ran out of money towards the end of it, only the robbery scenes had not been shot, and then the negative 'disappeared' and Jim White claimed he had destroyed it. Then it came out later - I guess he and the investors had got together and finished it. All the sex stuff I had nothing to do with, so even though I directed the stuff on the sound stages and out on location I'd just as soon not have my name on it. There was a distribution contract signed with American General Pictures for ninety-nine years so they are in violation of contract. I own all those pic-

tures but it doesn't make any difference to me. You sue someone, what are you going to get? Look how bad the picture turned out.

I was equally surprised to learn of another little-seen Hewitt film that is unavailable on videocassette.

DLH: I made an adult documentary called *Sexual Freedom and Permissiveness in America* and that did very well and got nice reviews in *Box Office* magazine. Although it was X-rated (*containing six minutes of graphic footage*) it was not an exploitation film. We talked to prosecutors and defence attorneys, even filmed in the Supreme Court. A real in-depth study.

In 1972/1973, Ken Hartford's production/ distribution company Cine-Fund Incorporated had had some success with Mohy Quandor's *The Spectre of Edgar Allan Poe* and began production on several new films. One of these was *The Women of Stalag 13* (later retitled *Hitler's Wild Women*), on which David Hewitt was the director, co-producer and writer. Once again things did not go as planned.

DLH: It went over-budget and never got finished. We shot with three or four cameras for many hours on the Culver City Studio sets with tanks, guns and extras. I think it got sold by the lab because I was told that a guy bought it and then brought in an editor to patch it together from the script. There were enough sections still missing from the screenplay (that were still in rewrite!) that they couldn't figure out how the picture went together. Anyway, my contract as director and writer said that I had the rights to all the stock footage of the Sherman tanks and the mob scenes - all of the scenes minus the principal actors. Two months after we had finished shooting I heard they were going to tear the Culver City (*studios*) backlot down, so I took some fences from the *Hogan's Heroes* TV show, some windows, bunks - a couple of trucks-worth of stuff. I also had about sixty Nazi uniforms that I had bought when a Burman's costume company sold out their office in Los Angeles.

SX: Were you able to use the footage?

DLH: Well; now I had footage, sets and costumes so Ken Hartford approached James Flocker, a producer who was dealing with Hartford selling some foreign films that he had made. Myself and a writer named Dale Skillicorn wrote a real interesting script and we had a new movie. But one week before shooting the producer slashed the budget and we lost thirty-five whole pages from the script. Ken Hartford was the director for the first three days, then he got replaced and I (originally I was the production manager) took over for the next three and a half weeks. At the time I owned a big, 14,000 square foot inserts studio called Burrindo Sound Stage, where we shot the interiors. *Cinderella 2000* (Al Adamson), *Rattlers* (John McCauley) and some of *Psychic Killer* (Ray Danton) were shot there. We shot everything but the opening and the ending for *The Lucifer Complex* when the producer said, "That's it. I'm out of money. We'll have to finish later" and later never happened. The picture got released with a full ten minutes of someone walking around on the hillsides of Hawaii at the beginning and end. It was ridiculous.

SX: You seem to have worked a great deal with Ken Hartford. What can you tell me about him?

DLH: Ken Hartford is a very (*pause*) unique person. There's no-one else like him in Hollywood. He's creative, he's ingenious and he's very dynamic. He puts

deals together and was active in the video part of the business. He was very big on foreign sales, had quite a few companies and sold a lot of pictures. He represented American General Pictures overseas for a while. I always got my money from Ken Hartford.

Hewitt was also involved in what eventually became the Herbert Strock/Ken Hartford film *Monster* (aka *Monstroid*). Hartford first had the idea for the film in 1975 and Hewitt helped him create some photographic publicity material for the film.

DLH: I did the clay sculpture for a two-and-a-half foot monster with goats' eyes (from a taxidermist's suppliers) and buffalo teeth which I put in upside down so the roots stuck up through the mouth. I also made a tail section. Ken Hartford took photos of that to create the monster and then had some people make it out of rubber. They made a promo where a girl was in a farmhouse and it smashed through the roof.

SX: John Carradine was the grandfather in the promo but played a different role (as a priest) in the finished film. Why was that?

DLH: I think they went in a different direction when they actually made the thing. Ken Hartford went to New Mexico to do the picture and I wasn't involved with it.

In the mid-'70's Hewitt created Hollywood Optical, a company specialising in photographic special effects. Consequently Hewitt's name can still be glimpsed, albeit a little further down the credits, on such films as *The Lamp* and *Superman IV: The Quest for Peace*.

DLH: I've been doing this for about fifteen years. I own the place. I've always liked special effects and I like the equipment. We do a lot of bluescreen composite shots, a lot of Vistavision work. We did a bunch of bluescreen work recently in *Millennium*. We did *Honey, I Shrunk the Kids*, all the visual opticals on *The Wicked Stepmother* and all the bluescreen work for *Evil Dead II*.

I was later delighted to learn that Hewitt will soon be back in the director's chair - older, wiser and still out to have fun, he assures me. In fact he has two fantasy films in development: one, *The Mask of Zantar*, he refers to as a film set at the end of World War Two concerning aliens, dinosaurs, Nazis and Anthony Eisley as a 105 year-old man. Hewitt says that some of the process photography and special effects are already under way and it could shoot in February 1991. This movie I have to see... ■

DAVID L. HEWITT: Filmography

THE TIME TRAVELERS.
USA 1964.
Dir, Scr & Co-Story: Ib Melchior. P: William Redlin. Co-Story & Sp Eff: David L. Hewitt. Ph: Vilmos Zsigmond. Camera operator: Laszlo Kovacs. With: Preston Foster, Philip Carey, Merry Anders, John Hoyt, Dennis Patrick, Forrest J Ackerman.

MONSTERS CRASH THE PYJAMA PARTY.
USA 1964.
Dir, P & Writer: David L. Hewitt. With: Don Brandon. (Running time: 45 minutes.)

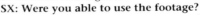

(Above) Cannon manage to misspell part of their rotten ad.

(Below) Cannon can't even get the title of the film they're exploiting right...

THE WIZARD OF MARS
(aka HORRORS OF THE RED PLANET, US video title: ALIEN MASSACRE).
USA 1965.
Dir, P & Scr: David L. Hewitt. Ph: Austin McKinney. Technical advisor: Forrest J Ackerman. With: John Carradine, Vic Gentry, Vic McGee, Jerry Rannow, Eva Bernhardt. A Borealis Enterprises Inc. Production.

DR TERROR'S GALLERY OF HORRORS
(aka THE BLOOD SUCKERS, UK video title: GALLERY OF HORROR, US TV title: RETURN FROM THE PAST).
USA 1966.
Dir & Co-P: David L. Hewitt. Co-P: Ray Dorn. Scr: David Prentiss, Gary R. Heacock & Russ Jones. Ph: Austin McKinney. With: John Carradine, Lon Chaney, Rochelle Hudson, Roger Gentry, Vic McGee, Joey Benson, Ron Doyle. A Borealis Enterprises/Dorad Corp. Production.

THE GIRLS FROM THUNDER STRIP.
USA 1966.
Dir & Co-P: David L. Hewitt. Co-P: Michael Mehas. Scr: Pat Boyette. Ph: Gary Graver. With: Jody McCrea, Maray Ayres, Mick Mehas, Casey Kasem, Lindsay Crosby. A Borealis Enterprises Inc. Production.

HELL'S CHOSEN FEW.
USA 1967.
Dir & P: David L. Hewitt. Co-Scr: John McCarthy & David Prentiss. Ph: E.M. Brown. With: Jody Daniel, Kelly Ross, Bill Bonner, Vic McGee, Joe Folino Jr, Gary Kent, Mick Mehas, Titus Moody, Jan Arlen, Shirley Cash. A Borealis Enterprises Inc. Production.

JOURNEY TO THE CENTER OF TIME.
USA 1967.
Dir & Co-P: David L. Hewitt. Co-P: Ray Dorn. Scr: David Prentiss. Ph: Robert Caramico. With: Scott Brady, Gigi Perreau, Anthony Eisley, Abraham Sofaer, Austin Green, Andy David, Lyle Waggoner. A Borealis Enterprises Inc. Production.

THE MIGHTY GORGA.
USA 1969.
Dir & Co-P: David L. Hewitt. Co-P: Robert Vincent O'Neil. Scr: Joan Hewitt & David Prentiss. Ph: Gary Graver. With: Anthony Eisley, Kent Taylor, Scott Brady, Gary Graver, David L. Hewitt. A Borelais Enterprises Inc. Production.

HORROR OF THE BLOOD MONSTERS
(aka VAMPIRE MEN OF THE LOST PLANET).
USA 1970.
Dir & P: Al Adamson. Scr: Sue McNair. Ph: William Zsigmond & William G. Troiano. Sp Eff: David L. Hewitt. With: John Carradine, Robert Dix, Vicki Volante, Joey Benson, Jennifer Bishop, Gary Graver, Al Adamson.

THE TORMENTORS
(Shooting title: THE DAY THE ADULTS DIED).
USA - No production date available.
Dir & Co-P: David L. Hewitt (credited to 'Boris Eagle'). Co-P & Writer: James Gordon White. Ph: Bill Davies. With: James Craig, Chris Noel, Anthony Eisley, William Dolley, Bruce Kemp, Inga Wege, James Gordon White.

SEXUAL FREEDOM AND PERMISSIVENESS IN AMERICA.
USA 1971.
(Documentary.)
Dir: David L. Hewitt.

DOOMSDAY MACHINE
(aka DOOMSDAY, Shooting title: ARMAGEDDON 1975).
USA 1973.
Dir: Lee Sholem & Harry Hope. Co-P: Harry Hope. Co-P & Scr: Stuart James Byrne. Ph: Stanley Cortez. Sp Vis Eff: David L. Hewitt. Eff Ph: William C. Davies. With: Bobby Van, Ruta Lee, Henry Wilcoxon, Mala Powers, James Craig, Mike Farrell, Grant Williams, Casey Kasem, Denny Miller.

1,000,000 AD.
USA 1973.
(Promo.)
Dir: Joseph Mazuka. Exec P: Ken Hartford. P: S. Lee Lieb. Scr: Shelly Silverstein & Allen Foster. Ph: William C. Davies. P Manager: David L. Hewitt. With: John Carradine, Anthony Eisley, Jo Morrow.

THE WOMEN OF STALAG 13
(aka HITLER'S WILD WOMEN).
USA 1973.
(Unfinished.)
Dir, Co-P & Co-Scr: David L. Hewitt. Co-P: Peter Joy. Co-Scr: David Prentiss. With: Jack Mills, Lynn Hawkins, Peter Redgrave.

HITLER'S WILD WOMEN

MONSTER.
USA 1975.
(Promo.)
Dir: 'Andre Faro'. Based on the novel by Peter Crowcroft. Creature design: David L. Hewitt. With: John Carradine, Liz Winslow, Anthony Eisley, Don Robinson.

THE LUCIFER COMPLEX.
USA 1976, released 1979.
Dir & Scr: David L. Hewitt. Orig Dir: Ken Hartford. P: James Forsher. Ph: David E. Jackson. With: Robert Vaughn, Aldo Ray, Merrie Lynn, Keenan Wynn, William Lanning, Victoria Carroll, Glen Ranson, Gustof Unger, Bertil Unger.

THE DEVONSVILLE TERROR.
USA 1983.
Dir, P, Scr & Ph: Ulli Lommel. Sp Eff Ph: David L. Hewitt. With: Suzanna Love, Robert Walker Jnr, Donald Pleasence, Paul Willson, Deanna Haas.

David Hewitt owned Borealis Enterprises Inc.

HOLLYWOOD OPTICAL SYSTEMS: Selected Filmography
1985	The Lamp, aka The Outing (Tom Daly)
1986	Evil Dead II (Sam Raimi)
	Low Blow (Frank Harris)
1987	Superman IV: The Quest for Peace (Sidney J. Furie)
1988	Honey, I Shrunk the Kids (Joe Johnston)
	Willow (Ron Howard)
1989	Wicked Stepmother (Larry Cohen)
	Millennium (Michael Anderson)
	Shocker (Wes Craven)

THE BIG MAMAS BATTLE WILD CHOPPER JOCKEYS, THRILL KILLERS CALLED HELLS CHOSEN FEW SHE TAUGHT THEM A NEW GAME ON TOP OF A POOL TABLE!

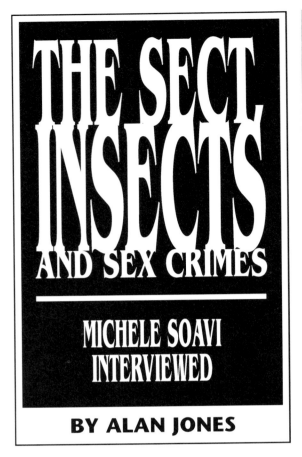

THE SECT, INSECTS AND SEX CRIMES

MICHELE SOAVI INTERVIEWED

BY ALAN JONES

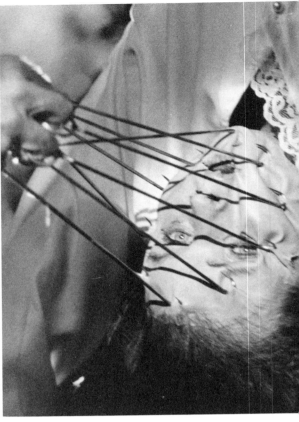

As the millennium approaches, a fine red line of blood and terror spans two decades, slowly spreading from a parched Californian desert's hippie commune to Europe. Ritualistic killings from the distant past make headline news again as devotees of an esoteric evil cult - The Sect of the Faceless Ones - make a final appointment with the Devil to change the destiny of a chaotic world. An appointment they have no intention of missing and in the name of which they are prepared to torture and murder. Adepts come from all parts of the world, from all social levels, united by their blind

fanaticism, their craving for Absolute Power. And they close in on a fragile, timid, young German schoolteacher named Miriam.

Suddenly everything around Miriam is tinged with blood and fear. She's forced to witness the deaths of all those dear to her. Her forest chalet, once a peaceful sanctuary, overnight becomes a demonic funhouse as mysterious forces emanate from a cellar well. Normal people turn into savage assassins who cut out their victims' hearts. A possessed Holy Shroud provokes madness in whoever contemplates it. Insects extinct

for eons reappear, feeding on human brains in which they deposit their eggs. And Miriam is at the centre of this vortex of escalating horror, trapped in a web of terror from which there is no escape. For she is the most important pawn in the Antichrist's grand design for Hell on Earth and she has no choice but to await her preordained fate in an epic battle with evil.

The Sect (aka *La Setta*) is the third feature from Michele Soavi, a director single-handedly revitalising the stale spaghetti horror film industry. If *Stagefright* (aka *Bloody Bird*, aka *Deliria*) was Soavi's thematic revamp of Dario Argento's solo breakthrough, *The Bird with the Crystal Plumage*, *The Church* (*La Chiesa*) continued the tradition with a new take on *Demons'* mythology. To all intents and purposes *The Church* was *Demons 3* in disguise, a Gothic horror which, like *The Sect*, was produced by Argento, and, for want of a better analogy, is *The Wicker Man* Italian style. No matter how hard he tries to play down the fact that he's Argento protégé *numero uno*, thirty-four year-old Soavi will never be able to escape the comparisons he now reacts to with resignation. His career to date has been inextricably entwined with the *giallo maestro* and will probably remain a constant, if annoying, factor throughout his entire working life. What Soavi has yet to realise is worse similarities could be made: *Stagefright* was produced by Joe D'Amato (aka Aristide Massaccesi), with whom he scripted both *Ator* movies, and that would be an even greater cross to bear!

A former actor in various slices of pizza schlock - *Alien Terror*, *City of the Living Dead*, *Anthropophagus*, *Atlantis Interceptors*, *A Blade in the Dark*, *Endgame* and *Caligula-The Untold Story*, a role in the 1979 drama *Bambule* led to Soavi assisting director Marco Modugno on the production side. Then he met Argento just after the troubled *Inferno* was completed.

Argento gave helpful suggestions about one of Soavi's screenplays and they became good friends. When Argento began preparing *Tenebrae* he made Soavi his second assistant, promoted him to first assistant on *Phenomena* (aka *Creepers*) and asked him to direct the rock promo for Bill Wyman and Terry Taylor's 'Valley' theme from the soundtrack. Soavi encored this position on Lamberto Bava's *Demons*, directed the Claudio Simonetti title track video, and played the metal masked man handing out preview tickets. Then came the Japanese TV documentary *Dario Argento's World of Horror* which made Soavi's name and led to his critically acclaimed début feature *Stagefright*.

Although set in suburban Frankfurt, the main location for *The Sect* was Monte Gentile in the Marino Hills, an exclusive residential area 30km from Rome where Sophia Loren and Carlo Ponti scandalised *la dolce vita* society with their infamous *paparazzi* love affair. Kelly Leigh Curtis, Jamie Lee's younger sister, Herbert Lom, Tomas Arana, Michel Hans Adatte and Mariangela Giordano star in another of Soavi's eclectic mixes of favourite movies and concepts. *Rosemary's Baby*, Charles Manson, *Phenomena* and *The Omen* are just a few of the ideas lifted into the script co-written by Soavi, Argento and Gianni Romoli, Italy's foremost comedy writer. Originally titled *Catacombs*, Romoli initially wrote the treatment for director Luca Verdone, superstar comedian Carlo Verdone's brother. As they had produced *Opera* and *The Church* and because they couldn't finance the feature on Verdone's name, producers Mario and Vittorio Cecchi Gori turned to Argento for help. Soavi takes up the involved genesis: "Dario hated *The Sect*'s story. He thought it was too similar to *Inferno* - which it was - although it began in ancient Rome and led to the present day. But he loved Vittorio's new title, which was a very commercial one, and we wrote a totally different narrative with a Manson cult as the basic thread. As the final script stands there isn't one detail remaining from Romoli's original draft."

Around this time Soavi was trying to write a script about a haunted well. He lamented, "But *The Well* didn't pan out and I started seriously thinking about remaking *The Golem* in modern dress. I'd liked what Romoli had done with *Catacombs* and we tried to co-

(Above) Herbert Lom and Kelly Leigh Curtis recoil with horror at something too ghastly for words.

(Above left) A minor character meets a major fate in **The Sect**.

(Bottom left) Michele Soavi profiled.

(Above left) Soavi supervises a bit of torture on **The Church.**

(Above right) Soavi and Asia Argento on the set of **The Church.**

write a script together, but getting to grips with the Jewish myth was hard. I spent Christmas 1989 in Prague scouting locations, shooting footage of the Romanian revolution for Italian TV news networks in the accidental process, until Dario decided *Blade Runner*'s replicants had taken the mechanical man to the limit and finally vetoed the idea. Then Luca's interest waned, Dario didn't like or want him anyway, and I was offered the project."

The Sect comprises three sections. Argento wrote the opening, set during the '70s hippie era, showing guru Tomas Arana brutally murdering a desert commune while chanting key dialogue lifted from Rolling Stones songs. Romoli wrote the middle section outlining the cult's master plan for Kelly Curtis. And Soavi's input is her basement cellar pit where most of the supernatural action takes place. Soavi joked, "I had to

put *The Well* in somewhere! I couldn't expand the idea into a full feature so it plays a pivotal part here instead. I like all that sort of stuff. My favourite sections of *The Church* took place in the dark subterranean vaults."

Set in Germany because "Dario has a passion for the country", Soavi outlined the reasons why the exact locale is described as being "twenty-three minutes east of Frankfurt in the small town of Seligenstadt." He continued, "It translates as 'the place of rest and peace'. That's my additional subtext and *The Sect* will be my most personal film due to those sort of weird touches. Many of my own belongings, like the ceramic rabbit ornaments which come to life at various junctures, have been used to dress the set. I recently found out that my great-grandfather was Irish too. I've read volumes on Celtic myths and Druids to discover more about my roots and I've put as much reality-based information as I can into the narrative. *The Sect* started out as just another routine job for me but my personal research has turned it into something much more and now I'm really caught up in it."

Nor is Soavi worried or paranoid about what he's doing. He was on *Stagefright* and *The Church* because he felt he was stumbling into unchartered territory. But with *The Sect* he acknowledged, "I'm in full control. I'm more relaxed. I like Kelly Curtis. I went to America to cast the lead and chose her for her obvious intelligence and special facial qualities which burn a hole in the screen. She's not beautiful in the classic sense. She looks more like her mother Janet Leigh than sister Jamie Lee, which I felt was important. But she's interesting to watch and the whole film centres on her ability to be totally believable. I love the location. I like the compactness of the script. And I no longer give a shit if Dario lurks around the set. I'm not paranoid anymore about the tension he creates which puts the crew on edge or his offers of advice which I may or may not take. *The Church* did me in because, after one week's shooting, I was two weeks behind schedule and Dario drove me increasingly crazy, especially during the editing. He's extremely happy with the moody atmosphere of the rushes so far and I finally feel he trusts me to work fast and turn in a good piece of work."

Argento is famous for his working relationships turning hot and cold. You can be 'flavour of the month' one day and then for no apparent reason be ignored and not contacted for up to a year. This has happened to Soavi on numerous occasions: while making *Stagefright*, refusing to desert his second unit post on Terry Gilliam's *The Adventures of Baron Munchausen* to direct episodes of Argento's universally panned TV game show *Giallo*, and when he bowed out of assisting Argento on *Two Evil Eyes* because the Pittsburgh production office's air-conditioning system caused him increased asthma attacks. And both strong-willed personalities have clashed again during *The Sect*. One major skirmish concerned Soavi's insistence on filming exteriors with May blossom floating in the air similar to Ridley Scott's *Legend*. He sighed, "The story is set in spring and revolves around the fateful day of May 6th... Having this feathery snow-like substance wafting in the breeze added a unique strangeness Dario refused to understand until I underlined its symbolism. Herbert Lom's preordained arrival at Curtis' house signals the nest building he's starting on behalf of the sect's ultimate aim - to enforce her immaculate conception of Satan's son. It's curious stuff and I want *The Sect* to work on a number of weird planes to engage audience attention."

That's why Soavi has filled every available inch of screen space with Druid iconography, Celtic metaphors - "The turquoise ribbons tied on the trees are what you do if you want a baby boy," he explained - and personal in-jokes which will keep Soavi trainspotters on their attentive toes once more. But *The Sect* sees Soavi mainly paying homage to Argento again thanks to the scarab-style insects crawling out of various human orifices. He added, "That's a reference to *Phenomena*, my first major assignment with Dario, and the start of my film career."

What sets the $2 million production apart more, though, is Soavi opting for a youth-plus personnel ethic. He said, "I needed to be surrounded by a young enthusiastic crew. The director of photography is Rafaele Mertes whose work so far has been confined to television and *Giallo in Venezia*. Although I insisted on doubling as cameraman - it was important for me to look through the lens at all times especially during the hand-held camera sequences - I wanted a very naturalistic look. Rafaele is using only available light redirected by angled mirrors to achieve a soft, understated tension. Steadicam operator Giovanni Gebbia is carrying out the major objective though. *The Sect's* theme is a continual spiral, a hypnotic vortex sucking you into the horror like the water in the cellar well. Every time there's a tense moment or shock the camera moves in a circle. At first it's ninety degrees, then it's 180. Only during the conclusion will the camera move 360 degrees to complete the terrifying ring of deception. I'm not using camera tricks for their own sake. They have a deliberate and very real underlying purpose."

Bearing in mind the criticism he faced with *The Church*, that there weren't as many horrific set-pieces as in *Stagefright*, Soavi has considerably upped the horror quotient in *The Sect*. There's a gory face-ripping ritual after a female victim has been rivet-gunned to the floor of a supermarket storeroom. Kelly Curtis is savagely pecked by a prehistoric bird and insects crawl out of the wound in a dream sequence. She gives birth to an insectoid foetus and watches in terror while Mariangela Giordano is suffocated by a linen death

mask soaked in Herbert Lom's sweat. And Giordano turns into a possessed human blood fountain after cutting open her hospital stitching when raped and slashed by a truck driver. Argento's special make-up effects regulars, Rosario Prestopino and Sergio Stivaletti, are the men responsible for all the splatter mayhem - a brief which also included remote-control rabbits and a larger-than-life nasal passage. Soavi's camera can therefore follow the evil insect up Miriam's nostril as it prepares to burrow into her brain, conceptualised as the surreal optical light show similar sequences in *Opera* should have been.

Soavi admitted, "I don't think *The Sect* is anything too startling or that original. But it offers me a great opportunity to pull it through on my directing ability alone. Shooting in English hasn't been that difficult, although sometimes I do lose track of the script. That's where working with Terry Gilliam has really come in useful. *The Sect* will be my first movie to show a definite Soavi style. *Stagefright* wasn't my story although I added all the stuff with the key. *The Church* was drenched in a Gothic atmosphere because that was the mark Dario wanted to make on it. I've gone for more nail-biting suspense and scalp-freezing scares with *The Sect*. I want the audience to be really wound up over Kelly Curtis' fate. She and Herbert Lom are real people, not stars, and I'm lucky to have them both in the picture. Their quest for realism has been extraordinary, helped by the fact they think the script is really well written. Hopefully I'll be taken far more seriously after *The Sect*. I do want to work for other producers rather than stay in Dario's shadow. I want new challenges to grow as an artist in my own right above being told to do this, or do that - and quickly! *The Sect* is something unusual. I feel that. There's a maturity and depth to it you don't normally find in horror fantasy. I think it'll shape up as quite a unique little picture." ∎

Kelly Leigh Curtis after a midnight visit to Highgate Cemetery...

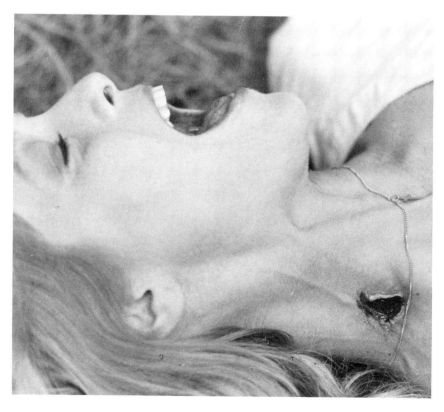

SPAWN OF TARANTULA!

A CAREER IN BRITISH SLEAZE

BY DAVID McGILLIVRAY

David McGillivray was responsible for some of the better British exploitation/horror film scripts of the '70s. Here, in the first part of an autobiographical retrospective, he talks about the early days of his career in sleaze.

(Right) Would you buy a Pete Walker interview from this man?

(Opposite page) Sheila Keith and the appropriately named Kim Butcher get down to business in **Frightmare**.

Jack Arnold made me do it. Or Nigel Kneale. If it hadn't been for people like this I would have entered for the Duke of Edinburgh's Award Scheme and I expect I would now be producing *Beadle's About*. I still feel a tug in that sort of direction. But things turned out rather differently.

Stop me if you've heard this one, but I decided that showbiz was the life for me after I saw my first film, *Singin' in the Rain*. That Technicolor swirl of glamour and gaiety set my head aspinning. Months later, however, I was intrigued to find that entertainment had an equally exciting Dark Side. In 1955, just after my eighth birthday Nigel Kneale's *Quatermass II* serial was screened on television. I suppose my parents must have been quite enlightened because they let me watch the first episode. Whatever it contained, it achieved its object by giving me nightmares and I was not allowed to watch any more. A cliché, I know, but horror really did take on an even more alluring cachet because it was forbidden.

Horror, needless to say, was very difficult to experience at an age when my gloves were still sewn to the ends of my coat sleeves. Whenever my father took me for a trip to London's West End, I would guide him away from the buildings of interest and into Piccadilly Circus because there I could gaze in fearful wonderment at the old London Pavilion, where United Artists used to première their monster movies.

The one I remember best is Jack Arnold's *Tarantula*. It seemed to offer an inconceivably horrible experience, featuring as it did a one hundred foot tall spider *and* hideously misshapen men. And there they were in huge photographs, bearing down on the hapless John Agar and Mara Corday. I fretted about their plight for months afterwards.

By the time I was twelve, my peer group was managing to bluff its way into 'X' films, off limits in those

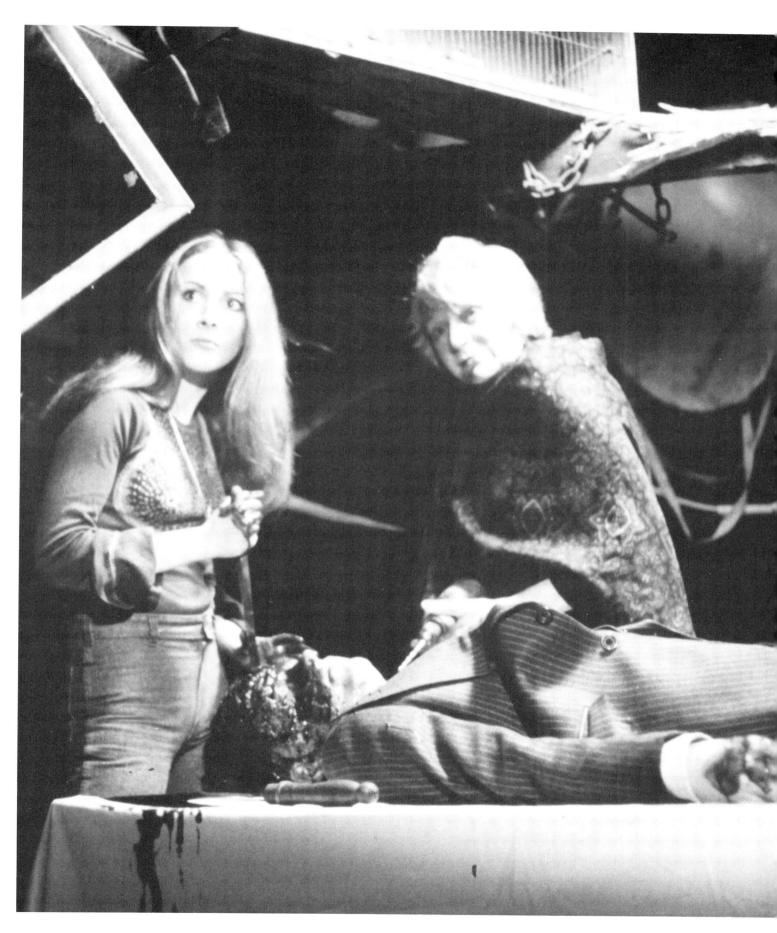

days to the under-sixteens. It sounded easy. "I know you're not sixteen, but I'm letting you in because we need the money," the cashier at the Rex, Wood Green, told my friend Derek Gray. But I was too lily-livered to join these escapades. I thought that I would be frightened to death, a possibility, which, according to the posters ('£10,000 if you die of fright!') was all too likely.

When I turned fourteen, I felt that the time had come to face up to the challenge. My mother took me to see *Gorgo* in which a dinosaur trampled London. She thought it was ridiculous and I realised for the first time that most horror films are like Christmas: anticipating it is better than experiencing it. I think this is what Karl Boehm meant in *Peeping Tom* when he said, "The most frightening thing in the world is fear itself."

Not long afterwards, however, I saw a film called *Night of the Eagle*, which really did scare the bejesus out of me. During one particularly tense scene my heart pounded so fast that I thought it was going to explode and when the lights came up the usherette would discover me lying in a pool of gore. When I walked from the cinema unscathed I felt exhilarated, as though I'd survived the initiation I'd desired/dreaded for so long. Of course I wanted more of the same. And what soon developed was the ambition to create the

experience for others.

Less than a decade later that's what I did. In the '70s I enjoyed my fifteen minutes of fame writing such horror films as *House of Whipcord* (1974), *Frightmare* (1974) and *Satan's Slave* (1976). If a cult consists of having the title of a film you've written painted on the ceiling of the Scala cinema in King's Cross then *House of Whipcord* is a cult. But if the title means nothing to you, don't worry. It was all a long time ago and there's been nothing since. I seem to have gone overnight from screenwriter in the first flush of youth to has-been wheeled out at conventions to reminisce about the good old days.

My excuse for raking up past glories yet again is only to assure the incredulous that there really was a time within living memory when Britain supported a large community of film-makers producing several horror films every year. Today, when the British film industry consists almost entirely of Channel 4 drama in which two people in a room fail to communicate, this may be hard to believe, but take it from me that the sleaze business once boomed.

I got into it almost before I knew what was happening. Hoping to play the parts Gene Kelly was now too old for, I went to drama school, but I wasn't a very

MIRACLE FILMS present
HOUSE OF WHIPCORD
COLOUR   Cert **X**
BARBARA MARKHAM
PATRICK BARR   RAY BROOKS
and introducing **PENNY IRVING**
PRODUCED and DIRECTED by PETER WALKER

good actor and even when I was reduced to extra work the assistant director put me at the back of the crowd. I began to say yes to any interesting sounding job and that's how I came to the assistant editor of the British Film Institute's *Monthly Film Bulletin*. It was swinging 1971 and my work mostly entailed reviewing the sex films that the likes of Nigel Andrews and Tony Rayns didn't want to see.

I was a bit like Charlie in the chocolate factory because, prior to my BFI appointment, I actually used to pay money to see this kind of film. That's how I discovered an independent film-maker called Pete Walker. He began by making useless skinflicks with titles like *Strip Poker* (1967) and *School For Sex* (1968), but gradually his technique improved, and when I saw *Cool It Carol* (1971) and *Die Screaming, Marianne* (1971), I knew that it would be only a matter of time before the critics hailed him as a major new talent. I wanted to be the first to interview him.

I think I managed to make an impression on him. Mind you, he'd never been interviewed before, and he wouldn't have been able to compare me to anyone else. But I did know who Russ Meyer was and I dropped his name into the conversation. Walker raised an eyebrow. "You know your movies, don't you?" he said. Well, that kind of movie, yes.

Walker also impressed me. To survive the cut-and-thrust of the softcore porn industry in Britain up until the end of the '70s, a film-maker had to have the mentality of a used car salesman. But whereas the rest of the pack would have been at home on the forecourt of Len's Motors, Walker would only have been found selling Ferraris in Park Lane.

A former grammar school boy, he was intelligent, nicely spoken and impeccably dressed. He loved every aspect of the movies, even down to the smell of the celluloid in the can. And he was stinking rich. He had an office in Mayfair, far away from tawdry Wardour Street, the heart of British movieland; his other properties included a mansion in Esher with a pool and acres of manicured lawns; and he gave me a lift somewhere or other in one of his vehicles, a Rolls Corniche with a telephone and electrically operated windows, unheard of in 1971. I returned to my rented bedsit and chronicled Walker's entire life story. I wasn't to see him again for a couple of years.

Back at the *Monthly Film Bulletin*, editor Penelope Houston smelled a rat. She had been monitoring articles I'd been writing for other magazines. Apparently the topic in each case had been low-grade smut of various types and never had I made so much as a passing reference to the Hungarian masterpieces so esteemed by the Institute. I was sacked.

It was 8 September 1972. I thought I'd better look for another job, but I didn't know what to try next. As it happened, no effort was necessary. On 7 November a friend of mine named Ray Selfe asked me to beef up a screenplay he'd written called *Albert's Follies*, with which he was due to make his début as a director.

I'd known Selfe for some years. He was a huge, bearded man who wore Max Miller suits and lived in a house stacked from basement to attic with old movies. There were even film cans in the shower. I would listen for hours while he held forth on every conceivable aspect of film-making. I wasn't quite sure what he actually did for a living, but it was something between mending projectors and running ITN.

It seemed quite feasible in those days that a back street distributor should give Selfe £60,000 to direct a

sex comedy. The story concerned striptease dancers being sold as white slaves. It was written for The Goodies, but they didn't want to do it and the honour fell instead to up-and-coming comedian David Jason. I jumped at the chance to rewrite the dialogue for £100.

I think my maiden experience as the writer of a low budget exploitation film was pretty typical. My new version of the script was prepared in three days and I seem to remember that everyone thought it was terribly amusing. Then everyone changed their minds and wanted alterations.

At the beginning of 1973 there were murmurings that a "foreign backer", whoever that may have been, thought the script didn't have enough sex. Jason, on the other hand, thought it didn't have enough gags and began making helpful suggestions. When I went down to Twickenham Studios to play a small part I'd written for myself, I met an old codger of an actor named Hugh Lloyd, who showed me his rewritten version of the first scene. His jokes were terrible, but he'd added an extra line for me so I kept shtum. Lloyd and another buffer called Tim Barrett went on to rewrite the whole of their parts, which began to get bigger than Jason's.

The rough cut was received in stony silence. Selfe thought the film could be salvaged by the addition of another sex scene, but the shooting of it was scuppered by buxom starlet Sue Bond, who announced when she arrived on the set that she'd promised her boyfriend she wouldn't take her bra off.

Albert's Follies was released at the end of 1973 as *White Cargo*, a second feature for the raincoat trade. I went to the first performance in the Charing Cross Road. It was much the film I was expecting, albeit a shorter one. In an effort to make it playable, the distributor had cut it from ninety-five to sixty-two minutes. I recognised very few of my lines.

My companion at that screening, who left afterwards in a taxi without a word, was Pete Walker. By that time I'd already written two screenplays for him. Walker and Selfe knew each other; and when Walker needed somebody to write a script in a hurry, Selfe recommended me. If the article I'd written about Walker had appeared in print, he wouldn't have employed me. I didn't know it in the early days, but in fact he hated criticism.

When he read a piece I wrote about him in 1982, he stopped speaking to me, a situation that persists to this day. But publication of my original article was held up for three years during which time I remained *persona grata*.

Since our first interview Walker had made an Old Dark House thriller called *The Flesh and Blood Show* (1972) and wanted to try something similar. At an early meeting with me to discuss the new project he described his work method, actually that of Roger Corman before him: first he would think of a title, then he would design the poster, and only at this stage would the story be worked out.

The title he had now come up with was *House of Whipcord* and the poster he envisaged was "a girl's face screaming through a noose" (this was indeed the poster that eventually advertised the film). Alfred Shaughnessy, who wrote *The Flesh and Blood Show*, had already devised a story around Walker's new title that promised a potent mixture of thrills and titillation: in a private prison on the moors offenders are starved, flogged and hanged.

For reasons I can no longer remember, Shaughnessy

What terrifying craving made her kill... and kill... and kill...?

FRIGHTMARE X

Rupert DAVIES · Sheila KEITH

DEBORAH FAIRFAX
PAUL GREENWOOD
KIM BUTCHER

Guest Stars
LEO GENN
GERALD FLOOD

COLOUR

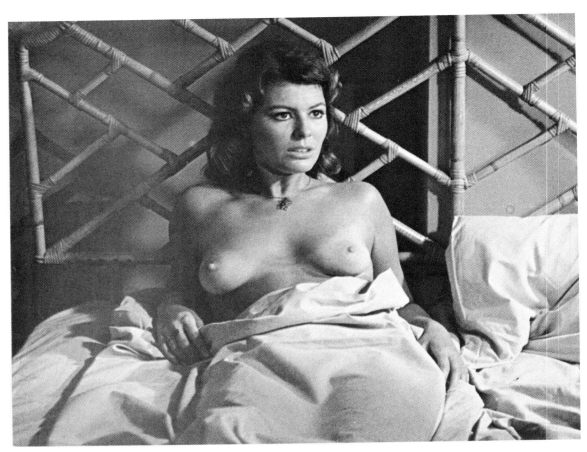

*An artistically valid still
from* **House of Whipcord.**

was unable to complete the screenplay. Walker showed me Shaughnessy's first twenty pages of dialogue and a synopsis of the rest of the plot. To my delight, it was the kind of screenplay I'd been longing to write. My diary entry for 16 March 1973 read, 'Surprisingly I rather like it. It's nightmarish horror which unfortunately degenerates towards the end into standard chase thriller. I want to change that.'

Walker soon made it clear that I was not required to change anything. For £200 I would flesh out the plot as it stood, and preferably by the end of next week. So that's what I did. The job took exactly two weeks, longer than I expected, but simultaneously I was directing a stage play and appearing in *Albert's Follies*.

I delivered the completed manuscript to Walker's Esher mansion. After reading it, he decided that he wanted to simplify the climax and add extra scenes. I wrote them in a few hours, Walker accepted them and had the script printed. My screenplay was filmed virtually word-for-word as I typed it, an experience that was to be repeated every time I worked for him. No other director had more respect for the script, and writing for Pete Walker spoiled me for life.

The casting for Walker's films always followed the same pattern. He was besotted by the screen goddesses he grew up watching in the '40s and his first move would always be to try and tempt Peggy Cummins, Pat Kirkwood, Susan Shaw, Sandra Dorne and suchlike into making comebacks. According to Walker, there was always some kind of snag that prevented him signing them. I expect they wanted too much money. Right up until a week before shooting was due to start, Peter Cushing, Trevor Howard and Jack Palance always wanted to play major roles. Then they would mysteriously drop out and we would be left with Patrick Barr,

Gerald Flood and Anthony Sharp.

Walker always offered the young male lead to Ray Brooks, who was hot in the early '60s because of *The Knack* and *Cathy Come Home*, but had since taken a tumble and had no better offers than Walker's. He was undeniably good and Walker didn't seem to know who else to try when Brooks began turning him down. He had a keener eye for young actresses and went on to make wise choices with Susan Penhaligon, Stephanie Beacham and Lynn Frederick.

Walker's casting for *House of Whipcord* makes it the only one of my films I can still watch today. The actors' names didn't bring in a penny, but I thought they were all wonderful and they never changed so much as a comma. Walker's chief discovery was Scottish character actress Sheila Keith, who played - I suppose it was an in-joke - Walker, the sadistic lesbian prison wardress. In an attempt to establish her as a British horror queen, Pete Walker put her in another four of his films, but no other director saw her in the same light, and Sheila Keith returned to playing magistrates in TV sitcoms.

I was glad I didn't have the responsibility of finding a location to double as a prison. The eventual solution was to shoot the interior in a disused asylum in South London. The exterior was a private residence a hundred miles away in the Forest of Dean. When I first saw the film, I thought that the brooding atmosphere created in these locations by Walker and his tiny crew of regular collaborators was almost harrowing.

Once again I wrote myself a part, this time one that required me to be on the set for three or four days. Everything Walker did - or didn't do - fascinated me. He was the fastest director I had ever encountered. On my first day I was in and out of make-up, went on to the set and finished an entire scene by 10.00am. Walker was an equal opportunities employer - he was rude to everyone. "All actors are egotistical poofs and all actresses are pompous prostitutes," he informed me. The crew called him "sir." He seemed to know a lot about lenses and focal lengths, which baffled me.

What his direction consisted of, however, was hard to pin down. He rarely told his actors anything apart from where to move. And he followed the script to the letter, even down to the camera angles. Nowadays I tell budding screenwriters not to include camera directions because directors don't want this kind of advice. But Walker never told me to stick to writing dialogue. If I scripted a scene from a low angle through a window, that was how it was shot.

And yet Walker must have been doing something. No matter who wrote the script, his films are instantly recognisable from the first scene. His way with suburban menace is uniquely his own. He was in fact a model director, slick and efficient and exerting a subtle influence to get what he wanted.

Shot in four weeks, *House of Whipcord* was whipped through post-production at a similar pace. It was cut, dubbed and scored in just over three months. Only one piece of additional material was shot. Walker needed some rats for the solitary confinement cell. Ray Selfe hired three from his local pet shop and we filmed them in somebody's garage.

The first preview was just over three weeks later. Walker reported that Stephen Murphy, lenient Secretary of the British Board of Film Censors (he allowed both *Straw Dogs* and *A Clockwork Orange*) wanted the whipping scenes 'reduced'. Eventually the film was passed with one token cut (a whiplash). Today its distribution on video in this country is forbidden.

Apparently Murphy saw *House of Whipcord* as an attack on the Festival of Light, a vociferous group of moral reformers. He thought the prison governess, Mrs Wakehurst, was in reality Mary Whitehouse and that her blind, senile husband, Justice Bailey, was anti-porn campaigner Lord Longford. This was news to me. Walker hoped that others might jump to the same

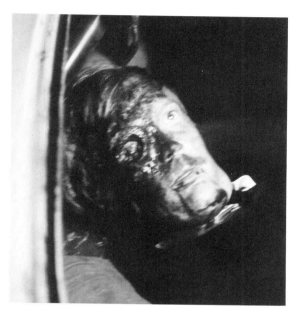

(Above left) A victim from **Frightmare**.

(Below left) The inmates are revolting in **House of Whipcord**.

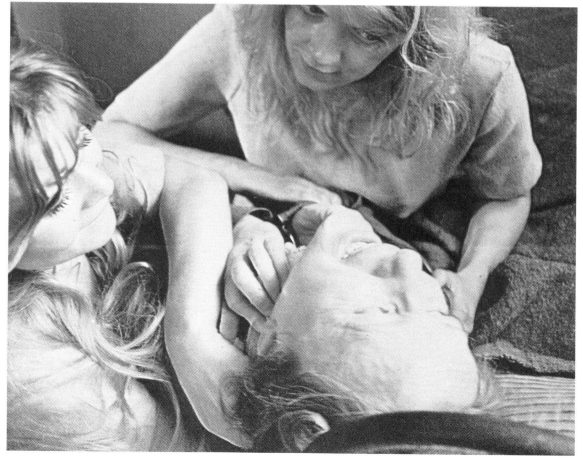

mistaken conclusion and egged them on by adding a title before the main credits: 'This film is dedicated to those who are disturbed by today's lax moral codes and who eagerly await the return of corporal and capital punishment...'

When a couple of intellectual critics swallowed the bait (Tony Rayns thought that 'House of Whipcord charts the dark side of the Festival of Light with a pop-Freud vengeance') I seriously thought in my naivety that this lurid shocker would rock the world. Fat chance. Russell Davies in *The Observer* summed up the opposing view when he dismissed the film as 'a feeble fladge-fantasy' and, after a good opening at the London Pavilion, takings fell off. What a thrill, however, to have my name plastered all over the cinema that had first fired my boyish imagination. It's a shopping mall now.

While *House of Whipcord* was still shooting, Walker told me to come up with an idea for another film, something "to hang your coat on." I hadn't got a clue. Opportunely my sound recordist friend Godfrey Kirby dropped by. He drew my attention to a current shock-horror story in the newspapers: apparently survivors from an aeroplane crash in the Andes had stayed alive by eating the nutritious brains of their dead companions.

I telephoned Pete Walker and said, "Cannibalism."

He loved it and began designing a poster. You must remember that this was 1973, seven years before the cannibal holocaust of the early '80s. On 20 July he set up a screening of one of his favourite *film noirs*. It was *Build My Gallows High* starring Robert Mitchum. Walker was intrigued by the character played by Jane Greer: seemingly innocent and charming, she's actually cunning and unscrupulous.

Over lunch we tried to tie the two ideas together and an embryonic plot took shape before dessert. My diary entry for that day: 'The story concerns an apparently innocent and charming girl who is in fact killing men for her mad cannibal mother to eat. It's outrageous enough to be another winner. Sheila Keith will be the mother.'

Briefly titled *Covered in Blood*, the film was shot as *Nightmare Farm* and released as *Frightmare*. The main object of this exercise was to be nastier than *House of Whipcord* and some people felt we succeeded. I think that, up until that time, no one in a British film had ever had his head drilled open so that his brains could be extracted.

The story was so ridiculous that it took a very long time to instil it with any credibility. By December, time was running out and Walker had instructed me to "just start writing." We made up the story as I went along and five days before I reached the last page I still didn't know how it was going to end.

The plot formulated at the first script conference over lunch in July evolved thus: apparently innocent and charming Jackie tries to satisfy her Mum's abnormal cravings by supplying her with pig's brains purchased at the butcher. On the quiet, however, Mum is enticing human victims to her nightmare farm by advertising in *Time Out* as a tarot card reader. (The plug for the London listings magazine *was* an in-joke. Simultaneously I was earning £6 per day compiling their film section.)

Packed into my customary fourteen day writing schedule were my customary attempts at in-depth research. I telephoned the National Association for Mental Health and asked if there was any such condition as pathological cannibalism. I was told there wasn't. I had no option but to invent it and even coined a non-existent medical term, 'caribanthropy', to describe it. I also had no idea how Mum was going to get the brains out of her victims' heads. I asked a nurse and she told me about a surgical saw called a trephine used for brain operations. This inspired me to come up with the Black and Decker wielded so memorably by Sheila Keith, the screen's first driller killer.

At first *Frightmare* was going to take place in a fairground because Walker and I both love them. This was soon rejected as impractical, but I was allowed to use a fairground for the prologue, in which Andrew Sachs (later to become Manuel in *Fawlty Towers*) meets a messy end. The main locale was first changed to an out-of-season holiday camp and finally to a farmhouse in Hazlemere, Surrey, which was more suited to Walker's budget.

As with *Whipcord*, Walker was lucky to find the perfect, sinister setting. It was the archetypal House That Dripped Blood and the art director didn't have to change a lampshade. Even the gargoyle-like plaques on the walls were *in situ*. I hung around the set, observing Sheila Keith sitting in corners practising her mad glints, and once again I thought we were going to give people the screaming habdabs.

Once again we didn't. It was partially my fault for

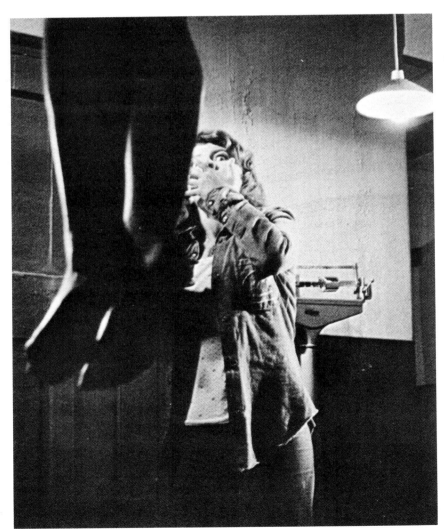

House of Whipcord - 'a feeble fladge-fantasy' (The Observer).

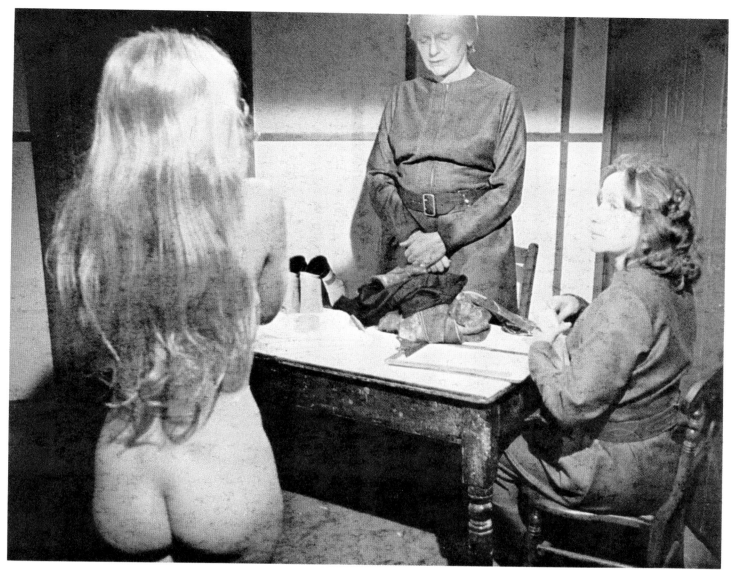

putting in too many chatty scenes in flats and streets. Later I saw the film in a deserted cinema in Victoria and was mortified to hear somebody behind me say to his friend, "Slow, isn't it?" But I also felt that Walker was defeated by his breakneck three week, four day schedule. This time I wished he'd given himself more time to crank up the tension.

As always, 'sir' would brook no criticism. He told me it was the best thing he'd ever done. Down the years many of his followers have agreed. But at the time *Frightmare* was a tough film to sell. During production Walker thought he might advertise it as 'An everyday story of country folk', but later chickened out of such a soft sell. I wanted to put a caption on the poster reading, 'When you find out what Dorothy does with this drill...don't tell your friends!' Walker wasn't having any of that. He said that graffiti artists would scrawl underneath, "She sticks it up her snatch."

When *Frightmare* was released in London at the end of 1974, the critics slaughtered it. In a long article headed 'What are stars like these (*a reference to Leo Genn and Rupert 'Maigret' Davies*) doing in trash like this?', Fergus Cashin in *The Sun* branded the film 'disgusting, repulsive, nauseating rubbish.' He quoted liberally from my 1971 interview with Walker, which had just been print-

ed, three years late, in *Films & Filming* magazine. Taken out of context, Walker's remarks made him appear a stupid, talentless hypocrite.

At eight o'clock on the morning the newspaper came out, I was awoken by a phone call. It was Walker and he was furious. "I don't deserve this treatment," he whimpered with some justification. I tried to save the day by pointing out that words like 'disgusting' and 'repulsive' wouldn't necessarily deter the film's target audience.

Later he agreed to my suggestion to take out a brash advertisement in the evening papers that listed every pejorative comment made about *Frightmare*. It made an awesome sight: 'Nasty... horrible... repellent... despicable... gruesome... a moral obscenity...' Surely that would do the trick? Today it might. But not in 1974. On 24 December the take at the 1,186 seat London Pavilion was £23.

Certainly *Frightmare* was not an ideal Christmas attraction. But its failure, coupled with the tiff with my employer, made me concerned that I'd blown it already. I hadn't. There were another seventeen screenplays to come. ∎

(To be continued)

Smut.

BLACKBOARD JUNGLES
AND LIBERATED LATRINES

SOME WRITINGS

BY GEORGE KUCHAR

Named as a major influence by John Waters ("I decided to make films after I saw his early movies... [George Kuchar] made 'cheesy' an art form."), George Kuchar was born in Manhattan in 1942. With his twin brother Mike (one hour older than George) he began making 8mm movies on their apartment block roof and in their Bronx neighbourhood, using old curtains for costumes and friends as stars. By 1965 the brothers' different approaches to cinema led them to split. As director, writer, photographer, editor and producer George has make over fifty films in 8mm and 16mm. Since the mid-80s he has also worked in video, producing over forty titles.

Portrait of the artist as, oh, something or other...

Growing Up in the Bronx

The only person who ever told me that I was lucky to have grown up in the Bronx was a famous and well respected director of big budget movies. He was premièring his newest film which dealt with exactly that topic and I had the fortune to chat with him at a reception highlighting the opening of the Mill Valley Film Festival. His movie was a sellout. My show featured one of the most spectacular examples of unoccupied seating I had ever witnessed. While addressing that vacant cavern I stood behind a podium that towered above a floral arrangement like a vertical coffin that had just expelled its tenant - me! Oh well, the ticket price was kind of steep...two dollars more than it cost to see that other stiff, King Tut, who was being exhibited in San Francisco at the time.

Let me not sip at these sour grapes any longer but continue my narrative about growing up in the Bronx.

The director had told me, while we imbibed wine and nibbled on cheese, that he envied me for maturing into manhood during the '50s in the only New York borough attached to the US mainland. Whether I had ever reached manhood in this borough or anywhere else is still a hotly debated question, with maybe only a few hairdressers knowing for sure; but I thanked him and we talked freely, as the cheese was not that awful, foul-smelling garbage usually served at these functions and so I felt free to open my mouth real wide and issue coherent sounds. I did not tell him the whole story, such as how I was treated like a leper

in that borough because of my hefty buttocks and pyramidal pectorals softly mounded in white meat - attributes (?) I acquired by noshing on kosher franks and kasha knishes. How could I tell him that my body was looked upon as an example of baby fat being ravaged by dermatological disasters and unsightly erections below the belt? Even the hair on my head was not immune to scorn, being compared to a Brillo pad, or, when uncut for some time, to the bristles on a toilet brush. Friends would tell me that I had legs like a horse and something that looked like a spare tire around my waist. Is it any wonder that I spent most of my youth tucked away in the dark sanctity of neighbourhood movie houses getting lost in a shifting mosaic of lean males with non-flapping pectorals and rear-ends that kept a low profile as if in respect to the big assed, leading ladies? The starlets were free to puff-up their attributes but I had to sit on mine and hope that all those hours in a theatre seat would flatten it out. It was during those turbulent times that I realised my only chance to be an actor was if I was willing to be a nude stand-in for the actress whenever a rear shot was needed to show an exposed butt. In fact, I had actually done this in an 8mm movie my brother directed: I donned a wig and a dress worn by the girl in the movie and did her nude scene, as she would never have permitted my brother to shoot her in this condition. The friend who told me that I had legs like a horse saw that film and became enraptured by all the extravagant, voluptuous meat - my meat, not hers, only he didn't know that! Well, I eventually told him who it was up there on the screen and the guy turned beet red. It was then that I realised that in another dimension or medium the flesh God gave me was not a curse...but a temptation to the self-righteous and a damnation to the chaste.

Art World Exposure

While very young I was given paper and pencil by my mother and told to have fun. In the ensuing years I developed a drawing style, comic book in nature, and depicted our neighbours being mowed down by machine gun fire or pushed out of sixth floor windows. With this talent I eventually gained admission to a vocational art school in Manhattan that specialised in commercial art. Fine art was frowned upon as a wonderful idealism that led to starvation. I remember one morning sitting in class and the teacher reading a synopsis of Paul Gauguin's life. The grossly abbreviated traumas he endured in that synopsis had us all rolling in the aisles with laughter: surely it would be better to rot away in some advertising art office than to get a Polynesian social disease and then botch-up a suicide attempt! To we students, art museums were some place you never got into with your work unless the suicide was successful.

Vocational art high school, to me, was nothing more than a crucible of white hot puberty with the greatest creative impulses centred in the region of the genitals. What my hands created was labelled mediocre. What that other part of me generated was never even discussed. There was only one student, in my opinion, who unconsciously understood all this. He was a soft, somewhat effeminate black boy and he'd sit all day in class erasing the clothes of newsworthy individuals whose photographs were reproduced on newsprint paper - the surface rubbing off easily with strokes from a pink pencil eraser. With the other end of that pencil he'd fill in a voluptuous and unabashed rendition of what, hopefully, was under those clothes. The serenity and composure of that black youth was inspirational to behold.

During all those years of vocational art training - and the following winters of discontent in the commercial art world itself - I kept making movies...8mm dramas that I financed with paychecks from hell. It was through these movies, and not suicide, that museums opened their doors to my visual work, displaying the fruits of my labour on a canvas of beaded or lenticular material reflective to light. Those years in school and in the world of the working-dead had fanned the flames of frustration into a raging inferno hot enough to boil over whatever simmered, unfulfilled, in the depths of George Kuchar. My contemporaries did not desire me in the flesh, the flesh being too loosely distributed on an ungainly frame. They desired the handiwork of that flesh. It was because of this handiwork that the doors to their bedrooms opened allowing me to enter with an unzipped camera case and a dangling light meter. Through the twin, cyclopian eyes of camera and projector a stereoscopic view of libidinous dimensions came into focus; a view perhaps best left myopic by obscure symbolism and heavy diffusion filters. The actual living man behind the camera was only desired by dark strangers who populated the shadow world of Beelzebub's bestialised buggers. It was into this world that the man behind the camera

plunged...in a nose-diving suicide mission of drugs and doughnuts, culminating with a crash on the Pacific coast as a California pervert.

Holding this photo in front of a mirror and looking at it over your shoulder will cause hidden Satanic messages to appear. Honest.

California Concoctions

In the early '70s I was offered a teaching position as film instructor at a California art college. My last movie, made in New York, was like a desperate scream for help and so I knew that it was time to move on and enter a new phase - however frightful this might turn out to be. Well, it turned out that biggish buttocks and knish-bloated derma were considered erotically stimulating in the city of San Francisco. My West Coast career was off to a good start!

Young people in this city by the bay were aiming their movie cameras at exposed chakras left and right as the sexual revolution was in full swing at that time. This was fine with me as it made sitting through their films that much more enjoyable. One quiet youth used to screen his super 8mm movies in my morning class and we'd all munch on croissants and sip coffee while we watched his latest epic on how to play with your pecker in 101 ways.

Students would come to talk with me about cinema, articulating expressively in the air with long, purple fingernails - these were just the male students. One female in my class was up on the silver screen being sodomised by a latex novelty while indulging in a

(Right) George consults his **Good Enema Guide to San Francisco!**

(Below) Artwork by George.

4 **BIG** PROGRAMS of **ACTION** and **ROMANCE**

GEORGE **KUCHAR** FILMS

MOVIES made with his students at the **SAN FRANCISCO ART INSTITUTE**

coke of non-carbonated powder. The person on the other end of that rubberised protrusion was a female classmate of lesbian persuasion obeying the direction of a unisexed, university urchin who looked like Hermaphroditos incarnated.

Eventually I fell victim (happily) to this quagmire of heaving and humping viscosity and embarked on an orgy of flesh-debasing delinquency that knew no bounds. A youth who admired my cleavage whenever I bent over too far in the classroom became my part-time partner in these escapades and we both fed off the sweat of each other's genitalian gyrations. It was not only a vicious circle but a concubined cube, a testicled triangle and a rectumised rectangle of abstruse abscesses.

The students, curious about the effects of chemical pollution in frumpy faculty, would inject me with psychedelic substances powerful enough to subjugate schizoid pachyderms. I found myself groping indiscriminately in a twilight zone of blackboard jungles and liberated latrines, unable to find what was me and what was my partner. It was during those turbulent times that I produced the bulk of my California motion pictures (1973-1976).

When, much to my horror, a clearer image of the real me emerged from the steam and cigarette smoke my first instinct was to reach for an enema bag. Fortunately there were enough degenerates in this Californian city to handle that nauseating chore for me. I recovered, refreshed to some extent, but then almost immediately fell victim to a cosmic caper that resurrected once again the deities and superstitions I thought I had buried in the rubble of my shattered Christian faith: on the surface it looked like Earth versus the flying saucers but deep underneath, in the now evacuated bowels of my being, it spelled the rebirth of my religious life as another dimension opened its crack and a ton of shit hit the fan!

Tips on Directing

In directing narrative, underground films it is important not to be well prepared: the reason being that when you witness your well thought-out plans degenerate to utter chaos the tendency to throw a temper tantrum becomes very great. As a film director I am usually a fun-loving human being; as a man I am a wretched and obscene creature...a creature of perverted instincts and revolting hungers. Save all these drawbacks for the characters you create for the screen, as once they are projected these flaws become 'big box office potential'. In being unprepared you are never sure of what you are going to do and the sudden chance for discovery and inspiration becomes greater. If this creative spring does not start flowing or suddenly dries up, just excuse yourself from the set by stating that you have to go to the bathroom. Once in there, get your 'shit together', as they say.

If you develop a stock company of actors they eventually become familiar with your quirks and no longer beg for morsels of character motivation and plot development: "Just tell me what to do" becomes the most commonly heard phrase. Then you tell them what to do and you act it out. God forbid that they should follow you to the letter! An actress from Brooklyn once mimicked me exactly and it was like looking at a National Geographic TV special on autistic chimps.

Never have auditions for actors. If you like the way they look, use them. As for acting, well, if they stink just have the person stand around in a stylised pose. To be turned down and judged as rotten for a creative project is a very painful experience. It is better to have a rotten picture than a trail of tears shed by a rejected human being. But, if they really are awful, there can always be a sudden plot twist featuring a hit-and-run accident, a freak bolt of lightning, a carelessly flung banana peel, etc.

If a performer's thighs are too textured with cellulite, light the offending limb with a combination of Marlene Dietrich and Bela Lugosi lighting: one bright spot aimed down from on high, the other blasting upward from a low angle. If the performer needs a face-lift, hang the person upside down while doing close-ups. Gravity will then do the job of pulling all that meat scalpward.

Never dress your stars in the current fashion mode. Always mix styles in reckless abandon, as this way your film will never become dated but will retain a sort of ambiguous freshness. If material is hard to come by, plastic trash bags make very futuristic gowns when used sparingly. Unfortunately the subjects sweat heavily under the hot lights and if you're shooting in sync-sound there's all this squeaking and razzing noise when they bend down.

Make-up should be used to full advantage. In black and white filming, instead of administering red lipstick, use an eyebrow pencil and colour the lips black as sometimes red goes light, especially if you are using an orange or red filter in the camera. Of course black lips can be used in colour shooting too if the character is a victim of strangulation. When a performer has difficulty in expressing emotions, these emotions can be drawn on the face by changing the contours of the eyebrows for each scene. The edges of the mouth can also be painted either up or down. If an actor has badly spaced teeth, a strip of glossy, white cardboard can be inserted into the mouth producing a dazzling smile when the lips are parted. Trouble develops when the performer has to recite dialogue; in that case the trick only works if the person is portraying a stroke victim.

Yes, all this information is offensive. Please excuse me, but making movies can be a pretty offensive and humiliating endeavour. But I think it is a lot better than being a creature in the jungles, because whenever I watch documentaries on the natural world it turns my stomach! All these bugs are climbing out of their flaky skins, laying eggs in manure, while these blistered reptiles chomp on gummy bubbles filled with palpitating tadpoles. It is enough to make you sick and appreciate your own obnoxious secretions...be they celluloid or otherwise.

Editing

Many films are 'made' in the editing room and it is a very fascinating part of film-making. It is not easy to sit for twenty-four hours at a time while editing picture and sound so that image and audio are married for ever after. Because of the ensuing artistic pressure, the sweat glands exude a particularly overbearing stench (which smells like an odd mixture of apricots and old nylon stockings). Always have incense in your carrying case and matches handy as visitors to your editing station are a distinct possibility. Socks should be fresh also, as

shoes are discarded early on in the editing process. Acne is an ever threatening event due to long hours in a dark, stagnant cubicle. The urge to pick at the acne is quite strong, especially during crisis periods when the decision for a proper cut must be made. Keep your hands away from your face or you will come out of the room with hideous, bleeding sores along with the sickening stench previously noted.

Never edit your film while wearing those flimsy, white editing gloves. You should touch the processed film stock as much as possible with bare hands - hoping that more of yourself will rub onto the project. Of course, when you are working in negative film you do have to edit it with gloves and work in a dust-free room. Since the only gloves I have are heavy duty rubber ones, for use in wringing out a floor mop, and being that dust settles on my furniture like manna from heaven, I think that working in negative is ridiculous. Not that I am that much of a filthy individual. Yes, I have pride in my home and in my personal attire but never forget that dirtiness was, in times of old, a sign of great holiness. There was once a saint whose presence was detected by olfactory nerves way before his image appeared on the retina. The sense of smell has always featured strongly in the world of international cinema. The smell of buttered popcorn and wet umbrellas in theatre lobbies. The

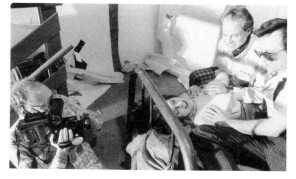

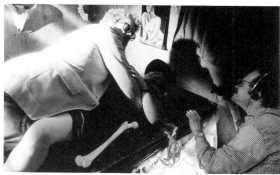

I'm afraid that you, the reader, must supply your own captions for these photos...

George (left) and Mike Kuchar, with a painting by George.

you have a mate already, undoubtedly he or she will feel neglected if you spend too much time on your film project; so, in order to concentrate and be a film-maker, you'll have to be a really miserable and unhappy person, preferably castrated, and someone who likes boiled chicken and potatoes.

An inferiority complex helps because you will then have a desire to struggle against all odds in order to create something superior; something that will put you on the map of human culture. A fetish comes in handy too and proves to be an incentive for many elaborate shots. A dirty bed helps keep you working late because who wants to retire on stained, gummy linen?

If you are a male homosexual and have a lover who edits film also, never visit him at his editing station after swimming in a municipal pool. The heavily chlorinated water causes your hands to smell like semen and the hard-working editor freaks out thinking that you have been fooling around while he slaves over a hot splicer.

Music helps in concentration but avoid a disco beat like the plague! The jackhammer beat is designed for movements below the waist and the musicians mix in Satanic messages, in reverse, under that beat. Not only will you find your pelvis jerking uncontrollably, but, if someone foolishly interrupts what you are doing that person is likely to have his jugular vein ripped out.

It is no good trying to concentrate when your body is poisoned with either tobacco, drugs or alcohol. Before working, check into a public sauna and steam room. You'll work up a good sweat fighting off all the groping perverts and in no time at all concentration will be clearer than ever. Sometimes the reverse is true and you must debase and poison yourself in order to break down intellectual and spiritual constipation. I really don't know why this is so except maybe that we need depravity and spiritual filth for mental health reasons. You might as well bring it all to the surface every once in a while and face the demons. In either case, get the poisons out of your system the next day and maybe say the Rosary for good measure.

What has all this to do with film-making? Well, perhaps a great deal, as making movies is a magical enterprise and you will be exorcising a lot of personal devils and charting your own perversities. Speaking of devils: did I ever tell you about the time I was almost possessed by something horribly evil? Well, it happened while I was washing underwear, I believe. My hands were in the water and wringing out the garments when suddenly what seemed to be the real me - the essence of what I knew to be George Kuchar - shrunk inside the centre of my head and appeared to be just two, tiny eyes encased in a cavernous skull that was part of a huge body washing underwear (although at that point I lost all physical sensation and could not feel the water). My body was suddenly an unguarded shell and to my horror I realised that something monstrous and evil, something invisible, was now beginning to press into it from outside. I felt absolutely helpless against this penetrating onslaught and began to panic as it dawned on me that whatever was about to take over my body had a lust for murder via a serrated bread knife. The panic caused my heart to beat wildly as I fought the intruder. My fear was very great, but in a matter of seconds I seemed to gain control once again and the real me began to reoccupy the body - pushing out the alien force. Dear Lord, protect us from things that go bump in the night when we do our laundry. Amen. ■

aroma of that chunk of solid deodoriser that lay at the bottom of urinals as you take aim and splash yellow. The sweet, sticky smell and feel of Coca Cola underfoot as you try and make it to your seat amid the sucking sounds produced as leather soles pull free of muck. The dizzying perfume of lacquered hair that obscures whole areas of screen in a mound worthy of a home for African termites. The ever faint, ever threatening cloud of released flatulence that attempts to pull you back to reality just as movie magic begins to weave its spell. All these, and more, make up the moviegoing experience.

How to Concentrate

In order to buckle down and get to work on your project you'll have to try various techniques to focus your energies. It helps if you live in a boring environment and there are just reruns on television. Too many friends are not advisable because they always want to come over and chew the fat. If you eat an excess of hot and spicy foods you'll always be horny and want to go out and mate with what's available. If

GEORGE KUCHAR:
Selected filmography

1957: The Naked and the Nude
(with Mike Kuchar)

Screwball (with Mike Kuchar)

1958: The Slasher (with Mike Kuchar)

1959: The Thief and the Stripper
(with Mike Kuchar)

1960: I Was a Teenage Rumpot
(with Mike Kuchar)

A Tub Named Desire (with
Mike Kuchar)

1961: Pussy on a Hot Tin Roof (with
Mike Kuchar)

1962: A Town Called Tempest

1963: Lust for Ecstasy (with Mike
Kuchar)

Tootsies in Autumn (with
Mike Kuchar)

1965: Corruption of the Damned

1966: Hold Me While I'm Naked

1967: Eclipse of the Sun Virgin

Color Me Shameless

1968: House of the White People

Encyclopedia of the Blessed

1969: The Mammal Palace

1970: Pagan Rhapsody

1971: Portrait of Ramona

1972: The Sunshine Sisters

Destination Damnation

1973: Devil's Cleavage

Carnal Bipeds

1974: I Married a Heathen

1975: The Desperate and the Deep
Thundercrack (actor only)

1976: A Reason to Live

Nudes (actor only)

Weiners and Buns Musical
(actor only)

1977: Wild Night in El Reno

KY Kapers

I, An Actress

1978: Forever and Always

The Mongreloid

1979: Symphony for a Sinner

Blips

1980: The Woman and the Dress

Aqueerius

1981: Yolanda

1982: The Oneers

1983: Ms Hyde

Cattle Mutilations

Mom

1984: The X-People

Club Vatican

Screamplay (actor only)

1985: Ascension of the Demonoids

1986: The Legend of Thelma White

Motel Capri

PRC Musical

1987: Insanitorium

1988: Summer of No Return

(Left) Hold Me While
I'm Naked.

Connoisseur have compiled *Hold Me While I'm
Naked, The Mongreloid, Forever and Always* and *A
Reason to Live* onto a video entitled *Color Me Lurid.*

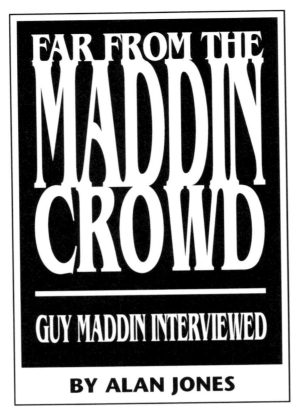

FAR FROM THE MADDIN CROWD

GUY MADDIN INTERVIEWED

BY ALAN JONES

He's been called the Canadian Jean Cocteau, David Lynch's bastard Russian son and the new Bunuel by way of Eisenstein. Guy Maddin has only directed two and a half movies to date but his unclassifiable slices of tortured realism have made him the hottest name on America's Midnight Movie cult circuit. Words simply cannot do justice to this thirty-two year-old's unique body of work. The half-hour short *The Dead Father* (1987), and his two twisted features, *Tales from the Gimli Hospital* (1988) and *Archangel* (1990), are 'silence is golden' surreal tapestries of precisely pitched tableaux blending absurdist satire, warped horror, eccentric gore and wrenching melodrama to fashion directional new forms of macabre intensity in the magical process.

Maddin's trademark brand of eerie silent movie nostalgia and expressionist symbolism, strained through a contemporary filter of '90s awareness, is very much an acquired taste. Apart from Lynch and Tim Burton, he's the sole purveyor of off-off-mainstream non-conformity at work in the industry today. A wilfully unconventional director, although he'll argue the contrary, Maddin's grudging destiny would seem to be shaking up the staleness the no-budget, low-rent amateur arena has slowly slid into since the advent of video. That Maddin is the most exciting individual to make weird and wonderful cinematic waves in over a decade is without question. So too is unshakeable global opinion that his stature and importance will keep growing. For each mind-boggling ball of confusion contains enough of his unique simplicity, chilling charm, dizzying dynamics and brain-scorching imagery to make each lovingly wrought miniature an exquisitely hypnotic work of art. Fasten your seatbelts for a twin peek at Maddin's mad, mad, mad, mad world.

Tales from the Gimli Hospital

At a hospital in the small Canadian town of Gimli, an elderly woman tells a story to her grandchildren as they wait for their mother to die. It tells of two men, Gunnar (Michael Gottli) and Enair (Kyle McCulloch), affected by an unspecified epidemic at the turn of the century. Both men share the same hospital room and Gunnar tells Enair a dark secret about how he 'murdered' his beautiful bride Snjofridur (Angela Heck) by passing her the deadly plague during their courtship. Enair has a tale to tell about Gunnar's wife too. But his shocking story will both unite them in grief and eventually make them sworn enemies.

SX: Did you purposely set out to make a cult movie?

GM: No, I just made it really. I shot it at weekends spread over a few months. Sometimes I got bored and didn't film for a while, and I was very relaxed and informal in my approach. It was the easiest film-making experience I'll probably ever have. I didn't have any market in mind as I come from Winnipeg where

there's a tiny film community and, when I started making *Tales*, no homegrown films were being shown outside the city. So I had no intention of pushing it anywhere. I just wanted to make a home movie my friends could be in and see. People ask me if it's a massive put-on or a serious movie. All I can say is whenever I see a movie that amuses me, the more straight-faced it is, the better.

SX: *Tales* makes provocative use of necrophilia, Icelandic myths, AIDS, synchronised dance routines, anaesthesia by glove puppet, surgery by scythe, tinted black and white photography and all manner of silent movie icon madness...

GM: I was always forced to spend teenage summers in Nordic communities to understand my heritage. I would attend speeches given by Icelandic elderly women elected as Festival maidens. *Tales* is my revenge on those people and so is the buttock wrestling. That's part of Icelandic culture and the object is to hoist your opponent up with all sorts of nimble foot movements required of the combatants. My actors couldn't do any of those so they just grabbed and hugged each other warmly. The movie ends with an Icelandic diplomat's speech about the evils of drink. Well I think that's what it is anyway! When I was scoring the movie I decided the only music I wanted for that scene was bagpipes. Don't ask me why, I just felt in a Scottish mood! I got synchronised swimming out of my system the same way too, as I love going to swimming pools to watch teams practise. *Tales* was invited to the Reykjavik Film Festival. I've heard nothing since but I'm probably excommunicated and my picture is a wanted poster at all Icelandic airports!

SX: What about the many references to fish?

GM: The actual town of Gimli in Manitoba is a good old middle-of-the-prairies fishing village. They are fish crazy and seafood is served with everything including Christmas dinner! I didn't go out of my way to include all the fish. It's part of the Gimli culture. In truth I tried to cut most of the fish references down but somehow they remain to the fore.

SX: Why did you decide on the silent movie form?

GM: I've always liked the minimalist style. My favourite kind of movie is the curious part-talkie genre. You know, the ones made in December 1927. *The Jazz Singer* opened in November and directors scrambled to add soundtracks to catch the new wave. I always liked dialogue in the form of quickly shot monologues. I'm charmed by the free movement back and forth between the, then, new and old mediums. It was a far simpler process for a beginner to handle too. I would have done exactly the same if I'd had a million dollars.

SX: *Tales* practically represents the whole history

(Above) Michael Gottli as Gunnar in **Tales from the Gimli Hospital.**

(Opposite page) *Guy Maddin.*

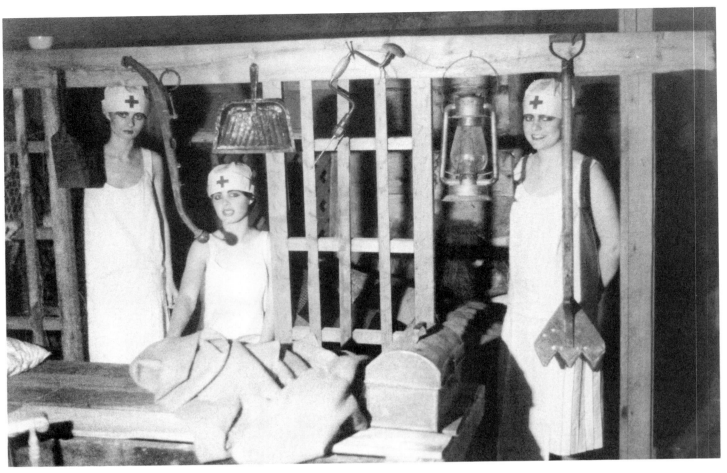

of cinema thrown into seventy-two minutes as a result.

GM: I'm not against modernism, I just found myself returning to the wonderful world of the past time and time again as I had access to this great film archive at Winnipeg University. I watched old movies constantly and *M, Birth of a Nation* and D.W. Griffith homages are all included in *Tales*. I'm totally sick of modern cinema and I just made what came naturally. Since I hadn't seen a colour movie for three years at the point I made *Tales*, the language and rhythm of silent black and white features came as second nature. I liked tinting the print to alter the mood indicating a change in emotion - a heavy influence from Griffith's *Broken Blossoms*. I'm glad the film looks about sixty years old. In many ways I wish it looked older. For some late night engagements the 16mm print has been blown up to 35mm. Funnily enough it works even better as it's scratchier and grainier. One reviewer said *Tales* looked like rotting images of past cinema. And, boy, in the 35mm version, does it look it!

SX: Kyle McCulloch plays a dual role in black face. Is that another nostalgic throwback to the past?

GM: I'm glad audiences are seeing it as nostalgia. It's an uncomfortable convention, one I've always liked. I've never thought about it until now but I suppose it could be another connection to *The Jazz Singer*. Kyle insisted he wanted to play a part in black face as well as the Enair character. Just do it, he said, and then decide later if you want to keep it. So I did. It was a potentially touchy subject but no one's ever complained.

SX: Have you had any formal film school training?

GM: No, I just worked in a bank one day and quit the next to fool around with a camera. I've been a film-maker for three and a half years now but only recently could I look my Mom in the eye and say, "I'm a director." Now she won't talk to me!

SX: Another major *Tales* influence is your love of vintage music.

GM: I'm a huge buff. Old 78rpm records are full of mysterious scratchy layers and often you can never get through them to actually hear the performers underneath. This creates a really strange world for me. When you're working with low budgets you need all the help you can get to create an ethereal netherworld. I was happy to recruit it by proxy from my scratchy record library.

SX: You hint at there being many more *Tales from the Gimli Hospital* to tell.

GM: I actually hope it doesn't come to that although I may get desperate. Certainly there are a million Icelandic myths to investigate. But with any luck you won't see them!

SX: You say you made the movie solely as a calling card to make new friends?

GM: And it worked! I made *Tales* in 1988 and Ben Bazenholtz saw it. He was the man who distributed *Eraserhead* and he immediately put it into the Quad cinema in New York. It is still doing very well and across America audiences keep growing. I'm pleased *Tales* has found any place at all in today's theatrical market. Let's be realistic - it hardly threatens *The Rocky Horror Picture Show* in terms of Midnight Movie greatness. Throwing fish at the screen is bound to upset the theatre owners! But I can still remember sitting all alone at the editing

table dreaming of the best and worst possible things that could happen with *Tales*. And the best happened surpassing all my wildest dreams.

Archangel

During the Bolshevik Revolution in the Russian city of Archangel, the love lives of three people unfold whose senses have been afflicted by severe memory disorders due to mustard gas apoplexy. Dashing one-legged Canadian Lt Boles (Kyle McCulloch) is in love with Iris. But she's dead and when he meets Soviet nurse Veronkha (Kathy Marykuca) he assumes she's his late beloved. Unfortunately Veronkha is already married to Belgian pilot Philbin (Ari Cohen) who keeps forgetting this fact. And Veronkha, assuming Boles is Philbin, falls deeper in love with him. Then landlady Danchuk (Sarah Neville) falls for Boles too, so disgusted is she with the behaviour of her obese husband Jannings (Michael Gottli). Which woman does Boles love or lust after the most - Veronkha, Danchuk or Iris? Guided by an ancient treasure map where X marks the spot for retro romance, Boles hopes his terminal catatonia will eventually defog to unearth the epic answer.

SX: As *Tales* slowly built late night word of mouth throughout the summer of 1989 you made *Archangel*. Was it easy to raise the money?

GM: Based on *Tales'* reception, very easy as it turned out. But whereas that cost only $22,000, and making a profit on such a sum obviously isn't hard, *Archangel* cost the Canadian tax payer $350,000. Telefilm Canada, formerly the Canadian Film Foundation,

backers of David Cronenberg's early work, matched the independent money I raised from distributor advances and Arts Council grants. I suspect it won't make too much of its budget back though.

SX: *Tales* garnered you an instant cult reputation. Did you receive any Hollywood offers as a result?

GM: Loads and I turned them all down. I had no intention of nipping my career in the bud with such appalling lapses in taste. They were all along the lines of 'Beverly Hillbillies from Outer Space' type movies. They'd say, "Here's a script just for you - you're weird and zany." Except they'd have discovered I was an impostor on the first day when I didn't know what end of a megaphone to yell into! Friends told me I should have directed under a pseudonym. But what's the point? They were diseased from the word go.

SX: What were the major differences between shooting *Tales* and *Archangel*?

GM: I shot *Archangel* in twenty-nine leisurely days and edited it during Fall 1989. It was the first time I'd made a movie on an actual shooting schedule. *Tales* was shot over a few months at weekends, or on Wednesday nights after the hockey game, at my mother's beauty salon where the interiors were hastily built. *Archangel* was all studio based in a huge disused warehouse. We drew out a floor plan arranging each set like a jigsaw puzzle so they'd all fit in. Very cosy. I closed in the frame to make each set look cramped with stylised shadows curving in on top. Once more I had to rely solely on cleverness rather than budget.

SX: *Archangel* represents the return to a juvenile passion for you doesn't it?

GM: I often ask myself, do I have to account for my work in this way? But as a kid I loved the uniforms of World War One with their toy soldier quality. I still find it hard to believe anyone got killed in that war because they all look so toy-like. I would always imagine them curled up in the trenches getting ready for bed more than battle.

SX: *Archangel* is far more tongue-in-cheek than *Tales*.

GM: Is it? I honestly didn't know what I wanted half the time. The whole shoot was a blobby mass in truth. My directing style was a bit laid back, yet I'm pleased with the tone and feel I accidentally achieved. Because I was worried the actors' styles would be all over the

(Left) Kyle McCulloch as Einar in **Tales***...*

(Below) David Falkenberg, Sarah Neville and Michael Gottli in **Archangel***.*

Angela Heck as Snjofridur in Tales...

that they'd be offended for certain.

SX: Why did you choose mustard gas as a narrative device?

GM: Because it serves a dual purpose. *Archangel* is about fogginess and forgetfulness. Mustard gas was a neat visual equivalent for the cloud of confusion the players find themselves in. I made it up for fairytale purposes to give the movie a folklore feel, hence the Iris, apple and eye symbolism. Filigreeing on simplicity with careless boldness is the basic freedom a storyteller has. It's also an excuse for the story being more unfocused than I had initially hoped. There's a very complicated, very real narrative there which some people see while others don't. *Archangel's* main failing is I don't give viewers a chance to get back on board if they get lost. There are no checkpoints anywhere to re-enter the story. That's a major screw-up on my part. It's great I can rationalise that as an underground film-maker by hiding behind all manner of artsy banners. But I'm honestly regretful that it's as unfocused as it is. There's no real punchline yet I hope there's enough to engage the attention despite there not being quite the expected pay-off.

SX: Rabbits stand in as metaphors for Bolsheviks who are 'half man, half beast with great big eyes and great big claws'. There's discreet cannibalism, enforced war medal eating and a strangulation by spilled intestine. The stylised gore is more upfront than in Tales.

GM: I strove for the artificiality of violence - like kids fighting in the back yard. I needed a savage punctuation mark and I wanted Michael Gottli to cram his guts back into his stomach to conquer his cowardice and shine better than the rest of the characters. I always welcome laughter in my entertainments. If audiences laugh or are puzzled by this false note, I think the sequence acquits itself once he forces his guts back in. Does it look convincing or fake? My rule of thumb is try your hardest and you'll still end up with something that falls short. I had hired a make-up effects guy to sculpt an intestinal panel. He wanted to charge $1,500 and I could tell he'd be a problem. "Shit," I said, "let's get a pack of sausages and do it ourselves." We untied the links, smoothed them out, and it cost $30.

SX: You didn't actively pursue 'rotting images of past cinema' this time. You highlight Cecil B. DeMille-style judgemental intonations and signpost the narrative with deliberately wacko title cards instead.

GM: Don't forget the blotching that suddenly appears. That happened because the print laboratory accidentally water-spotted the negative. They were apologetic and didn't want to bill me but I told them to print it anyway. It suited me fine. Any time people tell me they've ruined something, I get excited. It's almost always the best stuff! I shot *Archangel* on Kodak Plus X black and white negative because it gives a harsh, high key lighting effect. Some of the movie is speeded up too. That's another happy accident. I used my 16mm Bolex and because the spring is shot it kept adjusting to slow motion. I never clean it and abuse it all the time. I really must retire it soon! More confessions from a director whose art comes from calculated carelessness! My work ethic tends to infuriate the workers. But so what!

SX: How have the ultra-enthusiastic reviews of your movies affected your life?

GM: I'm a grade D celebrity back in my hometown.

place I decided to shoot the movie in sequence. Then if any feeling changed it would represent an on-screen evolution. I never really felt the performances were unified until we came to dub the picture. Because the studio sound was so crystal clear, the actors ended up whispering their lines in a relaxed Barry White sort of way. That's what brought the movie together. I didn't make the voices old, scratchy, or disembodied. I made them clean and upfront because I'm tired of being accused of simply imitating silent movie strategies.

SX: The publicity manual describes Archangel as 'A tragedy of the Great War. A melancholy dreamlike world of long-ago lost love. A Goya war painting etched upon a child's window pane in frost.' You say it's more a cross between Dr Zhivago and Battleship Potemkin.

GM: *Archangel* utilises Soviet editing techniques and minimal camera movement - both Eisenstein influenced. But I don't copy anything intentionally, it's subconscious plagiarism. The silent era used a whole roster of similar phrases repeated in each film. I'm conversant with that vintage vocabulary as my visual experiences tripled weekly watching one great classic after another courtesy of the Winnipeg University archives. My style may have a familiar quality, but why should I go out of my way to correct it? To be honest I've used up all my cherished silent images now. I was wondering the other day what would be the feeling if I showed *Archangel* to anybody still alive from that golden heyday. I came to the conclusion

I'm getting mentioned in the local press enough to be resented now.

SX: What's your next project?

GM: It's a wholly studio based movie, titled *Careful*, set in the Swiss Alps which we've built in papier-maché. I'm aiming for a Michael Powell/*Black Narcissus* look. I'm filming in black and white again with the intention of computer colouring it for TV and video release because I'm tired of distributors whining about the non-commerciality of monochrome. If I'm in full control of the operation from the beginning it will look like a hand tinted picture. It's about an anxious Swiss community in the timeless '30s who are far too careful for their own good. They live in constant fear of avalanches and this over-caution insidiously infects every part of their lives. It's partly autobiographical. My family are infuriatingly cautious - like the whole of Canada. As with *Tales* and *Archangel* I've written the script, with George Toles again, from the standpoint it's an unsung opera set in that most neutral country of all, Switzerland. Heated passions come to the fore when an incest scandal seeps out through the commune's cracks. I have a one-and-a-half million dollar budget, meaning I can sign up higher profile actors alongside my repertory actor stable. I promise you it will still have the now expected, pretty cheesy Maddin quality to it.

SX: Are you sick of the constant comparisons to David Lynch?

GM: The only thing we have in common is we've both made a couple of monochrome pictures. I'm a gentle, quiet director who seeks viewer involvement. I'm working towards beauty, placidity and exquisite strangeness. I don't think that's what Lynch is about at all. His work is far more contrived than mine.

SX: Looking back over your meteoric career rise what strikes you most in retrospect?

GM: That *Tales* and *Archangel* are an inventory of my movie-making mistakes so far. Now I want to sit back, take stock, and put everything I've learnt on this artistic collision course in dramatic perspective. My growing legion of admirers, and I still can't believe I have any, will see a development in the direction they like with *Careful*. The story is clear, yet peculiar. It's about people who love each other but who can't express their affection. They are tormented by Hamlet-style jealous passions and it ends up poorly, very much like life itself. Hey, I've had some good times but I'm not the only writer who thinks that way. Look at Chekhov. Anyway I like my characters being left the way I feel every morning!

SX: Will you ever 'Go Hollywood'?

GM: I don't think so because my movies speak for themselves. I'm not a commercial film director. I have no passion for it. I couldn't make one if I tried, I'm not that versatile. I'm well aware my movies are considered strange, offbeat and uncategorisable. But I'm proud of that. So I'll keep working in the areas that interest me and, who knows, maybe one day they'll stray into the commercial arena. But I doubt it! ∎

Kyle McCulloch in
Archangel.

THE DAMNED AND THE DEMENTED

ROGER CORMAN AND THE FILMGROUP

BY MIKE WATHEN

Set up towards the end of the '50s, The Filmgroup was Roger Corman's first attempt to run his own movie production and distribution company. Financially it appears not to have been a great success, surviving only until 1964. Corman waited nearly ten years before trying another similar enterprise - the rather more successful New World.

The Filmgroup was financed with money made from Corman's films for companies like American International Pictures and Allied Artists - it was his intention to have a rather larger slice of the pie than was possible while making films for others.

"I wasn't trying to be my own AIP," he is quoted as saying in Mark Thomas McGee's *Roger Corman: The Best of the Cheap Acts* (McFarland, 1988), "but I felt I was making these films that they were distributing and they were getting a disproportionate share of the proceeds. And I had a little bit of money invested so I thought I could continue to produce and direct while I ran my own company."

Corman's protestations to the contrary, The Filmgroup certainly looked like a cut-price AIP. The original intention was to produce and release quickly made exploitation double bills and, providing each film cost no more than $50,000, make a little money.

Whether any money was made or not is probably arguable after all this time - given the short life of the company, massive profit seems unlikely. What is certain is that in its few years of existence, The Filmgroup was responsible for more than its fair share of worthwhile pictures, including what may be Corman's best film as director (*The Intruder* - also his greatest flop) and his most famous (*The Little Shop of Horrors*) as well as several others now considered more interesting for who worked on them than how they turned out (*The Terror, Dementia 13, Beast from Haunted Cave*).

Juvenile delinquency was Filmgroup's first area of interest and they knocked out enough films in this subgenre to fill three double bills in their first few months.

T-Bird Gang (Richard Harbinger, 1959) was the new company's first production. Corman regular Ed Nelson plays a high school graduate who infiltrates the titular gang ('Fast cars, fast girls and nowhere to go' according to the ads) to avenge the death of his father. Released in Britain as *The Payoff*, it was described by the *Monthly Film Bulletin* as being without '...a vestige of promise.' Its co-feature was *High School Big Shot* (1959), written and directed by Joel Rapp. It also had to be retitled for British consumption. Teenagers in

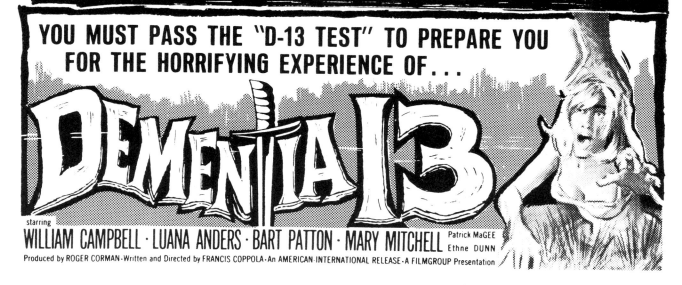

ENTER THE DOMAIN OF
THE DAMNED AND THE DEMENTED!
HOW MUCH HORROR? CAN YOU TAKE?

FROM THE DEPTHS OF AN EVIL MIND CAME A DIABOLICAL
PLAN OF TORTURE... INCONCEIVABLE... UNBELIEVABLE!

American International presents

BORIS KARLOFF
STARRING IN

THE TERROR
in
COLOR and VISTASCOPE   A FILMGROUP PRESENTATION

JACK NICHOLSON and SANDRA KNIGHT
... a new classic of horror!

SCREENPLAY BY LEO GORDON AND JACK HILL · PRODUCED AND DIRECTED BY ROGER CORMAN

YOU MUST PASS THE "D-13 TEST" TO PREPARE YOU
FOR THE HORRIFYING EXPERIENCE OF...

DEMENTIA 13

starring
WILLIAM CAMPBELL · LUANA ANDERS · BART PATTON · MARY MITCHELL   Patrick MaGEE   Ethne DUNN
Produced by ROGER CORMAN · Written and Directed by FRANCIS COPPOLA · An AMERICAN-INTERNATIONAL RELEASE · A FILMGROUP Presentation

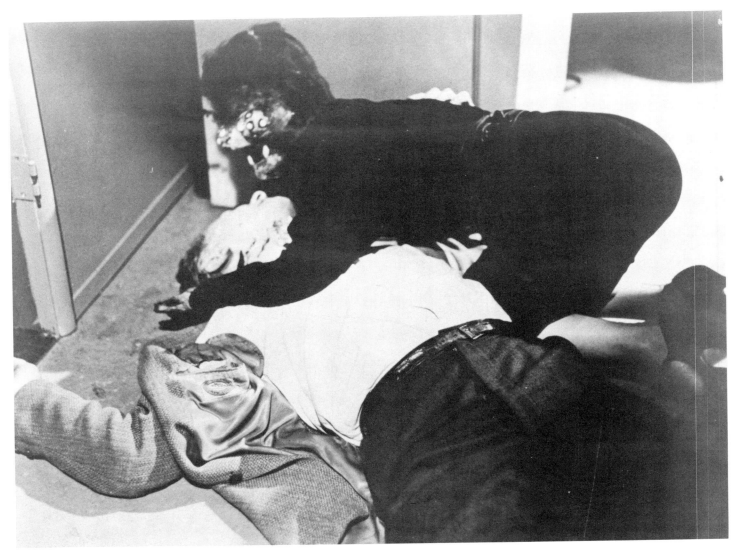

the UK obviously couldn't be expected to understand these strange new Americanisms, so if they wanted to see the film it had to be as *The Young Sinners*. The big shot of the title (or chief sinner, if you prefer) tries to impress his ex-girlfriend by planning and executing a daring perfect robbery. She remains unimpressed, tells her current boyfriend all about it and he tells the cops. Everyone descends on the scene of the crime and carnage results...

High School Caesar (starring John Ashley - 'Mob rule in a high school - He had more rackets than Al Capone') and *Date Bait* ('Too young to know - Too wild to care - Too eager to say I will') appeared in 1960, both produced and directed by O. Dale Ireland, a school drama teacher who used many of his students as actors.

The Girl in Lover's Lane (Charles H. Rondeau, 1960) combines a sleazy-romantic view of juveniles on the road with small town psycho-killings, sort of like a murder mystery by Jack Kerouac...Brett Halsey plays the young hobo who falls in love with the small town flirt. Soon she is dead and most of the town is out to lynch the wanderer, but as Jack Elam plays the town weirdo, they might be after the wrong guy... Its co-feature was *The Wild Ride* (Harvey Berman, 1960). Starring Jack Nicholson, it does for *The Wild One* what Nicholson's earlier film *The Cry Baby Killer* did for *Rebel Without a Cause* - steals most of it. In its brief (sixty-three minutes) running time Nicholson runs over a cop or two, kidnaps a young woman in order to wreck her boyfriend's life, wins a drag race by unconventional means (killing the competition) and is then chased around by the majority of the cast.

The first Filmgroup production with which Corman had any great personal involvement was also their first horror film. Produced and directed by Corman from a script by bad-guy actor Leo Gordon, *The Wasp Woman* (1959) concerns Janice Starlin (Susan Cabot), owner of a famous cosmetics firm. When she discovers that her fading beauty is not only causing problems in her personal life but harming her business as well, she becomes easy prey for pseudo-scientist Eric Zinthrop (Michael Mark), who is developing a new medical cosmetic from the enzymes of wasps to renew aging skin. Acting against the advice of her PR man Bill (Fred - later Anthony - Eisley) and secretary Mary (Barboura Morris) she agrees to back Zinthrop's experiments - with herself as a human guinea pig. At first the treatments work, but there are certain indications all is not well. An earlier experimental subject, a cat which Zinthrop's enzyme turned into a kitten, reverts to its true age, then turns into a cat/wasp mutation. Stunned by this turn of events, Zinthrop wanders into the path of an oncoming truck and spends the majority of the film either in a coma or suffering from amnesia. Aging again, Janice cannot find the formula for the wasp enzyme - she changes into The Wasp Woman and starts killing people and drinking their blood...

Extremely slow for a Corman film, *The Wasp Woman* at least has an engagingly silly monster - Cabot wears an insect head-piece seemingly modelled on *The Fly* (although it is never seen clearly) but is otherwise human from the neck down. She even retains her high heels, making her sudden, rushing attacks look even odder.

Despite a stunning, if irrelevant, poster ('A beautiful woman by day - a lusting queen wasp by night') and an entertaining trailer ("The most fiendish, the most fierce female that ever lived") the film was not successful, and was leased to Allied Artists for reissue, who cut it from an already brief seventy-three minutes to sixty-six.

Billed with *The Wasp Woman* was *Beast from Haunted Cave* (1959) ('See screaming young girls sucked into a labyrinth of horror by a blood-starved ghoul from hell!'), the first film directed by Monte Hellman, a film-maker who seems to have spent his career permanently on the fringes of greatness. His occasional features are usually critical successes, box-office failures, and often go on to become cult favourites. This one has never managed the first or third category because, despite having reasonably intelligent plotting, it finally seems too rushed and contrived. Neither is the script particularly original, being a thinly disguised rewrite by Charles B. Griffith of his own *Naked Paradise* (aka *Thunder Over Hawaii*) with a goldmine robbery in Deadwood replacing the Hawaiian plantation job.

Three small-time hoods - Alex (Frank Wolff), Marty (Richard Sinatra) and Byron (Wally Campo) have a simple plan for lifting Deadwood's bullion deposit - let off a timebomb in the mine and rifle the safe while everyone is out investigating the explosion. Marty is chosen to plant the bomb, but while fooling around in the mine with barmaid Natalie, he discovers the remains of a recently hatched egg - and not long afterwards the thing that came out of it. He panics and flees, leaving Natalie to her fate. After the robbery the gang join Alex's mistress, Gypsy (Sheila Carol), who has been keeping company with ski-instructor Gil (Michael Forest), who has unsuspectingly agreed to guide them across the snow-covered mountains to his cabin in the Black Hills, where they will await the arrival of a pre-arranged light plane. When night falls they break their journey; while on watch Marty hears a weird wailing sound, and searching for its source finds Natalie encased in a cocoon, hanging from a tree. As he looks at her she opens her eyes; he shoots her and is attacked by the beast, but escapes and returns to the camp. The monster follows them to the cabin and seizes Gil's Indian house-keeper. Byron sets out to find the house-keeper while Marty, who is in almost telepathic communication with the monster, sets out to find it. Gil and Gypsy try to escape from the by-now megalomaniac Alex, who pursues them. A blizzard commences and the cast (and monster) take shelter in the haunted cave. Byron finds the house-keeper cocooned and stuck to the cave wall but the beast kills him. Alex and Marty catch up with Gil and Gypsy at the cave; the monster kills Alex and mortally wounds Marty, who nevertheless manages to kill the monster with a couple of well placed signal flares as the film comes to a jarringly abrupt conclusion.

'They turned a white hell red with enemy blood' ran the tagline for *Ski Troop Attack* (1960), produced and directed by Corman back-to-back with *Beast*, the Black Hills location this time standing in for the Huertgen Forest in Germany. Set just before the Battle of the Bulge near the end of World War Two, good visual use is made of the snowy landscape as an American ski patrol trapped behind enemy lines battle their way to their objective, a mountain bridge which must be destroyed. Corman plays his largest acting role as the Commander of the German patrol in hot pursuit.

Filmgroup's other war film, *Battle for Blood Island* (Joel Rapp, 1959), caused a minor controversy among theatre exhibitors. They were somewhat dismayed to find that, despite the usual bloody poster, this story of two GIs hiding out on a Japanese-held island had no battle.

Both the legend and the reality of the making of *The Little Shop of Horrors* ('the best film ever made in two-and-a-half days') have been gone into in such detail that there is little that need be added here. The cult surrounding Corman's 1960 movie, a semi-remake of his earlier *A Bucket of Blood*, was slow in growing. The film was a flop when first released and many exhibitors refused to book it on the grounds that much of the humour was anti-Semitic. Filmgroup tried releasing it

They fought for the Ultimate Prize!

THE LAST WOMAN ON EARTH

NEW
Eastman 52-50
COLOR
VISTASCOPE

Starring
ANTONY CARBONE
BETSY JONES-MORELAND
EDWARD WAIN

to art houses with little success. Eventually it was leased to AIP where it became a frequent co-feature to *Black Sunday* and began to get noticed.

Little Shop went on to become a successful stage musical with its own bloated and unfunny film version. The first (unofficial) remake was Carl Monson's *Please Don't Eat My Mother*, a nudie-comedy with one or two hardcore scenes, starring Buck Kartalian (aka Monson) and René Bond. Variously known as *Hungry Pets* and *Sexpot Swingers*, it was made by Box-Office International who, of course, had never heard of a film called *The Little Shop of Horrors* and couldn't understand how their film had come to have almost the same plot.

Atlas (Corman, 1960) was, to say the least, a somewhat compromised production. The original intention, to make a *Hercules*-type picture on real locations with partial Greek financing, must have seemed wonderful. However, much of the Greek money was not forthcoming and the size of the warring armies shrank in proportion. Also, Michael Forest (from *Beast from Haunted Cave*) was one of the skinniest muscle men ever, though Frank Wolff (also from *Beast*) is great as Praximedes and the scenery is tremendous. Once again the advertising was more noteworthy than the movie. The poster features a very muscle-bound Atlas holding up his name while a scantily clad slave girl attempts to castrate him with a scimitar.

The Last Woman on Earth (Corman, 1960) was notable for being Robert Towne's first screenplay - not

that that stops it from being dull, talky and pretentious. Gambler Harold Gurn (Antony Carbone), his wife Evelyn (Betsy Jones-Moreland) and their attorney Martin Joyce (Edward Wain, aka Robert Towne) have escaped to Puerto Rico to avoid the attentions of New York's finest. Surfacing from a spear-fishing trip they discover that the air is unbreathable without aqualungs. The air regenerates but all life appears to have been destroyed. The trio engage in all the usual end-of-the-world self-preservation scenes while bickering furiously. Evelyn comes to prefer Martin and they run off together pursued by jealous Harold. He catches up with them and the two men engage in a fist fight that takes in most of the city of San Juan. There is some hefty symbolism as Martin goes blind and dies in a church, leaving the other two to continue the race.

Made back-to-back in Puerto Rico with *Battle for Blood Island* and *The Last Woman on Earth* (three films in three weeks!), *Creature from the Haunted Sea* (Corman, 1960) reunited Carbone, Jones-Moreland and Wain in the third version of *Naked Paradise*'s script. The most obscure of Corman's horror comedies (presumably because it was advertised as a serious film) (*and perhaps also because it sucks. Ed.*), it runs barely an hour but packs a hell of a lot into it. On a revolution-torn island, a group of loyalists enlist Renzo Capeto (Carbone) to transport them and the entire national treasury away from trouble. Capeto has his own schemes, however. He intends to take the money for himself, kill the loyalists and blame the deaths on a legendary sea monster. Several murders later and after the 'accidental' running aground of his ship, Capeto is surprised to discover 'his' monster is real.

Needing a co-feature, Filmgroup acquired *The Devil's Partner* (Charles H. Rondeau, 1958, released 1961) from Grand National Independent Pictures. Ed Nelson plays a dual role as an old man, Pete Jensen, and his young nephew, Nick. When old Pete dies, Nick arrives in the small Texas town to take care of the funeral arrangements. The townspeople soon realise that the younger man has as many peculiarities as the old, but whereas Pete was always disliked and dislikable, Nick tries to ingratiate himself with everyone, even lending money to David (Richard Crane) and Nell (Jean Allison) so they can get married. But Nick is up to something... In old Pete's cabin he kills a goat, draws a pentagram on the floor and begins chanting weird incantations. He changes into a wild stallion and tramples an old wino to death, then 'becomes' David's dog, attacking him and scarring his face for life. David turns against his friends and Nell turns to Nick for comfort, which is exactly what Nick was after. Investigations into the weird occurrences keep leading back to old Pete's cabin, where David and the sheriff find blood on the floor, freshly slain animal carcasses and a very large rattlesnake that tries to bite David. The sheriff shoots the snake and it changes into Nick, then changes into old Pete as the 'permanent' scars on David's face fade away.

Infrequently seen and even less frequently written about, *The Devil's Partner* is, even in its truncated form (Filmgroup cut it from seventy-five minutes to sixty-one) a genuinely eerie little picture, well worthy of rediscovery. As usual it was given a totally irrelevant but still wonderful ad campaign. 'Half Man, Half Beast, He Sold His Soul for PASSION' accompanies a picture of a naked woman on a centaur while Satan looks on. 'We do not recommend this picture for those who are easily shocked' is written on a tombstone.

half man, half beast, he sold his soul FOR PASSION

THE DEVIL'S PARTNER

WE DO NOT RECOMMEND THIS PICTURE FOR THOSE WHO ARE EASILY SHOCKED.

A HURON PRODUCTION
PRODUCED BY HUGH M. HOOKER
DIRECTED BY CHARLES R. RONDEAU

An ahead-of-its-time story of hatred and violence, *The Intruder* (1961) is also supposedly Corman's biggest financial loss. Scripted by Charles Beaumont from his 1959 novel and apparently inspired by newspaper reports of outside agitators, it concerns one Adam Cramer (William Shatner), a smiling and seductive spokesman for the Patrick Henry Society. Clad in sunglasses and a white suit, he charms his way into a small southern town and persuades locals to rebel against the court-ordered integration of ten black students into an all-white high-school. "The NAACP is a communist front," he tells them, "headed by Jews who hate America." Opposed by Tom McDaniel (Frank Maxwell), the local newspaper editor, Cramer at first pleads for non-violent revolt. Trouble soon starts, however, and swiftly escalates. A preacher dies when his church is bombed, a family is attacked and McDaniel is beaten up. Cramer spends time with McDaniel's daughter and convinces her that her father will be killed unless she accuses a black school friend of raping her.

Cramer by now has another enemy in Sam Griffin (Leo Gordon), who knows that his wife has been seduced and shamed by the bigot and has sworn to break him. He believes the rape story to be untrue and tries to persuade the girl to retract the lie.

A great-looking black and white film made very much on the run on location, *The Intruder* was perhaps too realistic for the early '60s. There are great performances from Leo Gordon, Frank Maxwell and Robert Emhard, with Shatner turning in the best performance of his career. Writers Beaumont, William F. Nolan and George Clayton Johnson all have roles in the film. Reissued as *Shame* and *I Hate Your Guts* it still didn't succeed with the ticket-buying public. In 1963, as *The Stranger*, it played a few dates in England before disappearing, though it has finally been released on video (under its original title) by Connoisseur.

A very much lighter and more obscure Filmgroup release was *The Mermaids of Tiburon* (John Lamb, 1962), filmed in Mexico as a vehicle for top nude model Diane Webber (aka Marguerite Empey) - 'the Uschi Digart of an earlier skin-magazine generation' according to Dean Chambers. She plays a mermaid queen thought to be the guardian of a fortune in rare pearls. Filmgroup picked the film up from Lamb, sold it to AIP, who sold it back to Lamb. He shot some additional footage of Webber and sold it to Arts Films International, who released it in 1965 as *The Aqua Sex*. The picture may well have been owned by more people than have actually seen it.

A mermaid of sorts figures in *Night Tide* (Curtis Harrington, 1961, released 1963), a watery variant on *Cat People* filmed largely on and around a run-down amusement pier in Venice, California. At least as worthy of rediscovery as *Carnival of Souls*, which has a similar atmosphere, *Night Tide* stars Dennis Hopper as Johnny Drake, a lonely sailor on leave who becomes fascinated with Mora (Linda Lawson) a girl who plays a mermaid ('The girl in the fishbowl') at a pier sideshow in a small coastal town. He is warned off by the owner of the sideshow and told that she believes herself to be descended from the Sea People who become the killers at the time of the full moon. Two men have died after being with her, possibly more.

Pushing his luck, Johnny goes swimming with her on the night of the full moon. While underwater Mora shuts off his air and leaves him to his fate. But he survives and returns to the pier. Mora's dead body is on display in the water tank, murdered by her boss who, insanely jealous, had planted the Sea People legend in her mind to keep her by him.

Apart from one unconvincing nightmare sequence (Hopper attacked by a rubbery octopus), the film is a fine atmospheric chiller spoiled neither by the apt explanation (there is a nice little twist) or the low budget. It was briefly released in England in 1964, first on a double bill with Julien Duvivier's *The Curse and the*

Coffin, and later with *Hamburg, City of Vice*, before falling into ill-deserved obscurity.

Niebo Zowiet (usually translated as *The Heavens Call*) was a Russian SF film made in 1959 and translated by Aleksander Kozyr and Mikahil Karyukov. It was acquired by The Filmgroup because Roger Corman liked the special effects and message of brotherly love. He had Francis Coppola rewrite the dialogue and add scenes. In the American version, retitled *Battle Beyond the Sun* (released by AIP in 1963 and credited to Thomas Colchart and Alexander Kozyer), Earth is divided into two parts, North Hemis and South Hemis, both engaged in space exploration. Both sides launch spaceships, but something goes wrong with one and the crew has to be rescued by their rivals. Coppola's additions involved a fight between space monsters - one resembling a penis and the other a vagina. The vagina monster wins the battle by swallowing the

penis monster whole. The character who witnesses all this is thought to be suffering a hallucination.

Coppola had been working for Corman for some time, as well as making adult films like *Tonight For Sure* and *The Playgirls and the Bellboy* starring June Wilkinson, and desperately wanted to make his own feature. While the Corman unit was in Europe making *The Young Racers* he convinced Corman that now was the time and at the end of shooting he went off to Ireland with half the cast (William Campbell, Luana Anders and Patrick Magee) and a Gothic script derived from *Psycho* and lots of others.

Dementia 13 (1963), the result, starts with a small boat on a lake at night. In the boat are Louise Halleron (Anders) and her husband John, arguing about John's mother's will. In the heat of the moment John suffers a massive heart attack and dies. Fearing that his death will cause her to be struck from the will, Louise pushes the body overboard, throwing his pop music-playing radio in after. Back at Castlehalora she types a letter, forging his signature to explain his absence. If the rest of the picture cannot live up to this moody and cynical opening, it's not for want of trying.

Every year the Halloran offspring gather at their mother's behest to commemorate the death by drowning of their younger sister, Kathleen. Louise ingratiates herself into the mother's confidence by claiming to be in contact with the dead girl's spirit. Scheming to crack the old woman's mind she takes some of Kathleen's dolls out to the lake where she drowned. Swimming underwater to secure the toys, she finds a likeness of Kathleen at the bottom of the lake. Panicking, she comes up for air and is abruptly axed to death by a tall figure. The family doctor (Magee, delivering his usual splendid, carpet-chewing performance) takes over the investigation. He orders the lake drained and narrows his list of suspects, but not before another murder takes place at the lakeside, this time a poacher.

Reputedly Corman wasn't very happy with the completed film and fixed it up himself by shooting the second murder. When released in the UK (with *The Crawling Hand*) the title was changed to *The Haunted and the Hunted*, a more subtle title for what had become a more subtle film, the censor having all but removed both murders. A couple of years later UK viewers did get to see most of the missing bits in the film-within-a-film sequences of Coppola's *You're a Big Boy Now*.

In the USA, *Dementia 13* was co-featured with another Filmgroup presentation, *The Terror* (1963), advertised under the joint tag-line 'Enter the Domain of the Damned and the Demented.' By now the company had given up all attempts to release their own films and were simply leasing them all to AIP.

Finishing *The Raven* early and with Boris Karloff still contracted for another two days, Corman and Leo Gordon quickly concocted a partial script, then rushed around filming all the interiors before *The Raven*'s sets were struck. What they ended up with didn't add up to much - just Boris and the usual Poe-movie atmosphere. (Shot under the more moody title of *The Lady of the Shadows*, *The Terror* is often considered an undisclosed addition to the Poe series. Certainly it is closer to, say, 'Annabel Lee' than *The Raven* is to *its* source material.) Rather than waste what had already been shot, a bunch of Corman folk spent the next few months, on and off, writing and shooting additional scenes and trying to fit it all together and make some

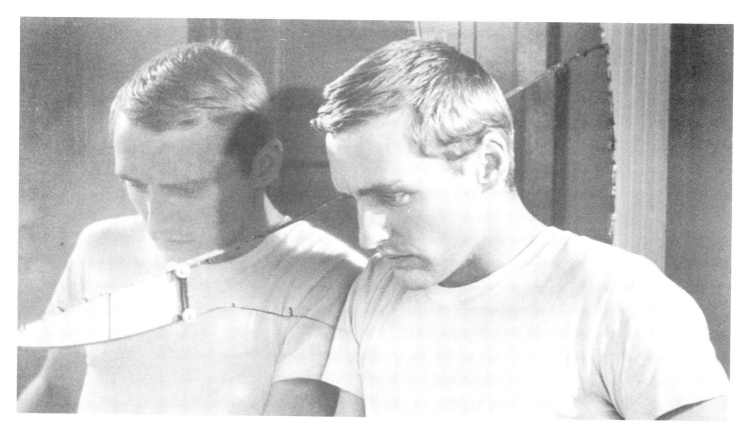

sense of it. Francis Coppola, Monte Hellman, Dennis Jacob, Jack Hill and Jack Nicholson all shot footage, with Hill and Nicholson contributing to the script in the vain hope of concocting some sort of story to accompany the visuals.

Separated from his regiment, André Duvalier (Nicholson, sporting a uniform several sizes too big), an officer in Napoleon's army, collapses from exhaustion somewhere on the Baltic coast. A beautiful woman (Sandra Knight) revives him and leads him to drinking water, then vanishes like a ghost. André is cared for by an old witch (Dorothy Neumann) and her idiot servant Gustav (Jonathan Haze). The girl appears and disappears at will and seems to be able to change herself into a bird. Searching for a solution to the mystery, André goes to the nearby castle of Baron Von Leppe (Karloff), who has been living like a hermit for the last forty years since the death of his wife, Ilsa. André sees her portrait - it is the mystery woman. The witch hates Von Leppe for having murdered her son, Eric, Ilsa's lover, and is using the ghost to torment him. But she's got the wrong man. According to Von Leppe's servant, Stefan (Dick Miller), Von Leppe *is* Eric. In the fight over Ilsa, Eric killed the Baron and assumed his personality. Which doesn't matter much anyway, because the ghost is now out of control. She appears before the Baron/Eric and urges him to flood the crypt and join her in death. The witch gets struck by lightning after entering hallowed ground, the Baron/Eric drowns and Andre rescues the girl, only to see her rot away in his arms.

From its pre-credit sequence, where a puzzled Karloff follows a trail of blood to a hanging skeleton, to its last image of a bird in flight (possibly the spirit of the dead girl) *The Terror* is nothing if not stylish. Nor is it as incomprehensible as some reports would have us believe. On the contrary, it has one of the most over-explained horror movie plots. Whenever one of the many hands who worked on the film wanted the audience to know what was going on, he got a member of the cast to beat up Dick Miller and demand to know what's happening. Miller gets beaten up by nearly everybody, and the audience is always clued in to when one of these scenes is about to take place - Miller suddenly gains several pounds in weight and his sideburns get longer and more bushy, an unfortunate side-effect resulting from the months-long, stop-start shooting schedule.

And you can fool some of the people all of the time... In *Castle of Frankenstein* no. 4, a nameless critic (could it have been Joe Dante?) writes: 'Roger Corman establishes himself as a highly creative producer/director with this excellent film. Much atmosphere, chills and mood in tale of drafty castle, witchcraft, haunted woods, tombs and corpses that aren't really dead. Ingmar Bergman-like in some ways, this is the least heralded, most important film in many years.' Well, it ain't that good, but it's much better than its detractors would have you believe.

A few months later The Filmgroup was wound up, although a few subsequent AIP releases like *Queen of Blood* and *Blood Bath*, both 1966 fix-ups of foreign films, have enough Roger Corman connections to make one wonder if The Filmgroup hadn't initiated them.

At their best, The Filmgroup productions often show a rare intelligence and humour which is constantly undercut by the lack of resources, talent, time and/or interest expended on the production. The pictures are often too clever for their own good, outstripping budgetary limitations and the abilities of those involved. This attitude of 'try anything, even if it doesn't come off' is the root of their continuing fascination. Taken together, they might almost stand as a microcosm of Roger Corman's entire career. ■

Dennis Hopper experiences mermaid lust in **Night Tide.**

PESSIMISM DEPRESSION
AND A DIMINUTIVE GODZILLA

JOE DANTE INTERVIEWED

BY KIM NEWMAN

Originally a fan writer - a contributor to *Famous Monsters of Filmland* and *Castle of Frankenstein* - Joe Dante entered the film industry working for New World in the trailers department, where he was responsible for making many Filipino movies look more exciting than they were by inserting a stock exploding helicopter shot whenever he could. His first feature, co-directed with Allan Arkush, was *Hollywood Boulevard* (1976), a brisk and breezy satire on low budget schlock pictures that features cameos by director Paul Bartel, cult actor Dick Miller and superstars Godzilla and Robby the Robot,

Joe Dante and the Boy Next Door (Steven Spielberg, left).

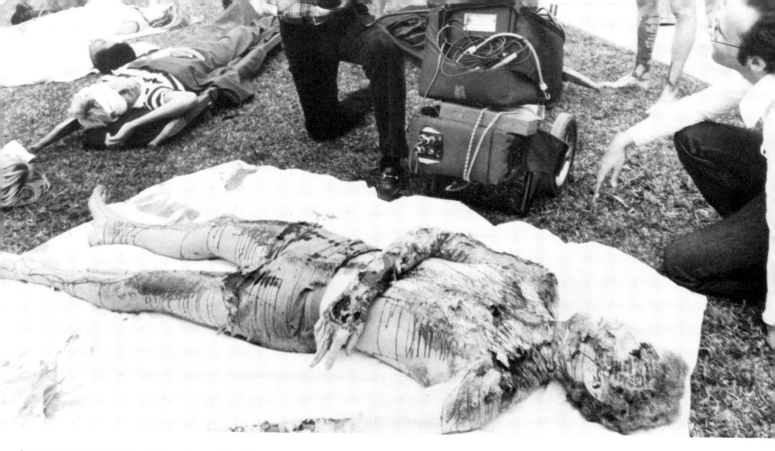

inaugurating Dante's tradition of movie buff in-jokes. With writer John Sayles, he made *Piranha* (1978) and *The Howling* (1981), a pair of amusing and effective monster movies, and then he gravitated into the orbit of Steven Spielberg to handle an episode of *Twilight Zone - The Movie* (1983) and the highly successful *Gremlins* (1984). Subsequent to the box office disappointment of his most personal film, *Explorers* (1985), Dante has made *InnerSpace* (1987), *The 'burbs* (1989) and *Gremlins 2: The New Batch* (1990). In addition to his feature work, he has contributed episodes to the omnibus comedy *Amazon Women on the Moon* (1987) and to the TV series *Amazing Stories* (1985-87), *The Twilight Zone* (1985-87) and *Police Squad* (1982).

SX: Your most recent film is *Gremlins 2*...

JD: (*gloating*) I read your review in the *Monthly Film Bulletin*. The one where you said it was my 'least creditable film.'

SX: (*back-pedalling furiously*) **Um, ah, actually, I do quite like it, but I think you can do better.**

JD: Considering what I had to work with, I thought I did great. An empty page in front of me.

SX: It was something of a come-down after your recent works, *The 'burbs* and *Explorers*.

JD: Well, my recent works have been vilified in my country of origin.

SX: Is this why you changed and did a sequel after sensibly staying away from *Piranha II* and the five *Howling* sequels?

JD: Warner Brothers asked me to do it, and I had resisted for all these years and they said, "We'll let you do whatever you want." They're so restrictive in general that it just seemed to be an offer I couldn't refuse. I proceeded to anger them mightily with the movie that I made, which made me feel all the better.

SX: It did much better overseas than in America.

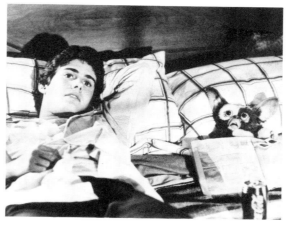

*(Above) The aftermath of a **Piranha** attack.*

*(Left) Major brand-name advertising in **Gremlins**.*

JD: Well, they had the brilliant idea of releasing it the same day as *Dick Tracy*. Whenever they pull out their marketing sheets, I swoon I tell ya, but the research showed them *Dick Tracy* was not a good picture and not going to be a big hit. I suggested otherwise, but they don't listen to the people who make the movies. So it opened the same day, and it never recovered.

SX: In Britain, it outgrossed *Dick Tracy*.

JD: Actually, it outgrossed *Dick Tracy* all over Europe, but I think that has to do with people being more familiar with *Gremlins* than *Dick Tracy*. Ever since *Gremlins*, all my pictures have done better in Europe. Except for *The 'burbs* which flopped there too. I'm thinking I should just go to Europe and direct pictures there.

SX: What do you think it is in the European sensibility that goes for your movies more than an American audience?

Some **Gremlins.**

JD: I'm not so sure that that's the equation. I think that the reality is that the advertising for the movies in America has been so abysmal that they've had to change it when they went to Europe and couldn't help but do better.

SX: *Explorers* **was critically acclaimed in the UK after being reviled in the US.**

JD: It was reviewed in the USA as if it were a pro-Nazi movie. They just despised it. The critics were particularly nasty that summer because there had been so many teenage science fiction movies. The fact that it seemed to be one movie for part of it and then turned into this other movie was too much for them. It was a very strange experience making it, because we rushed through it and didn't really finish it, but it was directly out of my psyche, we didn't have a finished script - which was what we kind of did in *The 'burbs* too, made it up; when we started shooting *Explorers* we really didn't know what the aliens were going to look like, or indeed what they were going to do because in the script they just played baseball. And it sort of developed into this stream-of-consciousness movie. I quite like it, and it's the only movie I've ever made where people, total strangers, come up to me and tell me it's their favourite picture. But it is devastating when you make a movie and it's so decisively rejected. It's hard not to take it personally. You start to question

yourself and whether you're doing the right thing and whether you should make pictures like this anymore. That's really what lead to me do *InnerSpace*. I thought I can't make another one of these movies that nobody understands. Then I made the movie and I made it so strange that the studio was worried that it was another one of these weird movies, but audiences loved that picture. They just didn't go see it because the ad was so terrible.

SX: On *Gremlins 2*, **how did you approach the challenge of doing what you'd already done once?**

JD: By trying not to do the same thing. And boy have I been raked over the coals for it by the more auteurist critics. David Chute was railing about how I have turned my back on my initial promise, that I don't make these black horror pictures any more, and what's the matter with me, how could I have sold out like this? It's just not interesting to remake the same movie, so the idea of remaking *Gremlins* and doing another black comedy was just not interesting. I was much more interested in trying to make a big Saturday matinée movie out of it, sort of a giant Warners cartoon, than I was with repeating anything, thematically or any other ways.

SX: It reminded me more of *Hellzapoppin'*, **with the interruption of the film...**

JD: That's one of my favourite movies. *Gremlins 2* is

a little different on video. I changed it. I took out that scene, and added a scene that makes it look like the VCR is kaput.

SX: Are you ever tempted to do a real cartoon?

JD: I was one of the people who was talked to about *Who Framed Roger Rabbit?*, but that was a different Disney administration, and at the time they didn't have the rights to all the characters. And I wasn't very taken with the original material so I didn't do it. When I saw the movie I really admired all the effort and technique that had gone into it, but I still wasn't very taken with the material. Roger is such a jerk. All the great cartoon characters are smarter than everybody else in the movie, and he's stupider than everybody else. He's such a schlemiel that he's not a lot of fun. Ah well, here we are, trashing somebody else's picture.

SX: You're one of the only American directors to have used Godzilla in a movie, in *Hollywood Boulevard*.

JD: That's true, although my Godzilla was a little diminutive. I like to think I contributed to his career resurgence. When he was down on his luck and he was working with me, he actually went out on a publicity junket with me. We walked the streets of LA passing out leaflets. That's actually true.

SX: Did it help the movie?

JD: Well, no. *Hollywood Boulevard* was not what you would call a massive success.

SX: That too has been sequalised recently.

JD: It's actually a remake. That and *Rock 'n' Roll High School*; Roger Corman just remade them and called them sequels. I guess that's what everybody does now.

SX: Do you still keep up with exploitation pictures?

JD: I try, but it's really hard because they're almost all on video now. When there's a really unusual one, I try to see it in a theatre, but it's real hard. Roger's pictures now play token theatrical engagements to justify their video releases. I went one day to see *Munchies*, which was made by a friend of mine, and it was playing at this big theatre, and I went at seven o'clock and it wasn't playing. It only played once, at one o'clock in the afternoon, and that allows Roger to advertise the picture as playing at a big theatre. Apparently, that's quite a typical way of doing it.

SX: Did you find it ironic that Roger Corman backed *Munchies*, an imitation of *Gremlins*?

JD: Oh no, I encouraged him. I didn't encourage it to be so bad. The effects guy on that picture just ought to be arrested. It was an opportunity for my editor, Bettina Hirsch, to direct, so I tried to be as supportive as possible, but the picture didn't turn out so well.

SX: Did you see any of the sequels to *The Howling*?

JD: Christopher Lee spent a great deal of time apologising for one of them. That was the one that I saw first, and I must say my mouth was open for a long time afterwards. And I saw the one with the kangaroos that was, um, not bad, and then there was the one - I get the numbers mixed up - where the kids are trapped in the castle, but nothing happens at all. That's *awful*. And then I heard that they went back to the original book, and the book was just atrocious, but apparently they filmed it.

SX: One of the few distinctive things about the series is that until number five, each one was made on a different continent. But they skipped Antarctica.

JD: I guess they were run out of most of the places they were in. Where do these pictures make money? It just seems hard to believe that after number five you

(Left) An irritating rubber whatsit from **Explorers**.

(Below) One of these actors is the late, great John Carradine.

would be able to generate enough interest and money from investors to be able to make another one of these movies. Maybe I should get back into the *Howling* sequels. Number nine. I could do number eleven, I'll be on the skids by then.

SX: I take it there won't be a *Gremlins 3*?

(Above) Exploitation stalwart Dick Miller (right) and Belinda Belaski (star of the classic Till Death) in The Howling.

JD: If there is, I certainly won't be involved with it. They've made sequels to less successful movies, but it's such a pain in the ass to make those pictures, they're just so hard to make.

SX: They could probably get Philippe Mora.

JD: Gasp, no. That's very humorous...heh, heh, heh.

SX: How do you feel about *The 'burbs* now?

JD: What's disappointing to me about *The 'burbs* is that the picture had an ending, before we hired Tom Hanks, that made sense, a sort of Hitchcockian twist ending. It ended up with the hero getting killed, and as soon as we hired Tom Hanks, the studio said we can't kill him, you can't use this ending. My ending originally was that I didn't want to reward these people for having been wrong the entire course of the movie, so at the end of the picture they were chastened. It was sort of a sad ending. Art, the big fat stupid guy, ends up lost, alone on the street at the end of the picture, and nobody likes him. And we ran it for previews and audiences were annoyed, because we've just spent an hour and a half with these people and now we're gonna have to feel bad at the end of it. So there was this quest for a new ending. We shot two other endings, and I'm not sure if the one we used was the best one. That part of it bothers me, but there are a lot of things in the movie that I like. While I was making it, I thought of it, heh heh, as kind of an art film.

SX: Do you feel strange about the fact that your movies do a lot better when they are miserable and mean-spirited?

JD: I don't know. I've never thought of it that way. I don't think *The Howling* is mean-spirited.

SX: It ends with the heroine turned into a monster and shot on live television.

JD: I think there's a sort of tragic grandeur to that. Although, even when I was making *Explorers*, I remember talking to Jerry Goldsmith about the music, and saying I want a lot of sad music in this film. I'm basically a kind of melancholy guy. Everybody says, "Oh, he's so cheery", but I'm not. Basically I'm pessimistic and depressive, and I guess the movies that it shows up in are the movies that are more personal.

SX: Do you see yourself going back to that next?

JD: What I'm trying to do is get away from these fantasy things. It follows me everywhere, and every time I've tried to make a film that was not in this genre, it hasn't happened. I got within two weeks of shooting on *Little Man Tate*, which is now being directed by Jodie Foster, and they pulled the plug because I wouldn't hire a forty year-old actress to play a twenty year-old lead. So I never got to make it. It would be nice to get away from the fantasy angle. I'm interested in real people - nobody ever believes that, but I really am - but I would like to try my hand at something that's different from what I've been doing. I'm not foolish enough to think it'll be completely different because, as with *InnerSpace*, it will turn out to be strange and odd. But that's the fun of it. There just won't be a guy turning into an animal every five minutes, and there won't be any rubber puppets or complicated blue screen work. Or maybe there will, I don't know. That's what I said about *Explorers*. What a nice little movie this will be, about these three little kids, it'll be such a change from *Gremlins*, and it was three times as expensive. I like to think there's more to me than being able to photograph rubber so it doesn't look like rubber.

I've got something with Orion that I hope will get made, which is a small-scale drama, a comedy with a movie theatre background. Hopefully, it will be different. It's very hard to get to do different things. People typecast you, and they want you to do the same thing. Even when I was making *Gremlins 2*, there was a tremendous pressure to make it like *Gremlins*, and whenever I would do something that was different - when I put in the joke with the film breaking - I thought they were going to die. Warner Brothers said, "You can't do this, this just isn't done", and I said, "Did you people ever see the cartoons you made, did you ever watch that picture you made, *Blazing Saddles*?" But conventionality is what they want, and I'm not interested in that, and so it makes for a tense relationship. ∎

FROM CHRIST TO SATAN

SEAN MANCHESTER'S BOOKS REVIEWED

BY RAMSEY CAMPBELL

'What kind of person would be the best for the job of vampire killer?' asks Ellen Datlow in *The Year's Best Fantasy and Horror*. Her answer is Pat Cadigan's excellent story 'The Power and the Passion'. I imagine that one quality which Ellen admires in the tale is the way the narrator reveals more about himself than about vampirism. This at least it has in common with *The Highgate Vampire*, Sean Manchester's account of his experiences with vampirism.

'No one, named or unnamed, bears any responsibility for what I have written,' the first page declares. This sort of candour is to be found throughout the book, and there's a similarly inadvertent aspect to the puff by Paul Spencer Vickers, of the

Department of English Literature at University College, London (a graduate student, apparently, who then taught there for a while): "I found the book fascinating in its subject matter and magnificent in the quality of its prose. Sean Manchester's literary style is refreshingly reminiscent of the Gothic genre." Reminiscent, certainly; or as Manchester puts it in his foreword, 'I commit pen to paper in what is hopefully the last frenzied flutterings of a force so dight with fearful fascination that even legend could not contain it.' Having met him twice on television, where I was invited as the voice of reason, I can confirm that no frenzied fluttering is visible.

The early pages continue to be reminiscent - 'Circumstances have brought me to many a strange, unchartered place in my endeavours as an occult investigator...the threshold of a vast, shadowy world...I am already beginning to wonder if the whole adventure were not some part of a frightening, fragmented dream - a nightmare in which the door between us and another world was almost ripped off its hinges...' This sort of thing may just be decoration, but we can hardly use that as an excuse for the pages (ten to fifteen) which attempt to define and prove the existence of vampires. These start soberly, quoting history and dictionaries, but when they try to demonstrate why a vampire can't simply be an artificially preserved corpse the writing can no longer contain its enthusiasm: 'When the stake pierces the heart, fresh blood will jet and spurt forth in all directions as the quivering, writhing body shudders to a halt.' At this point the style seems to have spent itself for a while, and tries to be sober again: 'Another point that all scientific explanations overlook is that when a vampire is exorcised it will emit a blood-curdling scream and, where many years have elapsed, will turn immediately to dust,' an attitude to science and scientists worthy of von Daniken.

It would perhaps be unreasonable to expect too

The Reverend Sean Manchester.

The Highgate Vampire

SEAN MANCHESTER

much hard information from a writer who admits 'It was while being bathed by an attractive nanny at the age of seven that I learned of the blood-sucking undead,' but any book should at least exhibit internal consistency. There isn't much of that here. The author first became convinced in 1967 that there was something amiss in Highgate Cemetery when, after two sixteen year-old convent girls saw bodies rising from the graves, an employee of an acquaintance of Manchester's saw someone standing behind a locked gate, 'an expression of basilisk horror on his face.' Why the sight of someone looking horrified inside a graveyard should have made the young man (who later joined the army) and his girlfriend flee isn't clear, but in the space of another four lines the intruder in the graveyard has become 'the thing' and then 'the spectre'. Sean Manchester elects himself to investigate and makes his way to the 'large, pulsating heart' of the graveyard. From this a path leads directly to the gate beyond which the intruder was standing, which might suggest to the careful reader that his appearance beyond it was of no great significance. However, the

soon-to-be soldier climbs over the wall near the gate one night, presumably rather than use the path to it, and sees a dark shape. For no reason he can think of he recites the Lord's Prayer aloud and jumps back over the wall. It is to be hoped he does well in the army.

Denied the chance of visiting the cemetery at night with someone who had seen the someone/thing/ spectre, our investigator lets the case drop for two and a half years and concentrates on other matters, until by chance he meets Elizabeth Wojdyla, one of the convent girls. She is anxious to speak to him and displays all the symptoms of anemia and somnambulism. She tells him one of the experiences that have been troubling her: "Midnight had struck...Something is outside my window...My arms and legs feel as if weights have been attached to them...I see the face of a wild animal with glaring eyes and sharp teeth, but it is a man....The face is gaunt and grey...There is a strange, falling sensation and I remember no more..." Now, if an eighteen year-old brought me that story I should say she'd pillaged several fictions about vampires, but clearly Manchester takes her more seriously. Some weeks later her boyfriend Keith (a tall young man of Scottish descent whose help is to prove invaluable) phones him for help because she is being 'overcome by something.' They both observe two small holes in the side of her neck. Three days later Keith writes him a letter - 'The full horror of the situation is too much for her to accept at the moment,' he writes - and feeds her broth. "Take a look at this," Manchester tells him, and hands him a photostat of an extract from *Dissertatio de Vampyris Serviensibus*, Duisburg, 1773, which Keith slowly reads aloud. Shaking his head he adds, "Can such things really be? Can they?" and is persuaded by our investigator to seal the door and window of Elizabeth's bedroom with garlic and a crucifix, write the first fourteen verses of John's gospel on a piece of paper and slip it under her pillow, and sprinkle the room liberally with holy water while reciting the Creed three times at the top of his voice, among other activities. In case she's alarmed or thinks they're crazy Keith doesn't tell her why he's doing all this. For about a week she is 'especially restless during her sleep', but then the fever goes away, and so does our investigator, though not without taking some photographs of Keith waving a Bible at her and of her smiling at the camera while poking a hand towards the lens 'in her bedroom towards the end of her nightly visitations.'

In February 1970 the *Hampstead and Highgate Express* publishes an account of three sightings of a figure inside the same old gates. The writer (unidentified, at least in the book) of the account 'can think of no other explanation than this apparition being supernatural.' The letter column then breaks out a rash of sightings, all of the writers being identified only by initials. Someone who didn't write to the press was supposedly attacked by a tall figure with the countenance of a wild animal - a description which, Sean Manchester admits, 'was somehow not altogether unfamiliar.' Indeed. At the end of the month Manchester decides after much soul-searching to tell the paper that a vampire is abroad, and is contacted by the sister of a twenty-two year-old woman whose name is apparently not Lusia. Why Manchester should conceal her real name isn't clear, since the book prints a photograph of her, emphasising her cleavage, on the cover and repeats it inside above the caption 'beautiful and innocent as a child.' Lusia has started to go in for sleepwalking and has two marks on her neck. Soon her sister Anne leaves Manchester a note: 'She is now at the front door and undoing the locks...You know where she will be heading.'

Off they all troop to the pulsating heart of the graveyard, where Lusia heads for an iron door and collapses. Our investigator decides on an official vampire hunt, but alas, freelance vampire hunters are beginning to get in the way, possibly because Manchester has referred in the *Hampstead and Highgate Express* to staking and decapitating the vampire just after dawn between Friday and Saturday. Despite his declared aversion to publicity, Manchester then plans to appear on a television show introduced by Eamonn Andrews, but things go wrong during the shoot outside those cemetery gates: the camera director falls over; the wind howls and screams; the generator wires lash to the ground. Of course. Nevertheless the programme, including full instructions for destroying vampires, is broadcast on the eve of the vampire hunt, and to our investigator's surprise a crowd worthy of a football match arrives at the graveyard, including 'all manner of freelance vampire hunter,' not least one Alan Blood, a history teacher from Chelmsford or Billericay with an interest in the black arts. Manchester, together with one hundred official assistants, gamely ventures to the iron door and has himself lowered through the roof of the tomb. He finds three empty coffins and blesses them, but the vampire must be shy of publicity. All Manchester can do is continue the official investigation, and has himself lowered through the roof again in August. One of the coffins has gone.

Nothing will do except that he take Lusia to the iron door and use his hypnotic powers. "You should never have come here," she says in a deep voice, but obligingly walks to the doors of a nearby vault. Here he and his three hand-picked assistants find a monstrous black casket in much better condition than the others, and we must imagine for ourselves why he didn't notice this beyond the iron door on the night of the vampire hunt and how it has been transported to its new home. Inside the casket is something gorged and stinking with the the life-blood of others, burning red eyes, long sharp teeth, you know the kind of thing. Our man poises a stake over the heart. "Is there no other way?" an assistant says, and our investigator senses the vampire's dreadful aura of triumph, but decides against hammering the stake. Instead he hangs around until sunset, performs an exorcism and decides that bricking up the tomb with garlic in the cement will do. Lusia sobs on his shoulder and hugs him with all the strength she has left, having dropped a Bible which falls open at the words 'For the blood is the life.'

However, we are less than halfway through the book. Once again overcoming his dislike of publicity, our investigator appears on a national BBC television programme about the Highgate Cemetery events, though he finds it "difficult to focus his mind" on the questions he is asked by the interviewer. Watching the programme reminds him that he neglected to hammer in the stake. Meanwhile a mail order clerk, one Barry Edwards, explains that at the time of the sightings in the graveyard he and the Hellfire Film Club were filming an amateur vampire movie there. Our investigator hasn't much time for amateurs, of course, nor for the objection that human canines can't leave vertical punctures on a neck: "During my various lecture tours and talks on the subject, I have satisfactorily demonstrated - using a live model - that the canines can in fact sink into the jugular vein on the neck." In any case, perhaps vampires have hollow teeth, and besides, his critics fail to mention that werewolves become vampires after death, and we should also remember that there is anti-time just as there is anti-matter, not to mention that the atomic weight of the vampire's body can be raised above the level of the earth's vibrations, though "this is looking at it scientifically." So much for science.

The BBC programme rouses more amateurs. Some wander through Highgate Cemetery banging on tombstones with stakes and shouting "Come out vampire, we are coming to get you." Our man's adversaries begin to proliferate: David Farrant, who lives in a coal-cellar and who has the temerity to found the British Psychic and Occult Society, apparently in opposition to our investigator's British Occult Society, before he is convicted of interfering with corpses and sent to Blunderstone Prison; John Pope, a fire research assistant from Barnet who tries to raise Dracula in a Transylvanian hotel room ("I wish he'd throw away all this rubbish and find himself a girlfriend," his father, once an RSM, apparently said); Jean-Paul Bourre, a black magician who dresses 'predictably in black from head to foot.' Also abroad are a whole bunch of Satanists, 'the vampire's living emissaries,' who desecrate an Anglican Church in Islington. The Reverend Pauley of that church calls our investigator, and over a bottle of Napoleon brandy they agree that Manchester should exorcise the church (why him, rather than the diocesan exorcist, isn't clear). Lusia is brought along to the exorcism, and before long she needs to be hypnotised, sending our investigator to Highgate Wood. There he seems to see a robed figure in an old pavilion, and when he returns in daytime with an assistant and a camera he finds signs inscribed on the floor. Lusia is brought along to be hypnotised and utters remarkable utterances - "must go to the old house" and so forth. Our investigator decides it's time to return to the cemetery, 'indeed to the undead tomb itself,' for apparently a house which used to cast its shadow over the (pulsating) heart of the cemetery was occupied in the early eighteenth century by a nobleman who was brought to England in a coffin, after which there were tales of 'hobbs, ghaists and daemons' and a grey giant that walked through walls. No doubt Nigel Kneale came across these tales while researching *Quatermass and the Pit*. Our investigator has two workmen reopen the bricked-up tomb. What is his surprise on discovering the coffin has gone!

Two years later he finds it, in a house at the edge of Highgate where 'whatever walked the broken staircases, walked alone.' Surrounded by clichés, he and a clairvoyant (Veronika) and a skeptic (Arthur) enter the building, which the residents of the adjoining Jewish old folks' home call the House of Dracula. They probe the darker recesses with enthusiasm and try to settle down for the night, only to suffer a further onslaught of clichés and for Veronika to announce that the tenant won't let them leave. Perhaps it is fed up with being mislaid by our investigator. He gives Arthur a cross, and the trio sit outside in their car and fill the window spray with holy water, seemingly from inside the vehicle. Manifestations cause Arthur to cry "I'm off" and be so. Manchester runs after him and gives him another cross, but they are assailed by an apparition 'nearly impossible to describe,' hence not described at all. More apparently fed up than ever, it allows them to go next door to the old folks' home for some buckets of water. An old lady looks somewhat

SECRETS OF WITCHCRAFT AND SATANISM
REVEALED IN A STORY OF SALVATION

From Satan To Christ

Written by
Sean Manchester

astonished. Back outside Hill House or whatever it's called, Manchester chunters for a page and a half at Arthur while an apparition forms behind him. "What does it all mean?" says Arthur. Veronica falls asleep. The sun comes up. Before heading for the basement of the veritable temple of a dark force which has permeated the very wood and stone with living evil they see Veronika home, but the vampire has also nodded off. They drag the enormous black casket upstairs and out of the house, and Manchester poises the stake. "In God's name strike!" cries Arthur. Terrible roar from bowels of hell, sluggish flow of inhuman slime and viscera, etc. Arthur tries to use the camera but has to turn away. The old folk next door are presumably catching up on their sleep. The house is subsequently demolished to make way for flats, but the Bodgers who live there speak of "a presence".

In 1981, while filming a documentary about vampirism, our man is called back to England by a telegram. Animals are being drained of blood in Finchley in what the local paper calls 'the local mid-night rabbit kill.' Clearly one of the vampire's victims is on the rampage, and the best thing for our investigator to do is to climb over the wall of Highgate Cemetery at night with Sylvaine Charlet, an actress. Nothing comes of this visit, but before Sylvaine returns to Paris they attend a masquerade at a stately home, since she likes to dress up. Here, by a lake during a fireworks display, our investigator thinks he sees Lusia dressed in white, a scene so cinematic I'm surprised that nobody - Roger Vadim, let's say - has used it in a vampire film. Then he meets Lusia's sister, who tells him that Lusia died seven years ago from leukemia.

Our investigator locates her and her activities in the graveyard in New Southgate where she was buried. Here a boy was lured out of a park nearby and bitten by a 'lovely lady all in white' who can be none other than Lucy Westenra - than Lusia, I mean. In order to avoid publicity our man adopts the name of George Byron, recalling a family legend that he is the great-great-great-grandson of Lord Byron. Before long he is forced to disguise himself in order to campaign against a council plan to develop part of the graveyard, and gives a television interview among the graves. Spike Milligan is the first to sign his petition, which Byron plans to deliver to the Prime Minister, having ridden along Downing Street on his horse Thunderbolt. After posters appear advertising him as a council candidate under his assumed name, his phone is tapped and Special Branch officers are cautiously polite as they interview him in his room full of vampire repellents. He is astounded to be subjected to such an interview. He is also troubled by dreams of Lusia 'caressing her silky skin in rhythm' and licking her lips until he raises a stake and she uses it for 'a ferocious masturbation which leaves her spurting blood out of every orifice at the moment of orgasm.' Perhaps things are getting on top of him, not least the local newspaper reports of the council election under the headlines 'Vampire Slayer Fighting Election' and 'I'll Oust the Living Dead, says Candidate.' He is unsuccessful at the election, but forgives those who didn't vote for him - "Their heart was not in their sword when the day of battle arrived" - and quotes Kipling's 'If' to himself.

It remains only for him to deal with Lusia. He takes her sister to the grave and tells her "The night is full of her voice calling my name." Nevertheless Anne won't let him dig up the corpse, and so he sets about invoking the vampire at the grave during the hours of darkness. Having performed various rituals he strips naked, feeling like 'a schoolboy on his way to meet his first real date.' After a good deal of Wheatleyish conjuration he is rewarded by the appearance outside the magic circle of a spider the size of a cat. He shoves a stake through the centre of the spider. 'Something wet and glutinous oozed stickily as I pressed the stake further.' The spider turns into Lusia's corpse, which he holds until dawn, at which point he returns the quickly decomposing remains to the ground, presumably by digging up the grave.

While *The Highgate Vampire* was published by the British Occult Society the sequel, *From Satan to Christ*, comes from Holy Grail, but both are available from the same address. The sequel is less a book than a prolonged contradictory footnote. Our man has usually been able to trace any attempts to discredit him back to Satanists, not least David Farrant of the coal-cellar and of what Manchester calls the symptoms of someone with an identity crisis. Having dressed in a robe and carried a nine-foot cross through the West End and fed his followers on Hampstead Heath with fish and bread, Manchester is called upon to save one Sarah from Satanism. The book says she has 'a child's heart in the body of a woman,' and a good deal of the latter, emphasising cleavage, is visible on the cover. While at primary school she used to preach to the neighbours about their shortcomings, but became disillusioned with the church after the parish priest tried to give her a French kiss and his successor ran off with a nun. On leaving college with an arts degree Sarah decides to move to London in search of a coven.

Meanwhile Manchester is hard at his mission of rescuing stray sheep, which apparently began in the '60s. The Satanists are too busy to have become aware of him: David Farrant stands in the Hornsey election as the Wiccans Awake candidate; John Pope (the ex-RSM's son) consults Farrant for a ritual to use against David Crawford, organiser of the Bedford branch of the Brotherhood of the Ram, and later tries to join the Orthodox Temple of the Prince but receives a letter calling him 'a fly on the backside of occultism.' Where our investigator obtained this letter and much else besides is unclear, but perhaps it has something to do with Sarah, who has joined the Croydon Order of the Star and Snake.

We are told this was run by Mark Pastellopoulos (the Great Beast, or Lucifer, or son of Mercury) and Samantha Courtenay-Devonshire, who preferred to be addressed as the Whore of Babylon. Sarah is initiated in a temple with black candles and a statue with a goat's head and an erection, but doesn't realise she's involved with Satanism. (One tip the book offers is that you can recognise Satanists by their untidiness.) Soon she gives birth to the Antichrist which is named Arianne Julianna Xanthi Dea. Luckily she encounters our investigator, whose aversion to publicity has prevented the coven from hearing about him, and he recognises her peril from the weird, discordant music on the stereo in her flat. He confronts the Beast and Whore at Sarah's birthday party, where the guests dress as vampires and ghouls and so on, and our man comes as Lord Byron. Eyes blaze and voices grow cold and snarling while our investigator ripostes, the Beast unlocks his chubby fingers and rolls forward on the sofa and sweats a lot. Our man is unable to prevent Sarah from undergoing an impregnation by a demon, but the ritual apparently doesn't work, and the book trails off; Sarah marries our hero; David Farrant has a last confrontation with him in a wood before they 'each dissolved into the night's shadows in opposite directions.' The final pages, however, warn us not to fail to recognise the Messiah, so perhaps all is not over.

If these books are less fun to experience at length than to read about, this can't be said of the illustrations. The Satanists seem to have been happy to be photographed; we have David Farrant at his devilish altar in Highgate, Sarah stripped to the waist for a ritual, and the Satanic coronation of John Pope. The vampire book offers a 'remarkable picture of Lusia somnambulating,' for some reason shot from floor level, as well as a buxom wench throwing out her chest in the pulsating heart of the graveyard, some freelance vampire hunters, a large black casket, Caroline Munro and our investigator (wearing a Marvel Comics badge) discussing vampirism 'before an astonished audience' at a horror film convention, our investigator surrounded by vampire repellents, our investigator with his box of accoutrements, our investigator's official portrait displaying his esoteric shield which boasts three bats, our investigator on his horse

(Left) Dick Smith's make-up for **Dorian Gray.**

Thunderbolt, and much else. Most striking of all is 'a representation of the vampire in its final moments of dissolution,' which is nothing of the kind; it is an early makeup by Dick Smith, featured in *Famous Monsters of Filmland,* for an American television production of *Dorian Gray.* But enough. I should respect Sean Manchester's aversion to publicity. I just wish he'd told us what happened to Arianne Julianna Xanthi Dea. Surely he can't be planning another sequel. ■

Manchester, Sean: THE HIGHGATE VAMPIRE (British Occult Society s/c, £7.50) (Gothic Press, revised h/c, £19.99).
Manchester, Sean: FROM SATAN TO CHRIST (Holy Grail s/c, £4.50).
Available from Sean Manchester, Holy Grail, PO Box 542, London N6 6BG.

(Below) Ramsey Campbell.

Ramsey Campbell is Britain's most respected living horror writer. He became a full-time writer in 1973 and has since written hundreds of short stories and the novels The Doll Who Ate His Mother, The Face That Must Die, The Parasite *(aka* To Wake the Dead), The Nameless, Incarnate, Obsession, The Hungry Moon, The Influence, Ancient Images *and* Midnight Sun. *A multiple winner of both the World Fantasy Award and the British Fantasy Award, he has also edited several anthologies, broadcasts frequently on Radio Merseyside as a film critic, and is President of the British Fantasy Society. He describes his latest novel,* The Count of Eleven, *as a comic novel about a serial killer. His latest collection is called* Waking Nightmares.

THE ACT OF SEEING WITH ONE'S OWN EYES.
USA 1972 .
Dir: Stan Brakhage.

If Pasolini's *Salo: The 120 Days of Sodom* is narrative cinema's darkest work then this must be the avant-garde/underground's equivalent, as it relentlessly offers the audience thirty-two minutes concentration on the grim process of the human post-mortem.

Brakhage is a film-maker who found favour in the early '60s with both hard-line structuralist critics and writers connected with the counter-culture, most notably *Film Culture* magazine's Jonas Mekas. A permanently blissed-out buffoon, Mekas would embrace any old piece of 'underground' garbage, as long as it was non-narrative, and (his favourite phrase) "life-affirming". One wonders what he made of *The Act*...! It's not hard to imagine him back-pedalling up his own mystic fundament to find a way of describing even *this* bleak opus "a life-affirming work".

Brakhage begins by showing us in clinical detail the preliminary examination of a number of dead bodies. Blood collects in the lower regions, according to the way in which the body was positioned; collects in the buttocks, in the back...pressing down hard on the flesh of the forearm leaves a precise indentation that doesn't spring back into shape, as it would on a living body, and so on. It isn't long before such documentary details are left behind, however; the camera and editing increasingly conspire to depict abstract alignments of form and colour - and suddenly pull back to reveal some further dishevelment of the human form. Strangely, for almost twenty-five minutes it seems that Brakhage has decided to spare us (and himself) the shock of the 'unzipping': that astounding and outrageous image of the first incision. Juan Logar's *Autopsia* builds a heavy cinematic edifice around this moment, employing dramatic build-up and appropriately nauseating swathes of music to get maximum shock treatment from it. For some perverse reason (doubtless some twisted anti-narrative thing - an autopsy should have a beginning, a middle and an end, but not...) Stan saves it for the last few minutes of his film. This time, the offal bag being slit open is a 200lb plus negro woman, not far removed from Grizelda (Jean Hill), the incredible black maid from John Waters' *Desperate Living*! But what really lifts this film above movies like Logar's *Autopsia* or SPK's *Despair* and the associated human post-mortem video

is the compulsive, jittery camerawork and dark-hued, sombre colour photography. Here there is a kind of disconcerting beauty pervading certain sections: flayed cadavers, their skins thrown open at the waist like discarded scuba diving suits, begin to resemble giant pink clams, or muddy dug-out canoes; gaping soup tureens are filled with barbecue spare ribs; internal organs become limp coral formations; opaque jellyfish try to pass livers, spleens; duodenal tracts become bloated eels... Amongst all this, Brakhage's sweeping camera movements and repeat edits, his nervous cross-cutting and frantic plunging of the lens into the most grisly details seem to indicate a predicament, perhaps comparable to that which I experienced while watching. There's a conflict between wanting to face death without recourse to the romantic, to escapist tactics - and the desire to re-interpret, re-associate, re-write death ("the atrocious end of life" as that guy in *Autopsia* calls it), which is perhaps the driving force of all art. Terry Gilliam's marvellous *The Adventures of Baron Munchausen*, for example, is suffused with this desire to rewrite the final chapter. Art, to borrow from Norman O. Brown, is Life *against* Death. At times Brakhage does become rather evasive, seemingly tempted to wander down the formalist corridors of his earlier work; the camera gazes at chrome fittings or out-of-focusses its way over various surgical accoutrements, but the avant garde tendency to go to the zoo and film the guttering is thankfully held in check.

Watching a completely silent film with a theatre full of people is an experience which often threatens to collapse under the weight of its own absurdity, especially in larger cinemas - as anyone who has sat through screenings of early Warhol movies in the National Film Theatre will know. But the claustrophobic back-room of London's ICA Cinematheque proved an ideal location, and effective impromptu soundtrack was provided by the muted groans, long exhalations and departing footsteps of various audience members - at least two-thirds of whom suddenly remembered previous engagements.

Elsewhere, bone-particle smoke rises from the rotating blade of a bone-saw...an albino-white cadaver with purplish, irregular stains displays an advanced case of *wobble-mortis*...one severely decayed, wet-look corpse looks as if it has been tarred, feathered and had its penis substituted by a greenish pancake roll. But conducting such introverted image-associations was not the main strategy adopted by the audience for coping with the film. Several would-be hipsters broke avant-garde etiquette (I was shocked!) and made banal wisecracks: "They're only actors" and "Phew, what a haircut" during a scalp-peeling scene. I did find one girl's parting shot amusing - after the film ended and the audience were filing dejectedly out of the theatre, she turned to a companion and said, in the outraged tones of an irate consumer, "Well, that does it - *no way* am *I* going to die!"

Stephen Thrower

THE AMBULANCE.
USA 1990.
Dir: Larry Cohen. With: Eric Roberts, Eric Braeden, James Earl Jones, Red Buttons, Megan Gallagher, Stan Lee, Laurene Landon. Sarlui/Diamant/Entertainment in Video.

Larry Cohen closes the cell doors on Maniac Cops and paroles a Maniac Medic in a terrific urban paranoia thriller dosed with black comedy, super stuntwork and sudden terror. With another impressive cast featuring Hollywood has-beens, old girlfriends and Bel Air neighbours, Cohen's cleverest concept since Q - *The Winged Serpent* finds him exercising vice-like control over the escalating mayhem, elevating non-stop medical madness into a top level funny bone operation with traumatic side effects.

Taking advantage of some unusual Manhattan locations, the best B-movie helmer in the business follows a vintage red killing machine (disguised as a vehicle of mercy) around New York as it picks up sick locals. One of these is a working girl that comic artist Roberts has been trying to date. But she doesn't arrive at any known hospital, as Roberts discovers when he tries to locate her - she's been abducted by psychotic surgeon Braeden (the great Dr Forbin from *Colossus*) and taken to a hi-tech lab for illegal diabetic research above a downtown club. The evil quack considers animal testing *passé* and uses kidnapped patients as guinea pigs in trades with global Frankensteins...

Doubting detective Jones, hard-bitten journalist Buttons and lovelorn officer Gallagher surface as Roberts' unlikely allies as he investigates other ambulance appearances for leads, while the mad doctor's male nurse contingent eliminates everyone around him. A wild disco climax, witty repartée, unpredictable plot twists, cynical dialogue, high action, quirky characters and Cohen's furiously paced direction all add up to a first rate fright delight, exploiting first aid fears with an accent on syringe-sharp satire. Cohen's creepy cure for terminal boredom comes recommended as worthwhile shock treatment.

Alan Jones

ARACHNOPHOBIA.
USA/Venezuela 1990.
Dir: Frank Marshall. With: Jeff Daniels, Julian Sands, Harley Jane Kozak, John Goodman, Stuart Pankin, Brian McNamara. Hollywood Pictures/Amblin.

Slick reworking of *Kingdom of the Spiders* that marks the feature directing debut of Spielberg alumnus Marshall. Big city doctor Daniels moves into Small Town USA and discovers that a series of mysterious deaths are the work of a mutant strain of prehistoric spider. Other possible victims of the pissed-off creepy-crawlies include Sands' aloof arachnid expert, veteran Henry Jones as a cranky old codger, and *Roseanne*'s Goodman, raising the yuk factor as a homicidal pest controller. Impressive production values, excellent special effects, but very little bloodletting, which makes this a sanitised horror film for those who don't normally like 'that sort of thing'.

Stephen Jones

THE BEAST OF YUCCA FLATS.
USA 1961.
Dir: Coleman Francis. With: Tor Johnson, Douglas Mellor, Barbara Francis, Bing Stafford, Larry Aten. Cardoza Productions.

Is this no-budget obscurity a carefully cloaked warning for the approaching nuclear age? Don't bet your rent money on it! Sure, it's coated with a wafer-thin theme of atomic irresponsibility, but deep down the concept is simply a grainy variation on The Incredible Hulk, featuring another appearance by one of the greatest schlock personalities of all time: Tor Johnson (*Plan 9 from Outer Space*, *The Unearthly*, and so many other ungodly awful movies that your brain would haemorrhage if you tried to watch them all).

The story begins with Tor as Joseph Javorsky, a famed Hungarian scientist on his way to Yucca Flats to pass secret Russian information to the US Government. But as the bald, 300lb professor is waddling across a field in an effort to escape the murderous Soviet agent -

oops! - off goes one of those pesky A-bomb tests, and Tor is turned into The Beast! Don't expect any special effects or disfiguring make-up though - not when the entire budget is only $34,000. Instead, the film-makers simply rip Tor's clothes a bit, pour some talcum powder on his face and turn on the camera.

Tor isn't really given much to do, and half the time all we're shown is a ground-level shot of his size fourteen feet. But at least he isn't a stupid monster, since the first thing on his agenda is kidnapping a woman and taking her back to his secluded cave where they can swap radiation poisoning in private. It's one of Tor's last (not to mention least) performances, and he's so weak that he becomes the first monster in film history to use a staff to get around the rough terrain. Sad.

A few dumb sub-plots are also tossed in to pad out the running time (and they *still* couldn't get it past the sixty minute mark). A posse of lawmen search the desert for the crazy killer, just as a pair of obnoxious brats get lost in the same area, so after a while the trigger-happy cops begin shooting at the innocent dad. Just another "victim caught in the wheels of justice." Talk about metaphor overdose! The film concludes with a so-exciting-I'm-surprised-I-kept-my-eyes-open

saddled with a constant narration - a monotone drone that explains every insignificant action in an attempt to create a semblance of continuity. Though never up to Ed Wood Jr's acclaimed level of pretentious incomprehensibility, it's damned close, with hackneyed lines like, "Joseph Javorsky. Respected scientist. Now a fiend, prowling the wastelands. A prehistoric beast in the nuclear age. Kill. Kill, just to be killing." The type of script-writing that makes Norman Mailer look subtle.

It's inconceivable to even consider the acting in a film such as this. Characters come and go with little rhyme or reason - with the annoying narrator informing us of who they are, just in time to watch 'em killed off or simply forgotten. But what more could you expect from writer/director Coleman Francis, whose only other claim to fame was playing 'Rotund Drunk' in Russ Meyer's *Beyond the Valley of the Dolls*?

It would be much too easy to continue nitpicking - the underlit photography, generic score, and the utter banality of the whole project, etc, etc. In other words, this is a massive mess! But still, there's a certain charm in seeing ol' Tor trudging across the sands, scaring the population. You gotta love the big guy!

Steve Puchalski

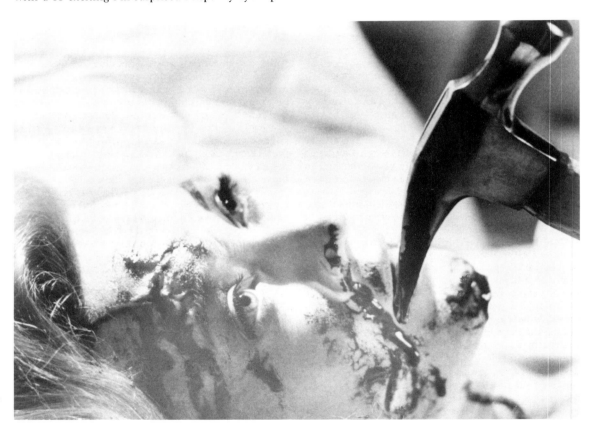

Eat hardware and die!
Blood and Lace.

pursuit on foot, as Tor chases after the pair of little boys. The only logical problem is that the ultra-hefty Swedish Meatball on Two Legs would have trouble getting out of a chair, much less chasing two ten year-olds at top speed. (Not that a little thing like logic ever stopped me from enjoying a trashy movie.)

But as with most clinkers from the past, the plot has little to do with the memorability of the final product - it's the idiotic *method* in which the creators pull it off and paste it together. In this case, since the budget didn't afford them the luxury of synched-sound, we're

BLOOD AND LACE.
USA 1971.
Dir: Philip Gilbert. With: Gloria Grahame, Milton Selzer, Len Lesser, Vic Tayback, Melody Patterson. AIP.

When teenage Ellie is sent to an orphanage after the death of her prostitute mother, she discovers a web of corruption and cruelty presided over by nasty old Gloria Grahame. Young people (children would hardly be the word for these long-tooths) are beaten, maltreated and eventually killed, mostly off-screen, by the superintendent's shovel-faced male sidekick. There's not much help either from the crooked welfare inspector who makes out with Grahame, or the kindly police chief with a suspiciously friendly interest in school-age girls. Excitement mounts as Ellie squares up against another girl, the improbably named Bunch, for the attentions of the thirty year-old teenage hunk Walter, a gymnasium monkey with the face of Bobby Ewing's retarded twin brother. One mediocre plot twist springs a man in a Larry Buchanan-level rubber deformity mask upon the heroine - after a frantic chase through the woods the pursuer is revealed to be...the police chief, working undercover with a rubber deformity mask. He asks Ellie to marry him in return for which he'll turn a blind eye to the fact that *she* is her mother's killer...

Goodness knows where this dreary effort gained the reputation it enjoys in some genre publications. With photography little better than a bad episode of *Prisoner Cell Block H* and a grade Z melodrama soundtrack chiselling away constantly, there seems to be little to recommend it other than its curious GP rating. Despite infrequent, minimal drops of blood, and the prolonged dwelling upon a hammer brandished stiffly before a subjective camera, *Blood and Lace* is an irritating, creakingly old fashioned effort. The idea of a murder thriller set in an orphanage has some potential and Grahame does come across as a quite convincing bitch, but when the interiors look like a Ted V. Mikels production and the tone is so 'afternoon TV', who cares? In *The Aurum Horror Encyclopedia* some loser favourably compares *Blood and Lace* to Sade. Well, I'll take it in preference to 'Smooth Operator', I suppose...

Steve Thrower

THE BLOODSUCKER CONDUCTS THE DANCE
(aka LA SANGUISUGA CONDUCE LA DANZA).
Italy 1975.
Dir: Alfredo Rizzo. With: Femi Benussi, Giacomo Rossi-Stuart, Krista Nell, Patrizia de Rossi, Luciano Pigozzi.

Ireland 1902: Count Marnak (Rossi-Stuart) welcomes a modest theatre company to his isolated castle. The star of the travelling group is Evelyn, a beautiful young woman who bears a striking resemblance to the Count's late wife. She and Marnak begin an affair, but their happiness is cut short by a series of brutal murders in which the victims are decapitated. Initially, the killings are blamed on an ancient family curse, but the real culprit is revealed to be the supposedly dead Countess - hopelessly insane and kept hidden in the castle chapel by a loyal servant.

Although hampered by excessive talkiness and scenes that would be more appropriate in a cheap sex farce, this low key return to the spaghetti Gothics of the '60s is not without a certain degree of charm. Tolerably shot and with a mock-classical synthesizer score by Marcello Giombini, the picture creates an effective ambiance through well-chosen locations and ornate set dressings. Of course the actual murders take place offscreen, but the discoveries of the severed heads - with one being gruesomely mounted on a wall - provide adequate touches of the macabre. Sections featuring a pair of gossiping kitchen maids are particularly annoying, especially a ridiculous scene in which one girl invites the other to grope her blithely bouncing breasts! Other unfortunate episodes, such as the voyeuristic gardener (Pigozzi) falling from his vantage

point outside a bedroom window, and an unbearably drawn out sequence which introduces a police inspector, are thankfully redeemed by the sensitively handled ending: the Count leads his tragic wife out of the chapel and lovingly places a coat around her shoulders before watching a carriage take her away forever. An unexpectedly poignant moment, it perfectly captures the bizarre tenderness which underscores most of the better Italian genre product.

Pasta sleaze fans will find several things in this minor entry to pique their interest: Rizzo found regular work as an actor in classic potboilers like *Bloody Pit of Horror*, whilst sex queen Benussi enjoyed a varied career - from working with Pasolini to directors like Andrea Bianchi! It's always a pleasure to see the terminally handsome Rossi-Stuart, and the sight of Pigozzi (aka Alan Collins) skulking around on the sidelines evokes a pleasing sense of *déjà-vu*.

Mark Ashworth

THE BOGEYMAN AND THE FRENCH MURDERS
(aka MURDER IN PARIS, aka THE PARIS SEX MURDERS, aka CASA D' APPUNTAMENTO).
Italy 1973.
Dir, Co-P & Co-Scr: F.L. Morris (aka Marius Mattei). With: Anita Ekberg, Rosalba Neri, Evelyn Kraft, Howard Vernon, Barbara Bouchet, Robert Saachi.

What madness possesses a soul to title a movie *The Bogeyman and the French Murders*? What a title! And what a movie! Sure, the French Murders take place under the shadow of the Eiffel Tower, but who is the Bogeyman? Why, he's nothing more than a Humphrey Bogart impersonator! I kid you not - meet Police Inspector Robert Saachi, 'The Man with Bogart's Face' himself.

A number of prostitute slayings put jewel thief Antoine Gottvalles under suspicion of murder. Gottvalles is chased by the police through the Parisian backstreets. When he stops in mid-chase to accept a cigarette from a stranger (who turns out to be the Bogey police inspector), Gottvalles is captured and taken away cursing, kicking and quite incredulous that he has in fact been caught. Later in court Gottvalles swears, "From the grave I'll come back!" and promptly escapes. A kind of Mack Sennett chase follows as he steals a motorbike and bumbling police are knocked over and scattered everywhere in their attempts to recapture him. A head-on encounter with a lorry carrying sheet metal decapitates Gottvalles. After this incongruous mishap, stranger things begin to happen...

Anne-Marie (a story nobody) sings a terrible song in a nightclub. Gottvalles' severed head is taken to a lab for 'experiments' (!). In a house of ill-repute, the 'beautiful' Madame Colette receives an unexpected caller; the caller kills her. The Bogeyman investigates. Miles away in the nightclub, a lady struggles to keep an amorous drunk at bay as Anne-Marie finishes another terrible song; when the song is finished everyone in the club - including the drunk - stops to applaud.

Bizarre murders continue. A TV newscaster reads the news in French when everyone else is speaking English. Pointless telephone conversations take place. Back at the lab someone walks in and asks, "How are the experiments going with Gottvalles' head?" And the experimenting physicist has hallucinations in which Gottvalles' eyes *move*, and the physicist has to *kill* accordingly...

It doesn't matter that the real title of *The Bogeyman and the French Murders* lies on some cutting room floor, or that director F.L. Morris is labouring under a pseudonym, *The Bogeyman* is great anyway. How can anyone fail to be charmed by the fact that the Killer Physicist carries Antoine Gottvalles' eyeball around in his jacket pocket; or that Police Inspector Saachi looks, dresses and acts like Humphrey Bogart for no plausible reason whatsoever!? These 'facts', coupled with ample doses of decapitations, eye gougings, nudity and crass stupidity intercut with moments of high weirdness (like the courtroom sequence being shown in negative), make *The Bogeyman* a solid slice of class trash.

David Kerekes

Buster Keaton in BOOM IN THE MOON.
An Alsa Film Production.
Screenplay by Victor Trivas and Jaime Salvador. Music by George Tzipine. Production Manager, Alfonso Dominguez. Produced by Alexander Salkind. Directed by Jaime Salvador.

Keaton's career may be said to have begun to head downhill after the failure of his most ambitious film and arguably his masterpiece, *The General*, which was a commercial disaster as well as being disliked by the reviewers. (*Herald-Tribune*: '...long and tedious...' *Daily Telegraph*: '...trite and stodgy...' *Daily Mirror*: '...slow, very slow...') He was unhappy working with the director James Horne (who would later direct *Way Out West* as well as some of Laurel and Hardy's best short films) on his next feature. What Keaton thought of having to work with the Three Stooges' directors Del Lord and Jules White, on the shorts he made for Columbia before the attack on Pearl Harbour, appears not to have been recorded. One of them, *Pest from the West*, consists largely of Keaton dressing up in a variety of idiotic ethnic costumes and falling off a boat, and as a group they tend to be regarded as the low point of his career.

According to Tom Dardis' book on Keaton, he was persuaded by Alexander Salkind to film *El Moderno Barba Azul* in Mexico just after the end of the war. Dardis lists the cast as Keaton, Angel Garasa, Virginia Street, Luis Bariero and Fernando Sotto, and the running time as ninety minutes, adding that it was unreleased in America and is 'reputedly extremely poor'. All the same, an English-language print running about eighty minutes was broadcast on Granada TV, under the title *Boom in the Moon* and with only the credits listed at the beginning of my review. The film is all that Dardis feared it was, but it is also pretty peculiar.

Keaton plays an unnamed American soldier whom we first see paddling a rubber dinghy until a plane drops a canoe by parachute near him. At this point (signified by a headline and a shot of the signing of the treaty) Japan surrenders. Keaton rows to Santa Cruz, accompanied by a mickey-mousing score which doesn't let him drop a single item of army equipment without a musical comment. Despite the signs in Spanish and the fact that people keep saying "Vamanos" Keaton assumes he is in Japan, and surrenders. Once in jail he is taken for a serial murderer who never eats any sugar (in terms of any plot, a wholly mysterious reference) and who disguises himself with a long blue beard. Some disguise. On this basis he is applauded by his cellmate and by the chief of police,

though he can't understand why, insofar as though they are speaking English on the soundtrack it is supposed to be Spanish. The police chief also has a fine time miming having his throat cut and being strung up at every opportunity. In the midst of all this the director seems to have left Keaton alone to stage a few gags, and so Keaton falls off a table while trying to climb into a top bunk, and makes a mess of eating a tortilla (though to be fair, the tortilla gag eventually harks back to Keaton's unique style, the comedy of competence rather than of slapstick).

Meanwhile a Mexican scientist has invented a moon rocket and needs someone to put in it, since he has to launch it the next day. His niece suggests Keaton, who is about to be tried and executed (pretty rough, the law in Mexico), and so a group of men, presumably bandidos, hold up the police station and bring Keaton and his cellmate to the scientist. By now the orchestra on the soundtrack seems to have been playing Mexican dance music for hours. Keaton gets to drop some eggs and fail to milk the scientist's cow before the launch. There's plenty of air on the moon for the astronauts to breathe, the scientist tells an audience of his colleagues, so long as they breathe through their noses. He accompanies Keaton and partner into the rocket to give them the operating instructions to read and to explain that they must pull "this lever" in precisely two minutes and four seconds, after which he spends more than that amount of screen time in the rocket. But the rocket stays grounded, so his niece climbs into the rocket to check the ignition ("That chick'll fix it," the scientists say, and "Oh yeah, she's an expert.") only to have it take off with her on board. Radio Mexico calls the rocket to announce that Keaton and partner have been cleared of the Bluebeard murders (odd, since the partner wasn't accused). Soon a *Washington Post* headline tells us that the rocket is approaching the moon, apparently "changing orbit" automatically in order to land, but it crashes with a display of special effects Edward D. Wood might have been ashamed of (and don't anyone tell me they were meant to be funny). From this point the film goes into a decline. "Let's put our moon suits on now," the scientist's niece says. "Let's take a walk. Maybe we'll run into the man on the moon." The moon suits look exactly like costumes for pantomime magicians, and since (surprise!) the astronauts never really left Mexico, they soon find themselves in the care of a psychiatrist specialising in "lunar hallucination", a performance which I take to be that of a Mexican comedian making a bid for international fame but which I would cross several streets to avoid. From there it's back to the police station and eventual release, at least for the audience. Keaton, however, is claimed by his Mexican wife who hasn't seen him for twelve years (no, I don't understand this either) and who proves to be so wizened that he locks himself back into his Mexican cell, a fitting symbol for the whole film.

Of course, this wasn't the end of his career. He had yet to make haunting appearances in *Sunset Boulevard* and more substantially in *Limelight*, as well as starring in Samuel Beckett's *Film* (with his back to the camera) and a Richard Matheson episode of *Twilight Zone*. God forbid, though, that *Boom in the Moon* should be anyone's first taste of his work.

(*Note: The film is listed in both Walt Lee and Don Willis, as* The Modern Blue Beard *in the former, and* A Modern Bluebeard *in the latter. Willis gives its date as 1946, Lee as 1947 but unreleased until 1950. Neither pro-*

vide a running time. Lee's cast list includes the following additions and variations to Dardis: Virginia Serret, Luis G. Burreiro, Fernando Soto, Jorge Mondragon. Willis adds one 'Mantequilla' to the cast. Both refer to Famous Monsters of Filmland no. 31, Lee also to a 1966 Spanish volume entitled Imagen y Cienca-Ficcion by Luis Gasca. Ed.)
Ramsey Campbell

BRAIN DEAD.
USA 1989.
Dir: Adam Simon. With: Bill Pullman, Bill Paxton, Bud Cort, Patricia Charbonneau, Nicholas Pryor, George Kennedy. Concorde/New Horizons/MGM Video.

Three pretty weird actors - Pullman, Paxton and Cort - here team up for a seriously weird movie: apparently, cheapskate Roger Corman had this script by *Twilight Zone* veteran Charles Beaumont kicking around the office for twenty years, and he finally decided to dust it off for his ex-wife Julie to produce. In fact, the direct-to-video result is pretty impressive, with Pullman playing a brain-obsessed doctor who finds his reality unravelling when he becomes involved with a mysterious corporation. There are some flashes of *Re-Animator*-type humour, while the second half is one extended paranoid schizophrenic nightmare. Add to all this a blockhead cameo by George Kennedy plus talking brains in jars and you know you've got a low budget classic.
Stephen Jones

BRIDE OF RE-ANIMATOR
(aka RE-ANIMATOR 2).
USA 1989.
Dir & P: Brian Yuzna. With: Jeffrey Combs, Bruce Abbott, Claude Earl Jones, Fabiana Udenio, David Gale, Kathleen Kinmont. Wildstreet/Medusa.

This limp sequel to Stuart Gordon's outrageous *Re-Animator* wasn't worth the wait. It picks up where the first film left off as this time Herbert West (Combs) and Dan Cain (Abbott) return to Miskatonic University to use spare body parts to create life instead of just trying to reanimate it. The result is far too much of Screaming Mad George's predictable prosthetics, although the creation of the Bride faithfully echoes the classic scene in James Whale's *The Bride of Frankenstein*. Not helped by heavy censor cuts in the UK and a stupid title change for the moronic video industry, this has less that zero to do with poor old H.P. Lovecraft.
Stephen Jones

COCAINE COWBOYS.
USA 1979.
Dir & Co-Scr: Ulli Lommel. With: Jack Palance, Andy Warhol, Tom Sullivan, Susanna Love, Peter Huckabee, Richard Young.

Ulli Lommel's first American film, made just prior to *The Boogey Man*, managed to avoid any reviews on its

Bride of Re-Animator:
eat your heart out, Elsa
Lanchester, or words to that
effect...

US release and belatedly turned up in the UK on video. Filmed at Andy Warhol's striking Montauk home it is a strange amalgamation of low budget action film and music documentary, and is consequently of little interest to fans of either. The Cowboy Island Band and their manager (Palance) have a nice side-line in supplying dope to a gangster named Vince. When a consignment fails to arrive after a courier is forced to dump it in the ocean, Vince becomes suspicious. After several rehearsal sessions and much snooping around by all the characters, Palance is killed by Vince's hired assassin and the real culprits are themselves double-crossed by their drugs contacts.

In trying to find a vehicle for the band's talents, Lommel must have decided that an action movie was their best bet at commercial success. But the two strands never combine and the plot grinds to a halt while the band perform their songs. The music is passable but its filming is pedestrian, while the simple narrative soon becomes horribly confused and the audience learns nothing about several characters significant to the plot. The bookend structure of having lead singer Dustin (Sullivan) relating the events to interviewer Andy Warhol is unnecessary and makes no sense in terms of the narrative since Warhol figures prominently in the story himself. As expected from a Lommel film the technical aspects are more than adequate and the bleak location is well-used. Unfortunately the directorial style is highly conventional and generates little audience identification or excitement, while the band's lack of charisma hardly promotes involvement in the plot. Jack Palance here essays a sympathetic role but seems a very unlikely band manager; his striking appearance and powerful acting style serve to draw attention to his character, yet in the event he doesn't actually do very much - it is the other performers that suffer in comparison. Warhol looks his familiar pale and fragile self and it is to be assumed that he is on hand to provide the musicians with some degree of legitimacy. This movie comes across as a genuine oddity but that's not enough to sustain interest for a full ninety minutes.

Julian Grainger

No-one expects the Spanish Inquisition! (© 'We've used this caption before but let's hope no one will notice' dept.) **The Demons,** *if you must know...*

DEMON OF PARADISE.
Philippines 1987.
Dir: Cirio H. Santiago. With: Kathryn Witt, William Steis, Laura Banks, Frederick Bailey, Lesley Huntley.

What - no Vic Diaz cameo? In Hawaii, dynamite fishing awakens Akusa, a scaly rubberoid creature of legend, from its sleep in the deep. "That's a carnivorous lizard man of the early Triassic...it's also the link between mammals and reptiles." Or is it a mutation? "All the pan-fried toxic muck we throw at this planet...you never know what it might throw back at you." A hotelier and a sleazy hippie journalist try to turn the monster into a tourist attraction, the *Connoisseur* magazine babe for January poses in a bikini and snorts coke, the monster mauls a few natives and the local cop teams up with a lady scientist to trash the beastie. At one point, the high standards of tabloid journalism are upheld by the headline 'AQUATIC BEAST DEVOURS DAD WHILE HE'S TRYING TO FEED STARVING KIDS.' The monster's favourite method of killing people is to scare them so badly that they drop things that happen to be on fire near sticks of dynamite. After a long, boring stretch, the army turns up and totals the creature with bullets and grenades. As Gill-Man rip-offs go, this monster looks better than the one in *The Swamp of the Lost Monsters* but not as good as the one in *Destination Inner Space*.
Kim Newman

THE DEMONS
(aka LOS DEMONIOS, aka LES DEMONS).
France/Portugal 1972.
Dir: Clifford Brown (Jesus Franco). With: Anne Libert, Britt Nichols, Howard Vernon, Alberto Dalbes, Karin Field, John Foster, Doris Thomas.

Set in England during the reign of Charles II, but dressed in mainly Elizabethan costumes, this sex-horror item trails a long way after *Matthew Hopkins -Witchfinder General* and even *Mark of the Devil* in the witch torturing stakes. Typical of Franco's mix-and-match of literary and historical references is the way the villainous Judge Jeffreys (Foster) is partnered by Milady De Winter and a servant called Renfield, and an artist called de Quincey is called upon to act as the hero. Anne Libert and Britt Nichols are the convent-raised daughters of an executed witch; they spend the film panting in the nude, being tortured or seeking vengeance, while period muzak or sub-'Shaft' disco burbles on the soundtrack. As usual, Vernon slices himself the best dialogue: "A woman weeping is like a melodious modulation...both touch my sensibilities and stir my spirit and blood to weaken me." Cut by over twenty minutes, this still retains vestiges of tongue-pulling and nipple abuse, but the supernatural horror is confined to an unimpressive trick whereby a witch's kiss reduces a victim to a polished skeleton. The script attempts to work in some 'history' - at a ball, a guest remarks, "there is some speculation that the Earth is round...that it is shaped like a globe", and Jeffreys is supposed to be conspiring with William of Orange to take over the country. The message would seem to be that witches ought to be burned just to be on the safe side, and that a similar fate should be accorded to whoever gave Jesus Franco a zoom lens.

(*Note: Due to an apparent misprint in the* Monthly Film Bulletin *this film has been erroneously listed as* Os Demonios *in various sources. Ed.*)
Kim Newman

DERANGED.
Canada 1974.
Dir: Jeff Gillen & Alan Ormsby. With: Roberts Blossom, Cosette Lee, Les Carlson, Micki Moore, Pat Orr, Marion Waldman, Marcia Diamond, Arleen Gillen. AIP.

Deranged is a neglected gem of '70s horror. Its surprising appearance, uncut, on Sky TV was a boon to fans who may have despaired over seeing anything but a handful of stills. Cut by two minutes for its 1976 UK release, *Deranged* more than lives up to the grim reputation it has accumulated since. Even the rather silly interruptions provided by an on-screen narrator are tolerable when one recognises none other than *Videodrome's* Barry Convex (Carlson) lurking beneath the sideburns and heavy glasses!

The film is based fairly closely on the antics of Wisconsin necrophile Ed Gein, a farmer who in the late '50s was discovered to have robbed graves of female corpses. As well as preserving them, he also fashioned masks, musical instruments and full-body aprons from the skins he'd collected. And, as any *Shock* readers will know, his activities provided inspiration for both *Psycho* and *The Texas Chain Saw Massacre*. Despite changing Gein's name to Ezra Cobb, however, Ormsby's screenplay sticks closer to the facts than either of its more famous fellows.

Ezra Cobb lives with his sick mother (Lee) in a remote farmhouse; he's pathetically attached to her, despite being well into middle age. His mother's fanatical religious convictions spew from her in a constant invective which links sex with sin, disease and death. Ezra swallows this poisonous diet completely. When she dies, Ezra can't stand being alone and digs up her putrefying corpse, returning it to the house. Despite dropping casual remarks about his necro activities, which gradually extend to a collection of other corpses, no one believes him to be anything other than a rather eccentric old man with an odd sense of humour. Ezra strikes up a brief relationship with tubby spiritualist Maureen Selby, the one woman of whom his mother had approved. But after succumbing to her suggestion of a seance, he is repelled by her sexual advances and shoots her dead. A waitress from a nearby bar accidentally stumbles on Ezra's 'friends' arranged around a dining table and is forced to sit with them for supper. Ezra beats her to death with a human thigh bone when she tries to escape. A final victim is chased and trapped in the snowbound woods near Ezra's farm. A handful of local men converge on the farmhouse, too late to rescue the girl who hangs eviscerated in the barn.

Although *Deranged* approaches its subject with less velocity and viciousness than *The Texas Chain Saw Massacre*, certain set-pieces are just as effective in their own way. Chief among them is the prolonged sequence depicting the fate of Mary, the unfortunate cocktail waitress who stumbles into Cobb's madhouse. After dropping in on a supper time gathering of mouldy corpses, she stares in incomprehension as a raddled old cadaver twitches spasmodically to life and begins turning the handle of a decayed barrel organ. A cracked tuneless drone fills the room. The 'corpse' is actually Ezra himself, dressed in a decrepit old woman's hair, facial skin and breasts, the latter tied around him like an apron. In a scene echoing Hooper's film, the girl is subjected to a hideous dinner party with Ezra's collection of stuffed old women lolling at the table.

And, like *Texas*, the film here allows moments of macabre hilarity to surface - as fuel for, rather than

Ezra gets down to business in **Deranged**.

respite from, the horror of the situation; such as Ezra's attempts to impress his pretty captive by prancing around in a ludicrous war dance, beating a drum made from human belly-skin with a human thigh bone. "I'm jus' tryin' to show you I got talents too," he says. However, in contrast to *Chain Saw's* speed-freak frenzy Ormsby and Gillen opt for a surprisingly effective slow-motion dénouement to the scene, the sequence coming to a freeze-frame dead-end on Cobb's warped, grinning face as he bludgeons his victim to death.

Ormsby's script is replete with queasily observed black humour, leaving memories of his puerile *Children Shouldn't Play with Dead Things* well behind. Exchanges between Ezra and his dying mother unite hilarity and disgust as he crams spoonfuls of pea soup into her mouth while she coughs up globs of blood. "Don't bleed, mama," he cries, spooning blood frantically back into her mouth. This element of pathos is followed through later as we hear Mrs Cobb demand to be dug back up from her grave, whilst the camera pans around the poverty stricken kitchen to reveal Ezra huddled on a palette near the stove - his lips moving in imitation of his mother's voice. It's this abject quality that gives *Deranged* its distinct atmosphere. Unlike the unknowable lunatics of Hooper's *Chain Saw*, Cobb/Gein is given a horrible pathos, as well as fleeting moments of awareness of his revolting obsession. And it's the sheer loneliness of his madness which the final scenes capture as we see him eviscerate a girl's corpse hanging by its heels from a beam in the barn. The emptiness of the experience registers and his long moan of despair echoes over perspective shots of rusting farm machinery and a rickety wooden gate swaying listlessly ajar.

Ormsby brought a similar emotional chill to Bob Clark's excellent *Dead of Night*, which he wrote before moving into the mainstream with scripts for *My Bodyguard* and Schrader's shapeless remake of *Cat People* (still better than the dull and over-rated original though!). His script here shows surprisingly subtle inflections, touching briefly but succinctly, for example, on one of the problems encountered in defining whether someone like Gein was actually insane. After

(Right) A bunch of dummies (mummies?) from **Deranged.**

(Below) Erica Blanc sees her wardrobe for **Devil's Nightmare.**

digging up his mother's corpse, Cobb is shown driving home in his truck singing to himself, his mother's corpse hidden in a large sack. When he is pulled up for speeding, however, his crazed carousing stops abruptly. The police officer comments on the rotten smell in the truck, and Ezra quickly claims it is due to a hog he's slaughtered that has "gotten to smellin'." Even in the furthest throws of his mania he is portrayed as being able to spot a risk to his freedom. Immediately after, though, he turns to his mother's corpse and says, "I apologise for callin' you a hog, momma!" (A similar float between cognizance and repression characterised the case of Dennis Nilsen, resulting in his defence of schizophrenia being rejected.) Furthermore, Ormsby deserves credit for filling in the personality of Gein's mother, passed over completely in *Chain Saw* and only drawn on in *Psycho* through Perkins' schizoid impersonation. Ma Cobb's spluttering tirade against "filthy black-souled sluts with pus-filled sores" is a tour-de-force of maternal gross-out that makes Gein/Cobb's necro habits seem almost inevitable. And of course, the success of *Deranged*'s squalid scenario depends largely on actor Roberts Blossom, who animates his gaunt features with varieties of childish glee, wretched sorrow and gnomish cunning, managing to throw light on the man's sick mind without letting the horror and disgust evaporate. Perhaps Gein's case will act as inspiration to other film-makers some day, but for a reasonably accurate evocation of Wisconsin's finest son, one need look no further than Blossom's unnerving performance in *Deranged.*

Steve Thrower

DEVIL'S NIGHTMARE
(aka AU SERVICE DU DIABLE).
Belgium/Italy 1971.
Dir: Jean Brismee. With: Erika Blanc, Jean Servais, Daniel Emilfork, Jacques Monseau, Ivana Novak, Shirley Corrigan.

Along with *Shapely Brunette Seeks Super-Endowed*, this tight sweaterful of tacky terrors is one of my favourite highlights from La Blanc's classic 'top slut' period. Like some awful mating of *The Exorcist* and *Are You Being Served?*, Brismee's directorial debut is a scream-a-minute ride through a nightmare landscape of tangerine nylon sports jackets and wet-look PVC luggage. Voluptuously squeezed into a black bell-bottomed trouser suit - with keyhole detailing to show off her comely navel - Erika turns into a ghoulish succubus to murder the guests at Baron Von Rhumberg's (Servais) gloomy ancestral schloss. To give the proceedings a touch of contemporary relevance, each of the guests represents one of the seven deadly sins, and the Devil (Emilfork) arrives to lead a handsome young priest (Monseau) into temptation. In the end, the night's events are revealed to be a bad dream, but Satan is on hand to take his due when the priest's libido is aroused by the feel of Blanc's curvaceous body beneath her figure-hugging maxi-coat...

Featuring such delicious lines of dialogue as, "Do you think I'm lascivious? Shameless? What if I were to get completely undressed in front of you? Do you think I could be...a succubus?" and characters that would seem more at home in a cut-price situation comedy, *Devil's Nightmare* is high camp at its transcendental highest. The sickly green tint of the pre-credits sequence, in which the Baron is shown stabbing his baby daughter to death, sets the mood perfectly for the string of hokey killings that provide the picture's brief burst of low-key gore. In a saucy variation on Julie London's 'Cry Me a River' scene from *The Girl Can't Help It*, Brismee has Blanc do a laughable 'now you see her, now you don't' vanishing act. The twist is that instead of wearing a *different* costume each time she reappears, leggy Erika is simply wearing *less* costume and ends up totally naked! The pleasantly garish Gevacolor photography and the baroque art direction manage to fill in the gaps with some striking images, and Alessandro Alessandroni's fabulous score, complete with eerie, wailing female vocals and twangy electric guitar, contributes further to the atmosphere of Biba Gothic. The splendidly cadaverous Emilfork sends a few genuine shudders down the spine, but the overall tone is pure 'Twenty Great Hits, But Not By the Original Artists'. I love it - if the Rubettes had made horror films instead of wonderfully sugary teenybop singles, movies like *Devil's Nightmare* would have been the result...(*Of all the perverse assertions to appear in* Shock Xpress *over the years, this has to be one of the most twisted...Ed.*)

Mark Ashworth

THE DOORS.
USA 1991.
Dir & Co-Scr: Oliver Stone. With: Val Kilmer, Frank Whaley, Kevin Dillon, Meg Ryan, Kyle MacLachlan, Kathleen Quinlan, John Densmore. Carolco.

Miserable dullards who know less than zero have castigated this movie for its self-indulgence, misogyny, excessive running time and general addle-patedness - I think we can afford to be liberal and only subject the blinkered philistines to short, relatively painless deaths... *The Doors* not only contains pretty much every image, anecdote and/or apocryphal tale I've read, heard or *imagined* about Jimbo Morrison over the past twenty years, but puts them into a context where one can finally (vicariously) *be there* as Morrison immerses himself in every Satanic excess Babylon has to offer. It's a wild, acid-frenzied sprawl of booze and dope-induced madness, charting Morrison's rise from beach bum to cock-rock poet of the '60s to bloated Lizard King, dead in the bath at the age of twenty-seven. Besides the non-stop drugs and sex (Jimbo and a *buxom* Nico?!?) and astonishing reconstructed concert footage, there's Kilmer's definitive 'rock star' performance, MacLachlan mugging it up as arch-goon Ray Manzarek (anyone foolish enough to subscribe to the notion of Manzarek as the unsung genius of The Doors should check out their two post-Morrison

efforts or his solo albums) and Crispin Glover as Andy Warhol! With its swooping, swirling camerawork (one of the steadicam operators is *Street Trash* director Jim Muro) and mind-blowing editing (both sound and photography), *The Doors* is a total cinema experience, a two-and-a-half-hour trip as compulsive and cathartic as *Apocalypse Now* or *Videodrome*. Yeah, I liked it...

Stefan Jaworzyn

EDWARD SCISSORHANDS.
USA 1990.
Dir: Tim Burton. With: Johnny Depp, Winona Ryder, Dianne Wiest, Anthony Michael Hall, Kathy Baker, Vincent Price. 20th Century-Fox.

A transcendental experience. A romantic fantasy classic. A delicate, timeless fable not to be missed. You want more? Tim Burton's bewitching *Edward Scissorhands* is a magical, mystery tour-de-force, a heart-felt masterpiece representing his finest hour. Revealing his genius imagination, camp surreality and visual story-telling talents at the peak of their audacious perfection, *ES* is Burton's *E.T.* - a wildly original magnum opus topping everything he's done to date.

Created by inventor Vincent Price, who dies before he can replace the Punkenstein's razor-sharp prototypes with proper hands, Depp is taken from his gloomy gothic mansion into Avon Lady Wiest's candy-coloured suburban home. Becoming the talk of the bored Stepford wife community for shearing hedges, grooming dogs and cutting hair, he falls in wistful love with Winona Ryder. But the tide of concerned friendliness turns when he's framed for robbery and, in time-honoured Torch-Bearing Villager finale, is hounded out of town back to sad, yearning, cursed isolation.

Framed as a bedtime story explaining why snow falls each tropical Christmas, Burton's masterful fusion of poignant fairy-tale themes with brilliant contemporary slants packs an emotional wallop certain to float you out of the cinema on a spellbound high with tears in your eyes. Potent heart-breaking symbolism, with exact measures of meanness and strangeness, is the entrancing secret of this *Elephant Man* meets *Hairspray* enchantment, easily matching the tales of Hoffman, Brothers Grimm and Hans Christian Andersen in terms of sheer haunting power, exquisite charm, dark romance and palpable mythic qualities. Burton's bravura blizzard of dislocated Disney imagery simply glows with mesmerising performances, fabulous art direction and a glorious Danny Elfman 'Sugar Plum Fairy'/Morricone score. *Edward Scissorhands* is a dazzling triumph, a slice of unbridled magnificence and the best fantasy treat I've seen in years.

Alan Jones

Tim Burton is Edward Scissorhands: the misunderstood artist, whose prodigious imagination, romantic soul and basic decency can find no place in the dark heart of modern America.

Well, I'm sure that's what Mr Burton would like us to think.

However, *Edward Scissorhands*, both film and character, paints a far more candid portrait of its creator than he might have intended - not so much childlike as childish and not so much self-sacrificing as self-absorbed.

For all its lyrical yuletide trappings and tragic overtones, there is something distinctly unpleasant at the

The British distributor of **The Doors** *refused to provide any stills from the film. Here's a snap of Jimbo's grave instead.*

Johnny Depp as **Edward Scissorhands.** *A work of unmitigated genius or unspeakable self-indulgence? Do you dare to disagree with Alan Jones? Is David Taylor criminally insane? Do you care?*

heart of *Edward Scissorhands*; viewing it is rather like pulling a Christmas cracker and finding a dead mouse inside. Taking its cue from seasonal classics like *A Christmas Carol* and *It's a Wonderful Life*, the film follows the revelatory adventures of the title character as he departs his Gothic sanctuary for the mixed blessings of a holiday in suburbia. At first welcomed with open arms for his artistic abilities and charming eccentricity, Edward's other-worldliness (or should that be lack of worldliness?) soon begins to strike deeper and deeper notes of discord in the community. So far, so good - this is the very stuff of high tragedy. But it is at precisely this point that Burton scuppers his own intentions by mistaking gratuitous self-pity for genuine pathos. Edward's petulant fit of vengeful vandalism on the neighbourhood and his miraculous winning over of the affections of the prettiest girl in town are as unlikely, given all that has gone before, as they are self-indulgent. And whereas Ebenezer Scrooge and George Bailey were ennobled by their exposure to the harsh realities of life, Edward is too ungenerous a character to have any option but to slope back to the womb of his dark castle and indulge his own

juvenile fantasies. In this modern fairy-tale's most badly judged (and grotesquely bathetic) moment, the pretty heroine renounces her love for Edward in favour of the kitsch and tedium of suburban life.

If *Edward Scissorhands* fails on a dramatic level, this is in no way compensated by its technical achievements. Burton's roots in the two-dimensional world of animation have become painfully apparent as the years roll by, rendering even the most impressive of sets (such as Edward's gothic castle or the noirish labyrinth of Gotham City in *Batman*) about as visually exciting as the painted backdrop in an amateur pantomime. If the quite wonderful sets are wasted because Burton refuses to explore them, that's nothing compared to the short shrift given to his film's characters. Depp is left floundering in his role because he hasn't been given anything positive to do, just events to react against. Ryder's character is robbed of any of the nuances which might have rendered her transformation from cheerleader bimbette to sensitive lover even remotely believable. And pity poor Vincent Price, whose performance is stretched so thin as to be almost transparent. It is indicative of Burton's complete lack of a sense of direction that the flashback scenes of Edward's genesis seem to have been thrown in at random to somehow give the film a dramatic resonance which it patently has not got. One rather gets the impression that the director spent more time deliberating over the exact design of Edward's scissor hands than he did developing a coherent script. Which only goes to prove that no amount of gimmickry can compensate for the lack of a plot, characters or a genuine cinematic vision.

It has become increasingly apparent since his debut feature, *PeeWee's Big Adventure* (which at least made a virtue of its own free-wheeling structure), that Tim Burton cannot even be dubbed a promising talent. On the strength of *Beetlejuice*, *Batman* and *Edward Scissorhands* there is precious little ability there worth developing. Unfortunately it would be too much to hope that, like his creation, he would just lock himself away and make movies in private so that people wouldn't have to waste their time, energy and money in actually going to see them.

David Taylor

FOOD OF THE GODS II.
Canada 1988.
Dir: Damian Lee. With: Paul Coufos, Lisa Schrage, Michael Copeman, Colin Fox, Frank Pellegrino, Frank Moore. Carolco/Rose & Ruby/Guild Video.

For every *Total Recall* you've got to remember that Carolco also turns out laughable rubbish like this direct-to-video turkey. It's apparently an uncredited remake of Bert I. Gordon's *The Food of the Gods*, about a growth serum that goes haywire and results in a swarm of unconvincing mutant rats chomping on guests during the gala opening of a campus swimming pool. There's also a giant boy, a huge tomato and a melting scientist. Even Bert's dime-store effects were an improvement over what's on show here. At least they didn't bother to credit H.G. Wells' novel this time.

Stephen Jones

HIJOHKAIDAN: LIVE AND CONFUSED.
USA 1990.
Alchemy/RRR Video.

'Music' lovers unable to take the demands of *Men Behind the Sun*'s 'complex narrative' might care to subject themselves to this ludicrous document of Japanese performance art/confrontational noise retards on the rampage. Featuring live performances spanning 1981-1988 (I defy anyone to spot the 'progression') with some studio bilge thrown in, its main claim to fame is the inclusion of yet *more* autopsy footage (ho hum). Well, this autopsy footage *is* actually different (for one it's Japanese) and contains an edit which provides a genuine shock - a cut from some solarised porn to a nude girl of almost the same build as the porno starlet being opened up. The live material is variable, but seeing these clowns perform *does* provide more than a few laughs (plenty of po-faced bashing, crashing, instrument destruction and sundry carnage) and there are a couple of priceless clips (not least their version of 'Purple Haze', committed to vinyl on the *Limited Edition* LP). Musically Hijohkaidan sound like primitive, unstructured Whitehouse colliding with Lou Reed's *Metal Machine Music* - if that's your poison then you can safely relax for an hour of pure bliss with this demented offering.

Stefan Jaworzyn

HOUSE OF TERROR
(aka FIVE AT THE FUNERAL).
USA 1972.
Dir & P: Sergei Goncharoff. With: Jenifer Bishop, Arell Blanton, Irene Byatt, Jacquelyn Hyde, Mitchell Gregg, Irenee Byatt.

This is one of those obscure movies that almost frightens you into believing that the output of the US independent exploitation scene is complete garbage. While this is manifestly not the case, *House of Terror* is a depressing squib of movie with few redeeming features. Director Goncharoff's only notable previous credit was as editor on Al Adamson's *The Female Bunch*. The story concerns strange goings-on in a Californian mansion where Jenifer Andrews (Bishop) accepts a job as nurse to the wife of millionaire Emmett Kramer (Blanton). The usual murder-mystery characters are all present (ailing wife, jealous sister, psychopathic

boyfriend) and of course the bodies soon pile up. There are several fake suspense sequences to irritate the viewer ("It was only a joke, honey") as well as the all-too-familiar ghostly apparitions of murder victims. Byatt plays Kramer's wife Marsha and her identical twin sister Dolores in a cast that totals six persons, just one of the ways Goncharoff kept his production costs to a minimum. The final revelation that mute maid Norma (Hyde) is a psychopathic maniac - when she has heretofore done nothing except creep around scowling - throws narrative logic straight out of the window. The one decent action sequence, where Kramer's car careers through the streets with no brakes, was probably handled by second unit director John 'Bud' Cardos. At the time Cardos was primarily a production manager and actor for Al Adamson and there are other Adamson connections; Jenifer Bishop (who here turns in a passable performance) had appeared in his *Horror of the Blood Monsters* and *The Female Bunch* and would later feature in the 1975 revenge western *Jessi's Girls*. Other personnel include cinematographer Robert Maxwell (*The Zebra Force*) and Phedon Papamichael, now directing films for Roger Corman's Concorde Pictures. It would be difficult to find a more preposterous, wretched tale than this. It has no hooks for a potential genre audience because it is neither horrific nor suspenseful, and there is no pleasure to be had from the characters since they are all unremittingly ghastly; boyfriend Mark is a murderous thug, Jenifer thrives on his abuse and Kramer is just unbelievably stupid. All you have is an uninteresting tale of nasty people killing each other. I am sad to say that I wasted ninety minutes of my life sitting through this.

Julian Grainger

KING OF NEW YORK.
USA/Italy 1990.
Dir: Abel Ferrara. With: Christopher Walken, Steve Buscemi, David Caruso, Larry Fishburne, Victor Argo, Giancarlo Esposito. Rank.

A career 'high' for Christopher Walken as the dope-addled crime kingpin in King of New York.

A sleazy roller-coaster ride through *Fear City*'s criminal underworld, this is Ferrara's best movie since *Ms. 45*. Because *The Driller Killer* director pushes his deep love of the Big Apple's mean skyline more than any storyline, ultra-violent thumb nail sketches get thrown together like a heap of gory road accidents as an outrageous plot excuse. But who needs a narrative structure when Ferrara delivers the goods in a lurid series of mind-blowing - and nose-blowing - set-pieces revolving around paroled Walken reinstating his drug baron position and using the money to fund a hospital in his old Bronx neighbourhood.

As Walken's homophobic, sexist and racist henchmen continuously off Mafia hit-men, Triad trash, *China Girl* stool pigeons and immigrant junkies, the police finally resort to underhand methods to entrap the good fella godfather culminating in a strangely moving finale set in Times Square. With "motherfucker" the every other word uttered and kinky splatter way over the usual limits, *King of New York* is a startling, darkly amusing social shockumentary.

Walken is perfect as the cool king-pin too psychologically fragile to deal with real life, hoist by his own self-obsessed petard as a result of believing his own publicity. With a cocaine party massacre and a back alley torture being major highlights, Abel Ferrara's bloody valentine to his Manhattan hometown is one offer you can't refuse.

Alan Jones

Leatherface shows off his tool.

LEATHERFACE THE TEXAS CHAINSAW MASSACRE III.
USA 1989.
Dir: Jeff Burr. With: Viggo Mortensen, William Butler, Ken Foree, Joe Unger, Kate Hodge, Tom Everett. New Line Cinema.

New Line's attempt to turn Leatherface into another money-making merchandise vehicle like Freddy, Jason and Michael Myers may have backfired due to massive studio cuts, problems with the MPAA and a tagged-on happy ending. However, this second sequel to Tobe Hooper's 1974 cult hit is a hell of a lot better than *2* as two Californian yuppies and a weekend survivalist square off against another family of crazies. Despite his vociferous complaints, the script by splatterpunk author David Schow remains faithful to the backwoods weirdness of the original and there are some nasty touches with a brain-bashing machine and a homicidal little girl. Director Burr (*Stepfather II*) gives

the film a classy look, with one of the most atmospheric studio swamp sets since *Son of Dracula*. Incredibly, the BBFC still stupidly refuses to grant certificates to any of the *Chain Saw* films.

Stephen Jones

THE LUCIFER COMPLEX.
USA 1979.
Dir: David L. Hewitt & Kenneth Hartford. With: Robert Vaughn, Merrie Lynn Ross, Keenan Wynn, Aldo Ray, William Lanning, Ross Durfee. Vista/Gold Key.

Here's a real obscurity, as co-writer/co-director Hewitt proves that he's learned nothing about film-making since *The Wizard of Mars* back in 1965. After an interminable discourse on the futility of war, a near-future viewer of a video 'time capsule' watches as toupéed secret agent Robert Vaughn (still trying to relive his *Man from UNCLE* days) tries to stop Fourth Reich Nazis Wynn and Ray, under the command of an aged Führer, from creating an army of clones to conquer the world. In the end he fails. This looks as if it was pieced together using footage from several other films, and the result is so inept that there's even a shot of the clapperboard edited into a fight sequence! For completists only.

Stephen Jones

MANIAC COP 2.
USA 1990.
Dir: William Lustig. With: Robert Davi, Claudia Christian, Michael Lerner, Bruce Campbell, Laurene Landon, Robert Z'Dar. Movie House/Fadd/Medusa.

Look, okay, I admit it: I actually enjoyed *Maniac Cop*, and this nearly-as-good sequel reunites writer/producer Larry Cohen and director Lustig with another edge-of-the-seat action chiller. Z'Dar's horribly mutilated Matt Cordell joins the ranks of Freddy, Jason *et al* as a fully fledged nemesis who quickly kills off Campbell and Landon, survivors from the first film, and then goes on a psychopathic rampage with sleazy stripper killer Leo Rossi. Once again Spiro Razatos' breathtaking stunts are the high point, and what more can you ask from a film that includes Charles Napier as a talk show host and is dedicated to Joe Spinell..?

Stephen Jones

MEET THE APPLEGATES.
USA 1990.
Dir: Michael Lehman. With: Stockard Channing, Ed Begley Jr, Cami Cooper, Bobby Jacoby, Dabney Coleman. New World.

Can a tribe of giant Brazilian cockroaches infiltrate provincial Ohio and blow up a nuclear power station in protest over the destruction of the Amazon rain forest? You'll find out in Michael Lehman's witty, surreal send-up of '50s bug-eyed monster flicks and semi-detached suburban society. The *Hudson Hawk* and *Heathers* director turns his keen satirical eye on tacky sci-fi (complete with Kevin Yagher's squishy rubber creatures), brainless pop culture and trashy Americana in this hilarious eco-comedy.

Channing and Begley head the right-on pest-nest who transform chameleon-like into a typically average sitcom family based on a 'Fun with Dick and Jane' primer found in their jungle home. But while their creepy-crawly spirits may be willing, their flesh disguises are weak. For they gain the worst human foibles and forget their mission. Channing falls prey to credit card mania, blotting out rising debts with booze - grasshopper cocktails are her favourite. Begley indulges in extra-marital sex with his secretary and resorts to entomology magazines for page three excitement in times of frustration. Cooper gets pregnant, attends feminist lectures and turns lesbian - her birth-to-a-translucent-egg scene is ultra unpleasant! Jacoby falls in with Heavy Metal drug dealers and remains permanently stoned - "Pass the roach, man!" As the attic fills up with the cocooned victims of their excesses it's up to transvestite queen Coleman to get the sabotage plan back on course during a community staging of a 'People Are Neat' musical.

Meet the Applegates runs out of steam after a brilliantly energetic first hour, but this insecticide mixture of *Parents*, *Them!* and *Quatermass and the Pit* is still wild, weird and wonderfully funny. Definitely destined for cult classic status.

Alan Jones

MEN BEHIND THE SUN.
China 19??.
Dir: F.T. Mous. All other credits in Chinese.

Obsession with death leads us through strange, sometimes appalling territory. Although exceptional artists can achieve the desired state of morbid vertigo through simulation (John McNaughton springs to mind), the death obsessive often turns away from fiction, in search of kicks that diminish still further the space between voyeur-subject and death-object. Forensic footage provides a death spectacle which satisfies, for a while, by confronting us with images of the body *in extremis*; an autopsy film's conspicuous absence of cinema mechanism, of aesthetics, seems at first to allow closer inspection of the death-object. And yet, the matter-of-factness of a 'film' like the SPK-associated *Human Post-Mortem* (appropriated from medical sources) is a cinematic dead-end that can seem curiously flat and boring. Which leads us grate-

fully back to Art! It might be just a miniscule step back, to Brakhage's *The Act of Seeing With One's Own Eyes*. Or it might be a longer step, with one foot still in the video grave, to Juan Logar's mutant hybrid of autopsy footage and melodrama, *Autopsia*. Located in a single-space category of its own somewhere in between is *Men Behind the Sun*.

Men Behind the Sun is a Chinese propaganda/docudrama utilising real human corpses for added impact. Apparently made with the cooperation of the Chinese authorities, it depicts experiments carried out by the Japanese during World War Two in Manchuria, where research into bacteriological military capability was undertaken. Stories of Japanese cruelty were widespread after the war, and the puppet state of Manchoukou, or Manchuria, became synonymous with torture and criminal brutality. (Even the generally frivolous *Avengers* series turned grim when handling Manchuria in the episode 'Room Without a View'). By February 1945 the Japanese were suffering heavy battle losses and biological warfare became increasingly tempting to their command. Using local Chinese as test subjects, their research into such weapons allegedly outstripped even the Germans, with bubonic plague mutation just one of the notables on their agenda. Given that *Men Behind the Sun* was apparently conceived as a piece of virulent anti-Japanese propaganda, its array of facts may be open to argument. Certainly, a review of this sort can do little more than remind readers of the film's propaganda status - documentation of the period exists, but is too extensive to reprint here.

Director Mous has stripped the film down to its hideous basics, with little more than a cursory plot depicting the training and deployment of a fresh batch of recruits. As the Youth Corps become gradually calloused to the work they perform, a series of experiments on human subjects are shown in graphic, unflinching detail. Each Chinese victim's demise is catalogued by an on-screen subtitle listing their name, their date of murder and their age at the time of death. This matter-of-fact device, which mirrors the clinical detachment of the camp's Mengele-like doctors, brings the plot to a standstill, leaving us with only the casual sadism of the experiments to contemplate. Other subtitles offer bleak section descriptions of the building: 'Animal Breeding Unit', 'Bacteria Breeding Room' and 'Outdoor Frostbite Experimentation Section'. It takes another atrocity, the bombing of Nagasaki and Hiroshima, to nudge *Men Behind the Sun* out of its torture daze.

A trainee doctor rushes out of a laboratory and vomits; a colleague explains to a military onlooker that the man still isn't completely adjusted to his new work. No wonder - the work includes...

Tethering a woman outside in the snow (temperature -35c) with the outstretched arms bared. Freezing water

Ed Begley Jnr as 'Dick' in **Meet the Applegates.**

is poured over her arms until they are thickly encrusted with ice. After a lengthy period her arms are beaten with a stick to remove the ice and she is taken inside. There, her arms are plunged into hot water. When she is allowed to remove them from the tank, a doctor tugs the soggy flesh and skin effortlessly off the bones, as if removing a pair of elbow-length gloves. The woman screams helplessly at her ruined arms.

Forcing a young man to plunge his hands into super-cooled nitrogen. His brittle, frozen digits are shattered and snapped off by repeated blows.

Placing a naked man in a decompression chamber. In a shocking sequence that is hard to adequately describe, his prone body swells and prolapses violently through the anus; the rectum, bowels and much of the large intestine shoot across the floor. Frighteningly realistic, this scene appears to utilize a recently deceased human cadaver.

Killing a mute Chinese boy of about twelve, befriended by one of the soldiers, who plays ball near the camp. The head of the Medical Section suggests to the soldier that he bring him into the camp. Once in the laboratory he is shown around and asked by a benignly smiling officer to undress. The boy is placed on a surgical table and chloroformed unconscious. A full evisceration takes place immediately, while the boy is still alive. His organs and still beating heart are removed and placed in jars. Although the body in question isn't the child actor's, it *is* the body of a boy of almost exactly the same age and appearance.

There's more, but it's pointless to go on really. Dialogue constantly has superior officers stressing that the victims ("marutas") are just "material for experiments", "a log for making the fire", and so on. But there's a hint that the director found it impossible on the fourth atrocity described above - the soldier who befriended the boy organises a reprisal against the officer who initiated the killing and we see him take a severe beating from a gang of recruits wielding heavy sticks. He isn't finished off though, and is seen alive for the next scene showing a cat thrown into a room teeming with rats. Even by 'Mondo Shitto' standards this scene is utterly disgusting, and cat-lovers are advised to spare themselves the nauseating sight of the creature being eaten alive. I know they say Orientals are less sentimental about animals than most, but honestly...

With the knowledge that something very similar to this catalogue of horrors did actually take place, *Men Behind the Sun* is a gruelling movie to watch. Whilst it shares subject matter with the so-called 'Nazi cycle' of horror films initiated by the likes of *Ilsa, She-Wolf of the SS* and propagated by Italian schlock such as *SS Experiment Camp*, it really does show these tawdry Western efforts up for the witless garbage they are. *Men Behind the Sun* is *exactly* what you might have expected from things like Garrone's films before seeing them for the campy nonsense they turned out to be. There's no trace of the Nazi cycle's comically fiendish gloating or ridiculous ham histrionics. Here, the closest thing to a joke is the crematorium attendant who chops up real, decaying cadavers and throws them into a furnace, singing constantly in a cracked sing-song wail. He's portrayed as so completely off his trolley that he has to be carried bodily from the furnace room when the evacuation of the camp begins. But *Men Behind the Sun* is no joke. With the ever-present threat of chemical warfare in the Gulf and a still-incurable disease like AIDS springing up, suspiciously in synch with a Western right-wing backlash

against permissiveness and promiscuity, this Chinese film - made goodness knows when - strikes too many contemporary nerves to consume flippantly. For the obsessives described in the first paragraph (*aren't you glad you don't know any...? Ed.*) it's a disturbing must-see, but be sure you know what your tolerances are before checking out this one.

Steve Thrower

MISERY.
USA 1990.
Dir: Rob Reiner. With: James Caan, Kathy Bates, Frances Sternhagen, Richard Farnsworth, Lauren Bacall, Graham Jarvis. Castle Rock/Nelson/First Independent.

Stephen King's best novel for a decade also becomes one of his most successful film adaptations, as Reiner and scriptwriter William Goldman flesh out the claustrophobic terrors of the book's relatively simplistic narrative. Caan gives an impressive performance as injured novelist Paul Sheldon, imprisoned and tortured by his 'number one fan', Annie Wilks (Bates). As Annie's insane obsession turns to homicidal rage, Sheldon is forced to continue the exploits of his fictional heroine, Misery Chastain, while he attempts to contrive ever more complex methods of escape. The film-makers turn the screw slowly but surely, until by the climax the tension is all but unbearable. There are a couple of pretty nasty moments (including a genuinely shocking foot-hammering scene), and amongst a first-rate cast, Richard Farnsworth stands out as the wily sheriff.

Stephen Jones

THE MONSTER OF THE OPERA
(aka IL MOSTRO DELL' OPERA).
Italy 1964.
Dir: Renato Polselli. With: Giuseppe Addobbati, Vittoria Prada, Marco Mariani, Barbara Howerd.

Despite its ramshackle technique and feeble attempts at comic relief, this micro-budgeted sexploitation film contains several sequences of undeniable power - managing to build a far more convincing atmosphere of erotic menace than any one of Jean Rollin's turgid efforts. Obviously based on *The Phantom of the Opera* but looking more like a cross between Piero Regnoli's *The Playgirls and the Vampire* and a cheesy '30s backstage picture, Polselli's follow up to *The Vampire and the Ballerina* takes place almost entirely within the confines of an abandoned theatre. The eerie prop-strewn cellar houses Stefano (Addobbati), a ravenous vampire who soon begins to prey on a troupe of young performers rehearsing upstairs in the cavernous auditorium. Falling in love with the star of the show (Prada), Stefano spirits her away to his secret underground lair. In the movie's most impressively nightmarish scene, she is tortured with a pitchfork before being subjected to an attack from a bevy of chained, writhing vampire sluts. Predictably, Prada turns out to be the reincarnation of Stefano's long-lost paramour and eventually returns to the theatre to introduce the rest of her colleagues to the salacious delights of bloodsucking. At the chaotically staged climax, however, she is saved from damnation when her baleful mentor is reduced to a chalky skeleton.

Perhaps understandably, Polselli shows only a perfunctory interest in the half-baked plot, preferring to concentrate on the visualisation of the screenplay's sexually suggestive undertones. As a result, his evocation of the disturbingly sensual aspects of the vampire's existence is very persuasive, even when compared to more carefully mounted productions such as *I Vampiri* and *Brides of Dracula*. Similarly, *Il Mostro*'s quieter passages display a surprisingly sensitive feel for the creation of Gothic mood, and it seems a pity that the director's interesting - though rather muddled - sensibilities have been constantly shackled to the limitations of zero budget trashiness. Thankfully, the detrimental effects of the film's irritating lapses into slapdash amateurism are diluted by occasional bursts of truly bizarre campiness. One particularly surreal segment has practically the entire cast performing a ridiculous orgiastic dance whilst under Stefano's hypnotic control. To the accompaniment of a cringingly ritzy big band number, which strikes up from *absolutely nowhere*, everyone go-gos frenetically as Polselli randomly slings in shaky close-ups of Addobbati's wildly staring eyes. Other notable moments occur when the black and white camerawork achieves a crudely voyeuristic quality, which combines with the art direction and Aldo Piga's creepy score to produce an uneasy sense of claustrophobia, especially in the sections set in the vampire's smoke-filled dungeon. The picture's uneven nature can no doubt be traced to its stilted production history: begun in 1961 as *Il Vampiro Dell' Opera*, it was not finished and distributed until three years later. Since then, this curious little work appears to have languished in undeserved obscurity, consigned to the dumper of late night airings on Italian regional TV - if only such a fate had befallen *The Lost Boys*...

Mark Ashworth

NIGGER LOVER
(aka TOM, aka THE BAD BUNCH).
USA 1973.

Dir: Greydon Clark. With: Greydon Clark, Tom Johnigarn, Jacqulin Cole, Bambi Allen, Aldo Ray, Jock Mahoney. Dimension Pictures.

Jim (Clark) loses his best friend Clay Washington while on active service in Vietnam. Wishing to explain that he died a hero, Jim visits Clay's family - and is beaten up by hostile Tom Washington (Johnigarn) and his brothers. Jim is saved by the timely intervention of two racist cops, Lt Stans (Ray) and Lt Berry (Mahoney) who proceed to handcuff and brutally beat Tom. Jim is under pressure to marry the wealthy Nancy (Cole) but he doesn't wish to make a commitment. He meets the free-wheeling Bobbi (Allen) and they strike up a relationship immediately. Meanwhile, Tom is furious that his father still grovels to the white establishment and consequently beats him to death. Jim goes to the old man's funeral but once again his presence creates friction. Jim tells Nancy that although he loves her he cannot consider marriage and they agree to separate. Jim arrives at a party to find Tom waiting for him and a fight starts - which lands Tom in jail for a month. After sleeping with Bobbi, Jim decides to marry Nancy and tells her the good news. When he gets out of jail Tom and his brothers abduct and then beat up Bobbi. One of the brothers, sympathetic towards Jim, calls the police but it is the two racist cops who arrive. Stans is

beaten to death and Berry is shot. At his wedding to Nancy, Jim is shot dead by Tom.

This extraordinary feature from Greydon Clark is a triumph of offensive film-making. What first appears as a serious attempt to address some of the problematic issues of racism is rapidly revealed as an example of libido-induced film-making, with 'social comment' elements grafted on merely to exploit the (then) current trend of aiming movies at a black audience. Rather than promoting the benefits of cooperation, the logic of the plot suggests that Jim's attempts at communication lead directly to his death. The character of Tom is so full of hate that he becomes psychotic and most of the brothers are seen to participate in the lethal beatings dealt to the cops and Bobbi. The end-credits quotation from Martin Luther King only adds insult to injury. With an arrogance that crosses into narcissism, Clark the writer/director presents Clark the actor as an irresistible stud whose dilemma is simply that he cannot make up his mind between living with the hippie or marrying the society girl. Life is that tough. After spending most of the film screwing both he chooses the latter - the proverbial having your cake and eating it. This is blaxploitation in its worst possible sense; a patronising, pessimistic and reactionary statement about the futility of integration.

Julian Grainger

NIGHT OF THE BLOOD MONSTER
(aka IL TRONO DI FUOCO, aka EL PROCESSO DE LAS BRUJAS, aka DER HEXENTÖTER VON BLACK-MOOR, aka THE BLOODY JUDGE).
Italy/Spain/West Germany 1969.
Dir: Jesus Franco. With: Christopher Lee, Maria Schell, Maria Rohm, Hans Hass, Leo Genn, Margaret Lee, Howard Vernon, Dennis Price.

The success of Michael Reeves' remarkable *Matthew Hopkins - Witchfinder General* spawned a large number of rip-offs, of which the most famous (and unpleasant) are Michael Armstrong's *Mark of the Devil* and Adrian Hoven's *Mark of the Devil Part 2* (which owes a good deal to *The Devils* as well). Needless to say, both were banned in Britain.

Night of the Blood Monster is an addition to the cycle by the prolific and sometimes interesting Jesus Franco. Franco's Hopkins figure is the famous Judge Jeffreys, best known for his services to the restored English crown in the wake of the Cromwellian era. He was actively involved in the Popish Plot prosecutions and the trails of Algernon Sidney, Titus Oates and Richard Baxter, but his reputation for infamy rests largely on the 'bloody assize' which he held after the unsuccessful Monmouth rebellion. Monmouth was the natural son of Charles II and in 1685 attempted to seize the crown from James II. However, his forces were defeated at the battle of Sedgmoor, Monmouth was executed, and Jeffreys was appointed to punish his followers with the utmost severity. This film mixes torture, history, romance and courtly intrigue in equal proportions. As in *Witchfinder General* the charge of witchcraft is used as a means of persecuting political undesirables - in this case the enemies of James II. Chief amongst these are Seften (Hass) and his lover Charity (Schell) whose sister was burned at the stake by Jeffreys. After the failure of the Monmouth rebellion they both end up in Jeffreys' hands, and Charity gives herself to Jeffreys in an attempt to save Seften's life. In the end, however, they are saved by the arrival of William of Orange, whose reign put an end to Jeffreys' activities. In the final shot of Jeffreys we see him fearfully contemplating a scaffold which is being kept busy outside his prison window... (In fact the real Jeffreys was sent to the tower for his own good to protect him from the mob. He died there in 1689.)

Lee is quite impressive as Jeffreys, by no means a cardboard villain, though less complex than the extraordinary Matthew Hopkins. Again, the sexual power bestowed by the character's legal position is heavily stressed, from the moment that Jeffreys gazes at Charity's cleavage whilst sentencing her sister to death. However, the film lacks its model's tight structure and finely judged rhythmic sense. In particular there are too many talky scenes, which are suddenly punctuated by bouts of action such as torture, love-making or battles (something which Reeves couldn't afford - witness the build-up to the battle of Naseby, which never actually occurs on-screen). The torture scenes themselves are not particularly excessive - various floggings, a branding and someone being stretched on the rack. What is rather striking, however, is the revenge of the prisoners on the chief torturer, which seems to come out of a zombie movie as his former victims fall on him and proceed to rip him to shreds with their teeth! Needless to say, the vast bulk of the prisoners are women, chained females being something of a Jesus Franco hallmark. Incidentally, Jeffreys appeared again in Franco's

The Demons, but his best witchcraft film is probably *Les Possedées du Diable*.
Julian Petley

NULL: SONIC ACTION.
USA 1991.
RRR Video.

There's no information forthcoming on the box or the tape itself, but this thirty-minute performance was presumably filmed during K.K. Null's 1990 solo tour of the West Coast - Mr Null being Japan's leading practitioner of aural disturbance, both as a solo artist and with a variety of groups (Zeni Geva, ANP, YBO2, etc). This is a static camera observation of his set, in which he 'persuades' a guitar to make some of the most monstrous sounds imaginable. Utilising an unseen variety of effects (but without the aid of backing tapes) he produces some truly hellish music, each 'number' showcasing a different form of sonic mayhem. Rather unexpectedly, it's amazingly compulsive viewing with no tendency towards repetition, and it's fascinating to actually see how the great man operates. I've certainly wondered how many instruments he uses to produce his squall in the past; now I know it's only *one guitar* I'm even more amazed.
Stefan Jaworzyn

THE PACIFIC CONNECTION.
Philippines 1974.
Dir, P & Story: Luis Nepomuceno. With: Nancy Kwan, Dean Stockwell, Guy Madison, Roland Dantes, Gilbert Roland, Alejandro Rey, Vic Diaz.

Every year a lot of movies are made in the Philippines, often produced with American actors and directors filling in the gaps between their Stateside assignments, but until the advent of video very few were seen anywhere else. There are exceptions of course: the Eddie Romero-directed *Blood Island* films (with John Ashley) were given an extended release in the US, and Roger Corman has had various co-production deals going since the early '70s - co-financing and distributing films by prolific Filipino director Cirio H. Santiago. But usually these movies remain effectively invisible in the West, and actress Nancy Kwan had a second career in Filipino movies during the '70s that has gone almost entirely unrecorded. One film that does sometimes appear in lists of Kwan's work is *The Pacific Connection* made by Filipino mogul Luis Nepomuceno. It's a martial arts movie set in the mid-19th century and, with its locations and period galleons, must have had a relatively large budget by Filipino standards. Nepomuceno served as director, producer and writer and it was filmed at his own studio complex on the outskirts of Manila. The film is concerned with a vendetta between wrongly imprisoned farmer Ben (Dantes) and the Governor (Rey) who murdered his parents. Ben escapes to an idyllic island where he falls in love with beautiful local girl Leni (Kwan). Eventually the Governor hires a samurai assassin to hunt Ben down and he is forced to fake his own death. Ben is taught the higher martial arts by the mysterious Old Man (Madison) and eventually overcomes his adversaries. This is an immensely enjoyable movie; Dantes is an expert in arnis (combat using sticks) and his skills are used to great effect in several well-choreographed and brutal fight scenes. The film does have its sleazier moments (the Governor's fairly graphic castration as he tries to rape Ben's mother, for example), but unfortunately it is top-heavy with redundant dialogue and the narrative is frustratingly unfocussed and episodic - at one point Ben is sent on a quest to find a magical reed (that will provide him with protection from wounding) yet there was no previous indication of mysticism in the plot. While by no means a classic lost film, it is recommended as a fascinating curio and is a must for all devotees of martial arts on celluloid.

Julian Grainger

PREDATOR 2.
USA 1991.
Dir: Stephen Hopkins. With: Danny Glover, Gary Busey, Ruben Blades, Maria Conchita Alonso, Bill Paxton, Robert Davi. 20th Century Fox.

Faced with the seemingly insurmountable task of following a relatively uninspired Schwarzeneggar vehicle (John McTiernan might have been responsible for *Nomads* and *Die Hard*, but *Predator* was essentially a dull stalk 'n' slash picture with one incredibly choreographed and edited sequence - the attack on the rebels' jungle stockade) Hopkins acquits himself admirably, producing a much better sequel than one might have expected. His slick direction and camera pyrotechnics combine with non-stop effects and over-the-top set-pieces to keep the pace moving at a furious rate, while a great cast of 'who's who on the current

exploitation scene' blusters and hams through a script so cliché-ridden it's almost surreal. Certainly Glover is a poor substitute for Arnie, but the sleazy urban setting and the carefully maintained level of dismemberment, decapitation and general mindless violence is more than satisfactory. At this rate Hopkins may well emerge as one of the more interesting '90s exploitation talents.

Stefan Jaworzyn

ROBOCOP 2.
USA 1990.
Dir: Irvin Kershner. With: Peter Weller, Nancy Allen, Dan O'Herlihy, Belinda Bauer, Tom Noonan, Galyn Gorg. Orion/Tobor/Rank.

1990 was definitely the year of the shitty sequel, and they don't come much shittier than this comic book styled follow-up to the 1987 box office blockbuster. Co-scripted by Frank Miller (*The Dark Knight Returns*) and directed by Hollywood hack Kershner, the plot lines left over from the first film are ignored in favour of a simplistic shoot-out between the cyborg cop and drug-crazed criminal kingpin Cain (a nicely psychotic performance by Noonan). You'd never know it was Weller under Rob Bottin's Robo suit, Allen is totally wasted and even OCP's RoboCop 2 (animated by Phil Tippett) holds few surprises. The action scenes are suitably spectacular (so they should be for the money this cost), but the bad news is that they've already announced *RoboCop 3*.

Stephen Jones

*"Where's Arnie?" asks
Kevin Peter Hall in*
Predator 2.

SATAN'S BLADE.
USA 1982.
Dir & P: L. Scott Castillo Jr. With: Tom Bongiorno, Stephanie Leigh Steele, Thomas Cue, Elisa Malinovitz, Ski Mark Ford. MC Productions.

A mountain lake, peaceful in winter sunshine. Thrown from off-screen, a knife thuds into a foreground tree and begins to glow mysteriously. Cut to a bank robbery. Having shot two clerks, the robbers drive to a ski resort beside - gulp! - that lake. In their cabin they disrobe to reveal themselves as gunpersons (and in order to display some not particularly attractive skin). One girl shoots her partner for her share of the loot, but is herself stabbed by a shadowy prowler. That's four deaths in the first few minutes so, lest we get overexcited, it's time for the boredom quota.

The local police - all two of them - don't even bother to close the resort. When the manager suggests closing "to be on the safe side", his mother says darkly, "no one will be safe if it's what I think it is." "My mother has this crazy idea about some legend... the one about the mountain man whose spirit still roams through these hills."

Ah, *that* legend...

Guests arrive - two married couples and a bunch of girls. Mother gets into her stride, telling the legend in detail. The mountain man, forced from his land by newcomers, asked the mountain gods for help, but the Devil answered, giving him a knife which he put to good use. His spirit lives on in the lake.

Of course the guests don't leave, because then there wouldn't be a picture, would there, and we're not to be spared. The girls even take the cabin where the murders took place. So, in due course, all nine guests are slaughtered, mostly with the knife, though one girl is drowned in the sink for variety. The last victim, knifed in the stomach, staggers back with the succinct remark, "You! Why?", giving the killer his cue for the most excruciating acting yet.

"I - don't - know. All I ever wanted was the money. Something inside me I can't control. (*Voice changes.*) You have trespassed on my land..."

We see him throw the knife back in the lake, but afterwards a hand emerges and chucks the thing back into that tree, where it is seen by a passing fisherman. "THE CURSE CONTINUES."

Much of the picture is devoted to endless tedious conversation about the characters' uninteresting relationships. The un-gory killings have no impact thanks to slack direction by Castillo (*or could it be the three minutes thirty-five seconds removed from the picture by the BBFC? Ed.*), who was also responsible for production and original story. The bad acting is boring, not funny, although I suppose wandering about snowy landscapes makes marginally better viewing than, say, old houses or abandoned mines. The music, threatening tinkly keyboard stuff by Martin Jaquish, is effective in its monotonous way. The only goodish (*'goodish'? Ed.*) scene is a dream one of the girls has of a mad killer breaking in.

Closing credits record "Special thanks to Patrick McIntosh, without whose faith and support this film could not have been made." Where are you, McIntosh - there's something inside me I can't control...

Colin Davis

THE SILENCE OF THE LAMBS.
USA 1990.
Dir: Jonathan Demme. With: Jodie Foster, Anthony Hopkins, Scott Glenn, Ted Levine, Anthony Heald, Brooke Smith, Charles Napier, Roger Corman, George Romero. Orion/Rank.

The leanest, meanest psycho-thriller in ages earns Roger Corman protégé Demme his stripes as a top flight director. For once a bestseller comes to the

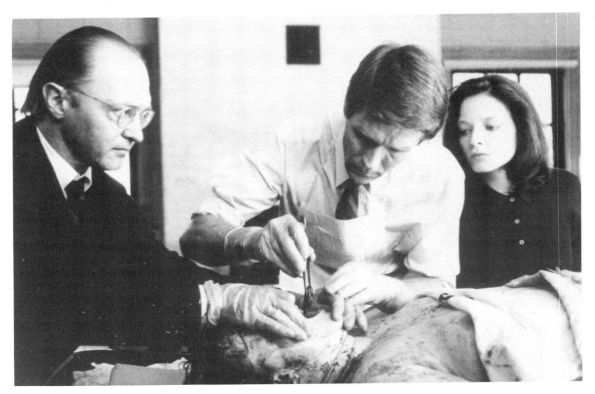

Jodie Foster (right) in **The Silence of the Lambs.**

screen with every outstanding ounce of disturbing brutality and chilling menace intact. Thank scriptwriter Ted Talley for a faithful, no-holds-barred adaptation of Thomas Harris' perverse companion piece to *Red Dragon* (filmed by Michael Mann as *Manhunter*). Eschewing Mann's splatter chic approach, Demme focuses on stunning performances and hard-hitting adult themes to generate maximum suspense without resorting to tired exploitation technique. The compelling result is quintessential, intelligent film-making evoking an immediate and intense response.

Tenacious FBI recruit Clarice Starling (Foster) tracks down Buffalo Bill, a transsexual serial killer who "skins his humps" with the aid of imprisoned psychopath Dr Lecter (Hopkins), who forces her to confront her own haunted past in the process. Instantly gripping, powerful and uncompromising, the hair-raising dialogue alone is enough to cause spine tingles. While it's hard to forget *Manhunter*'s Brian Cox as Hannibal 'The Cannibal' Lecter, Hopkins reinvents the role, making it his own with a wide-eyed, manic Oscar-worthy portrayal of blood-freezing evil. From the huge hall where Lecter is eerily caged (and makes his gruesome escape), through his airport arrival behind restricting bars and metal mouthpiece, to the dingy cellar where Buffalo Bill keeps his frightened quarries, every moment hits relentlessly on the high drama button. There's not a false note in Demme's flawless masterpiece - it's a must-see guaranteed to electrify every viewer.

Alan Jones

STREET HUNTER.
USA 1990.
Dir & Co-Scr: John A. Gallagher. With: Steve James, Reb Brown, John Leguizamo, Valarie Pettiford, Frank Vincent, Richie Havens. 21st Century.

Suckered again... With a trailer promising brutality and ultra-violence, a wise-cracking black vigilante, "motherfucker" every other word and "a terrifying array of weaponry", *Street Hunter* looked set to be some kind of minor blaxploitation classic. It isn't, of course. It's an amateurish effort with poor acting, a retarded script (co-written by James), slack editing (people stand around either waiting for the shot to end or to *be* shot), a two dollar synth score and the cheapest main titles seen since *Boardinghouse* or *Death Bed*... James (who apparently learned nothing from the excellent *I'm Gonna Git You Sucka*) is barely competent, Brown plays Colonel Walsh, a ridiculously batty Viet vet/mercenary closet case who worships Alexander the Great (well, it's a new angle), while Havens bumbles briefly about mumbling and looking embarrassed. Some solace might be found in watching *China Girl*'s lumpen Richard Panebianco have his brains blasted out, but that's about it. Makes *The Punisher* look like a lost Eisenstein classic.

Stefan Jaworzyn

TETSUO.
Japan 1989.
Dir, Scr, Ed, Sp Eff, Art Dir & Co-Ph: Shinya Tsukamoto. With: 'Tomorrow' Taguchi, Kei Fujiwara, Nobu Kanaoka, Shinya Tsukamoto, Naomesa Musaka.

A guy walks into a junkyard, sits down amongst assorted pieces of metal, cables and tubes, opens his leg with a blade and inserts a metal bar into his thigh, accompanied by a post-industrial score. So begins this black and white Japanese film, a mechanical nightmare, the ultimate techno-paranoia picture. It has a uniquely oppressive atmosphere, aided by its stop-motion and special make-up effects. It has neither dubbing nor subtitles, but has practically no dialogue anyway... Another character, an office clerk, is pursued by a robot-handed female on his way back from work and manages to escape after a brutal fight in an underground toilet! Back home he has a nightmare in which he kneels on the floor and is attacked by his wife, who has a cobra between her legs. He wakes up, serves dinner to his wife, and they start to make love - but he begins to mutate, metal partly covering his body, so he retreats to the bathroom. His wife enters, attempting to comfort him, and finds his reproductive bits are now a giant drill with a rotating conical head. After an epileptic tussle she dies, her body faithfully impaled.

Well, it's not exactly the clean-cut, stylised robots of *RoboCop* or *Metropolis* but rather a melting pot of flesh consumed by mechanics. With its traumatic effects, grim music (a Kraftwerk piece seems like a lullaby in comparison) and dark photography, *Tetsuo* is one of the top depressing movies of the '80s.

Lucas Balbo

Tetsuo, a common Japanese given name, can be written with the characters for 'metal' and 'man', and this astonishing 16mm black and white movie is the body-horror cyberpunk tale of monster mutants who fuse flesh and steel in an increasingly creaky and agonised ecstasy of transformation.

In an industrial Japanese hell, a scrapheap casualty who enjoys ramming bits of iron pipe into open wounds is trashed in a hit and run accident, and causes the couple responsible to turn into hideous half-man, half-machine, all-monster creations and to alternately indulge in frenzied and painful sexual congress or try to drill, slash, hack and splatter each

(Below) Twisted mania in **Tetsuo**.

(Over page) A tender and tastefully presented scene of marital bliss from **Tetsuo**.

other to bits. Finding a metal spike in his cheek while shaving, the driver gradually mutates in competition with the underground geek, and his girlfriend and an uptight female commuter are also dragged along the evolutionary path. With monster costumes that come across as the X-rated equivalent of the tatty grotesque outfits that used to crop up in *Dr Who* ('The Claws of Axos') or *Lost in Space* ('The Great Vegetable Rebellion'), this features some of the strongest stuff seen on the screen in recent years, especially when the nominal hero sprouts an uncontrollable pneumatic drill penis and his girlfriend rides him to a messy death, redecorating the wall behind her. It winds up with a pixilated battle, using some of the type of effects mastered by Mike Jittlov in *The Wizard of Speed and Time*, through the streets of town, as the two main mutants chase and hack each other with Marvel Comics verve, finally resolving to spread their biomechanical perversion across the city.

Painful, funny, pretentious and pointed, *Tetsuo* is made with a low budget flair that shows up Jorg Buttgereit for a fumbling amateur, but goes beyond almost anything currently being made in the mainstream, harkening back to the Kurosawa of *Dodes 'Ka-Den*, the Cronenberg of *Videodrome* or the Lynch of *Eraserhead*. In its stylised, shrieking kabuki horror (also slightly reminiscent of the 'industrial sodomy' of Sogo Ishii's Einsturzende Neubauten video *1/2 Mensch*), weirdo Shinya Tsukamoto, a fringe theatre director and outlaw rock promoter, is established as a potential dingbat genius.

Kim Newman

TILL DEATH.
USA 1978.
Dir & P: Walter Stocker. With: Keith Atkinson, Belinda Belaski, Marshall Reed, Bert Freed, Keith Walker, Jonathan Hole.

I like video cassette sleeves like *Till Death* that bear such legends as 'What is Paul's Terrifying Secret?' I like the fact that you know before you actually watch it that the chances Paul has a secret are going to be pretty slim, and that it should be a terrifying one even slimmer. But I like these legends and I like this movie.

For the most part *Till Death* is filmed on a soundstage. It is about the endless love between Anne and Paul and how this love reaches beyond the grave. The movie is divided into two definite parts: that of Paul and Anne when Anne is alive, and Paul and Anne when Anne is dead, the latter part taking place entirely in a mausoleum.

Paul Ryan (Atkinson) has a nightmare wherein he is in his car, trapped in heavy fog. He sees the distant shadowy figure of a woman dressed in white and follows her on foot. Before he knows it, Paul has followed the ghostly figure to a mausoleum. He goes in. Peering into an open coffin he sees the body of a woman with pasty make-up effects and runs away screaming. The woman rises from the coffin and follows. Everything moves into slow motion and Paul reaches the gate of the mausoleum, only to find himself locked in. As the woman closes in, Paul wakes from the dream, drenched in sweat.

The jolly *Till Death* theme song begins on the soundtrack and bright yellow puffed up words roll for the credits, giving the impression that something akin to *The Munsters* is about to begin...

Paul marries Anne (Belaski) and they head off on their honeymoon in the car, only to be caught in a thick swirling fog. They stop the car and exchange lovey-dovey sentiments, waiting for the fog to lift. In the distance, Paul sees a woman in white.

The fog disperses and the couple drive off...right off the side of the road, that is. Anne manages to fall out of the passenger door as the car makes its descent down a cliff.

Some months after the accident, Paul is still under observation in a mental hospital. He believes that his dead wife is still alive somewhere. Two doctors spend a good five minutes engaged in a rudimentary, somewhat pointless psychoanalytical exchange on whether Paul is abnormal or not. They decide not and discharge him.

Paul immediately heads for Anne's final resting place. Anne's tomb is just like the one in Paul's nightmare, but he doesn't appear to notice. Paul sits inside the mausoleum and falls asleep, despite already having been told that the graveyard is due to close soon. Paul has a flashback dream, recalling most of what we've seen in the film so far.

The mausoleum is locked and the graveyard closed. As he awakes - was that the sound of faraway laughter? - Paul resigns himself to waiting in the darkened mausoleum for morning. Suddenly the soundtrack has an attack of electronic blips and Paul thinks he hears Anne calling his name. Paul breaks open Anne's coffin - she's alive!

A storm breaks outside. Lightning sends an overhead power cable crashing onto the mausoleum gate, fortifying the only exit with electricity.

Looking somewhat detached, Anne says that she remembers falling out of the car and then going to sleep, only she didn't feel as though she was asleep. After a few kisses and cuddles, Anne talks of Paul's life being in danger. Nonsense, he says. They both exchange more sticky, lovey-dovey sentiments. The conversational stance between Paul and Anne veers wildly; one moment she wants him to leave her (how?), the next minute she wants to make love to Paul and begs him never to leave. Paul agrees, then disagrees, then questions Anne about her new fondness for cats, as the black cat that she has been stroking lunges for his throat. Paul kills the cat, but Anne screams, "That won't stop them!"

"Them?" asks Paul

"We're doomed!" replies Anne.

Once *Till Death* manages to slip past the agony of the sugary dialogue, of the "sweet torment" of Anne and Paul being reunited, then it really does begin to get pretty peculiar. While the dialogue never fully shakes off its saccharine content, it does take on a whole new perverse dimension as the movie finds its ground in the locked mausoleum, and it becomes obvious that Paul is in actual fact directing his words of love at nothing more than a corpse.

The couple wait for morning and release from the mausoleum. At one point Anne tries to explain to Paul that she is in fact dead. But, in keeping with the sentiment that has gone before, Anne forgoes this revelation for, "...in the brightness of our love we were brought together again."

Anne further deliberates that the two of them are suspended in the stillness of time in the mausoleum, and that there is no way that she can leave with Paul come morning. Or maybe she can, she's not sure.

"Take me, now," she begs Paul as she pulls him to the floor.

Belinda Belaski in a still not from **Till Death.**

Certainly, in part, this claustrophobia is the result of the film's swirling mists and use of closed sets - the abundance of which, however, also suggests a certain naivety on the part of director Walter Stocker. In the main, though, the atmosphere and claustrophobia of the movie is governed by the crazy situation in which Paul finds himself and the often stilted dialogue exchanged between himself and Anne. These incessant attempts to formulate an understanding of their situation in the mausoleum draw chokingly tighter around Paul as the *spirits of death* get closer; neither does Paul want to face the inevitable fact that Anne could be dead, and so he conjures these conversations of love, which in turn become increasingly irrational in the mausoleum's 'stillness of time'.

As movies go, *Till Death* falls into that small pocket of 'America's Strangest'. It is one of those small Stateside productions which is both unsure of itself and at odds with whoever may comprise its potential audience (let's face it - a *Nietzchean* ghost story?). It is also one of those small Stateside movies that doesn't quite manage to hit the mark it's aiming for - no mean feat considering it has more unrealised ideas than any number of box-office smashes could muster.

All of which makes it a sad fact that *Till Death* should remain an obscurity. And yet the reason it remains obscure is probably more to do with it being an American picture than it has with budget, distribution or word of mouth. *Till Death* should be acknowledged as an important piece of film-making if only because it proves, once and for all, that European directors don't hold a monopoly on weird shit cinema.

David Kerekes

WENDIGO.
USA 1978.
Dir & Scr: Roger Darbone. With: Ron Berger, Cameron Gornick, Victor Lawrence, Robert Steffen, Van Washburn Jr, Carol Cockerell.

"Sorry Anne, I can't, not here," says Paul.

At this point a shadowy superimposition in the graveyard outside makes its way across the screen. Before long Anne is seeing shadowy figures all over the mausoleum. These shadowy forms are the *spirits of death*, and they have come to take Anne back. Paul is going crazy trying to console Anne that there must be a logical explanation for all of this (though it isn't clear whether Paul himself can see the spirits or not). Anne screams. Paul tries to ward off whatever-it-is with a stick, accidentally cracking Anne a blow to the head. She's dead (again?) and the spirits leave.

Paul decides he doesn't want to live any longer and electrocutes himself on the live gate of the mausoleum.

With its minimalist settings and the fact that the movie really only has two principal characters, *Till Death* comes across as a kind of diluted Nietzchean morality play. (With its cyclic rehashing of the same conversation, it isn't impossible to envisage *Till Death* performed as a one-act stage play.)

The film has little of what could be called pace, and no action as such, and it would be vulgar to interpret the rather sorry story as a plot. But the movie is drenched with a feeling of impending desolation - that nothing good can come from any of this. Along with this desolation comes a nauseating sense of claustrophobia, so strong that at times it appears *Till Death* is curving in at the edges. (*Another invaluable addition to the lexicon of cinema there, Mr Kerekes. Ed.*)

Perhaps because it was assumed to be a retitling of *Ghostkeeper*, with which it shared some ugly video box art, this plodding item has managed to stay out of the reference books for an entire decade. Although anyone who sets out to adapt an Algernon Blackwood story (this may be a first) obviously knows something about the genre, this no-budget bore conveys little of the chills of a piece rated by H.P. Lovecraft and others as one of the two or three finest ghost stories in the language. Indeed, this bears all the hallmarks of the notoriously unprofitable 'Indian Curse' cycle of walking-around-in-the-woods duds. A group of enthusiastic amateur actors (one sports a particularly terrible Northwoods French accent) are stranded by a clumsily staged helicopter crash in the woods and bumble around spouting idiot dialogue ("When your business associate is also your lover, you can serve all the apple sauce you want but it's never apple pie.") for well over an hour without anything happening. Then an Indian is horrifyingly hung upside down from a tree and some of the characters get pulled into the air by smudges and ineptly torn apart by the barely-glimpsed wind demon (it looks a bit like The Great Gonzo). Finally the heroine's head catches fire for about half a second, the Wendigo waves a claw like Porky Pig signing off a Looney Tune and it's all suddenly and mercifully over.

Kim Newman

INDEX

OF FILM TITLES